OXFORD RESEARCH STUDIES IN GEOGRAPHY

General Editors

J. Gottmann   *J. A. Steers*
F. V. Emery   *J. Parsons*

Frontier on the Rio Grande

A Political Geography of Development and Social Deprivation

John W. House

CLARENDON PRESS · OXFORD
1982

Oxford University Press, Walton Street, Oxford OX2 6DP
London Glasgow New York Toronto
Delhi Bombay Calcutta Madras Karachi
Kuala Lumpur Singapore Hong Kong Tokyo
Nairobi Dar es Salaam Cape Town
Melbourne Auckland
and associate companies in
Beirut Berlin Ibadan Mexico City

Published in the United States by
Oxford University Press, New York

British Library Cataloguing in Publication Data
House, John W.
Frontier on the Rio Grande.—
(Oxford research studies in geography)
1. Geopolitics—United States
2. Geopolitics—Mexico   3. Mexico—Boundaries—United States
4. United States—Boundaries—Mexico
I. Title
341.4'2   FIZZ8.5.U6
ISBN 0-19-823237-3

Library of Congress Cataloguing in Publication Data

House, John William.
Frontier on the Rio Grande.
(Oxford research studies in geography)
Bibliography: p.
Includes index.
1. United States—Foreign economic relations—
Mexico.   2. Mexico—Foreign economic relations—
United States.   3. Mexico—Boundaries—United
States.   4. United States—Boundaries—Mexico.
5.Rio Grande Region—Economic conditions.   6. Rio
Grande Region—Social conditions.   I. Title.
II. Series.
HF1456.5.M6H68   303.4'8272073   82–3615
ISBN 0-19-823237-3   AACR2

Typeset by Oxprint Ltd, Oxford
and printed in Great Britain
at the University Press, Oxford
by Eric Buckley
Printer to the University

To
GEORGE W. HOFFMAN
and the
TEXAN GEOGRAPHERS

PREFACE

Fieldwork for this study was carried out in 1977–8 while an Oxford Exchange Visitor at the University of Texas in Austin. The theme explores the relationships, in structure, time, and space between Mexico and the United States across the international boundary of the Rio Grande. This distant and for the most part harsh environment has had a complex and turbulent history, but the focus here is upon contemporary issues and problems. In these, the dramatic past is but an essential ingredient for an appreciation of the present, and the prospects for a more harmonious future. The approach adopted is that of political geography by an observer uncommitted to any of the three distinctive cultural stances of Borderlands people. An applied perspective is intended, it is hoped, to increase understanding of the problems of one of the world's most contrasting frontiers with a deliberate view of contributing a little thereby towards their reduction, if not their ultimate solution.

University of Oxford,   JOHN W. HOUSE
April 1981

ACKNOWLEDGEMENTS

Tribute is due and gratefully extended to all those who have aided this work. To Marigo Broad who so skilfully prepared most of the cartographical figures and to Margaret Loveless for her valued contribution of the others. To my secretaries, Dinah Wood-Mallock and, more recently, Pauline Linières, who both worked indefatigably in libraries, at the typewriter and, in Pauline's case, in proof-reading as well. To my wife, for constant help and support, not least through many extremely hot, dusty days in summer-time along the Rio Grande.

Figures 22 and 23 are reproduced by kind permission of Dr John C. Day of Simon Fraser University; the cover-plate by authority of the United States Immigration and Naturalization Service; and Plates 5 and 6 by kind permission of Dr Robin Doughty.

CONTENTS

FIGURES

TABLES

PLATES

INTRODUCTION

On 3,000 km of frontier we are the most representative of North–South relations, a consequence of two growing civilizations previously separated by the desert, now linked together in a complementary way by conurbations and exchanges.

PRESIDENT LÓPEZ-PORTILLO, 1979

We must not follow the paths of either arrogance or submission. In their place I am confident that together we will take the path of dignity towards an interdependent future, sovereign co-operation, mutual respect and peace.

PRESIDENT JIMMY CARTER, 1979

What has traditionally been good for the United States in Mexico has not necessarily been good for tens of millions of the latter's citizens.

R. R. FAGEN, 1979, 700

When President-elect Reagan visited President López-Portillo in the Mexican Border town of Ciudad Juárez early in 1981 he opened a new chapter in the long-standing, hitherto turbulent relationships across the Rio Grande. This was the first foreign visit by the President-elect, a sure indication of the importance attached to good neighbourliness with America's southern, now oil-rich neighbour. That it took place in a Mexican city on the Rio Grande underlined the reality that the problems on the Border are indeed a microcosm of those long troubling US–Mexican relations in a wider setting.

Here we are concerned solely with that part of the US–Mexican frontier which lies along the Rio Grande, the international boundary between Texas and the few adjacent states of northern Mexico, for a distance of no less than 1,930 km from above El Paso–C. Juárez to the Gulf of Mexico. Along its entire length, the US–Mexican boundary is one of the most remarkable and abrupt culture contact-faces in the world, between the most affluent and developed country and one in the midstream of development, today undergoing a potentially dramatic shift from abject poverty towards a rich future based on its oil wealth, at least for some. Nowhere else in the world are there such steep economic and social gradients across an international boundary. By comparison the US–Canadian boundary is extremely permeable and, 'has a weak or non-existent Border culture' (Stoddard 1980, 2), whereas the boundary with Mexico is stringently controlled, by tradition more turbulent and, moreover, has hitherto been greatly neglected. Perhaps the boundary between Israel and the Arab lands offers the closest parallel, but it is, quite differently, a fortified, warlike zone of contact with deeply entrenched and bitterly conflicting concepts on whose ancestral home is Palestine.

The Rio Grande boundary was established a century and a half ago in the Treaty of Guadalupe Hidalgo (1848), ending the US–Mexican war. For both countries these Borderlands were the last to be settled and developed, within a harsh, and for the most part arid environment, remote from both national capital cities or major economic heartlands. This is the frontier between the advancing civilizations of Anglo-America and Latin America, but the Rio Grande has never been a clear-cut and finite cultural divide. The boundary of Spanish speech, and, even more that of the Spanish-surname population (see Fig. 5) lies well to the north of the river, not the only imprint of a rich and varied history in the landscapes and lives of the Border people. Furthermore, the twin-cities on the Rio Grande, artificial though their development must seem, have become significant international market-centres and meeting-places. Indeed, across the Rio Grande bridges there flows annually the greatest transnational human tide seen on any international boundary (158.4 million Border crossers in 1975). Southwards into Mexico there has long been a great but very selective diffusion of American life-styles, some would say also of US domination and exploitation of the very economic life of Mexico, which no protestation of a 'New Deal', an era of 'Friendship and Co-operation', or a 'Good Neighbour' policy could effectively gainsay.

To some the Border region reflects a unique and distinctive culture 'definable in historical, socio-political, psychological-cultural, economic and other terms' (Ross 1978, 380). The Border reality by no means begins or ends with the juridical line of sovereign demarcation on the Rio Grande. Others argue that in conditions of environmental adversity the Borderlands are unified only through the fatal logic of geography and the marginal nature of the economy. Yet this common economic life, too, may be seen as a neocolonialist form of exploitation by the US, extending deep into an oppressed realm of northern Mexico (Fernández 1977, 154). Without necessarily accepting this ideological reasoning the asymmetrical nature of relationships across the Rio Grande is inescapable.

The United States, a world superpower, is affluent and immensely influential at an advanced stage of Western capitalism. Her 3 million square miles (8m km^2) of territory, rich in all manner of resources, a population of 226.5 millions (1980), a national income of 2,081 billion dollars (1979), and a per capita income of 9,040 dollars per annum, all illustrate crucial aspects of this strength. The economy is orientated on market principles, with minimum governmental intervention, while, politically speaking, American democracy shows a distinctive blend of co-operative federalism, with an entrenched right for the State level to be consulted, and a strong expression of citizen power 'at the grass-roots'. On all counts, Mexico is demonstrably the weaker partner. Her 770,000 square miles (2m km^2) of territory reflect a much harsher upland or arid environment of which only 12 per cent is fit for farming. Her population of 67.3 millions (1980) is dependent on a limited range of scarce natural resources and, for some decades, has been growing at a rate which no provision of work could ever hope to match; during the 1980s, for example, around 700,000 new jobs a year will be required. Furthermore, the national income of 104 billion dollars (1979) and an annual per capita income of 1,500 dollars conceal deep internal extremes in 'a country of poor people living in the midst of an élite becoming rich at their expense' (Barkin 1975, 64). In Latin American terms, the Mexican economy would seem to have had a relatively balanced growth, in both the sizeable State-controlled and the private sectors. Yet there is a considerable foreign, mainly American, penetration into the most vital and dynamic industries and urban activities, a relationship that has been described as 'historically between a Mexican dependent bourgeoisie and foreign capitalists developing towards a new miracle of imperialistic domination' (Cockroft 1974, 284). In the process Mexico is left with many unsolved political dilemmas: unemployment, urban poverty and deprivation, depleted raw materials, low-productivity agriculture, and the need for many to emigrate clandestinely for the work they cannot find at home. Politically there is a strong and centralized Mexican federal bureaucracy directly responsible to a seemingly all-powerful President, ruling for six years, while effectively the electoral process has for long been almost exclusively dominated by a single party, the PRI (*Partido Revolucionario Institucional*).

The basic asymmetry of power between the US and Mexico is inevitably projected into their relationships across the Rio Grande, but the political perceptions on what is to be done are very different. These relationships are in the first place governmental, but they are also both economic and social, with the governments in that case holding a wary watching brief. In 1979 Mexico drew 71 per cent of her imports, by value, from the US and sent 68 per cent of her exports to that country. Yet the significance of this volume of trade, in an American perspective, is minimal. Though Mexico is the fourth-ranked client of the USA and the fifth-ranked supplier the proportions these represent of US trade are no more than 4.7 and 3.1 per cent respectively (Ojeda 1979, 11). Moreover, apart from the recent oil bonanza, Mexican exports have mainly been of non-essential items, whereas imports from the US have been vital to Mexico's industrialization and urbanization. Even taking positive *net* tourist receipts (737 million dollars in 1979) and emigrant remittances into account Mexico ran up a balance-of-payments deficit calculated at 3.5 billion dollars in 1980, and that for a country which had experienced a 30 per cent price rise in the same year, in spite of a steady 7 per cent GNP growth rate in 1979 and 1980.

Not surprisingly, this unequal, uneven, and US-dominated set of relationships has for a very long time aroused the strongest political feelings south of the Rio Grande. These are exacerbated by the extent of penetration into the Mexican economy by American investors, particularly through major multinational companies. Such penetration is not new: it first flourished under the Porfiriato (1876–1910), but since 1940 there has been an upsurge in its momentum. The textile, cement, iron and steel, and paper and pulp industries in northern Mexico were stimulated by wartime shortages. By 1957 one-sixth of Mexican manufacturing was in US-controlled enterprises, concentrated in the largest-scale, most dynamic growth sectors. The Mexican government import substitution policy, started in 1959, encouraged further US investment in the industries and cities of Mexico. From a book value of foreign investments at 1,080 million dollars in 1960 the volume had risen to 2,300 million dollars by 1968 (Barkin 1977, 71). By the late 1970s three-quarters of all foreign investment in Mexico was from the US, two-thirds of it in dynamic and strategic manufacturing, and one-half of this in capital goods industries (Ojeda 1979, 19). One-quarter of the 938 major firms today are foreign-controlled, and almost half the one hundred most important firms.

Given this situation it is less than surprising that the rhetoric of US–Mexican 'interdependence' has a somewhat hollow ring. Mexico's retarded and uneven development, or its continued misdevelopment are both laid at the door of a dependent State capitalism (Cockroft 1974, 259). Fernández (1977) formulates a model of historical materialism to explain this unsatisfactory state of affairs, highlighting the innate contradiction between the forces of production and the social relations of production. Barkin (1975, 77 *et seq.*) speaks rather of a Mexican model of secondary capitalism, in which there is 'systematic isolation of a substantial part of the population from the fruits of economic growth without creating unmanageable social unrest'. In this indictment the United States

advertises a life style few can achieve and exports the machinery to ensure that not many will be needed to work in the factories. It obtains aid and invests to pay for exports to Mexico, but in return obtains control over industry and a mortgage on that country's exports. It cooperates with an affluent local bourgeoisie, coopts an occasional recalcitrant politician and subsidises the loyal opposition, to promote its ideal of democracy and free enterprise.

Mexican political leaders 'bemoan dependence'. Some seem powerless to end it but 'most capitalists see no benefit from changing the present pattern'. The Mexican government tries to 'maintain the rate of economic growth but reforms social welfare, tries to decentralize regionally to solve the urban crisis, and sees tourism as the way to attract dollars and create jobs'.

These then are the protagonists on either bank of the Rio Grande. The economic and social issues between them are focussed and sharpened at the international boundary, and they are many, severe, and intractable. As President López-Portillo summed them (February 1979) they include: 'multilateral relations; the economic order; commerce and prices; population; finance; currency; drugs; fuel; land, sea, air, or gas pollution; and, not least, migratory rights for workers, or for humans — a specific but constantly changing agenda, and one on which American and Mexican priorities have often differed markedly. Both countries are concerned to stimulate adequate flows of goods and persons, to combat smuggling, and to increase trans-frontier co-operation generally. Under President Reagan the United States is likely to continue to place the illegal alien question at the head of its agenda, followed by access to Mexican oil and natural gas, then US fishing rights in Mexican waters and, finally, accord on Central American and Caribbean political tensions. The Mexican priorities are founded rather on more open access to US markets, a fuller and more regulated system for the entry of Mexican migrant workers to the US, and more American 'aid without strings' for Mexican development. These different bases for policy impact unevenly in the Borderlands and, as policy trade-offs take place between the two countries, they do so all too often without regard for the at-times disastrous effects on the frontier communities along the Rio Grande.

ARGUMENT AND ANALYSIS

During the past two decades the literature on aspects of the US–Mexican Border has grown steadily, with contributions by scholars in many disciplines (Stoddard 1970, 1975a, b). Historians (Almaráz 1975) concentrated on analysing the forces and events that shaped a frontier society, while geographers (Gildersleeve 1975) emphasized themes on the landscapes, urban life, economic problems, or the cultural character and diffusion of traits in the Borderlands. Anthropologists (Stoddard 1975b) highlighted community characteristics and problems, especially those of the Border 'twin-cities', with a particular focus upon immigrants from Mexico and migrants within that country. It is also to anthropologists that we owe the concepts of a Border culture, unifying both US and Mexican frontier-dwellers, and the valuable insights into the social costs of space in arid regions. Economists (Taylor 1975) focussed rather on issues of underdevelopment and conflict among socio-economic groups, with a deliberate perspective on the desirable policy mix for meeting such problems. Immigration issues and the Border Industrialization Programme received particular attention. Political scientists (Bath 1975) developed behavioural rather than ethical or ideological approaches, with a preferred orientation upon a political-systems approach. Political culture and political socialization were the inputs to the political system, public policies and their effects the output from the system. Such a perspective was overtly problem-oriented and helped to break down the nation-based stereotypes of Border life. The study of the exercise and dissemination of power was a particular focus set within the context of political culture. Two notable potentials for this type of work lie in the construction of a bureaucratic politics model for the analysis of decision-taking and in the development of linkage-related insights into the political system.

Most contributions to Borderlands studies have thus been systematic and from the perspective of a particular discipline. An outstanding exception is a collection of essays (Ross 1978) by American and Mexican scholars from several disciplines, 'intended to shed light on misunderstandings and misconceptions concerning the Border and the frontier zone'. This catholic overview treats culture, politics, economics, the migrants, health, the social psychology of the Borderlands, and the ecology of the region. On most issues there is an individual presentation by a Mexican and an American scholar, each focussing on his national side of the Border—an ironic reflection in an excellent work intended to develop a common concern for the Borderlands as a unified problem region.

A second recent important work (Fernández 1977) develops a politico-economic interpretation of the US–Mexican Border system. It seeks to 'understand current economic developments on the Border through an historical perspective', within the theoretical framework of historical materialism. Contrary to the previously mentioned study the conclusion is that 'the basis of the economic unity of the Border is founded on inequality, uneven development and domination (by the United States)'. Thus

to speak of a border economic regional unit *as we know it today* can only imply the continuation of the status quo in both the United States and Mexico. A better, more rational economic development future for this geographic area must signify the disappearance of the present economic elements of unity, i.e. the disappearance of imperialism and uneven development (p. 157).

To the dynamics of Borderlands analysis is thus added the strength of ideological commitment, but both recent works share in common a powerful social concern for the intractable problems of the US–Mexican Border.

The approach adopted here is novel in the literature of the Borderlands, using an *applied political geography* as the means of analysis and integration. Simply put, political geography is concerned with a systematic understanding of the complex interaction between political processes and earth space. It focusses upon the spatial and structural differentiation of habitat, economy, and society, which are concerns in common with general geography, but adds the extra dimension of polity to the systems-based investigation. The dynamics of development and change in structure and space are studied through time, with a direct, problem-oriented concern for the role, significance, and impact of policy and politics. The adding of an applied dimension to conventional political geography requires a disciplined focus on alternative futures, a commitment to problem-solving, policy-critique, and prescription. In this perspective, there is the maximum outgoing relationship with cognate social science disciplines, often using common concepts, methodologies, or techniques. This is a clear recognition that, given the complexity of Borderlands problems, no discipline alone may provide solutions, but each and every subject has a distinctive contribution to offer.

The application of political geography to the study of the frontier region is a particular and indeed a traditional focus in the subject (Minghi 1963; House 1969, 1980, 1981). During the past decade, however, there has been a shift in the focus of frontier studies, both methodologically and in terms of objectives (Guichonnet and Raffestin 1974; Sanguin 1976). Three novel perspectives are being developed. First, a thoroughgoing systems approach to the study of frontiers, setting this aspect of political geography on a convergent course with other social sciences. Second, the regional context of frontiers is becoming more fully recognized, giving fresh and direct impetus to the neglected study of the frontier zone and the trans-frontier region. Third, the positive aspects of co-operation across boundaries are being stressed rather than the negative aspects of barrier-like quality or closure at the outer limits (periphery) of sovereignty. If these newer approaches are to be consolidated they must be set within a dynamic framework, capable of measuring change and evaluating trends in space, place, and among people. The most useful theoretical frames for studying the policies and plans of political decision-takers need to be drawn from political science. Of these the most appropriate theories are those of conflict in power interaction (Boulding 1962), social communication (Deutsch 1963), and linkages (Rosenau 1969).

In this book the Rio Grande is the focus, a riverline international boundary. The study of riverlines in political geography is among the most traditional, often from a quasi-military, power-political standpoint, emphasizing division, difference, and dissociation. This study seeks to draw a balance between the potentially unifying and divisive qualities of a riverline boundary, grounding the analysis within the principles of private and public international law. On the side of unity are the merits of exploiting a scarce, multiple-purpose common water resource and the natural environment through which it flows; the possibility of 'twin-city' co-operation at crossing-points and the degree of openness in trans-frontier transactional flows which can be stimulated without detriment to either party. On the side of divisiveness, there is the complex reality of a finite line dividing sovereignties, with endemic conflict over delimitation, demarcation, and functioning of the riverline boundary through subsequently changed circumstances. Disagreements over even the common shared water resource may involve its proportionate allocation among international and national users, or priorities among alternative uses. The balance between potentials and constraints of a riverline limit of sovereignty illustrates both the empirical contribution of geographers to this topic of international law, and also the shortcomings of any attempts to impose solutions by principles of law, however admirable, formulated in different geographical conditions and sometimes misapplied to an arid environment.

The structure and argument of this book is formulated around an *operational model* (Fig. 1a & b) based on a disaggregated analysis of the total two-way transactional flows, of goods, services, people, capital, ideas, and policies across the Rio Grande. The model embraces the three dimensions of structure, space, and time. Its disaggregated elements can be fed into an input–output frame (Appendix) which, when calibrated, can be used to assess, in particular, events, intentions, policy shifts, and variable rates of change. From this the spatial origins, influences, and the impact of decisions upon the transactional flows and their milieu can be calculated. Specifically, the political effects of alternative policy or political scenarios can be tested within a system of total environment, economic, social, and political relationships. Central to the dynamics of the model is the theme of tension management in a complex, interacting political system.

Figure 1a demonstrates the structural and temporal ingredients of the model, Fig. 1b the working-out of relationships in variable geographical space, outwards from the boundary line and frontier zone (periphery), through the frontier States (intermediate) to the national (Federal) heartlands (core). The content and succession of chapters in the book is keyed into the developing structure of the model, but for readability explores the issues and problems in a more general as well as in a technical manner.

The first issue is to understand fully that missing ingredient in most US–Mexican Border studies–geographically differentiated space. Given the cutural complexity, the deep-seated attitudes in policies and politics across the Rio Grande, and the marked asymmetry in relationships which has resulted, a firm historical basis to development and

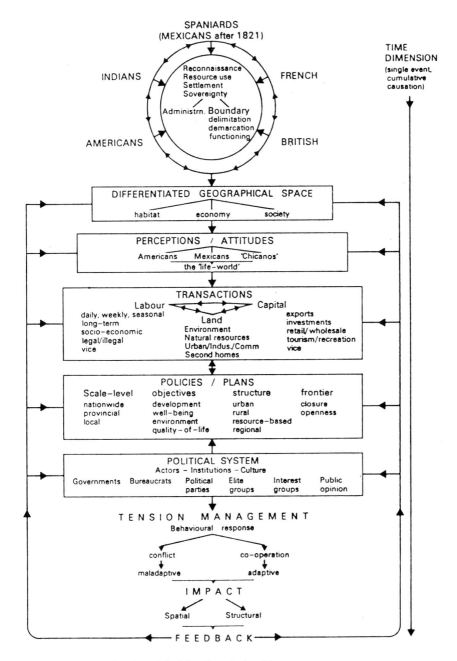

Fig. 1. An operational model of frontier relationships
(a) Structural and temporal

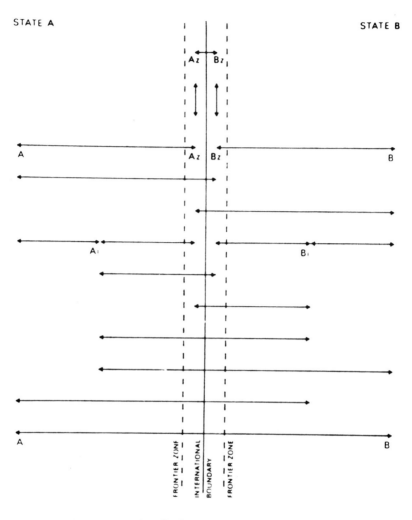

Az, Bz frontier zones
Aı, Bı regional (provincial) centres
A, B   national (federal) centres

FIG. 1. An operational model of frontier relationships
        (b) Spatial

sovereign interaction is an essential preliminary (ch. 1) to the study of
the frontier (Pt. I). The fixing of the international boundary along the
Rio Grande, its delimitation, demarcation, and the delicate and inflammatory problems to which it has subsequently given rise (ch. 2) focus
the range of international law questions on the riverline. Differentiated
geographical space is indeed the theme for much of Part II. The varied

connotations of the Borderlands, in time, manner, and space identify the geographical field of study and, in particular, identify the frontier zone, by various definitions (ch. 2), which is then set within the variegated physical and cultural landscapes of the region. From a consideration of habitat conditions the man–land relationship is then explored (ch. 3) through the characteristics of society and economy which provide the backcloth and meaning to present-day policy and political interaction in the Borderlands. From discrete geographical realities it is then necessary to turn to the more problematical theme of perceptions, attitudes, and opinions within the contrasting 'life-worlds' of the Rio Grande (ch. 3). Here there is a richly cosmopolitan spectrum of behavioural stances among Americans, Mexicans, and *chicanos*. Since these affect the ways people think, act, identify with or against one another, and provide the ground swell of continuity which politicians and policy-makers must take into account they merit close attention.

The body of the model is made up of the intricate web of total transactions across the Rio Grande (Pt. III) and the policies and plans to which they have given rise or within which they are imbedded. The model structure (Fig. 1a) shows the policies and plans segment as relating both to transactions which have taken place or are taking place but also to manipulation of those yet to come. In practical terms, the intermingling of policies, plans, and transactions means that they have to be interpreted in common, with any policy-making implications drawn together at the end. Transactional flows (Pt. III) include those relating to the environment (ch. 4), the labour market, including undocumented workers (ch. 5), illegal transactions (smuggling, the traffic in drugs, and prostitution) in chapter 6; and capital transactions (retailing and wholesaling, tourism, commercial development, and Border industrialization) in chapter 7. Each flow is complex and contributes to the problem mix along the Rio Grande, a mix which is further moderated by the varied geographical realities of space and place.

Part IV analyses the interacting political cultures in the Borderlands in terms of the actors and the institutions. The locus of power and decision-taking in the US and Mexican governmental systems is assessed at federal, State, and local levels (ch. 8). Power and influence relate to the contribution by politicians, bureaucrats, political parties, élite or interest groups, and finally, not negligible in the US, by the pressures of public opinion. The total interaction in the Borderlands is viewed as a network of tensions, creative as well as destructive in their purposes and effects. Public intervention is thus to be interpreted as a form of tension management, with behavioural responses in either a positive (cooperation) or a negative (conflict) manner. The interaction within the Borderlands system between the major political protagonists, with the third-party *chicanos*, involves maybe differing policy objectives or contrasting views on what constitutes adaptive or maladaptive behaviour. Through interaction, for good or ill, the system evolves and there are both structural as well as spatial impacts upon the Borderlands. In turn, these feed back into the system (Fig. 1a), transforming different-iated geographical space in the process, perhaps affecting perceptions and attitudes, certainly causing changes in the network of transactions, possibly shifts also in the character and mix of policies and plans. Evaluation of such changes is the operational purpose behind the model, which is capable of being recalibrated and used to project future impacts in the light of declared or postulated intentions of policy-makers. The time dimension is incorporated on the right-hand side of the model, covering single events or the cumulative causation of longer-term evolution. This may be envisaged as a form of diffusion process through the evolution of the system—a critical dimension since the timing of policy change or intervention is often crucial for its success.

Fig. 1b shows the spatial manifestation of trans-frontier interactions. Flows are disaggregated by distance and direction of interaction, dis-tinguishing: centre (core) of one State A (Mexico) to centre of the adjacent State B (USA); centre (A, B) to periphery (Az, Bz), the frontier zones, including also the periphery of the adjacent State (Az to B, Bz to A); regional (intermediate) centre (Ai, Bi) to core, regional centre and periphery within each State; and frontier-zone interaction (Az–Bz), both trans-frontier and, laterally, within the same frontier zone. Only thus may the true spatial significance of the impact of policies on the frontier zone be evaluated and the hierarchical relation-ships of power within two contrasting federal systems effectively put into perspective. In the input–output table for the model (Appendix) the spatial variables are integrated with those of structure and time, to form a three-dimension analytical system. The columns indicate the sequential structural elements of transactions and their context in the system, the rows the variable distances and direction of spatial linkages.

Chapter 9 offers a speculative look ahead on the Rio Grande frontier, and an epilogue considers some of the more general lessons for frontier studies at large.

REFERENCES

ALMARÁZ, F. D. (1975) 'The status of borderlands studies: history', *Soc. Sci. J.*, **12**, 9–18.
BARKIN, D. (1975). 'Mexico's albatross: the US economy', *Latin Am. Perspect.*, **II**, 2, 64–80.
BATH, R. C. (1975) 'The status of borderlands studies: political sciences', *Soc. Sci. J.*, **12**, 55–67
BOULDING, K. E. (1962) *Conflict and Defense: a General Theory* (New York: Harper & Row).
COCKROFT, J. D. (1974) 'Mexico: the struggle with dependency and beyond', in R. H.

Chilcote and J. C. Edelstein (eds.) *States and Societies in the Third World* (New York: J. Wiley).

DEUTSCH, K. (1963) *Nerves of government* (New York: Free Press).

FAGEN, R. F. (1977) 'The realities of US-Mexican relations', *Foreign Affairs*, **55**, 4, 685–700.

FERNÁNDEZ, R. A. (1977) *The United States–Mexico Border: a politico-economic profile (Notre Dame: Univ. N. Dame Press).*

GILDERSLEEVE, C. R. (1975) 'The status of borderlands studies: geography', *Soc. Sci. J.*, **12**, 19–28.

GUICHONNET, P. and RAFFESTIN, C. (1974) *La géographie des frontières* (Paris: PUF).

HOUSE, J. W. (1969) 'A local perspective on boundaries and the frontier zone', ch. 18 in C. A. Fisher (ed.) *Essays in Political Geography*, (London: Methuen), 327–44.

HOUSE, J. W. (1980) 'The frontier zone: a conceptual problem for policy-makers', *Int. pol. Sci. Rev.*, **1**, 4, 456–77.

HOUSE, J. W. (1981) 'Frontier studies: an applied approach', ch. 15 in P. Taylor and A. Burnett (eds.) *Political Studies from Spatial Perspectives* (Chichester: J. Wiley), 291–312.

MINGHI, J. V. (1963) 'Boundary studies in political geography: a review article', *Ann. Ass. Am. Geogr.*, **53**, 3, 407–28.

OJEDA, M. (1979) 'México y los Estados Unidos. Interdependencia o dependencia de México?', *Simposio Nacional sobre Estudios Fronterizos, El Colegio de México, Facultad de Filosofía y Letras de la UNAL* (Monterrey; Nuevo León).

RICO, C. (1979) 'La frontera Mexicano–Norteamericano, la retórica de la 'interdependencia' y el problema de las simetriás, *Simposio Nacional sobre Estudios Fronterizos, El Colegio de México, Facultad de Filosofía y Letras de la UNAL* (Monterrey: N. León).

ROSENAU, J. N. (ed.) (1969) *International Politics and Foreign Policy* (New York: Free Press).

ROSS, S. R. (ed.) (1978) *Views across the Border* (Albuquerque: Univ. New Mexico Press).

SANGUIN, A.-L. (1976) *Géographie Politique* (Bibliographie Internationale, Montréal: Presses de l'Université du Québec), 74–101.

STODDARD, E. R. (ed.) (1970) 'Comparative US–Mexico Border studies', *Occ. Pap. 1, El Paso Texas Border State Univ. Consortium for Lat. Am.*

STODDARD, E. R. (1975a) 'The status of borderlands studies: an introduction', *Soc. Sci. J.*, **12**, 1–28.

STODDARD, E. R. (1975b) 'The status of borderland studies: sociology and anthropology', *Soc. Sci. J.*, **12**, 29–54.

STODDARD, E. R. (1980) *US–Mexico Diplomacy: its latent consequences in the Borderlands.* Paper presented to 5th World Congress of Rural Sociology, Mexico DF, August 1980 (El Paso: Univ. Texas at El Paso).

TAYLOR, J. R. (1975) 'The status of borderlands studies: economics', *Soc. Sci. J.*, **12**, 69–76.

PART I
The Frontier

CHAPTER 1

Genesis of the Frontier

The developing Border grew from contact/conflict between two basically different socio-economic systems; the particular variant of feudalism developed in New Spain under Spanish colonial rule, and later under Mexican rule, and the predominantly market-orientated, capitalist US moving west.

R. FERNÁNDEZ

(Cortina) the man who would right the wrongs the Mexican had received; who would drive back the hated Americans to the Nueces, and some even spoke of the Sabine as the future boundary.

US CONGRESS, HOUSE 1861

The truth is, our government committed a great error in accepting the Rio Grande as a boundary line. We should never have stopped this side of that great natural boundary, the Sierra Madre range.

NEW ORLEANS *Delta*, 1850

FRONTIER PERSPECTIVES

Throughout its history the South-west has been a great realm for the contact and interaction of very contrasting cultures. Although it was initially seen as a wilderness by the would-be civilizers from Europe, whether from Spain, Britain, France, or the American colonies, it had been home for millenniums to the native Indians. Fewer in numbers, less politically organized and with lower levels of material technology the Indian contribution to the evolution of the South-west has been consistently underrated, even largely ignored (Spicer 1962). Spaniards, Mexicans, and Anglo-Americans interacted with the very diverse Indian cultures, sedentary and nomadic, usually to the great detriment of these native peoples. Subjugated, christianized, and forced to labour by the Spaniards, the Indian farmer for long fared little better under the seemingly more liberal Mexican policies on land and citizenship. To all Europeans in the Borderlands the Indian nomads were a constant threat during almost four centuries. Apaches and Comanches, in particular, influenced or retarded colonization and settlement over great tracts of the plains and plateaux, even until the late 1880s. Their ultimate condemnation to American reservations was a most unfitting end for these warrior-pastoralists.

It is, however, to the clashes of culture beween Spaniards, Mexicans, and Anglo-Americans that the South-west owes its complex political evolution. This was a culture clash expressed at different levels, in relations between governments, State and local, and in the turbulent contacts among frontiersmen, by their very nature at the margins or beyond the law of any land. Soldiers, ranchers, friars, and freebooters all made their contributions to the culture, the landscape, the myths, and legends of the frontier. This cosmopolitan sense of life-world and experience colours attitudes and, at times, helps to fuel antagonisms based on feelings of past injustices or present prejudices. To this past, the historians have added their own interpretations, on occasion quite differently and not unaffected by nationalist chauvinism. To the Turner school of American historians (Turner 1920) the westward advance from the Alleghenies was the progressive movement of civilization into the wilderness, a territorial extension of the Anglo-American frontier until its final closure around 1890. The frontier was not seen as a boundary, but rather 'an area inviting entrance into unsettled contiguous territory, constantly in pursuit of the lure of free land' (Webb 1933, 3). Indeed towards the end of American expansion, Turner (1920, 259) referred to El Paso as 'the gate of escape to the free conditions of the frontier'. American historians of the South-west (Bolton 1921; Bannon 1970) based their interpretations rather upon the intermittent northward movement of Spanish sovereignty, frontier, of dominion rather than settlement, from the Mexican heartland into the uncertain Borderlands of the so-called Great Chichimeca, and, later, towards confrontation with the French and the Anglo-Americans pressing in from the east. The Mexican historian Cosío Villegas (1956, 1968) was more even-handed in his analysis, allowing credits and apportioning blame where most justly due, in assessing a history common to all those who have travailed in the harsh, uninviting environments flanking the Rio Grande.

To some, the struggle in the Borderlands must be seen in ideological terms, of market-oriented capitalism and imperialism against colonial and post-colonial feudalism, contacts leading inevitably to conflicts between two basically different socio-economic systems (US Congress, House 1978, 807). Bustamante (1979) distinguished the progressive general instability on the frontier, resulting from closer contacts, from the social conflicts which grew from the very nature and range of such developing interactions. Certainly the perceptions, objectives, and methods of the Spaniards and their Mexican heirs differed greatly from those of the Anglo-Americans. The Spanish advance to the frontier took place irregularly, but in a centrally controlled manner, behind a reconnaissance screen of Franciscan missions and military *presidios*. The moves were 'carefully planned, minutely organized and regularly over-supervised' (Bannon 1970, 5). Secularization and selective economic development followed, promptly whenever possible, upon the pacification and christianization of the pioneer fringe. Church and State struggled for the labours of the Indian, but Spanish absolutism allowed the frontiersman little latitude, since frontier officials as well as laymen were regularly subjected to check by the *residencia* system. Spanish culture was implanted in 'the language, architecture, political administration, christianity and obedience to the King of Spain' (Spicer 1962, 5).

The French interlude on the South-west frontier lasted intermittently from the landing of La Salle on the Texan coast (1682) to the final sale of the Louisiana Territory to the United States (1803), but it was for the most part a peripheral impact. Though La Salle had grandiose ambitions, enough to spur the Spaniards to react vigorously, his dreams of a French route to the Pacific and ownership of the mines of Chihuahua (Bannon 1964, 55) expired ingloriously. French objectives were consistently more mundane, to open up eighteenth-century trade to Santa Fé and, later, to the Rio Grande and to expand influence with the Indian tribes by trade rather than by conversion or subjugation.

The Anglo-American penetration took place later, but has increasingly coloured the history of the past two hundred years. Involvement was much more individual, 'aggressive and inquisitive, in the hope of gain, for broader opportunities and personal advantage' (Bannon 1978, 6). Though much freer from central authority, the Anglo-American frontiersman was committed once he moved to the frontier and there he had to stay. English language and institutions moved with the frontier, land being held in individual title, improved farming methods practised, and the Protestant church and elementary school the basis of the neighbourhood community.

Cultural interaction in the Borderlands took place over a wide realm, with fluctuating currents in the directions and exercise of political authority. Apart from the southward diffusion of Indian peoples in early times, the spread of civilization was initially northwards from the Mexican plateau heartland, first by the Toltecs, and then by the Spaniards during some three centuries following upon the Conquest. By the mid-eighteenth century, there was pressure from the east and, to a lesser extent, penetration down through the Rockies and the Great Plains into Texas and the Borderlands. Early French trading contacts were contemporary with the predatory southwards migration of the Plains Indians into the great 400-km salient of the 'Apache corridor' (Spicer 1962, 233), a turbulent zone of raiding across the upper Rio Grande until the 1880s. In the mid-nineteenth century, the California gold-rush (1849) abruptly reoriented American trade east–west, reflected on the Rio Grande in the fortunes of El Paso, a potential confirmed by the Southern Pacific transcontinental rail link in 1881. In the twentieth century, the north–south linkage has been reasserted in the controversial era of an ever-increasing Mexican dependency on the United States.

Apart from the cross-currents, it is possible to interpret events partially through a simple centre–periphery model. Spanish or Mexican advances or retreats on the frontier took place in a remote land across a vast, barren, inhospitable country, distant in real terms from the core of the Central Plateau, but even more remote in the minds of men. On the Anglo-American side there was no such clearly defined core or base from which the frontier could be serviced or dominated. Lines of communication stretched far back from the Mississippi, but in a less centralized political society such remoteness carried fewer disadvantages. Chains of smaller bases sprang up behind the advancing frontier, to replenish it with men, materials, and such minimal sovereign authority as was tolerable in a turbulent pioneer society.

PRE-COLUMBAN TIMES

Remote from the complex early civilizations of Meso-America, the Borderlands during the early historic period were a vast realm with islands of settled Indian *pueblo* villages stretching up into New Mexico from cultivated patches on the eastern flanks of the Sierra Madre. More widespread, there were limitless open rangelands thinly peopled by the ancestors of the nomadic Plains Indians searching for loot and the bison. Between AD 1000 and 1200 the Toltecs had developed trading contacts with the distant Indian *pueblos*, but the frontier receded back to the Mexican core after the fall of Tula (Bernal 1978, 27). In Aztec times some trading contacts had been re-established with the *pueblos*, and there was during that period some indication of floodplain (*bañada*) agriculture on the upper Rio Grande (White 1968, 6). Essentially though, the vast zone of northern Mexico stretching up to the Rio Grande lay outside effective Meso-American civilization, and was to confront the Spaniards with an entirely novel and disturbing set of problems when they advanced northwards from the Central Plateau. A loosely organized culture contact zone was the best description for the undefined northern frontier in Pre-Columban times. Territoriality of the frontier was a non-existent concept and the use of the term 'boundary' entirely inappropriate in a turbulent marchland.

THE SPANISH MARCHLAND

For almost three centuries Spain exercised variable sovereignty in the semi-arid and mountainous realm of the South-west. Until the late seventeenth century her expanding northward frontier was uncontested by rival powers, though the Indians put up a spirited, widespread, and locally very effective opposition, most notably so on the approaches to the Rio Grande. After the implied French threat in the landing of La Salle on the Texas coast (1682) the Spanish view of frontier strategy became increasingly protective and defensive, first against the French, then in face of the Anglo-Americans. Spanish attempts to forestall Anglo-American political claims by a policy of land grants in the early nineteenth century came to nought, and her newly independent Mexican heirs were compelled to cede frontier territory in Texas (1836). After the US–Mexican War the Rio Grande first became the admitted international boundary in the Treaty of Guadalupe Hidalgo (1848).

In fact, early Spanish exploration towards the Rio Grande converged, by expeditions coming from the West Indies and along the Gulf Coast as well as northward from the Mexican heartland. The mouth of the Rio Grande was discovered as early as 1519, while in 1527 Cabeza de Vaca passed through the site of El Paso, and in 1539 Estevánico moved into present-day New Mexico (White 1968). Yet it was into the second half of the sixteenth century before any considered follow-up to these early reconnaissances took place. The *Camino Real* was pushed north to Santa Bárbara, in southern Chihuahua, by 1563, opening up a protected route to the lucrative silver mines (Bancroft 1884, 127). As the frontier advance continued the *Camino Real* followed, to provide a vital supply and reinforcement route to its ultimate northern terminus in Santa Fé. The spearhead of the frontier was the Franciscan mission and the accompanying military *presidio*. Behind, and often not far behind, there followed the rancher, the miner, and the civil authority, bent upon establishing towns, estates (*haciendas*), and an administration representing viceregal authority in Mexico City. But the frontier became ever more distant from the capital, and its advance, even its existence, was threatened by constant Indian troubles. Thus the pioneer phase of mission and *presidio* was longer lasting than intended, persisting indeed in the lower Rio Grande valley until planned colonization under Escandón in the mid-eighteenth century. As the frontier moved into Texas, after 1685, so the mission and the *presidio* continued their pionering role among fresh Indian tribes, but with greatly enhanced problems in an altogether different geographical habitat.

Though the Church resolutely opposed it, official policy saw the mission as a transitional frontier institution. It was to prepare the Indian for the loss of his land, his slavery in the mines, his subjugation as a *peón* on landholdings, or his virtual degradation in the towns. Though the friars had a vision of the Kingdom of God, others thought very differently – 'we came here to serve God, but also to get rich', as Bernal Díaz de Castillo so aptly put it (Horgan 1954, 238). The mission policy was to convert, and to preserve the Indian as a child of God, settling him on his own communal land, introducing him to sheep-rearing, irrigation farming, and the production of a communal surplus. The essence of the mission was, furthermore, to provide the 'religious, moral, social and industrial discipline' (Bannon 1964, 200) for the Indian to adjust to colonial society. The *presidio* was a small garrison, of from ten to two hundred men, often part of the mission compound, provided for local defence against the Indians, but in no way capable of stabilizing or protecting the vast northern frontier. Nevertheless, the tiny islands of relative security at the mission and its *presidio* were often the nucleus around which farmers and ranchers settled on land grants; retired *presidial* soldiers also added their quota to these local settlements (Bannon 1964, 50). Such 'islands', however, lay within 'a vast native sea of sedentary or nomadic peoples, who followed almost pre-Columban culture patterns' (Bernal 1978, 30).

On the approaches to the Rio Grande the *presidio*-mission took particular forms and patterns. The local Indians, Mansos, Sumas, and Apaches had few traditions of settled agriculture and, with the exception of the Jumanos (Spicer 1962, 230) could only be persuaded with great difficulty to congregate at the missions and accept a sedentary life. The friars sought to encourage by example, bringing with them christianized Indians from other parts of Mexico; at El Paso, for example, the mission was founded in 1659, using second-generation mission Indians from many tribes and *pueblos*. The heavy clays in the Rio Grande valley were first brought under the plough by the Franciscans, opening up fertile land for local irrigation. In the face of Indian raiding the *presidios* had to be stronger and settlement more concentrated than in more settled areas further south. Already in 1594 the marauding Apache had closed the Conchos–Pecos route to New Mexico across the buffalo plains (White 1968, 39). The Apache lived in separate semi-nomadic bands, hunting the buffalo and preying on settled farmers in the *pueblos* and missions. Throughout the eighteenth century, the Apache were increasingly compressed between the *pueblos* of the upper Rio Grande and their hereditary enemies, the Comanche, moving south through the Great Plains. In their battle for survival they constantly raided settlements for food and horses. In time the horse, and later the rifle, gave them mobility and fire-power which enabled them to dominate the 'Apache corridor' until the later decades of the nineteenth century. Curiously enough, the first mention of the Rio Grande as a boundary (1598) was between the tribal hunting lands of the Apache on the north bank and the Mansos to the south (White 1968, 73). In the same year, the provincial boundary between Nuevo México and Nuevo Vizcaya was declared to be in the vicinity of El Paso, but some years later neither provincial governor knew exactly where this boundary lay. When political power rested in Santa Fé rather than El Paso the jurisdiction of Nuevo México lay along the right bank of the Rio

Grande. At times that El Paso was the greater seat of authority the boundary was displaced northwards to El Bracito. In reality, the concept of a finite territorial boundary was real only in the minds of the military. For practical purposes, El Paso continued to be surrounded by vast arid lands over which no one held effective administrative sovereignty (White 1968, 81).

The potential threat implied by La Salle's expedition to the Texas coast in 1682, and the steady penetration of French traders from the Mississippi basin as far as El Paso and Santa Fé during the early decades of the eighteenth century, persuaded the Spaniards to colonize more positively northwards along the Gulf Coast to the Rio Grande, and beyond into their Texan marchlands. In mid-century, Escandón founded a string of typical Spanish colonial towns along the lower Rio Grande. Land titles were granted for large estates or ranches, also for smaller farms (*porciones*) and the missions were reinforced at Matamoros and Camargo (Smith 1961, 127). The delta lands were studiously avoided, but the basis was laid for the new frontier province of Nuevo Santander. The northern boundary of the province was commonly placed on the Nueces river, confirmed by royal *cédula* in 1805 (Cox 1902), though some maps showed the San Antonio river. In any event, there was no demarcated territorial limit to a vast tract of open rangeland north of the Rio Grande. The landowners usually lived in the river towns and had *vaqueros* (cowboys) on their land grants, stretching over plains regularly swept by Indian raiding bands.

Behind their advancing frontier the Spaniards sought to consolidate their administration (Fig. 2) (O'Gorman 1968). Provinces were fashioned from the loose frontier jurisdictions (1776) and *presidios* were strengthened by royal *reglamento*. The upper Rio Grande, which had been a boundary, between Tejas and Nuevo Vizcaya, was incorporated into the latter. Provincial boundaries in the lower Rio Grande remained unchanged, however, through into the Mexican period; in 1824 Texas and Coahuila were temporarily united. In 1796 the *Provincias Internas* were again integrated and once more withdrawn from the authority of the viceroy (Bannon 1970, 188) to strengthen central control of the entire marchland frontier.

Beyond the Nueces river lay the outermost territory of Texas, created a province in 1691, with a royal *entrada* in 1715 to open it up for settlement. The province lacked appeal to the Spanish colonizers, for it was a remote and dangerous frontier 'huge in area, vague in definition and, to the end, meagre in development' (Meinig 1969, 1). Beyond the San Antonio–Goliad line lay lands quite different from the Spanish colonizing experience in Mexico. The mission had again been the pioneer institution, from an early foundation in 1690, but the semi-nomadic Indians were reluctant to settle, had plenty of meat from the

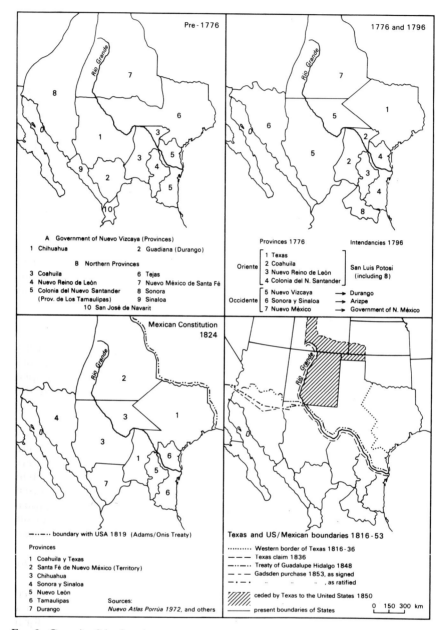

FIG. 2. Genesis of the frontier

buffalo hunt, and resented the Spanish intrusion. The missions were no more successful in the woodland country further east, where there was an added impediment in other troublesome settlers of non-Spanish origins. Although the eastern boundary of Texas was claimed to be on the Red river, later contracted in its southern part to the Sabine river, it was neither effectively nor continuously manned even in the early eighteenth century. In the first phase the occupation of Texas was sporadic, garrisons were intermittently withdrawn and missions closed as the French threat diminished; at one stage the frontier line was taken back as far as Nacogdoches. In the mid-eighteenth century, the Spaniards returned in greater force, establishing *pueblos* and making land grants. They reinforced their border outpost at Los Adaes, facing the increasingly active French trading post at Natchitoches. The French thereupon contested the Red river boundary, claiming a line farther west (Bannon 1970, 141), but at the outermost limits of empire both Spaniard and Frenchman lacked the powers to insist. In 1762 through a Treaty in Europe the Spaniards became heirs to the western lands of Louisiana, previously held by the French, thus moving their boundary east to its highwater mark on the Mississippi. Here after 1783 they encountered the Americans in growing numbers, both settlers and would-be territory-claimants, adding to the frontier turbulence which was soon to put the western boundary of Louisiana into dispute.

In the late seventeenth century, La Salle had claimed the Rio Grande (to him the River of Palms) as the western boundary of Louisiana, and in the Treaty of Retrocession (26 March 1802) by which western Louisiana was returned to the French by the Spaniards there was incorporated a secret instruction by which the French restated their claim to the Rio Grande line, 'from its mouth to about the thirtieth parallel' (Horgan 1954, 39). France guaranteed that she would yield Louisiana again only to the Spaniards, but in fact in 1803 the territory was sold in its entirety to the United States for fifteen million dollars. The French had never settled the western territory and their claim to the Rio Grande boundary had remained an entirely empty assertion. Nevertheless, on behalf of the United States Thomas Jefferson, as the legitimate heir to the French, claimed lands up to the Rio Grande. The Spaniards, scarcely in effective control of Texas, contested the claim vigorously, but the French declined to offer any assistance to the US, with the oft-remembered phrase of Talleyrand: 'The Americans have struck a good bargain and must make the most of it'. The Spanish eastern boundary lay effectively a few kilometres west of Natchitoches (Hackett 1931), but it was thinly manned and lay in woodland territory increasingly penetrated by unruly American settlers. The US–Spanish boundary was finally delimited in the Adams–Oñís Treaty, signed in 1819 but not put into effect until 1831, in which the US gave up its claim to Texas and the Rio Grande boundary (Miramontes 1979, 4). The agreed boundary line then followed the Sabine, Red, and Arkansas rivers to the Rockies (Fig. 2). The Texans felt betrayed by this and never again acknowledged Spanish sovereignty. Within a few years the Mexican War of Independence replaced the Spaniards by a new untested and untried nationalism astride the Rio Grande.

THE TEXAS REPUBLIC AND MEXICO

The newly independent Mexican government (1821) tried to do what the Spaniards had failed to achieve, namely to colonize and settle firmly the lands beyond San Antonio to the frontier. The traditional Spanish system of large-scale *empresario* land grants was reintroduced to attract entrepreneurs who, as agents of the government, would undertake to 'select and bring in colonists, allocate land and impose all the (civil and religious) obligations of citizenship' (Meinig 1969, 29). Apart from the well-known grant for Stephen F. Austin's colony, some 3,500 titles were issued and, by the end of the Mexican period, at least 25,000 people had settled, probably four-fifths of them Anglo-Americans (Meinig 1969, 31). These Anglo-American frontiersmen contained genuine settlers, but farther east in Texas there was a more turbulent element. 'East Texas was Mexican in soil, but Anglo-American in culture. Among its several districts were to be found the half-Indian hunter and trader, the restless and the shiftless, the earnest colonist and the crass speculator, the whisky peddler and the itinerant preacher, and all the other classic types of the Southern frontier' (Meinig 1969, 35).

The Mexican government tried to counter growing Anglo-American influence and increasing political pretensions, by strengthening the garrisons and creating three Departments in Texas: Bexar, around San Antonio; Brazoria, based on San Felipe; and Nacogdoches, on the eastern frontier. This threefold division implicitly reflected the waning power of Mexico with increasing distance from the Rio Grande. The Texan revolt, partly of east against west, quickly became a struggle with the Mexican State. 'The two great Anglo-American disasters, the Alamo and Goliad, took place beyond the margins of Anglo-American colonization, whilst their final triumph at San Jacinto took place deep within a country they had made their own' (Meinig 1969, 37). In the Treaty of Puerto Velasco (1836) with Mexico the Texas republic 're-claimed' the Rio Grande as its boundary line, from the Gulf to its very headwaters in the Rockies. Effective occupance by Texans, however, did not even extend southwards across the Nueces river, beyond which lay a no-man's-land deserted by the Mexican ranchers and exposed both to marauding Indians and roaming armed bands of Texans or Mexicans. Colonel Kinney's trading-post on the site of Corpus Christi (1839) was, indeed, on land purchased from a Mexican grantee. He obtained Mexican citizenship to acquire the land 'within the territory of the Republic of Mexico' (Taylor 1934, 21). Even so, the existence of his settlement was used by the Texans to claim *de facto* occupation of their rightful lands up to the Rio Grande. In the lower Rio Grande valley, however, the culture had remained totally Hispanic, based upon the river towns and their associated landholdings. Briefly, in 1839, the river towns rose in support of the Mexican Federalists, against the Centralists in Mexico City. There was also an economic base to this revolt since frontier trade was being strangled by excessively high Mexican fees and prohibitions (Smith 1961, 192). Though supported by the Texans, the Republic of the Rio Grande (Vigness 1951) was short-lived, crushed within the same year. Nor did the near bankrupt Texas Republic have much success in pushing expeditions out to their alleged territory of the upper Rio Grande. The Santa Fé expedition of 1841 across the Llano Estacado in search of Spanish silver expired miserably (White 1968, 107). Claims to such extended territorial sovereignty simply could not be made effective by the limited resources available, in the face of a harsh environment, hostile Indians, and a long-established, though weak Hispanic authority in New Mexico.

INTERNATIONAL BOUNDARY ON THE RIO GRANDE, AND WESTWARD

The accession of Texas to the United States (1845) abruptly changed the balance of power on the southern frontier, though it has been argued that 'the geographical patterns and trends of the Republic were simply extended and elaborated on into statehood with little interruption or alteration' (Meinig 1969, 38). The US–Mexican war, culminating in the Treaty of Guadalupe Hidalgo, confirmed the Rio Grande as the new international boundary line, and defined it as

commencing in the Gulf of Mexico, three leagues from land, opposite the mouth of the Rio Grande, or opposite the mouth of its deepest branch, if it should have more than one emptying directly into the sea; from thence up the middle of the river, following the deepest channel, where it has more than one, to the point where it strikes the southern boundary of New Mexico' (US Statutes 1848).

The Treaty had been hastily drawn up and, in its provisions on delimitation within the river course, showed a marked lack of understanding both of the nature of the river and the desert to semi-arid environment through which it flowed. The precedence given to navigation as a water use, though conventional in water treaties in humid regions at that time, and confirmed in the Treaties of 1853 (US Statutes 1853) and 1884 (US Statutes 1884) was altogether inappropriate for the Rio Grande. The definition of a water boundary to be demarcated in a braided, shifting channel was also to cause continuing friction and misunderstanding.

Even the termination of the international riverline boundary at the southern limit of New Mexico gave rise to considerable controversy. The Disturnell map (1847), upon which the Treaty provisions had been based in the upper Rio Grande, was proven to be altogether inaccurate: the location of the Rio Grande at El Paso was shown as 32° 15' N and 104° 39' W, whereas in reality it should have been 31° 45' N and 106° 29' W (Miramontes 1979, 9). Initially, the US and Mexican Commissioners agreed that the straightline boundary westwards should take off from the Rio Grande 8 miles (13 km) north of El Paso, but there was considerable uncertainty about the location, or even the existence of a clear east–west southern boundary of New Mexico. In any case, the Treaty made no provision that such a proven boundary, even had it been unambiguously established, would have taken precedence over the evidence on the Disturnell map. The Commissioners were thus driven to a further compromise, placing the starting-point of the boundary westward from the Rio Grande 67 km north of El Paso. The US Commissioner (Bartlett 1854, I, 8) claimed that he had 'yielded no land of value south of 32° 22' N, whilst gaining an area to the west containing copper and perhaps gold and silver'. He described the land which Mexico had gained there as 'a desert without water, wood or grass, where not one acre can ever be cultivated, where no military post can be sustained and which can never be inhabited' (I, 14). This land, however, a rectangle of some 56 km north to south and 280 km east to west, contained the best prospect for a transcontinental railway route south of the mountains, and in its Mesilla valley was later to become one of the most important long-staple cotton lands of the USA (White 1968, 138). In further negotiations for the landward extension from the Rio Grande the US Congress (US Congress, 1853) laid down that monies for the Boundary Commission might be spent only if 'the southern boundary of New Mexico is not established . . . further north of the town called Passo [sic] than is laid down in Disturnell's map'. In the final accord, written into the Gadsden Treaty (US Statutes 1853, Art. 1; Garber 1923), the boundary was redefined as 'up the river (Rio Grande) to the point where the parallel of 31° 47' N crosses the same, then due west one hundred miles, thence south to the parallel 31° 20' N latitude, then along the said parallel to the 11th meridian of longitude west of Greenwich . . .'. Thus the international boundary along the Rio Grande and its westward course by lines of reference across the desert were finally resolved, but agreement on the principles for this boundary line was merely the prelude to a host of problems and confrontations.

THE EARLY YEARS OF THE INTERNATIONAL BOUNDARY

Not all Texans were satisfied with the Rio Grande line as their limit of sovereignty: 'The truth is, our government committed a great error in accepting the Rio Grande as a boundary line. We should never have stopped this side of that great natural boundary, the Sierra Madre range' (quoted in Taylor 1934, 30). Yet in reality it was some years before the American hold on the lower Rio Grande was at all secure. In the upper Rio Grande Texas withdrew to its present limits in 1850, in return for ten million dollars of US Federal monies; the Texan boundary with New Mexico was fixed at 32° N (Fig. 2). In the lower valley there were raids and counter-raids, with the presence of lawless men from both Texas and Mexico. Evil stereotypes were implanted in the minds on both sides of the Border, while between the Rio Grande and the Nueces river, on Texan soil, the 'mustangers' ranged at will. 'While their ostensible employment is that of catching wild horses, they often add the practice of highway robbery . . . seizing any property that comes their way, murdering travellers and making descents upon trains and border villages' (Olmsted 1857, 443). Again, but only briefly successful, there was an attempt to set up an independent Mexican Republic of the Sierra Madre (1850), supported financially by American merchants and filibusters; in return for US aid the Mexican leader promised to pass a law for returning fugitive slaves (Taylor 1934, 38). Carvajal's attempt foundered within three years, but lawless conditions on the Border continued intermittently well into the 1880s. Trade nevertheless flourished, though much of it became clandestine. There was smuggling and counter-smuggling, for 'As might reasonably be expected in any country where the duties on foreign goods amounted to virtual prohibition, smuggling ceases to be a crime, identifies itself with the best part of the population, and connects itself with romance and legends of the frontier' (Emory 1857, 64). To counteract this, and also to encourage settlement, the Mexican government set up a Free Zone (1858) in the newly reconstituted State of Tamaulipas. Within this frontier tract goods could pass free of import duties, but, bitterly opposed by the Texans, this concession did little more than legitimate clandestine practices. The Texans opposed the Free Zone, as disadvantageous to their trade, and for twenty years and more the Free Zone became 'the haunt of fugitives and criminals, as well as of respectable merchants' (Smith 1961, 192). Indeed, at this time the Abbé Domenech (1858, 228) did not hesitate to describe the Americans of the Texan frontier as 'the very scum of society'.

At mid-century, the El Paso corridor on the upper Rio Grande became a major highway to the California gold-fields. Three routes converged: the *Camino Real* from the south, an important cattle and wagon trail; the overland trail from the Platte river far to the north; and the new San Antonio–El Paso road, opened up in the 1850s (White 1968, 145). In 1858, though, El Paso (then Franklin) was 'only a small adobe hamlet of about 300 inhabitants, more than three-quarters of whom were Mexican' (Miller 1962, 5). Across the river there were already around 13,000 in El Paso del Norte, the present-day C. Juárez.

The American Civil War had a very positive effect on development, most notably in the lower Rio Grande valley. In spite of a non-intercourse decree under President Juárez the Confederacy continued to export a vast volume of cotton to Europe through the Mexican port of Matamoros, which temporarily became the world's greatest cotton market (Dillman 1971, 30). Furthermore, the Confederate government continued to meddle in the affairs of the northern Mexican States. In 1861 General Sibley sought to persuade these northern states to join the Confederacy and, if Sibley had defeated the Union forces in New Mexico, Chihuahua might well have done so (White 1968, 163). At times there were overtures to the French party within Mexico, and even plans to resurrect the Confederacy within that country. Conversely, Mexican troops often operated locally with the Union forces on the Rio Grande, taking part, for example, in the attack on Laredo in March 1864 (Taylor 1934, 47). The Union was favourable to Juárez, who retired to El Paso in retreat from the French, 'a secure refuge with access to and from the US, for arms and provisions, protected to the south by a vast belt of dunes' (White 1968, 169).

UNITED STATES NEOCOLONIALISM

Following upon the Civil War there was a crescendo of development, and yet also of unparalleled turbulence on the Border, but it was development with a difference. Political domination of Mexico under the rule of President Porfirio Díaz (1876–1910), the Porfiriato (Cosío Villegas 1956), provided the stability for economic growth. The creation of vast large-scale landholdings by Mexicans was accompanied by the intrusion of US capitalist undertakings, on the land, in the mines, the cities and through investment in railways. Such large-scale growth took place on both sides of the Border, but it was more spectacular in northern Mexico. The land legislation of the liberal *Reforma* (1856–7) had transferred vast areas of ecclesiastical and other corporate lands to private ownership, establishing a powerful *hacendado* class. In the unsettled frontier areas the *haciendas* reached truly monumental proportions; in Chihuahua, for example, Luis Terrazas held no fewer than 2 million hectares (Carr 1971, 3). Within these baronial *haciendas* there were also medium and small-scale holdings of the rural middle class, a tradition from the seventeenth- and eighteenth-century settlements. There were also 'free villages' but peonage as servitude for debts, and virtual economic slavery were the more characteristic forms of rural society for the masses.

On the US side of the Rio Grande, economic development was no less rapid or large in scale. Mammoth land enclosures up to the Nueces river took place in the late 1860s to prevent landless cattlemen grazing herds; indeed, the King ranch (1870) came to rival the Terraza property in Chihuahua. Spring cattle drives began in the 1870s from South Texas to

Wichita in Kansas (Taylor 1934. 73) and the cattle industry spread rapidly westwards into more arid lands and turbulent Indian country (Meinig 1969, 66). In 1839 there were 100,000 registered cattle, but by 1870 five millions. It was, however, the railway boom of the last two decades of the nineteenth century that transformed the Border economy of both countries. Though bypassed by the first trans-continental route El Paso was linked east–west by the Southern Pacific in 1881 and northward through Santa Fé in the same year. Three years later the first through train from Mexico City to Chicago crossed the international bridge on the Rio Grande (White 1968, 181). American entrepreneurs (Fletcher 1958) eagerly took up railway concessions under the Díaz régime in Mexico, establishing a skeleton route network there by the end of the century. This was linked in part to the opening of copper, lead, and zinc mines in the northern frontier provinces, but also to the considerable American investment in landholdings and the cattle-ranching industry.

Railways opened up distant markets, led to land speculation and the introduction of settlers, diversification of farm products, and the industrialization of the growing riverside towns on the Rio Grande. At El Paso it was said (White 1968, 215) 'there will now be ample markets for table grapes, alfalfa and onions'. In the American lower Rio Grande valley Europeans as well as Americans came in to settle cheap land, purchased by speculators, and the irrigation acreage spread under land investment companies, who cleared and put the fields under intensive cultivation (Dillman 1971, 33). Initially sugar cane, but later citrus fruits and truck crops became the local specialities. On the Mexican shores of the lower valley, agricultural development was greatly re-tarded, by unilateral diversions of water by the Texans, by continuing insecurity on the Border, and by the restrictive nature of US tariffs, barring entry to the only likely economic market. Conversely, it was the favourable McKinley tariffs (1890) which stimulated the huge American investments in mining and beneficiation enterprises, par-ticularly in Chihuahua province (see Fig. 19). Copper, lead, and zinc mines and smelters were followed later by the iron and steel industry, founded in Monterrey by US capital. As a frontier base for this US economic penetration, El Paso grew to a city of almost 40,000 by 1910, 'the greatest rail centre in the American Southwest and the most important industrial centre in an 800,000 square mile area' (White 1968, 201).

The Rio Grande cities, on both banks, clearly benefited from the vigorous cross-currents of economic growth in the later nineteenth and early twentieth centuries, but there were also substantial adverse effects. In the first place, there was the concentration of vice in and around the Border cities, a tradition which has persisted. The ease of refuge, by slipping across the Rio Grande, had early attracted outlaws, and the lucrative waggon and stage-coach trails across the semi-arid lands offered tempting and often easy targets. This was the country of John Wesley Hardin, Billy the Kid, Bat Masterson, and Wyatt Earp (White 1968, 196). The constant stream of impoverished migrants passing westward through El Paso, in search of fame and fortune, mingled with the thousands of railway workers, Chinese labourers, Mexicans moving north and those stranded without means, to give El Paso its turbulent nineteenth-century reputation. 'Hell Paso' was a well-earned title for the 'sin city of the Southwest' (White 1968, 185) and a wide-open gambling town long after the State ordinances forbade it. 'Along the Border men were necessarily individualists, not part of a movement. They shot to take; they knifed from fear; they brawled because they were drunk. Only men, never leaders were shot on the Border' (Franz 1978, 41).

A greater problem, going back well before the Treaty of Guadalupe Hidalgo was that of marauding bands crossing the river in search of cattle, booty, or the security of an alien territory. These had traditionally been Indians far back in the history of the frontier, but in the nineteenth century both Texans and Mexicans were frequently involved. Bloody reprisals were as inevitable as were the certain counter-reprisals. This period, aptly chronicled as one of Blood on the Border (Clendenen 1969), coloured attitudes and promoted the bitterness which has for so long clouded Mexican–American relations. At issue constantly was the right of 'hot pursuit' an inevitably inflammatory topic once the international boundary had been located on the Rio Grande. Article IX of the Treaty of Guadalupe Hidalgo required the United States 'forcibly to restrain the savage (Indian) tribes, and prevent or punish incursions into Mexico'. This she had been powerless to achieve, least of all in the arid lands west of El Paso. 'In the desert the Indian was King'. The line of ruined *presidios* and abandoned missions, from El Paso through Janos to Tubac, was further if earlier evidence of the same basic truth. The Americans too had built a line of forts outward from El Paso, to block the movement of Apache and Comanche raiding parties, but it was a thin screen and, particularly in the remote Big Bend country, the Indians crossed the Rio Grande at will. After the Civil War, the US settled the Apache on reservations for in 1860 there had been an insurrection under Cochise and the later Gerónimo revolt was not finally suppressed until 1886. In spite of an 'iron fist' policy under Porifio Díaz Indian troubles continued on both sides of the Rio Grande (White 1968, 173). US troops were regularly sent across the Border in 'hot pursuit', until the 1882 agreement (Taylor 1934, 52). American black troops and 'Seminole' buffalo soldiers proved to be the most doughty Indian fighters.

The 1870s were an especially turbulent period. 'Hide-peeling', cattle-rustling and murder issued in a veritable reign of terror for many frontier communities. West of the Nueces river it 'was unsafe outside of the towns, and it was impossible to execute the laws at all ... the country was entirely in the possession of the cattle raiders'. In Nueces county 'large parties of mounted and well-armed men committed the most brutal outrages, murdering peaceful Mexican farmers and stock-men who had lived all their lives in Texas' (Jennings 1899). On the other hand, it was said 'the Mexican thieves and cut-throats who have collected on the Border think the killing of a Texan is something to be proud of' (quoted in Taylor 1934, 58). Both the US and Mexican governments were greatly alarmed by these events and commissions of enquiry followed in quick succession. It was possible to regulate 'hot pursuit' only in relation to regular forces under each sovereign authority. The US military were divided on the issue: local com-manders wanted action and they frequently ordered their men into Mexico on local, punitive retaliations. Invariably they regarded their distant federal superiors as 'sluggish and inefficient'. Forceful views, indeed, were not lacking that the permeable Rio Grande frontier was itself a cause of the problem and, to be secure, the international boundary should be moved further into Mexico. 'It is impossible to prevent these frauds unless you take the whole country and make the Sierra Madre the line', said one report (US Congress, Senate 1873, 12). According to another, 'Colonel Ford believes that the only security for the Texas frontier is to move the line west of the Rio Grande ... I believe the Sierra Madre is always the line we want to reach when we cross the Rio Grande' (quoted in Taylor 1934, 61). The local military view was clear, that 'full authority to operate in Mexico in any way we choose is the only way in which life and property can be made secure on this frontier', views which, fortunately, for diplomatic reasons were usually countermanded in Washington. Nevertheless, in the 1870s the practice of 'hot pursuit' over the Rio Grande was thought justified if in sight of the marauders or upon a fresh trail, in which case the raiders could legally be overtaken and punished.

The Mexican government preferred close co-operation between the military on both sides with a strong Extradition Treaty in the back-ground, but they had difficulty in imposing their will on the local Mexican Border bosses or *caciques*, many of whom were deeply involved in contraband and cattle rustling (Cosío Villegas 1963, 47). An unofficial force, the Texas Rangers, created in 1874, not frequently took the law into its own hands, and became the scourge alike of Indians and the Mexican frontiersmen (Jennings 1899: Webb 1935). The local Texans constantly asserted the superiority of their rangers over US troops in dealing with the Mexicans, a tradition derived from the achievements of the rangers in earlier Indian warfare (Taylor 1934, 59). General Sherman (US Congress, Senate 1877, 12) spoke rather differently: 'The Texas Rangers, so-called, have been a source of danger to the US, rather than of assistance in frontier defence.' Wherever the truth lay, Border attitudes hardened into hostility and intransigence on both banks of the Rio Grande. 'To the Texans, Mexicans were marauders, invaders, cattle thieves and murderers, and the international boundary should be moved to the Sierra Madre. To the Mexicans, the Texans were invaders, and thieves not only of cattle, but of land and territory' (Taylor 1934, 66). Behind this there lay a long-standing and basic clash of temperament and culture: 'The mingled Puritanism and brigandism, which distinguishes the vulgar mind of the South, peculiarly unfits it to be harmoniously associated with the bigoted, childish and passionate Mexican' (Olmsted 1857, 455).

It was with difficulty that the military on either side could contain such a situation, but the 1882 Protocol on the rights of 'hot pursuit' was a step in the right direction, at least for the regular forces. 'Federal troops might reciprocally cross the boundary line . . . in close pursuit of a band of savage Indians . . . only in unpopulated or desert parts of the said boundary line' (quoted in White 1968, 194). It is to be noted, however, that this said nothing about Mexicans or Texans, and, moreover, it did not apply in the Rio Grande valley proper.

THE TWENTIETH CENTURY

Revolutionary Mexico after 1910 put a new, more aggressive face on nationalism and, with the later nationalization of American oil assets (1938) under President Lázaro Cárdenas, there was a dramatic shift in relationships across the Rio Grande. The leaders of the Mexican north, the *norteños*, played a dominant role in the recurrent phases of revolutionary change (Carr 1971). The 'clever and ruthless young operators from the North' (Womack 1969) came to prominence in 1913–14 with the Huerta counter-revolution, followed by other Sonoran dynasts in Presidents Obregón and Calles. These were vigorous exponents of a nationalism nourished by fear and hatred of the foreigner, radical and later anti-clerical in direction and drive. Their rise to power also owed something to certain geographical advantages. The Mexican northlands were vast and remote from the governmental core on the Central Plateau. It was a distant mountainous or arid plateau environment, different too in its racial composition and social structure. The Catholic Church possessed few lands, but there was a wealthy secular land-owning class of *hacendados* and a well-funded middle class, on farms and in the towns. In Monterrey there was the strongest industrial and metallurgical base in the country and the nearby American hinterland offered abundant resources and a Border-lands refuge in time of need.

The early years after 1910 were exceedingly turbulent. The military warlordism of Villa on the northern Border, and Zapata with his southern peasants, threatened the regular government in Mexico city. Francisco Villa's last bid for power followed the US invasion of Vera Cruz (1914) and Pershing's punitive expedition of 1916; it expired with the intervention of US forces in the Battle of Juárez (June 1919). This finally brought military peace to a Border intermittently troubled by warfare, guerrilla activity, and Indian raids for almost four centuries.

Commercialized vice had become deeply engrained in Border life, but it paid handsome dividends. Referring to C. Juárez in 1921 the American consul reported: 'Juárez is the most immoral, degenerate and utterly wicked place I have ever seen or heard of in my travels. Murder and robbery are everyday occurrences and gambling, dope selling and using, drinking and sexual vices are continuous. It is a mecca for criminals and degenerates from both sides of the Border' (Martínez 1975, 57). On a more liberal note, four years later, we hear: 'I can find in all these towns no sin more gorgeous than those enjoyed by every Massachusetts Lodge of Elks at its annual fish-fries prior to 1921' (Aikman 1925). A case of double standards? Certainly C. Juárez became progressively transformed to a much more American urban landscape. New stores, shops, markets, factories, schools, libraries, theatres, auditoria and parks offered the acceptable face of develop-ment, whose obverse side showed bars, cabarets, brothels, and *zonas de tolerancia* where the wealth was often generated in the first place.

The major economic events of the twentieth century, two world wars and the great economic depression of early 1930s, each had a dramatic impact on the life and landscapes along the Rio Grande. During most of this period there were sharp and growing contrasts in conditions on the Mexican and United States banks, and in the differential course of economic development. For long it was the case that in Mexico 'the soil, the water, the climate and the labour are there but the all-important factor of a market is almost completely absent' (Timm 1941, 211). US tariffs on vegetables and fruit limited agricultural development south of the Rio Grande, and subsequent quota restrictions on the import of cotton textiles further hampered Mexican prospects. In the 1930s, grazing and dry-farming for cotton were characteristic land uses in Tamaulipas, in sharp contrast to the intensive and diversified cropland across the river, where winter truck crops, cotton and citrus fruit cultivation flourished in south Texas.

The spread of land reform and the creation of communal *ejido* farms broke up some, but by no means all the large landed estates in northern Mexico, while the plans for systematic irrigation (1926) under the

Calles administration ushered in an intensified and protracted interaction with the Americans on water management questions. Both
world wars stimulated the demand for Mexican labour in the US and
this led directly to the combustible social issues of the *bracero* farmworker programme and the subsequent waves of 'undocumented'
migration. From 1940 to 1965 there was an unprecedented economic
and demographic boom on the Rio Grande frontier, on both banks of
the river. The impact was the more dramatic in the Mexican cities
where the tide of migrants off the land flowed steadily stronger, in
search of city life or, even more hopefully, of admittance to the United
States, whether openly or clandestinely. The slum *barrios* proliferated at
the city limits, unemployment and underemployment became endemic,
and all the indicators of social deprivation mounted inexorably. After
the closure of the *bracero* farm labour programme in 1964 they became
even more severe, leading to progressive Mexican government intervention, with the enlargement of the 1961 PRONAF programme
(p. 209) and the 1965 Border Industrialization Programme (BIP).

The effective and comprehensive water management scheme for the
lower Rio Grande (1944) permitted the more rational and fuller use of
irrigation lands, particularly in the Mexican lower valley. Cotton
farming grew to monoculture proportions before waning during the
1970s. On the Texan Border the citrus industry gave place proportionately to more cotton and vegetables, most notably so after 1960
(Dillman 1971, 35), but there were problems too in Texas. Although
town populations grew in post-war years so did the drift off the land and
the progressive development of an economic and social problem area
along the Rio Grande. On almost all social indicators this was becoming a deprived strip, in living standards, social provision, quality of
life, availability of work, or long-term development prospects. This
situation was recognized in the granting of Economic Development
status to many of its districts during the 1960s and 1970s and in the
designation of the South-west Border Economic Development Region
in August 1977. Thus was born the Border paradox, whereby the Rio
Grande towns were a depressed area within Texas, but with fewer
problems and better prospects than their Mexican counterparts. These
Mexican Rio Grande towns, on the other hand, were not among the
most serious problem areas of that country and, indeed, on many
parameters showed up as being distinctly better than the average.

Since the mid-1960s, there has been a period of social and economic
adjustment between the two nations on their common frontier. The oil
crisis of the early 1970s emphasized the existing trends of instability and
decline. On the other hand, the oil discoveries in Mexico during the
same decade, for the first time promised an altogether different, more
prosperous future south of the Rio Grande (p. 261).

THE RIVERLINE BOUNDARY

The initial delimitation of the international boundary on the Rio Grande, in the Treaty of Guadalupe Hidalgo (US Statutes 1848), specified demarcation by the centre of the deepest channel, the well-known and long-established *thalweg* principle. Article V of the same Treaty also sought to give a degree of permanence to the demarcation: the link should be 'religiously respected . . . and no change ever made without the free and express consent of both nations'. Already during the reconnaissances to demarcate the river boundary (Emory 1857) it became clear that in a braided, frequently interrupted, and unstable channel the initial definition and demarcation of the boundary would prove difficult. Even more problematical was the evident short-term, lateral shifting of the channel within an unstable river bed. These processes the soldiers and diplomats at the Peace Conference had totally failed to take into account in their rigid belief in an immutable fixed-line principle.

The truth was that those drafting the 1848 Treaty had little notion of the wayward characteristic of the Rio Grande, and they thus sought to apply principles derived from widespread conventional experience in more humid regions. However, river courses in semi-arid or desert regions behave altogether differently, the product of low precipitation or run-off over the basin, markedly irregular flow régime, thin surface vegetation, and friable, loose soils. These characteristics increase the instability of slopes or river banks, and condition the development of an unusual longitudinal profile. As a result, rivers like the Rio Grande flow, when they flow at all, within broad, shallow valley-floors. Such valley-floors may be bounded by imperceptible slopes, as in the deltaic branches, or they may be enclosed by short, steep gradients up onto the nearby *mesa*, as along the lower Rio Grande or in the El Paso–Juárez valley. The gorge tract of the Rio Grande, through the Big Bend country, is sharply defined and more conventional in character; it offers few demarcation problems. The issue of demarcation relates particularly to the shifting of the river course by the processes of accretion or avulsion. By legal precept accretion, or its counterpart loss by erosion, concerns a slow, gradual, but steady process of lateral movement in a watercourse. Avulsion, on the other hand, refers to sudden, abrupt shifts of course, often the result of flood surges, or the breaking-through of a meander-neck, as perhaps the final stage of what may have been a slow and cumulative process of change. Herein lies the problem, for international lawyers, as well as for statesmen or riparian owners. Tardily, but eventually, as will be seen, the permissible legal adjustments of a boundary resulting from processes of accretion or avulsion were separately codified, but, inevitably, it could not easily be determined when one process blended into the other in what was often a continuum of change.

The problem on the Rio Grande was compounded by the speed at which processes of accretion, erosion, or avulsion all operated. In more humid regions, the formation of meander cut-offs, or *bancos* in Rio Grande parlance, was a more deliberate and slowly evolving process, intermittently broken, usually during flood surges, by the formation of natural cut-offs across the narrow meander-neck. In semi-arid areas, the river channel may sensitively adjust to surges by a remarkable lateral shift in its configuration and location. Any aerial photograph of the lower Rio Grande will illustrate the almost unparalleled complexity of extreme curvatures of the river bed, past and present, superimposed one upon the other in the course of its evolution. Surprisingly, the Treaty makers of 1848, confirmed in 1853 and persisting to the 1884 Convention, failed to recognize the significance of this. Not at all surprisingly, those concerned with the resultant demarcation, and its persistence, very soon realized the formidable problem that confronted them. The advice of the then US Attorney-General, General Cushing, was sought as early as 1857 (Mueller 1975, 121). In the light of established Treaty practice elsewhere, though invariably in more humid conditions, he gave the opinion that changes by accretion could legally permit the boundary to be moved, those by avulsion could not, but it was a unilateral viewpoint on which the Mexicans had not been consulted.

Though not implemented until after the 1884 International Convention (US Statutes 1884) had jointly agreed the principles involved this ruling led to the greatest difficulties and maximum local friction on the riverline. Article I of the Convention confirmed 'the centre of the normal channel, notwithstanding any alterations in the banks or in the course of the river, provided such alterations be effected by natural causes through the flow and gradual erosion and deposit of alluvium and not by the abandonment of an existing river bed and the opening of a new one'. Article II stated, equally categorically: 'Any other change, wrought by the force of the current . . . shall produce no change in the dividing line as fixed by the International Boundary Commissions in 1852; but the line then fixed shall continue to follow the middle line of the original channel bed, even though this should become entirely dry or be obstructed by deposits'. Rights of property in land which might have become separated under Article II should be unaffected and such land continued to be under the jurisdiction of the country to which it previously belonged (Art. V). There should be no attempt to dredge or construct works to influence lateral movement of the river, though protection of the banks by revetment was specifically permitted (Art. III). This arbitration by Man against Nature was bound to lead to countless problems. 'Rapid erosion in some sections carried the boundary with it; in others the river avulsively severed its meanders, leaving the boundary dry and distant from the new channel. By 1890, there were stretches along the lower Rio Grande where the international boundary was actually two or three times longer than the river' (Mueller 1975, 121).

Five years later the International Boundary Commission was created (US Statutes 1889), to clarify changes in the river course and recommend any consequential adjustments of the demarcated boundary. The Mexican government had not been content with the 1884 Convention, denying its authority to rescind prior claims and asserting continued Mexican rights to title by prescription, through continuous previous occupancy, or asserted historic rights. The IBC introduced a better climate for negotiation, but in 1895 Mexican claims to land in the tract known as 'El Chamizal' (p. 41) were still being based on historic rights of occupation, by the Mexican García family, going back to 1827, rights which, it was asserted, could legitimately be sustained on 'American' soil, since the river east of El Paso was alleged to have moved by avulsion during previous flood surges (Peters 1951, 414).

By the end of the nineteenth century the uncertain sovereignty and the difficulty of policing the many *banco* cut-offs led to further Treaty legislation (US Statutes 1905). *Bancos* had retarded development and many isolated parcels of land were, as a result, abandoned by farmers. Those separated by the new river course from former territory of the adjacent State ceased to be under effective jurisdiction (e.g. El Horcón, Fig. 4), and characteristically became refuges for bandits, smugglers, and ne'er-do-wells from both nations. Typically, a *banco* of disputed sovereignty near El Paso was used (1899) for a much publicized but prohibited prize-fight between Maher and Fitzsimmons, in defiance of the authorities on either bank (White 1968, 207). Quite early in its life the IBC recommended reduction, if not elimination of the many *banco* disputes by an exchange of territory on an equitable basis throughout the Rio Grande valley, but such a recommendation was well ahead of its time. The Mexican government at that time felt bound by its Constitution, which expressly forbade the transfer of any national territory to foreign ownership, but in the so-called *Banco* Convention (1905) proposals involving land transfer for mutual advantage were accepted by both sides. The 1884 Convention principles were abandoned in favour of retaining the international boundary along the centre-line of the deepest channel of the river after the formation of *banco* cut-offs, land thus detached being transferred as sovereign territory to the newly acquiring State. Under Article II there was to be an exchange of parcels of *banco* land, provided none was greater in extent than 250 ha (617 a) or had not more than two hundred inhabitants. Article IX provided for protection of private property on transfer of sovereign jurisdiction: '. . . may remain or remove . . . either keeping property or disposing of it . . . If anyone chooses to remain he/she may preserve title and rights of citizenship of the country to which the *banco* formerly belonged, or acquire nationality of the country to which the *banco* will belong in the future.' This seemed clear enough, but though it was legally neat, it proved troublesome to the local inhabitants. In the first thirty-five years 172 *bancos* were eliminated: 9,786 ha were transferred, 6,434 to the United States and only 3,352 ha to Mexico, including the land in the El Paso–Juárez valley (1933) (Timm 1941, 90). Between 1941 and 1967 the total of land transferred was 1,341 ha, 647 to the United States and 694 to Mexico, clear evidence that regulation of the Rio Grande waters after the 1944 Treaty (p. 123), with its storage dams, greater withdrawal of irrigation waters, and better protection of banks (Day 1970, 150) had tamed the river considerably. As the exchange of *banco* land proceeded, the US government adopted a policy of limiting the process to the minimum, since land values on the American banks were so very much higher and, moreover, the transfer was seen as a means of gaining US citizenship for former Mexican *banco* 'residents'. There were additional complications where farms held land on the *banco*, but also elsewhere and, in any case, the principles did nothing to solve the major international irritant, the problem of El Chamizal (p. 41) which had more than two hundred citizens and was a long-lasting source of embitterment in Mexican–American relations.

Further steps on the *banco* problem were taken under the 1933 Convention (US Statutes 1933; Fitton 1934, Reinhardt 1937), applicable to the El Paso–Juárez valley. To eliminate the danger of flooding and to stabilize the boundary line the Rio Grande was to be confined in an 141 km channel between artificial *levées*; the previous 'natural' river length had been 250 km. Under Article III the costs of the operation were to be borne according to the benefits accruing: 88 per cent by the US, 12 per cent by Mexico. There were no stipulations limiting the exchange of individual land parcels, either in area or number of inhabitants, but all land transferred now passed into government ownership, after compensation, and there was thus no need to safeguard either private property rights or to transfer rights of national citizenship (Art. V). The total land area exchanged between the US and Mexico had to be equivalent and this amounted in each case to about 1,420 ha. The international boundary then followed the deepest channel within the rectified river course (Art. VI). The straightened boundary greatly increased powers of immigration control and customs enforcement by both countries, while government ownership limited encroachment on the river-banks by private landowners. The IBC undertook to restore the river to its rectified channel if it should escape, whether by avulsion or accretion.

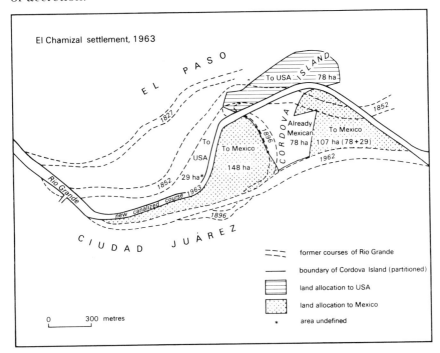

El Chamizal settlement, 1963

former courses of Rio Grande

boundary of Cordova Island (partitioned)

land allocation to USA

land allocation to Mexico

area undefined

FIG. 3. El Chamizal

EL CHAMIZAL

Men of goodwill, working together, can reach equitable solutions to mutual problems and, in working together, they will find friendship and gain understanding.
(Inscription on US monument at El Chamizal)

All the problems of defining and demarcating the Rio Grande riverline boundary became focussed in their most intractable form on a 600-acre site in the eastern outskirts of El Paso and C. Juárez, on the territory known as El Chamizal (Fig. 3). From being a local issue the Chamizal question became the dominant frontier problem in Mexican thinking for almost a century (Miramontes 1979), until its solution in the Treaty of 1963 (US Dept. of State 1963). As recently as the early 1960s, Communists in Latin America, to their advantage, were still citing the Chamizal as a typical case of American imperialism (Liss 1965, 83). There has, indeed, been more attention paid to the legal and diplomatic aspects of the Chamizal than to almost any other Border demarcation problem (Hall 1911; Hill 1965; Liss 1965; Wisner 1965; and Lessup 1973), but as an issue it never loomed large in the American popular mind.

PLATE 1. El Paso–C. Juárez from Ranger Peak, looking SE to El Chamizal

PLATE 2. El Chamizal. Mexican Border markers, pre-1963 boundary on Córdova Island

PLATE 3. El Chamizal. Re-aligned Rio Grande, seen through the 'tortilla' curtain

PLATE 4. El Paso, El Paso street, leading to the Rio Grande, looking back to the CBD

The problem arose directly from the considerable instability of the Rio Grande channel through the Chamizal. Prior to the major urban developments of the past hundred years the issue remained local. Disputes over private property rights, between Mexican and Texan farmers, had been the most prominent question, from the mid-nineteenth century onwards. During the 1850s, 89 ha shifted from Mexico, through movements of the river, and the land was promptly taken into possession by a Texan rancher. Southward swings of the channel continued through the 1860s, adding some 323 ha to the Texas bank, but not necessarily in sovereignty to that State (Liss 1965, 9–10). The most violent shift took place in the 1864 floods and within two years the Mexican government took up the problem of boundary demarcation on behalf of its nationals, but without response from the US authorities. The problem of sovereignty over the Chamizal lands became more serious in the late nineteenth century. El Paso was growing steadily and, by 1910, some 5,000 of its 40,000 inhabitants resided on the lands in dispute with Mexico. Taxes were levied by the municipality on five million dollars' worth of property in the Chamizal, and there was an escalating social problem of Mexican squatters (Lessup 1973, 431). Not only that, but there was lawlessness and a refuge for rum-runners or narcotics peddlers; armed conflict between US and Mexican customs agents was not uncommon, in 'hot pursuit' of such malefactors.

In 1910 an international arbitration took place (US Statutes 1910), in which a Canadian Commissioner acted in concert with American and Mexican counterparts. The arguments by each side and the ultimate arbitration indicated the continuing ambiguities of principle for re-defining sovereignty in a shifting river course. The Mexican case for recognizing her sovereignty over the Chamizal tract rested upon: the definition of the 1848 boundary, confirmed in 1853, as a fixed and invariable line; a denial that the 1884 Convention (p. 38) could be applied retrospectively; a claim that, in any case, the Convention took account only of slow erosion/accretion, or avulsion, whereas the channel changes had been abrupt, yet rapid and continuous; an argument that the Rio Grande was not a river, but a turbulent intermittent torrent, and could thus not be judged by normal legal precepts for rivers; and, finally, that the United States had no (historic) rights of prescriptive title to the lands. The US case was clean contrary, that: the 1848 and 1853 Treaties established a fluvial boundary, not a fixed and inviolate line; the 1884 Convention was retroactive; it also catered for all types of erosion; the Rio Grande was to be judged a river, within accepted definitions of international law; and a claim for a prescriptive US title to the Chamizal could be sustained in law.

The arbitrator ruled that the principles of a fluvial boundary, not a fixed and invariable line should apply; the 1884 Convention was retro-active; and that the US had not established a prescriptive title. On the most controversial question, slow erosion or avulsion he delivered a 'judgement of Solomon': from 1852 to 1864 the movement had been by slow erosion; from 1864 to 1868, in which major shifting of the river course had occurred, the process was a kind of avulsion. He therefore proposed a division of the Chamizal lands, including an apportionment of the major tract north of the contemporary Rio Grande channel, the so-called Córdova island (Fig. 3). Unfortunately, there was no clear measurement of the pre-1864 course on which to base a fair allocation of land but, in any case, the arbitration was rejected by the US. The rejection was based on: lack of jurisdiction for the arbitrator to make a divided award; and the vague and indeterminate nature of the argu-ments adduced, particularly those on slow erosion or avulsion.

There the matter rested for a further fifty years. During that time the problem became even more pressing. The eastward course of urban expansion at El Paso became distorted into a narrow corridor, with inconvenient detours around Córdova 'island'. West of the 'island' there was a congested industrial zone; to the east 'colourful residential neighbourhoods'. Parts of the 'island' were derelict and overgrown with weeds and refuse, a haunt of smugglers and illegal migrant trails. On its borders there was 'a honky-tonk row, with *tamale* shops, taxis and ramshackle houses' (Liss 1965, 2).

Finally, in 1963, the Chamizal problem was resolved (United Nations 1963). In the interests of amicable relations with Latin America President Kennedy declared that 'the Chamizal dispute is not a matter the US could continue to treat with indifference'. The sub-sequent Chamizal Treaty accepted the 1910 arbitration ruling, giving effect to its provisions under changed circumstances: 3,700 US citizens had to be compensated for land and resettled, at an estimated initial cost of twenty million dollars (Mueller 1975, 99). Article I of the Treaty provided for a relocation of the Rio Grande in a 7-km concrete channel, opened in 1968, which would become 'a fixed reach of the international boundary'. Location of this channel meant a complex transference of lands by both parties (Fig. 3), which involved some trade-off com-promises. To retain the river as boundary, in its new man-made course, it was essential to divide Córdova 'island' in order to allocate all the lands on one side of the river to one or other of the States. the new Chamizal channel was considerably longer than the natural channel had been and, as Mueller (1975, 101) put it: 'this is the only reach of the international Rio Grande that was lengthened, rather than shortened, by works of the Boundary Commission'.

The outcome has benefited both parties. On the American bank, a National Monument park has been laid out, a high school and vocational school built, and a spacious port of entry constructed. A multi-lane highway leads across a major new international bridge, into Mexican territory. There the lands acquired under the 1963 Treaty have been developed under the 1961 PRONAF programme, with parkland and a major tourist commercial centre. Far greater than this creative landscape impact is the marked improvement in general US–Mexican Border relations, which had been embittered for almost a century by the dispute over the Chamizal, and most notably so by the American rejection of the 1910 Arbitration.

THE 1970 BOUNDARY TREATY

This Treaty (US Dept. State 1970) was drawn up on the considered advice of the International Boundary and Water Commission to resolve all outstanding territorial differences along the Rio Grande valley. The major tract of land in dispute was in the Presidio–Ojinaga section, downstream from the confluence with the Conchos river. Here Mexico had claimed the entire valley section on the principle of prescription (historic rights of occupance) but also on grounds that the river had moved across the tracts by successive stages in a process of avulsion. A Mexican offer (1907) to compromise by offering 25.7 per cent of the land to the US was not acceptable at that time, but in 1970 the same offer was taken up and implemented, as part of a wider package deal in land along the river (Mueller 1975, 107). Approximately 650 ha were recognized as Mexican and 220 ha were confirmed as US territory, flanking a newly rectified river channel. The channel was completed and the lands transferred by 1977 (US Dept. State 1977a).

Downstream, other tracts of land and islands were exchanged. The Horcón cut-off (Fig. 3), a 170–ha plot of US territory, passed to the south of the Rio Grande channel when an American irrigation company illegally diverted the river bed near Mercedes, Texas in 1906 (Hill 1967). Effectively beyond local US jurisdiction for many decades, El Horcón was infiltrated by Mexican settlers at Rio Rico. Under the terms of the 1970 Treaty the tract was ceded to Mexico on 18 April 1972 (Mexico, Sec. de Rel. Ext. 1972), but in that same year there were numerous claims on behalf of Rio Rican residents to be permitted to enter the US as native-born citizens. The US Immigration and Naturalization Service contested these claims on the grounds that, though the land in question was US territory at the time the claimants might have been born, there had never been US jurisdiction during their lifetime, and there had been no giving of allegiance or obedience to the USA by the local citizens. No taxes had been collected, no local State or federal laws had been enforced by the US. The residents had freely taken part in the life of adjacent territory in Mexico, though they had remained outside Mexican jurisdiction until 1972.

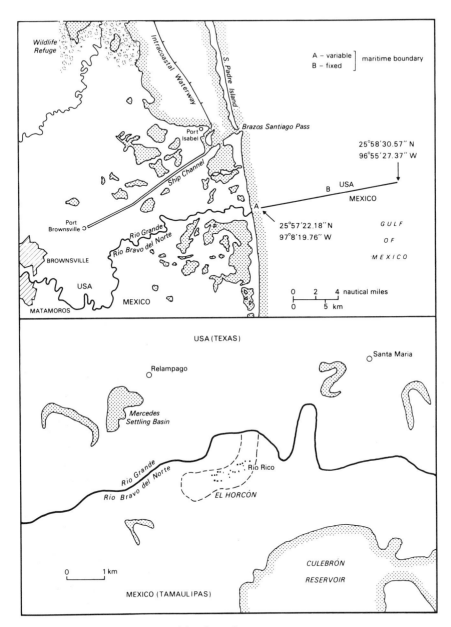

FIG. 4. Banco at El Horcón; maritime boundary

A further particular problem in the 1970 Treaty was the awarding of sovereign title to islands, many of them with a short-lived and ill-defined existence during the evolution of the river course (Mueller 1975,

108). In the Treaty, the allocation of islands was on principles similar to those of the *Banco* Convention of 1905: islands to the north of the main channel passed to the US, to the south to Mexico. The net deficit of 102 ha to Mexico was compensated for in the land allocation in the Presidio–Ojinaga valley section.

The 1970 Treaty recognized the natural channel of the Rio Grande as the permanent and stable international boundary, 'along the middle of the channel occupied by normal flow and . . . along the middle of the channel which in normal flows has the greater or greatest acreage width'. The definition by the widest channel, rather than the *thalweg* or deepest channel, makes for ease of recognition and demarcation, particularly with the control afforded by regular scrutiny of aerial photographs (Mueller 1975, 109). The processes of erosion and accretion are no longer defined in the limiting terms of 'slow and gradual', but it is in respect of the adjustment to avulsive changes that the 1970 Treaty breaks new ground. Under Article 3 the IBWC is charged with 'physically restoring the river to its pre-avulsive channel when the newly-formed tract exceeds either 250 ha or has a population of one hundred habitants'. If this is not feasible, credit is given to the losing country in a land bank, to be allocated in compensation at a later date along some other stretch of the river. Severed lands smaller in area or population may be awarded: (a) 'by the injured party restoring the channel to its pre-avulsive course within three years (plus a maximum one-year extension) if it wishes to retain the tract; or (b) if restoration is not made the land passes under neighbouring sovereignty and the river remains the boundary' (Mueller 1975, 110). In the latter case, compensation in an equivalent area of land is payable later, elsewhere in the Rio Grande valley.

A new problem faced for the first time in the 1970 Treaty was the location of the boundary in the chaotic area of the shifting delta outlets (Fig. 4). The heavy sediment load, almost imperceptible longitudinal gradient and northward longshore drifting, with an offshore bar obstructing the mouth, have moved the outlet of the Rio Grande into the Gulf of Mexico considerably over short periods of time. The problem of linking the variable location of the outlet with a fixed point defining the inner limit of the territorial sea some 609 m (2,000 ft) offshore was ingeniously solved. A variable line A–B was defined, pivoting on B as a fixed point defining the inner limit of the territorial sea and drawn to 'the center of the mouth of the Rio Grande, wherever that may be located' (Art. 5). From B, the permanent maritime boundary of the territorial sea and contiguous zone extends outwards for twelve nautical miles (22 km), defined by fixed positions of latitude and longitude.

In 1976 (US Dept. State 1976), Mexico and the USA each declared a

200-nautical mile (370-km) Exclusive Economic Zone (EEZ), extending outwards from the baselines used to measure the width of their territorial seas. This measure was directly related to fisheries conservation and management, and led in the following year to fisheries treaties (US Dept. State 1977b, c). Both nations were concerned with rational management, conservation, and optimum use of fish stocks in adjacent areas of the Gulf of Mexico. Each would have authority over the live marine resources above the continental shelf off the Rio Grande, and to 'anadromous species of fish of national origin during their migration'. Vessels of the sister nation required permits and must be subject to inspection by the country in whose waters they were fishing. Areas for fishing were designated, catches limited, and the number and types of vessel and their gear controlled, but traditional fishing rights would be respected whenever possible. The Mexican requirements were the more stringent, to protect local employment and develop the national industry which could not flourish under conditions of open competition. The scientific contribution of the Americans to Gulf fisheries was recognized in their allocation of fishing quotas, but by 31 December 1979 the lucrative shrimping industry was exclusively reserved for local fishermen.

The final transfers of parcels of land along the Rio Grande, completed in 1977, established a much simplified and clearly defined channel containing the river. For the first time since the 1853 Treaty there was an undisputed international riverline boundary at all points along the course. A fitting complement to the harnessing and management of its alternately turbulent and scarce water resources, similarly allocated in equitable fashion by mutual agreement under the 1944 Boundary Waters Treaty (p. 123).

REFERENCES

GENESIS OF THE FRONTIER

AIKMAN, D. (1925) 'Hell on the Border', *Amer. Mercury*, **5,** 17–23.

BANCROFT, H. H. (1884) *History of the Northern Mexican States* (San Francisco: A.L. Bancroft & Co).

BANNON, J. F. (1970) *The Spanish Borderlands frontier 1513–1821* (Albuquerque: Univ. New Mexico Press).

BANNON, J. F. (ed.) (1964) *Bolton and the Spanish borderlands, selections* (Norman: Univ. Oklahoma Press).

BARTLETT, J. R. (1854) *Personal narrative of exploration and incidents in Texas, New Mexico, California, Sonora and Chihuahua* (New York: Appleton), 2 vols.

BERNAL, I. (1978) 'The cutural roots of the border: an archaeologist's view', ch. 1 in S. R. Ross (ed.) *Views across the Border* (Albuquerque: Univ. New Mexico Press), 25–32.

BOLTON, H. E. (1921) *The Spanish Borderlands: a chronicle of Old Florida and the Southwest* (New Haven: Yale Univ. Press).

BUSTAMANTE, J. A. (1979) 'El estudio de la zona fronteriza México-Estados Unidos', *Foro Internacional*, **XIX**, 3, 471–516.

CARR, B. (1971) 'The peculiarities of the Mexican North, 1880–1928; an essay in interpretation', *Glasg. Univ. Inst. Latin Am. Stud., occ. Pap. 4.*

CLENDENEN, C. C. (1969) *Blood on the Border* (London: Collier Macmillan).

COSÍO VILLEGAS, D. (1956) *Estados Unidos contra Porfirio Díaz* (Mexico: Editorial Hermes).

COSÍO VILLEGAS, D. (1968) 'Border troubles in Mexican–US relations', *SWest Hist. Q.*, **72**, 1, 34–9.

COX, I. J. (1902) 'The Southwest boundary of Texas', *Tex. Hist. Q.*, **6**, 2.

DILLMAN, C. D. (1971) 'Occupance phases of the Lower Rio Grande of Texas and Tamaulipas', *Calif. Geogr.*, **12**, 30–37.

DOMENECH, Abbé E. (1858) *Missionary adventures in Texas and Mexico* (London: Longmans).

EMORY, W. M. (1857) *Report on the US and Mexican boundary survey*, House Exec. Doc. 135, 34th Congr. 1st Sess., Ser. 861.

FLETCHER, D. M. (1958) *Rails, mines and progress: seven American promoters in Mexico, 1867–1911* (New York: Cornell Univ. Press).

FRANZ, J. B. (1978) 'The Borderlands: ideas on a leafless landscape', ch. 2 in S. R. Ross (ed.) *Views across the Border* (Albuquerque: Univ. New Mexico Press), 33–49.

GARBER, P. N. (1923) *The Gadsden Treaty: a thesis* (Philadelphia: Univ. Pennsylvania Press).

HACKETT, C. W. (ed. & transl.) (1931) *Pichardo's treatise on the limits of Louisiana and Texas* (Austin: Univ. Texas Press).

HORGAN, P. (1954) *Great River: the Rio Grande in North American history*, (New York: Rinehart & Co.), 2 vols.

JENNINGS, N. A. (1899) *A Texas Ranger* (New York: C. Scribner's Sons).

MARTÍNEZ, O. J. (1975) *Border boom town: C. Juárez since 1848* (Austin: Univ. Texas Press).

MEINIG, D. W. (1969) *Imperial Texas* (Austin: Univ. Texas Press).

MILLER, W. W. (1962) *Forty years at El Paso, 1858–1898* (El Paso: Hertzog).

MIRAMONTES, R. C. (1979) 'Los tratados de límites de México con los Estados Unidos', *Simposio Nacional sobre Estudios Fronterizos*, UNAL (Monterrey: N. León).

O'GORMAÑ, E. (1968) *Historia de las divisiones territoriales de México* (México DF; Porrúa).

OLMSTED, F. L. (1857) *A journey through Texas* (New York: Dix Edwards & Co.).

SMITH, M. H. (1961) *The lower Rio Grande region of Tamaulipas, Mexico*, Ph.D. thesis, Univ. Texas at Austin.

SPICER, E. H. (1962) *Cycles of conquest: the impact of Spain, Mexico and the United States on the Indians of the Southwest, 1533–1960* (Tucson: Univ. Arizona Press).

TAYLOR, P. S. (1934) *An American-Mexican Frontier: Nueces County, Texas* (Chapel Hill: Univ. North Carolina Press).

TIMM, C. A. (1941) *The International Boundary Commission, US and Mexico*, Univ. Texas Pub. 4134 (Austin: Univ. Texas Press).

TURNER, F. J. (1920) *The frontier in American history* (New York: Henry Holt).

US CONGRESS, HOUSE (1978) Committee on Appropriations, *Depts. of State, Justice and Commerce, the Judiciary and related agencies. Undocumented aliens*. Hearings, 95th Congr., 2nd Sess. (Washington DC: USGPO).

US CONGRESS, SENATE (1853) *An Act making appropriations for the civil and diplomatic expenses of the government for the year ending 1853. . .*, US Congressional Globe, **XXIV**, 3.

US CONGRESS, SENATE (1873) *Report 166*, 41st Congr., 2nd Sess., (Series 1409).

US CONGRESS, SENATE (1877) *Exec. Doc. 19*, 45th Congr., 2nd Sess., (Series 1780).

US STATUTES (1848) *Treaty of peace, friendship, limits and settlement with the Republic of Mexico (Guadalupe Hidalgo)*, **IX,** 922–43, 2 Feb., 30th Congr.

US STATUTES (1853) *Treaty with Mexico (Gadsden Treaty)*, **X,** 1031, 10 Dec., 32 Congr.

VIGNESS, D. M. (1951) *The Republic of the Rio Grande: an example of separatism in Northern Mexico*, Ph.D. thesis, Univ. Texas at Austin.

WEBB, W. P. (1933) *The great frontier* (Boston: Houghton Mifflin Co.).

WEBB, W. P. (1935) *The Texas Rangers: a century of frontier defense* (Boston and New York: Houghton Mifflin Co.).

WHITE, R. A. (1968) *El Paso del Norte: The geography of a pass and border area through 1906*, Ph.D. thesis, New York, Columbia Univ.

WOMACK, J. (1969) *Zapata and the Mexican revolution* (New York: Knopf).

THE RIVERLINE BOUNDARY

DAY, J. C. (1970) 'Managing the lower Rio Grande', *Univ. Chicago, Dept Geogr., Res. Pap. 125*.

EMORY, W. M. (1857) *Report on the US and Mexican boundary survey*, House Exec. doc. 135, 34th Congr. 1st Sess., Ser. 861.

FITTON, E. M. (1934) 'The rectification of the Rio Grande in the El Paso-Juárez valley', *Geogr. Rev.*, **24,** 324–5.

HALL, C. V. (1911) 'The Chamizal Arbitration between the US and Mexico', *Am. J. Int. Law*, **5,** 3, 782–833.

HILL, J. E. (1965) 'El Chamizal: a century-old boundary dispute', *Geogr. Rev.*, **55,** 510–22.

HILL, J. E. (1967) 'El Horcón: A United States–Mexican boundary anomaly', *Rocky Mount. soc. Sci. J.*, **VI,** 1, 49–61.

LESSUP, P. C. (1973) 'El Chamizal', *Am. J. Int. Law*, **67,** 3, 423–45.

LISS, S. (1965) *A century of disagreement: the Chamizal conflict, 1864–1964* (Washington: Univ. Washington Press).

MÉXICO, Sec. de Relaciones Exteriores (1972) *Diferencias Fronterizas, Un Tratado*, Tlatelolco.

MIRAMONTES, R. C. (1979) 'Los tratados de límites de México con los Estados Unidos', *Simposio Nacional sobre Estudios Fronterizos*, UNAL (Monterrey: N. León).

MUELLER, J. E. (1975) *Restless river. International Law and the behaviour of the Rio Grande* (El Paso: Texas Western Press).

PETERS, D. W. (1951) 'The Rio Grande boundary dispute in American diplomacy', *SWest Hist. Q.*, **54,** 412–29.

REINHARDT, G. F. (1937) 'Rectification of the Rio Grande in the El Paso-Juárez valley, *Am. J. Int. Law.*, **31,** 44–51.

TIMM, C. A. (1941) *The International Boundary Commission, United States and Mexico*, Univ. Texas Pub. 4134 (Austin: Univ. Texas Press).

UNITED NATIONS (1963) *The Chamizal Treaty*, Treaty Ser. 505 UNTS 185.

US, Dept. of State, Treaties and other International Agreements (1963) *Convention for the solution of the problem of the Chamizal*, **15,** 1, 21.

US, Dept. of State (1967) *Demarcation of new International Boundary (Chamizal)*, 27 Oct., TIAS 6372.

US, Dept. of State (1970) *Mexican Treaty to resolve pend. bdy drifts and maintain Rio Grande and Colorado River as the international boundary*, 23 Nov., TIAS 7313.

US, Dept. of State (1976) *US–Mexican maritime boundaries*, 24 Nov., TIAS 8805.

US, Dept. of State (1977a) *Act appertaining to Minute 257 IBWC. Relocation of the channel of the Rio Grande*, 26 May, TIAS 8625.

US, Dept. of State (1977b) *Mexico: Fisheries off the US coasts*, 26 Aug., TIAS 8852.

US, Dept. of State (1977c) *Mexico fisheries*, 26 July and 27 Sept., TIAS 8853.

US, Statutes (1848) *Treaty of peace, friendship, limits and settlement with the Republic of Mexico (Guadalupe Hidalgo)*, **IX,** 922–43, 2 Feb., 30th Congr.

US, Statutes (1884) *Convention between the United States of America and the United States of Mexico touching the boundary line between the two countries where it follows the bed of the Rio Grande and the Rio Colorado*, **XXIV,** 1011, 12 Nov.

US, Statutes (1889) *Convention between the United States of America and the United States of Mexico to facilitate the carrying out of the principles contained in the Treaty of November 12th, 1884, and to avoid the difficulties occasioned by reason of the changes which take place in the bed of the Rio Grande and Rio Colorado*, **XXVI,** 1512–7, 1 March.

US, Statutes (1905) *Convention between the United States and Mexico for the elimination of the bancos in the Rio Grande from the effects of Article II of the Treaty of November 12th, 1884*, **XXXV,** 2, 1863–8, 20 March.

US, Statutes (1910) *Convention between the United States and Mexico for arbitration of the title to the Chamizal tract*, **XXXVI,** 2481–6, 61st Congr.

US, Statutes (1933) *Convention between the United States of America and Mexico: rectification of the Rio Grande*, **XLVIII,** 2, 1621–70, 1 Feb.

WHITE, R. A. (1968) *El Paso del Norte: the geography of a pass and border area through 1906*, Ph.D. thesis, New York, Columbia Univ.

WISNER, P. H. (1965) *The Chamizal problem: a study in political geography*, Master's thesis, Dept. Geogr., Norman, Univ. Oklahoma.

PART II
Man and the Land

CHAPTER 2

The Borderlands

The Rio Grande frontier is set within the Borderlands, a term which has almost as many territorial meanings as there are purposes for which it may be defined. This is not so surprising if the Borderlands are looked upon as a field of forces, changeable through time, within which there is economic, social, cultural, and political interaction between contrasting States, and even differing civilizations. The Rio Grande is a perimeter to both the United States and Mexico and, in that sense, there is interaction with the core areas of government, settlement, and economic development in each of those two countries. The core–periphery model of exchanges must be matched with the periphery to periphery interchanges which take place across the international boundary and within a more restricted frontier zone. Such inter-peripheral transactions introduce the concept of some more limited Border region, defined with zones of distance-decay into the heartlands to the north and south of the Rio Grande. The interpretation of the field of forces within the wider Borderlands is thus a matter of assessing the polarizing flows, on the one hand towards the frontier in each country, on the other in the centrifugal direction away from the frontier towards the cores of both Mexico and the United States. Whereas Mexico City is the unambiguous core in that country there are multiple candidates within the contiguous United States, from Dallas–Fort Worth and Houston in Texas to the Midwest and the NE Industrial Belt at a greater distance.

Perhaps the widest territorial connotation of the Borderlands (Bolton 1921) encompasses the total field of interplay between Spanish, then Mexican, and European, later American cultures and dominion. The fluctuating sway of this intermingling has already been discussed (p. 17), with intermittent but progressive northward diffusion of Hispanic culture encountering, and being finally overwhelmed by, the southwestward thrust of American power during and since the early nineteenth century. The complex ebbing and flowing of cultural influences has defined the Hispanic heritage lands north of the Rio Grande and also the penetration of American ways of life, values, and customs south of that river. To map this interpretation, by which each country has been complemented and enriched, is impracticable except in a very generalized way. Nostrand (1970) mapped the Hispanic–American Borderland as the area of greatest Hispanic population concentration, with a distinctive sub-culture (*chicano* in Texas), and the presence of

Anglo-Americans who have been hispanicized. Diffusion of American life-styles into Mexico is mainly an affair of the larger cities of that country and the immediate contact-zone along the Rio Grande. It is a more recent penetration but has produced some dramatic social tensions in a short space of time.

Beyond the confines of the Rio Grande valley, the Borderlands are neither sharply to be defined in landscape terms nor uniform in their physical characteristics (see Fig. 6). Aridity is a perennial theme in dry upland basins between high, dissected mountain chains flanking the upper valley, with scarce natural resources in a forbidding environment. The northward axis of the Mexican Sierra Madre Oriental cuts across the middle Rio Grande to expire in the Big Bend country. Below the Big Bend the Texan plateaux find no counterpart on the Mexican side, but both countries partake of the shallow scarplands and coastal plains flanking the slightly more humid lower valley. There is thus no clear northern or southern limit to the Borderlands on physiographic grounds alone.

For the purposes of this study, the Borderlands have been defined by several pragmatic criteria, and within this wider definition a frontier zone has been delimited, in statutory terms (Fig. 5). The chosen northern limit to the Borderlands within Texas generally follows the outer edge of counties which had 35 per cent or more people with Spanish surnames at the 1970 census, the best available surrogate indicator of existing Hispanic culture. Extensions beyond the defined Spanish-surname limit are to include the major central places, Midland–Odessa, San Angelo, and Corpus Christi, whose southward hinterlands extend virtually to the Rio Grande (Huff and DeAre 1974). To the south of the Rio Grande the entire Mexican provinces of Chihuahua, Coahuila, Nuevo León, and Tamaulipas have been included, since there are no clearly discernible intervening social or economic limits. The Borderlands thus defined include 2.5 million Texans, 22 per cent of the population of that State, and 5.8 million Mexicans, 12 per cent of that country's citizens (1970).

Within the Borderlands to be studied there is a kind of continuum outwards from the Rio Grande towards the northern and southern limits, across broad belts of thinly peopled tracts, but immediately flanking the river there is a distinctly different frontier zone. It is a zone of more concentrated urbanization, in asymmetrically paired cities on both banks, with higher ratios of employment in manufacturing, but most particularly in service occupations. Unemployment or under-employment is endemic, though unequally loaded on the Mexican side. Population growth has been rapid during the twentieth century, and most especially so since the Second World War. In the Mexican Border cities this escalating growth—the product of strong push-factors from

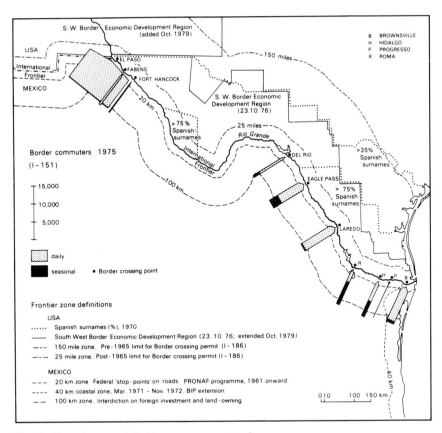

FIG. 5. Frontier zone definitions; commuter workers

the poverty-stricken countryside and no less powerful pull-factors from
the proximity of the United States—has produced tremendous social
problems. These have been compounded since the mid-1960s by the
return of the *bracero* farmworkers after the closure of that scheme by the
US in 1964, and the tighter US immigration policy ponding back a
floodtide of would-be immigrants in the Mexican Border cities.

THE FRONTIER ZONE

Statutory definition of a frontier zone, for special privileges or restrictions on either foreign nationals or local residents, goes back to the·
Mexican Free Zone (*zona libre*) policy of the mid-nineteenth century
(Fernández 1977, 76–80). This was introduced in Tamaulipas in 1858,
for a 12.5-mile (20-km) strip across which there were tariff differentials
intended both to benefit the Mexican border residents and traders, and
strengthen the prospects for settlement and economic development

there. All foreign goods could be imported free of federal, but not State or local taxes, and 'bonded' warehouses for imports could be established in Mexican Border towns. The Free Zone was an attempt to limit smuggling of cheaper US goods into Mexico, where taxes had kept prices artificially high. Quite early, British traders exploited the Free Zone to sell European goods in competition with American rivals. Apart from this, the US increasingly came to regard the Free Zone as a centre for smuggling, lawlessness, and practices unfair to American interests. By the 1890s the tariff differentials had become much reduced and the Free Zone on the Rio Grande was dissolved.

A similar 12.5-mile (20-km) frontier zone was reintroduced, on the Mexican side under the 1961 PRONAF programme and used in the initial phase of the Border Industrialization Programme (BIP). This zone defined the outer limit for the introduction of duty-free US machinery, equipment, raw materials, and components for use in an American 'offshore' ('in-bond') plant located within the frontier zone. For a short period, March 1971 to November 1972 a coastal zone 25 miles (40 km) wide was designated to enjoy similar duty-free privileges, but thereafter the so-called *maquiladora* (in-bond) plant programme was extended to the entire country. The 12.5-mile zone was retained, however, to control the movement of goods, particularly retail items, to and from the interior of Mexico. The customs and police posts along this inner boundary within Mexico have been in many respects, the *de facto* economic boundary of the country rather than the Rio Grande. Within the intervening frontier zone there was a considerable flux of transactions across the river to take advantage of price differences, quality, and availability of goods.

A wide statutory definition of the frontier zone in Mexico was the 62.5-mile (100-km) landward zone and a 31.5-mile (50-km) coastal zone, within which, under the 1917 Constitution, foreigners were forbidden to own property or to hold the majority in investments. On the US side of the Rio Grande the definitions of a frontier zone were for an altogether different purpose—to restrict the movement of short-term Mexican immigrants. The 'white-card' (I-186) permit-holders, entitled to visit US towns across the Border, were allowed to circulate within a 150-mile zone before 1965, thereafter limited to 25 miles without special permission. The 'green-carders' (I-151) who commuted to work were confined to circulation within the towns along the US bank of the Rio Grande. In practice, since there are no regularly manned US roadblocks on the inner perimeters, these limits are virtually unenforceable.

The US frontier zone is on many counts one of the poorest tracts in the nation (US Congress 1977, 298 *et seq.*), even though conditions in its Border cities are measurably better, in virtually all respects, than in their Mexican counterparts on the other bank of the Rio Grande. The

rate of unemployment in Texan Border counties is substantially above
the national rate and, in times of recession, has continued to grow at a
faster than average rate. Locally, rates of over 30 per cent unemployed
are not unusual and to these must be added the considerable underemployment characteristic of the rural areas. The median level of
family incomes is significantly below the national level, during the
mid-1970s about 40 per cent below overall, and in six rural counties
more than 50 per cent lower. These low levels relate in part to poor
returns in agricultural wages, in part to competition in the Border
labour market from Mexican commuters and illegal migrants (p. 141).
An additional source of weakness lies in the structure of the economy:
agriculture has been shedding labour steadily; the industrial base (US
Dept. Commerce 1968) lacks diversification, has a high rate of decline
elements, as in the garment trade, and is lacking in modern growth-
industries, for which the peripheral location and small local market are
both unattractive. The economy of the US Border cities has long been
buttressed by artificial stimuli from the nearby location of major
defence establishments. While these have had major beneficial multiplier effects since the Second World War one or two closures or run-
downs in recent years have correspondingly undermined vulnerable
local communities, for which no comparable volume of new jobs has
been remotely conceivable.

By the social parameters of housing, health, and education too the
US Rio Grande cities lag far behind the nation. Overcrowding in the
urban *barrios* is acute and has become steadily worse, as illegal immigrants flock in, birth-rates remain high, and the impact on housing
facilities is correspondingly severe. Health provision in the Border rural
communities is insufficient and many doctors and dentists do not speak
Spanish sufficiently well and are not familiar with Mexican culture.
Many children in the Texan Border counties do not speak English
fluently and may not speak it at all. Bilingual education programmes
are vital to equip children for later employment, but also to bring
parents into contact and thus avoid the clash of cultures within the
family. Inequalities in the distribution of public funds, due to gerry-
mandering of tax districts, have perpetuated gross differences within
the school system, while only vocational further education with its
limited professional opportunities has been the lot of most Spanish-
speaking school-leavers (US Congress 1977, 172–3).

Though plagued with no less serious social and economic problems
than its American counterpart the Mexican Rio Grande has enjoyed a
better national status, and plays a more significant role in the life of that
country (Mexico, Sec. de Indus. 1974, 1976; Urquidi and Villareal
1975; Berrueto 1979; Moreno 1979). Population in the frontier zone is
concentrated in the Border cities which have grown very rapidly since

the Second World War. This rapid growth, slackening during the 1970s, has been the product of high natural-increase rates locally, but pre-eminently of substantial migrant streams from the interior of Mexico. Significant proportions of those enumerated along the Rio Grande in the 1970 Mexican census had come, at some time in the past, from outside the province of residence (see Figs. 11 and 12). The age structure of the Border cities and their economic activity rates have been little different from the national average, but the structure of employment has been quite distinctive. Eighty per cent of the urban population is engaged in industry or service activities, rising to 90 per cent in C. Juárez. Thus these settlements have an occupational pattern similar to that of towns in advanced economies, but the rate of job provision has proved consistently inadequate to match population growth. Unemployment and underemployment have been persistently high, relieved in some measure by temporary or permanent migration, legal or illegal, to the adjacent towns of the USA. The development of the American 'in-bond' plants (maquiladoras) in Mexican Border cities and the tourist industry have helped to stabilize the local urban economy. Wage and salary levels on the Border have generally been higher than the average for Mexico and per capita real incomes have also been marginally better (1970: Mexico, 259 pesos; frontier provinces, 495; Border municipalities, 276). Municipal revenues have exceeded the national average and, though the rapidity of urban development has produced large slum barrios around the major cities the general conditions of heating, water supply, and public health are good in Mexican terms. Literacy levels are high: 76 per cent nationally, 88 per cent in the frontier zone; and both education and social provision are certainly better than in the surrounding rural areas.

The Mexican government has long been uneasily aware that economic conditions on the Rio Grande frontier have been artificially stimulated by the proximity of the US, and the lure of its Border cities in particular. A state of growing dependency underlined the vulnerability of the Mexican towns to shifts in American economic conditions or changes in a whole spectrum of policies. To counteract the state of dependency the Mexican government launched the PRONAF programme in 1961 to give a substantial 'face-lift' to the cities on the Rio Grande, and the Border Industrialization Programme (BIP) in 1965 to diversify the urban economy, promote economic growth, gain foreign exchange, and help in the training of Mexican workers.

The frontier zones on either side of the Rio Grande are thus contrasting in the range and degree of severity in their economic and social problems. Each government looks on the problems of its frontier zone in a rather different manner and, in their turn, the frontier populations are very conscious of their remote and peripheral location, the scarcity of natural resources, and the feeling that, on many pressing issues, their interests do not necessarily coincide with the national interest. Moreover these local interests tend to be disregarded whenever local and national issues are in conflict. The frontier dwellers thus have every incentive to promote the unity of a US–Mexican Border economy and market-place, to emphasize complementarity to mutual advantage, and to enhance the openness of the Rio Grande frontier in a growing network of transactions and trade.

BORDER LANDSCAPES

The variable degree of aridity and the extent of the vast open spaces have been principal constraints upon development within the Borderlands. In the drier mountain and high plateau zone of the west those constraints have been more sharply defined; in the Gulf Coast plains, scarplands, and low plateaux they have been rather less limiting. The Rio Grande valley cuts diagonally across the physiographic 'grain' of the country, with open flood-plain sections in the El Paso–Juárez valley (see Fig. 7) and the Presidio–Ojinaga tracts, upstream from the deeply dissected gorges through the Big Bend country. Below the Big Bend the course is through shallow scarplands to the Gulf coastal plains and the intensively settled irrigation tracts inland from the delta. By its direction of flow and the broken, uneven nature of its valley the Rio Grande has not acted as a corridor routeway, or a means of polarizing life from its vast hinterland. Concentration of settlement at a few major crossing-points is the counterpart along the river for the detached, scattered nodes of selective occupance within a virtual oasis society in the more arid west. Throughout the Borderlands distance has been the enemy of development, both in limiting the use of even the scarce resources available, and in rendering the area less attractive to would-be entrepreneurs from elsewhere. Communications have been built to link the Borderlands outwards, or to pass through, rather than to focus upon the area and its potentials for an integrated development.

Given the environmental constraints and the selective and scattered nature of human occupance, there has resulted a closer than usual correspondence between habitat conditions and the evolving cultural landscapes (Fig. 6). The diversity and uneven nature of environmental resources (Arbingast 1973; Bonine 1970) is, furthermore, reflected as clearly in the patterning of levels of economic development (see Fig. 9).

Within the Borderlands, the irrigated tracts in sections along the Rio Grande and in patches in its tributary valleys are among the most distinctive, intensively used lowland landscapes. The mosaic of rural land use is complemented by urban development crowding around crossing-points on the river. In the upper valley around El Paso–Juárez

PLATE 5. Rio Grande gorge in the Big Bend country (R. Doughty)

PLATE 6. Rio Grande valley downstream from the Big Bend country (R. Doughty)

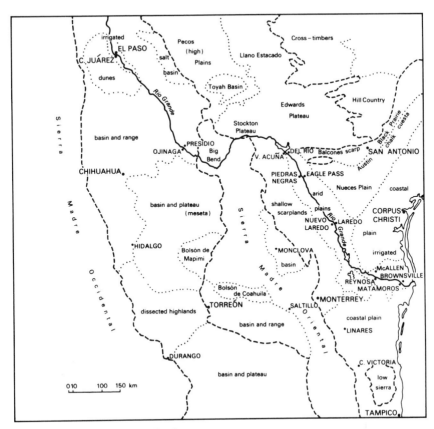

FIG. 6. Regions of the Borderlands

(Fig. 7) the landscape contrasts are vivid: the mosaic of irrigated fields, for cotton, alfalfa, and dairy products, more regular in pattern on the American side of the rectified Rio Grande channel; the lines of communication and rural settlements along the margins of the irrigated land; the desert shrub savanna and the arid wastes pressing in, Egyptian-fashion, upon the thin ribbon of development; and, finally, the dense urban concentrations of El Paso and C. Juárez, the regularity and spaciousness of the former contrasting with the limited but much more congested mass of the latter. The cultural landscape of the lower valley, west of Brownsville–Matamoros (Fig. 8), is even more intricate, an intensive riverain development set within a vast hinterland of *mesquite* and *chaparral*. The patterns of land use are complex, based on variations among citrus fruit, cotton, winter vegetables, sorghum, and wheat; the chain of small towns is almost equally diverse in its range of specialized activities. Everywhere the imprint of Man's careful management of water is reflected in storage and in distribution channels. Less apparent

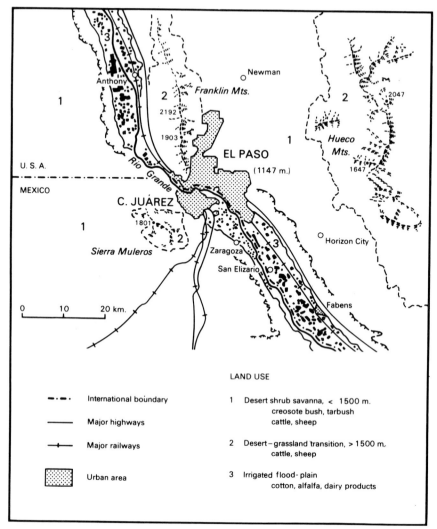

FIG. 7. El Paso–C. Juárez valley

but detectable are the relict field-boundary lines of some of the eighteenth century Spanish land grants running out at right angles to the river.

The great northward-trending mountain spines of the Mexican Sierra Madres dominate the physiographic skeleton of the Borderlands south of the Rio Grande. The higher, more humid Sierra Madre Occidental forms a barrier-like western chain, blocking access to and from the Pacific coastlands. This humid, subtropical mountain habitat nourishes pine forests, and oaks at higher altitudes, acts as a water-tower for the arid plateaux to the east, and is the home even today of

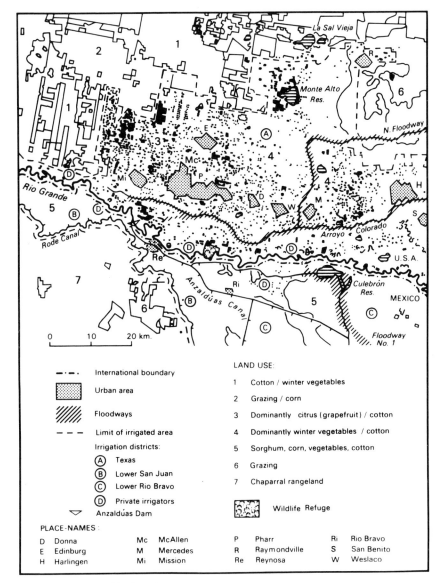

FIG. 8. The lower Rio Grande

small, scattered Indian groups (see Fig. 21), practising sedentary agriculture. Though less serious as an obstacle the limestone chains of the Sierra Madre Oriental act as an effective climatic divide between the Gulf Coast and the inland plateau of the *altiplano*. There is a sharp contrast between the inland drainage, limestone crests, and scrub vegetation of slopes facing west and the oak- and pine-clad slopes

overlooking the coastal plain (Bataillon 1967), 112). North of
Monterrey the chains of the Sierra Madre become more broken and, at
their northern extremity, die out in the Rio Grande gorges and the Big
Bend country. Both mountain habitats are thinly peopled, negative
bastions dividing and flanking the northward corridors of the *altiplano*
and the Gulf lowlands.

The high level plateau of the *altiplano* comprises a series of block-
faulted mountain sections with intervening flat-floored basins, or
bolsóns. This wide basin-and-range province, as it becomes known in the
US, stretches northwards across the upper Rio Grande into the Trans-
Pecos highlands. It offers a varied but, on the whole, a most unpropitious and arid habitat, discouraging to the Spaniards and only
tardily and selectively developed since their time. Sections are true
desert, others sterile surfaces of dried-out salt lakes; to the south of
C.-Juárez a vast dune belt deterred early traders and remains a wasteland to the present day. On the other hand, the better parts of the
basin-and-range country are true steppe-savanna land, with immense
potentials for the grazing of cattle. Settlement is at scattered sites, in
mining camps, or irrigated lands, or where a town has sprung up for
mining and at a nodal location. The lead–zinc and silver mines, known
early, were opened up rapidly by American capitalists during and after
the Porfiriato (1876–1910). Irrigation schemes for the most part came
later, in the Comarca Lagunera around Torreón, in the Conchos valley
near Ciudad Chihuahua, and in isolated patches in the northern desert.
These were grain and cotton-growing lands, broken up under the
mid-1930s phase of agrarian reform into many communal farms or
ejidos. Apart from the desert mining-camps there are major urban
centres along the one-time *Camino Real*, following the grassland fringe
northwards from Durango and Torreón through C. Chihuahua to the
frontier metropoli of El Paso–C. Juárez.

Unrepresented on the Mexican side of the Rio Grande the valley is
flanked in the middle Texas section by the flat-topped Edwards
plateau. This is an extension of the Llano Estacado, at the southern
extremity of the US Great Plains province; alongside its southern rim
the *Balcones* escarpment overlooks the piedmont and the coastal lowlands. The Edwards plateau is ranching land *par excellence* with very
large holdings, the home of huge herds of cattle and vast flocks of sheep.
It is a thinly peopled rural landscape of small market-centres, but along
the northern edge there is a belt of oil-rich towns from Midland–Odessa
to San Angelo. The interaction of oil wealth and cattle wealth in a
prosperous economy is an interesting indication of a symbiosis which
may soon be heralded in localities of an oil-rich Mexico.

The piedmont scarplands are not always clearly marked out along
the inner limit of the Gulf coastal plains. The shallow, grained country

of low scarps and mesas flanks the Rio Grande below C. Acuña–Del Rio, merging north-eastwards into the Black Prairies of south Texas. This is *mesquite-chaparral* country, which until cleared was a dense thicket and an impediment to early settlement and development. The Texas cattle industry had its origins here, between the Rio Grande and the Nueces river, spreading rapidly inland after 1860. In the lowlands east of Laredo the Winter Garden district has developed during the twentieth century, for vegetable and grain production. South of the Rio Grande the piedmont narrows southward from Monterrey, along the flanks of the Sierra Madre Oriental, with many small irrigated tracts for growing cotton or sugar-cane; on better-watered slopes orange groves are characteristic. The piedmont was the major routeway from Tamaulipas into eighteenth-century Spanish Texas. Its resources were developed late, but the agrarian landscapes of Texas and Tamaulipas grew very differently and are no less contrasting today. Texan lands have larger, more regular fields, intensely grazed or commercially farmed, with a more scattered rural settlement pattern; in Tamaulipas, the fields are smaller, less regular with more undeveloped land and greater concentration in a denser rural settlement pattern.

Monterrey and San Antonio are major metropoli within the piedmont, far removed from the Rio Grande, but important manufacturing and regional centres linked by the Pan-American highway, which crosses the Rio Grande at the two Laredos. With almost one million inhabitants in each city with its immediate hinterland these are the dominant urban nodes in the eastern Borderlands; furthermore, each is closely linked into the metropolitan network of its national territory. San Antonio has the more restricted range of manufacturing, concentrating on food-processing, the garment trades, and a diversity of metal industries. Monterrey, on the other hand, is the second most important heavy industrial and metallurgical base in Mexico, with iron and steel, engineering, and non-ferrous metals as outstanding industrial sectors. Both San Antonio and Monterrey have service hinterlands which intersect on the Rio Grande, but which also extend far into the interiors of Texas and Mexico respectively.

The coastal plain proper is narrow, the site of the compact intensively farmed and irrigated lowlands flanking the lower Rio Grande. The ports of Corpus Christi and Port Brownsville (see Fig. 4) are linked by the Intracoastal Waterway, through a succession of lagoons behind the offshore sandbars which fringe most of the coasts of south Texas and Tamaulipas. The tourist potential of this coastal strip has scarcely begun to be realized, though the string of developments along South Padre island, to the north of the Rio Grande delta, indicates both the wealth and the environmental damage which may result.

Figure 9 shows the geographical differentiation in levels of economic

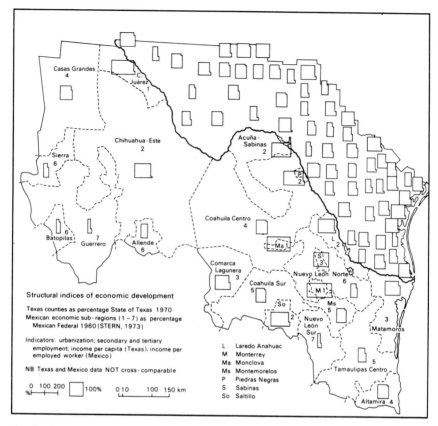

Fig. 9. Structural indices of economic development

development in the Borderlands, measured independently for economic sub-regions of Mexico (Batalla 1967; Stern 1973) and counties of Texas. The data is *not* cross-comparable between Mexico and Texas, but within each country the spectrum of differences is a crude but realistic indicator of development at the threshold of the 1970s. As such it is a useful summary of the evidence from the Border landscapes. In Mexico the contrasts are more extreme than in Texas, ranging from the deprived Indian areas of the Sierra Madres to the prosperous farming areas of the Comarca and the rangelands of eastern Chihuahua. But it is the Border cities along the Rio Grande and the manufacturing centres of Monterrey and Monclova which stand out as having the highest levels of economic development. In Texas the spectrum of economic development is compressed and is mainly within the higher ranges. There are poorer individual counties, among the *chicano* rural areas in the lower Rio Grande and in the more isolated parts of the

Trans-Pecos highlands. At the more prosperous end of the spectrum there are wealthy ranching counties in the west, oil-rich counties in the Edwards plateau and the piedmont. San Antonio and Corpus Christi also stand out, but the high average level of development there conceals immense problems of poverty and social deprivation among their *barrio* populations.

REFERENCES

ARBINGAST, S. A. (1973) *Atlas of Texas*, Bur. Busin. Res. (Austin: Univ. of Texas).

BATAILLON, C. (1967) *Les régions géographiques au Méxique*, Paris: Inst. des Hautes Etudes de l'Amérique Latine).

BATALLA, A. B. (1967) *La división económica regional de México* (México: Univ. Nacional Autónoma de México).

BEEGLE, J. A., GOLDSMITH, J. F., and LOOMIS, C. P. (1960) 'Demographic characteristics of the US–Mexican Border', *Rur. Sociol.*, **25**, 1, 107–62.

BERRUETO, E. M. (1979) 'Algunos aspectos socioeconómicos de la frontera norte de la República Mexicana', *Simposio Nacional sobre Estudios Fronterizos, El Colegio de México, Faculdad de Filosofía y Letras de la UNAL*, 24–27 January (Monterrey: N. León).

BOLTON, H. E. (1921) *The Spanish Borderlands: a chronicle of Old Florida and the Southwest* (New Haven: Yale Univ. Press).

BONINE, M. F. *et al.* (1970) *Atlas of Mexico*, Bur. Busin. Res. (Austin: Univ. of Texas).

FERNÁNDEZ, R. A. (1977) *The United States–Mexico Border: a politico-economic profile* (Notre Dame: Univ. Notre Dame Press).

HUFF, D. L. and DEARE, D. R. (1974) *Principal interaction fields of Texas metropolitan centers*, Bur. Busin Res. (Austin, Univ. of Texas).

MEXICO, (1974) Sec. de Industria y Comercio, subsec. de Comercio, *Zonas fronterizas de México: perfil socioeconómico*, México, DF.

MEXICO (1976) Sec. de Industria y Comercio, *Indicadores socioeconómicos de las zonas fronterizas*, México, DF.

MORENO, V. C. G. (1979) 'La economía mexicana y la economía fronteriza del norte', *Simposio Nacional sobre Estudios Fronterizos, El Colegio de México, Faculdad de Filosofía y Letras de la UNAL*, 24–27 January (Monterrey: N. León).

NOSTRAND, R. L. (1970) 'The Hispanic–American borderland: delimitation of an American culture region', *Ann. Ass. Amer. Geogr.*, **60**, 4, 638–61.

STERN, C. (1973) *Las regiones de México y sus niveles de desarrollo-socioeconómico* (México: El Colegio de México, Centro de Estudios Sociológicos).

US CONGRESS, Jt. Econ. Com. (1977) *Hearings before the Sub-Committee on Inter-American economic relationships*, 95th Congr. 1st Sess., 17–24 January, (Washington DC: USGPO).

US Dept. Commerce, EDA (1968) *Industrial and employment potential of the US–Mexico Border*, Nathan & Associates (Washington, DC: USGPO).

URQUIDI, V. L. and VILLAREAL, S. M. (1975) 'Importancia económica de la zona fronteriza del Norte de México, *Foro Internacional*, **XVI**, 2, 149–74.

CHAPTER 3

Peoples of the Rio Grande

PEOPLE AND PLACE

The location, structural character, and territorial movements of people over a formative period of time afford the most useful backcloth and barometer of economic and social change. The distribution and trends in the availability and types of work are key indicators in an interpretation of the shifting balance of man-environment relationships. Population change itself is both the product and the residual of the dynamics of birth/death rates, on the one hand, and the net movement of migrants on the other. Cultural and even political differences must also be taken into account in any analysis of the population–resources equation. For the present purpose attention is focussed on the dramatic changes in peopling of the Borderlands since the Second World War. During these past three or four decades there has been an unparalleled period of growth and development, waning during the 1970s, but its economic and social effects have been very uneven, both structurally and territorially. In particular, and directly germane to the study of the frontier, major contrasts may be drawn between the United States and Mexico, even within the pairs of cities facing each other across the Rio Grande.

Population growth-rates have consistently been higher on the Mexican side of the Border, the product of a higher natural-increase rate, by surplus of births over deaths, but also the result of considerable and persistent in-migrant streams from other parts of the country. While natural-increase rates in the US Rio Grande cities have traditionally been much above the national average, they are significantly below those for Mexico, and the currents of internal migration have been more complex. The characteristic movement of local residents has been away, northwards to other parts of the US (Weigand 1977), but this has been largely compensated for by in-migrant Border-crossers from Mexico, the 'alien tide' (p. 141), both legal and clandestine. By no means all these 'undocumented workers' show up in census figures; nor does anything like the full number of slum residents of the Mexican Border *barrios*.

The 1940s saw a second boom in the Borderlands. The US war effort led to the creation of large training bases along the Rio Grande, while an increasing labour scarcity on American farms ushered in the *bracero* or contract farmworker programme (1942–64), for Mexican immigrants. Illegal Mexican immigration reached a peak in the early 1950s, but the more effective Border controls under Operation Wetback (1954) cut this back very sharply (see Fig. 24). Post-war programmes of large-scale irrigation, commercialization of agriculture, and better financial provision for the communal farms, or *ejidos*, in northern Mexico both added to the attractiveness of the Borderlands in the eyes of immigrants and also led to considerable internal redistribution of population within the four Border provinces (Morrison 1963). On the US side of the Rio Grande reductions in farm labour in post-war years were very considerable, while the military training presence was sustained through the Korean and Vietnamese wars, artificially buttressing the prosperity of the Rio Grande cities. To the normal consumer demands on service industry in the American towns was added the multiplier effect of vice once the Border bridges were crossed.

During the 1960s the surging natural increase of the Mexican population at large was magnified in the Border towns, with their more youthful populations, the product of earlier immigrations. In the mid-1960s the closure of the *bracero* programme returned large numbers from the US to stagnation and unemployment just south of the Rio Grande. The migration currents off the countryside or from other provinces into these same Mexican towns began to slacken, but many more people continued to arrive than could be found jobs or given adequate living conditions (Martínez 1979), even admitting the beneficial effects of the government-sponsored PRONAF (1961) and Border Industrialization (1965) programmes. Unemployment swelled also in the Texan Border cities, as overseas competition hit the local apparel industry hard, population increase met a falling provision of new jobs, and the rural districts continued to lose their most able, younger people in the townward drift.

The 1970s heralded different trends. Rates of population increase in Mexico fell only slightly, but there was an abrupt falling-away of birth surpluses throughout southern Texas, most particularly in the ranching or farming country which had a lower ratio of Mexican-Americans. Migration to the Rio Grande from other parts of Mexico was further reduced, but the population dynamism of the Mexican Border cities continued little abated, from the reservoir of people who had entered earlier. The movement of undocumented workers across into the US became a floodtide (see Fig. 24), while others were 'ponded back' south of the river awaiting their turn or frustrated in their intentions. On the US side the closures or change in social structure of military bases withdrew support from the economy, while the onset of world depression following upon the 1973 oil crisis further weakened the already unstable competitive status of Border cities.

The most striking feature of population change in the Borderlands over the past few decades has been the progressive polarization of flows upon a few large cities, on the banks of the Rio Grande, or at San Antonio, Chihuahua, Torreón, or Monterrey, some distance from it. This distortion in the process of urbanization has produced a very uneven population pattern, with concentration at the extremes of the large city or rural dispersal. Such an 'oasis' distribution in semi-arid lands goes far back in the selective development of the Borderlands, but it has become emphasized during the period since the 1930s (Gutiérrez de MacGregor and Carmen Valverde 1975, 228). In 1900 only 9 per cent of Mexican urban population was located in arid and semi-arid zones, but by 1970 this had risen to 29 per cent. In 1930 Monterrey was the only city with over 100,000 people in the dry zone, but by 1970 there were no fewer than seventeen cities of 100,000 in the arid lands throughout Mexico. Town-dwellers in Mexico comprised 30 per cent of the total population in 1930, rising to 50 per cent in 1960, and 65 per cent by 1978. In the Borderlands these percentages were characteristically even higher.

Figure 10 shows the Borderlands distribution of people in 1970, some 2.5 millions on the Texan and 5.8 millions on the Mexican side of the Rio Grande. By 1980 the latter figure had risen to 7.88 millions, an increase of no less than 35 per cent in a matter of ten years, threatening even more serious pressure of population on scarce local resources. The irregular nature of the demographic pattern is clearly apparent. The dominance of large cities in a thinly peopled hinterland is most striking in the arid west, but San Antonio and Monterrey equally polarize life in the lower Rio Grande valley. In 1970, 45 per cent of the Borderland Texans and 47 per cent of Mexicans lived in cities of over 100,000 people, a sharp contrast in landscape and life-style to the wide open spaces beyond. The uneven chain of paired cities along the river is a typical frontier feature, the Mexican partner being invariably the larger and continuing to grow more rapidly. Otherwise, the rich variety of dispersed and greater rural densities in northern Mexico contrasts with the very thin equivalent in sparsely populated rural Texas. This is a country of large ranches and land-holdings, but very small, scattered central place settlements. The cluster of towns in the lower Rio Grande is a particular feature on both banks of the river.

Population mass, density, and pattern reflect the underlying differentiation of place. They also have important implications for social life, economic organization, and even political structure and the distribution of effective power. The dynamics of changing trends affect the future potential for such relationships, for good or ill. The age structure of communities directly influences crude birth- and death-rates, as well as the rate of formation of the prospective labour force.

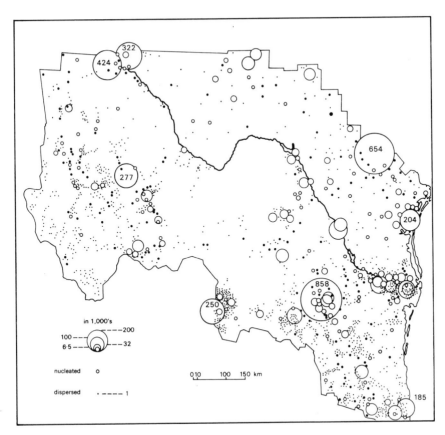

Fig. 10. Population, 1970

With a birth-rate of 42 per 1,000 in 1976 (34 per 1,000 1978), a death-rate of 9 per 1,000 (6 per 1,000 1978) and thus a natural-increase rate of 33 per 1,000 per annum (28 per 1,000 1978) Mexican urban communities have a youthful age-composition, and the prospects for further rapid population growth. In many isolated, poor rural settlements on the other hand there is the serious social problem of an ageing and dependent social structure. Texan towns with a high Mexican-American representation (Beegle *et al.* 1960) show similar vital statistics to those of Mexico: e.g. lower Rio Grande (1970), birth-rate 30.1 per 1,000, death rate 7 per 1,000, natural increase 23.1 per 1,000. This represents a fall from the natural increase rate of 28 per 1,000 only ten years earlier, but it is distinctly higher than among non-Mexican-American communities. For one such area, the Trans-Pecos economic sub-region, the figures in 1970 were, 21.0, 8.5, and 12.5 per 1,000 respectively. The societal implications of these figures are clear, in terms of the mounting but uneven need for social welfare provision, but they indicate a more relaxed problem for matching entrants to the work-force with the local availability of jobs.

Substantial natural growth of population *in situ* represents the second phase of urban development, which commonly follows a first phase of rapid in-migration. In the years since 1945 there have been turbulent tides of migration, in Mexico generally towards the Border, and in the USA northwards away from the Border to other States. This latter movement has often resulted in the permanent settling, notably in the Midwest or the Pacific North-west of formerly seasonal agricultural migrant workers from the lower Rio Grande (Stoddard 1978, 24). Two major internal processes have also provided strong migration flows: polarization on the towns (Unikel 1976; Greene 1978) and depopulation from the rural areas after the 'Green Revolution' in Mexico.

Table 1 shows the different growth rates for the major towns in the Borderlands (1940–78) and Table 2 illustrates the varied contribution of natural increase and in-migration to the process of change in selected cities (1950–70). These tables confirm previously described trends of change. Noteworthy specific features include: the remarkable population dynamism of C. Juárez, a sharp contrast to the trends of its twin-city of El Paso; the growth rates of Reynosa, from being a small stagnant market-town, to the status of a major industrial and petro-chemical centre; the characteristic slight net out-migration balances

Table 1. *Urban growth rates, 1940–78*

	Popn. (1,000s)		Growth rates (1940=100)			
	1940	1978 (est.)	1950	1960	1970	1978 (est.)
Mexico						
Monterrey	190	1,054	178	316	451	554
C. Juárez	55	597	239	503	770	1085
C. Chihuahua	78	369	142	236	351	469
Torreón	87	268	167	231	285	306
Saltillo	75	245	130	168	252	324
Matamoros	54	186	115	264	343	345
N. Laredo	31	214	189	304	480	· 680
Reynosa	23	218	300	582	651	945
Texas						
S. Antonio	253	773	161	231	257	304
El Paso	96	385	134	285	332	399
Corpus Christi	57	214	189	292	356	375
Laredo	39	98	132	154	175	251
Brownsville	22	72	163	217	237	364
McAllen	11	48	168	275	317	409

Sources: US, Census Reports; México, Censos General de la Población.

Table 2. *Composition of population change, selected Border cities, 1950–70*

	1950–60 (rates/annum)			1960–70 (rates/annum)		
	Total	Natural change	Migration change	Total	Natural change	Migration change
Mexico						
Monterrey	6.3	3.1	3.3	4.4	3.7	0.7
C. Juárez	7.3	2.8	4.4	4.5	3.0	1.5
Matamoros	6.7	3.9	2.8	4.2	3.4	0.7
N. Laredo	4.6	3.0	1.6	4.9	2.8	2.0
Reynosa	7.4	3.9	3.5	6.2	2.8	3.4
Texas*						
S. Antonio	3.6	2.9	0.7	2.1	1.9	0.2
El Paso	6.1	4.6	1.5	1.4	2.4	−1.0
Laredo	1.5	3.4	−1.9	1.2	2.7	−1.5
Brownsville	2.0	3.8	−1.8	−0.7	2.1	−2.9
McAllen	1.2	3.5	−2.3	0.3	2.6	−2.3

* SMSAs: Standard Metropolitan Statistical Areas
Sources: as Table 1

from the lower Texan Border cities, other than San Antonio, most marked from the lower Rio Grande valley; the general falling away of in-migration rates to Mexican Border cities during the decade 1960–70, and their continuing growth by natural increase stimulated from an earlier generation of in-migrants.

Migration to the towns has often been explained as the product of push factors from the land and pull factors by the job and social attractions of urban life. In reality the process is more complex and the balance of influences varies by both time and place, though there is a strong mutual dependence between migration and regional economic growth (Greenwood 1978; Margulis 1979). There is ample evidence on net lifetime migration, persons recorded as living in a province or town at one census but born elsewhere. Figures 11 and 12 illustrate the source origins and volume of such long-distance, longer-term movement, for each of the four principal Mexican crossing-places on the Rio Grande. A distance-decay effect is apparent and also the extent to which there is northwards 'corridor movement' along the *altiplano* and the coastal plains respectively. Part of the movement is certainly in transit, legally or otherwise, to the United States (p. 141). It must be remembered that there is also a compensating though a lesser flow in the opposite direction, of those born in the frontier province but now residing elsewhere in Mexico. Furthermore, and C. Juárez is a good case in point, the figures do not include the very considerable movement to each Border city from within the surrounding province. The study of a sample of migrants to Monterrey in the period 1940–65 (Browning and Feindt 1968, 184) showed that two-thirds came from surrounding rural

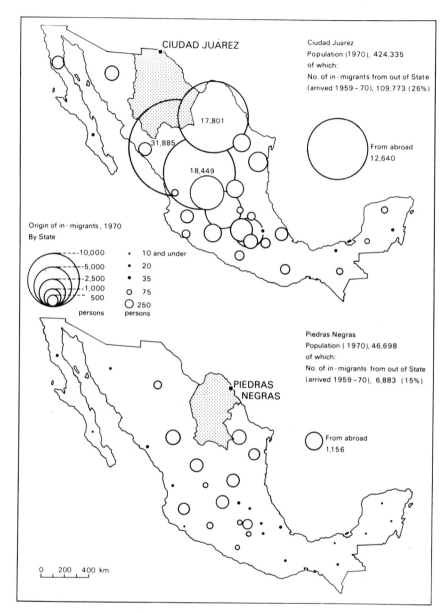

FIG. 11. Migration to C. Juárez and Piedras Negras

areas, more than half these in one direct movement; a further fifth came from small towns (5–20,000) and only 5 per cent from cities of more than 100,000 people. A high proportion of such moves were indeed over

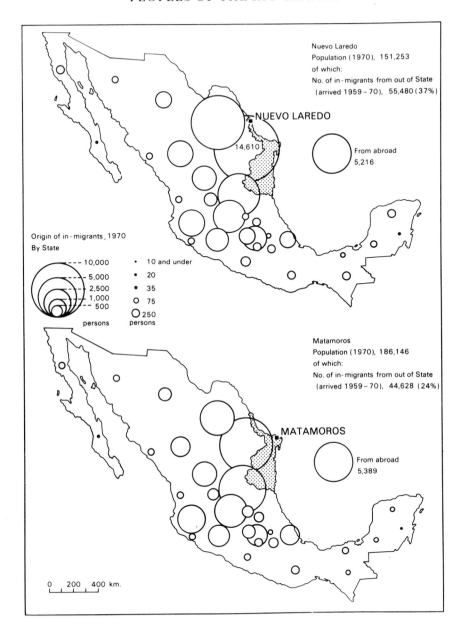

Nuevo Laredo
Population (1970), 151,253
of which:
No. of in-migrants from out of State
(arrived 1959–70), 55,480 (37%)

NUEVO LAREDO

14,610

From abroad
5,216

Origin of in-migrants, 1970
By State

10,000
5,000
2,500
1,000
500
persons

10 and under
20
35
75
250
persons

Matamoros
Population (1970), 186,146
of which:
No. of in-migrants from out of State
(arrived 1959–70), 44,628 (24%)

MATAMOROS

From abroad
5,389

0   200   400 km.

FIG. 12. Migration to Nuevo Laredo and Matamoros

short distances, illustrating a kind of gravity-model effect in the attraction by the city.

Out-migration from rural areas has been more variable in its social

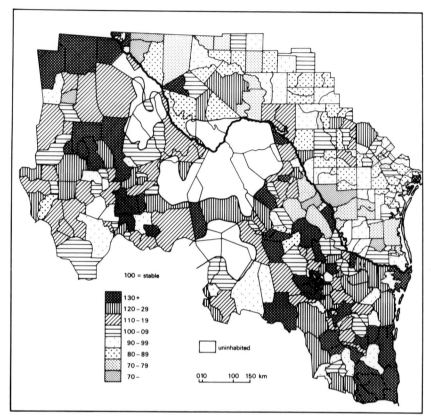

FIG. 13. Population change, 1960–1970

and economic effects (Whetten and Burnight 1956). Locally, very dramatic rates of out-migration underlie the widespread decreases in total rural population recorded on Fig. 13, between 1960 and 1970. Net out-migration within ten years of almost one-quarter of the 1960 base population are typical (Cabrera 1975) for vast tracts of the Sierra Madres, Occidental and Oriental, the Big Bend country on both sides of the Rio Grande, the western Edwards plateau, the south-west Rio Grande plain, and the lower valley. In Texas similarly high rates of rural loss had also characterized the previous decade (Bradshaw and Poston 1971), with cumulatively serious social effects. Such a dramatic exodus from the countryside must have had a notable destabilizing effect on rural communities, the more so if it had continued for two decades or more. However, in many isolated, poor lands in Mexico it is a mercy and a blessing that many migrate in search of betterment, instead of accelerating the cycle of diminishing returns by staying put.

On the other hand, rural out-migration has always been selective of the youngest, the most vigorous, and the most talented. Ageing populations left behind create a serious welfare problem of dependency, mitigated in part by remittances from the emigrants, and the periodic return of those who have earned and saved money in the United States.

Apart from poverty and substandard living conditions there are also technological reasons for the drift off the land. Increased size of holdings, the mechanization of operations, crop specialization, or large-scale irrigation all release labour, a process which has been in progress for longer in Texas, but has accelerated too in northern Mexico during the past three decades. In some Texan rural counties the farm-based population has been so reduced that any further losses might lead to land passing out of cultivation or reverting to savanna grassland. In the meantime, there are serious problems for social provision in such scattered small communities, even in a highly mobile and relatively affluent rural society.

SOCIAL DEPRIVATION

A sense of well-being may be culturally determined, but certain basic facts of deprivation and social difference are inescapable. Quality of life may be many-sided, but to be in work and the level of earnings are prime considerations. Alternatively, the incidence and level of poverty or unemployment are the hallmarks of social *malaise*. Basic differences in conditions and prospects on either side of the Rio Grande are a perpetual source of local discontents, and of large-scale illicit entry to the US in search of economic and social betterment.

To start with, more than 40 per cent of US families in the early 1970s had annual incomes of $15,000 or more, while the great proportion of Mexican families had only $3,000 a year or less. In Mexico $60 a month was a common wage for farm work, compared with $300 a month in the US. For industrial jobs the Mexican may earn $44 a week (1973) in contrast to the $165 a week of his American counterpart (Stoddard 1978, 54). The Mexican government decrees minimum industrial wages for each Border city, but these are not always paid and they are still well below US levels. With such differentials often starkly present in adjacent Border cities, it is less than surprising that the 'alien tide' of illegal migrants takes place. However, the outcome is often less than satisfactory. The illegal Mexican labourer may be paid $1.50 an hour plus free housing, but many are grossly exploited, without redress. Even so, to the Mexican, such low rewards north of the Rio Grande may seem a golden opportunity, measured against the most he could aspire to in his own country.

Unemployment and underemployment are indications of still more serious social deprivation. Figures for Texas and northern Mexico are not comparable but both sides of the river show disturbing trends. Even before the effects of world depression in the mid-1970s were fully felt, local unemployment in El Paso (1976) was estimated at 20–25 per cent, in Laredo over 25 per cent, and in Starr County 36.6 per cent (US Congress House 1977, D2). By comparison, data from Mexico at first looks innocuous, but figures for underemployment must be included, and very many remain outside official registration. For C. Juárez (1970) 5.6 per cent were unemployed, 25.7 per cent underemployed; for C. Chihuahua 4.6 and 26.4 per cent respectively (Reyes 1974, 731). Figuring strongly among the Texan unemployed are the *chicanos*, all too often with limited job prospects either on the land or in the city, and not infrequently in direct competition with the illegal Mexican immigrants (Briggs 1973), to their own detriment.

Poverty too is perhaps a relative term, but there is no doubting the social evil it represents on the Rio Grande. The per capita income levels of US towns in the lower Rio Grande valley made them the poorest in the nation, 'the poverty pocket of US urban society' (Stoddard 1978, 35). Income levels were only half those of the State or national averages, and in some rural tracts of south Texas income per capita ran as low as $1,300 per annum, a true indication of grinding poverty. The statutory poverty threshold of $6,200 per annum for a family of four in Texas (1978) seems very favourable when compared with a 10,000 peso ($450) equivalent in Mexico eight years earlier, or half the population of a *colonia* in C. Juárez who earned less than $1,500 a year (Ugalde 1974). The poverty endemic on the Mexican Rio Grande is nevertheless much less serious or deep-seated than in most rural parts of that country. It is however much worse than in the US towns across the river or in the south Texan countryside. There once again it is the *chicano* family which suffers most, with a likelihood of poverty four times greater than among their Anglo-counterparts.

Low income levels, unemployment and underemployment, or poverty are complemented by poor housing conditions, lower levels of educational achievement, and greater incidence of ill-health (p. 137) among the deprived groups or communities. The social tensions thus generated are cumulative, poisoning relationships between classes, setting Mexican-American against Mexican and both against Anglos. For the poorer *chicanos* the only relief alternative to 'endless poverty' (Stoddard 1978, 25) is to migrate northwards, but 'the disadvantaged Border residents who do move away will become disadvantaged urban slum residents, unless their capabilities are raised to permit them to enter the productive processes of the nation' (Nathan *et al*. 1968, 2).

The poorest of all living conditions on the Border are probably still in the slum *barrios* straggling up the ravines west of C. Juárez, or, by

American standards, the *chihuahuaíta* housing area in southern El Paso. Squatter invasions of the early 1960s brought an estimated 50,000 *paracaídistas* ('parachutists') into the *barrios* and *colonias* of C. Juárez (Martínez 1979, 202). The city authorities lessened the resulting grinding poverty by public land purchase and its resale for *colonia* housing projects at nominal prices, by selling food through discount stores of CONASUPO (a Mexican federal relief agency), setting up mobile vans for circulating low-cost provisions and a subsidized meat market for the poor.

THE BORDER ECONOMY

Figures 14 and 15 strikingly highlight remarkable contrasts in employment structure between the American and Mexican Borderlands. Within Mexico (Holt Büttner & Padilla y Sotelo 1976), at the national level, there has been a fall from 70 per cent engaged in agriculture in

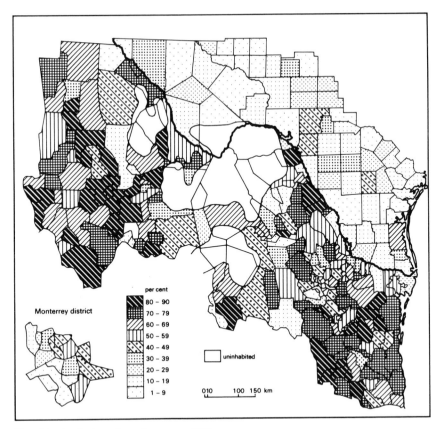

FIG. 14. Agricultural employment, 1970

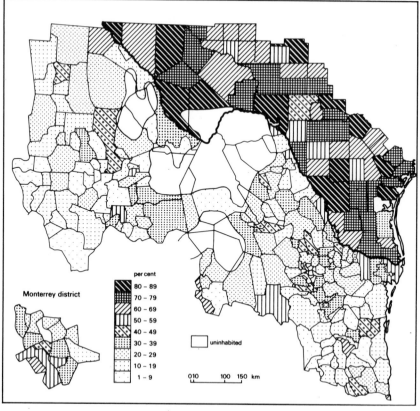

FIG. 15. Services employment, 1970

1930 to barely 38 per cent of the labour force in 1970. Yet it is clear that
in the Borderlands, over wide tracts of the Sierra Madres, the *altiplano*,
and the coast lowland more than three-quarters of those working are
still on the land (Fig. 14). In Texas, on the other hand, with a highly
efficient agriculture and ranching industry, the farm labour force has
dwindled to less than 20 per cent of all jobs in most rural counties. The
services sector of employment (Fig. 15) shows almost the reverse image.
Most Texan rural counties have three-quarters or more in non-farm
occupations, but in the less affluent, more self-subsistent way of life in
Mexico it is only in the more important towns that the services sector
employs a substantial proportion of those working. In the Mexican
countryside, fewer than 20 per cent and in the mountains under 10 per
cent are the hallmarks of a less-specialized, subsistent peasant society.
Mining (see Fig. 19) takes place in scattered locations, while manufacturing (see Fig. 20) is concentrated in the larger towns and has made
little impact in rural areas. The much more labour-intensive informal

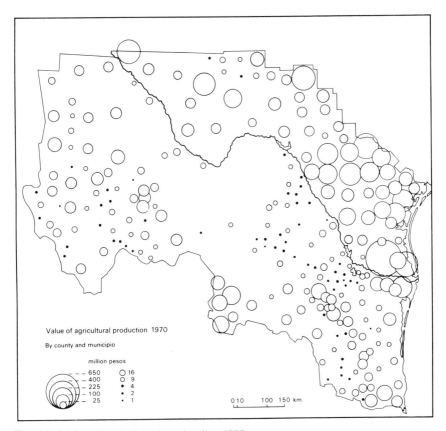

Value of agricultural production 1970

By county and municipio

million pesos

– – 650	◯ 16
– 400	◯ 9
– 225	• 4
– 100	• 2
– 25	• 1

0 10   100 150 km.

FIG. 16. Value of agricultural production, 1970

sector, including street vendors and pedlars, is widespread in northern Mexico, but rare within the more commercialized service activities in the USA.

THE RURAL ECONOMY

Figure 16 shows the aggregate value of farming output, while Fig. 17 indicates a clear correlation between the distribution of irrigation and the value of agricultural production. On both counts, the plains and scarplands of south Texas, the Comarca Lagunera, and the irrigated piedmont of the Sierra Madre Oriental stand out prominently. In the Trans-Pecos country and the *altiplano* there are more scattered localities of high-value output. The lower levels of production throughout northern Mexico underline the greater degree of subsistence and lesser marketable surplus in that economy, while the contrast in values along either bank of the Rio Grande is a further notable feature.

The type of farm economy conditions labour demand; its degree of

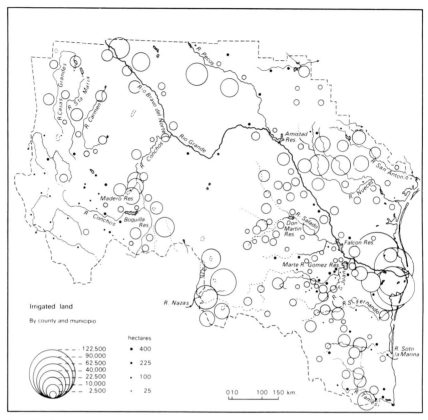

Fig. 17. Irrigation, 1970

prosperity in turn influences the structure of rural non-farm occupations. Thus distinctive forms of rural society have developed, with
built-in strengths and weaknesses. Society and economy are also formative in political attitudes, towards the significance of the frontier and
the alien national culture of those across the Rio Grande. These
attitudes are themselves the result of a long historical heritage, in which
there has also been constant intermingling of Mexicans in the Anglo
and *chicano* cultures of south Texas.

The Trans-Pecos country and the Edwards plateau are rangelands
par excellence for cattle in the west and a greater concentration on sheep
in the east. Almost all farms are larger than 800 ha, and indeed the
average farm size by county varies from 4,050 to 9,300 ha. This is a
highly prosperous stock economy with a small, skilled labour force, set
within a rural society of small, but diversified market settlements. Its
strengths lies in the long-term prosperity of cattle- or sheep-ranching,
its weakness rather the social effects of remoteness and small town *ennui*.

The south Texas scarplands and plains have a more varied rural economy. Cattle ranches, arable farms, and mixed farms abound. Stock densities are much higher and there is a larger ratio of irrigated land; farm sizes are intermediate, with average county sizes 300 to 800 ha. Rural settlement too is denser, labour requirements are greater, and there is a more developed network of market-centres. Mexican immigrants are numerous and there is a greater cosmopolitan social structure. Problems in such a prosperous rural society are few. Diversity of product is a source of strength in the economy, accessibility within the vast hinterland of San Antonio is good, but there are ethnic social tensions and a steady, continuing drift off the land.

The Winter Garden area east of Laredo and the irrigated lower Rio Grande valley have greater problems. Irrigated farms are characteristically smaller, often family enterprises, heavily capitalized and vulnerable to price and market demand fluctuations for a range of perishable products. Considerable seasonal labour is needed for harvesting, in midwinter (truck crops, citrus fruits), spring (onions), and midsummer (cotton). Pressure of demand for work keeps wages low, and illegal immigrants may compete unfairly in the local labour market. Rural population densities are high and there are numerous prosperous market-towns, but the social problems of housing, health, and education are often acute.

Any consideration of the diversity of the Mexican Border rural economy (Méx. Sec. Ind. y Com. 1974) must begin with a realistic appraisal of the land reforms. These were a principal aim of the 1910 Revolution, then and subsequently justified in social and political rather than in economic terms (Nguyen and Martínez Saldívar 1979a, b). *Latifundismo* and debt peonage were to be abolished, and land transferred to the peasants from the large landowners without full compensation. Each land grant to the peasants created an *ejido*, comprising pastures, forest, or wasteland to be held in common, and cultivable land which might be subdivided, temporarily or permanently, into private plots or farmed collectively. Title to land might pass to heirs but it might not be sold, rented, leased, or mortgaged, or otherwise peasant indebtedness would return.

Redistribution of land was slow at first, but gathered momentum in the 1930s and particularly after the Second World War. By 1970 the proportion of *ejidal* land in the four northern provinces had risen to one-third, but this was far below the Mexican average of 61 per cent. There were serious problems for *ejido* farming in arid and semi-arid areas (Stavenhagen 1966). Small individual land-units were simply not viable, there was insufficient credit available, and no worthwhile surplus accrued on other than irrigated land. There was a lack of any tradition of small-scale farming in the Mexican Borderlands, and the *minifundista*, usually on a farm of less than five hectares, was rare. Land reform alone could not change this state of affairs. Conversely, the land reform laws decreed that private ownership should be limited to 100 ha irrigated land, or 200 ha of rain-fed land. However, in 1946 the upper limit for a private holding of irrigated land was raised to 300 ha, if a remunerative commercial crop was grown (Chevalier 1967), but even this limit was commonly exceeded in the creation of large-scale *neolatifundismo*. Lands used for cattle-raising were held to be inalienable in any case and in the post-war years economic development became a more pressing priority for Mexico, taking precedence over social conditions. Under the 1971 Agrarian Reform Law (Fernández & Fernández 1971; Ginneken 1978) *ejidos* were permitted to contract out as private enterprises and to engage in small-scale industry, tourist enterprises, handicrafts, or even mining.

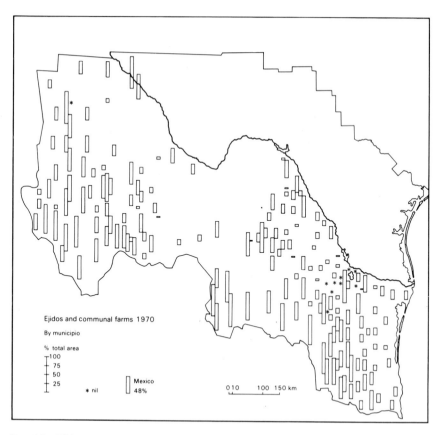

FIG. 18. *Ejidos* and communal farms 1970

Given the harsh nature of much of the Borderlands environment, the uneven application of land reform legislation, and its progressive modification the pattern of *ejidal* land seen on Fig. 18 is not altogether surprising. The high proportion of *ejidal* lands in the Comarea Lagunera and along the piedmonts of the Sierra Madres contrasts with their virtual absence in the Chihuahua and Coahuila ranching country. Curiously too the high ratio of *ejidos* in the irrigated tracts of the Rio Grande below C. Juárez, or near Nuevo Laredo, compares with a low ratio in similar irrigation land in the commercially farmed delta around Matamoros. *Ejidos* were introduced late into the uplands of the Sierra Madres but in the Indian country, of the Tarahumaras and Tepehuán, both farming or forestry *ejidos* have had considerable success.

The general balance of farm production in northern Mexico, or in southern Texas, changes from stock-ranching in the drier west to a higher ratio of arable farming in the more humid east. Yet there are major environmental, social, and cultural differences. Throughout, rural settlement densities in Mexico are higher, there is a greater subsistence element in production (the corn and beans economy), and the pattern of small central place settlements is more intricate. Nor is it only the Indian communities in the high Sierras that have no counterpart in Texas. Day-labourers or landless peasants are common in the Mexican Borderlands. Some came from *minifundias* or small *ejidos* which offer only sixty days' work a year while others are highly mobile in constant search of seasonal work, but most are unemployed for much of the year. It is from this deprived group that many of the *bracero* farmworkers for the US were drawn in the years 1942–64. The small farmer too is usually a depressed victim of merchants and moneylenders (Ginneken 1978, 54). Large landowners continue to exist, both in ranching country and in the irrigation areas, in spite of land reform, the result of priorities for economic development rather than social, or even political justice.

The rural service settlements south of the Rio Grande also contrast with their Texan counterparts. The informal sector, of street-traders, hawkers, pedlars, is strongly represented and the shops are small and variegated, with no images of the supermarket outside the large towns. Shopping is more of a social custom, and, like the church, has an important role in community solidarity in a less affluent, more self-subsistent rural economy.

MINING AND THE OIL INDUSTRY

The scattered, uneven, and unbalanced distribution of mineral resources (Fig. 19) underlines their limited, though occasionally dramatic contribution to Borderlands development. Total numbers employed are small and the mining or oil extraction settlements are

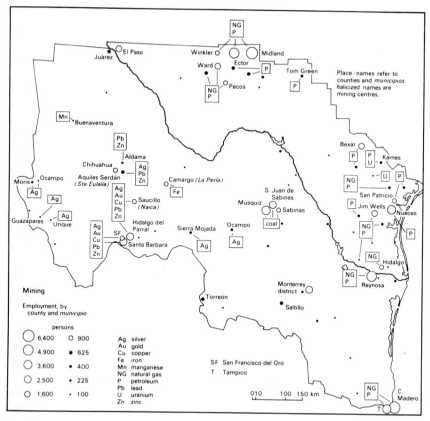

FIG. 19. Mining

usually isolated and not integrated into the local rural economy. Except for coal and iron ore, most mineral production is for export and, outside Monterrey, is of marginal significance for industrialization within the region.

The non-ferrous metal ores in Chihuahua and Coahuila provinces were opened up by American capital in the late nineteenth century (Bernstein 1964). Ores were processed locally rather than in the US to benefit from the McKinley tariff (1890), which discriminated against imported unprocessed minerals. Though beneficiation and refining still takes place *in situ*—and indeed the Mexican government also now discriminates against exports of lead and zinc—the regional industrial multiplier effect of mining is minimal. Coal from Sabinas serves the iron and steel mills of Monterrey, Monclova, and Piedras Negras. Only a minor fraction of the vast petroleum and natural gas reserves discovered in Mexico in recent years is located within the Borderlands, at

Reynosa and further south near Tampico. In the late 1970s natural gas was proven at Sabinas (N. León) and at two places in Coahuila province. Oil pipelines link these two producing centres and the petroleum products and natural gas pipeline up to Chihuahua is being extended to C. Juárez. Complex negotiations with the US for the export of vast quantities of natural gas into Texas were stalled in 1977, but reached fruition late in 1979 (Fagen and Nau 1978; Grayson 1978; US Congress House 1979).

Apart from limited supplies of uranium (Brent and Sandidge 1969) south Texan mineral resources consist of petroleum and natural gas, underlying the coastal plain and the northern Edwards plateau. These resources are linked into the State-wide distribution network. The post-war petroleum and natural gas boom was reflected in the sharp rise in population around Midland–Odessa in the 1950s and 1960s.

THE URBAN ECONOMY

The towns have been the growth points of the post-war 'oasis' society in the Borderlands. Their varied employment structure (Table 3) reflects the diversity of their hinterlands and the differing functional role which each plays. Accordingly, the urban economy too shows strengths and weaknesses, on both sides of the Rio Grande. The Texan towns have a more developed services sector, the Mexican towns a greater proportion employed in manufacturing, though it must be remembered that a high percentage of these latter jobs are in artisan workshops, or even in the informal industrial sector (Martínez 1978). These major contrasts show up particularly well in a comparison of San Antonio, the outstanding service centre, with Monterrey the most substantial and diversified manufacturing town. Along the Rio Grande twin-cities (Ladman 1979) face each other, the Mexican town invariably the larger. Between the

Table 3. *Employment structure, US–Mexican Border cities, 1970*

	Extractive	Manufs	Constrn	Utilities	Commerce	Tpt.	Services	
Texas								
S. Antonio	1.6	11.6	6.5	1.6	24.0	4.4	50.3	100
El Paso	2.8	17.1	6.5	2.4	25.4	5.3	40.5	100
Laredo	16.9	6.5	6.4	2.7	28.5	7.7	31.3	100
Mexico								
C. Juárez	6.8	22.3	10.9	0.6	20.8	6.0	32.6	100
N. Laredo	9.1	18.3	7.1	0.8	19.6	9.3	35.8	100
Matamoros	9.8	21.2	4.9	0.6	25.6	7.1	30.8	100
Reynosa	11.3	19.7	7.5	0.5	24.6	6.8	29.6	100
Monterrey	1.2	38.0	8.8	0.7	20.6	6.6	24.1	100
C. Chihuahua	3.3	20.5	14.3	1.0	20.3	8.1	32.5	100

Sources: US, Census Reports 1970; México, Censo General de la Población 1970.

pairs of cities there is a marked interdependence and complementarity in a common labour and retail market, distorted by the existence of the international boundary (Dillman 1969; Jeanjean and Revel-Mouroz 1972). The political implications of such interdependence and the policies which have resulted are the theme explored in Border Transactions (Pt. III) and The Political Imperative (Pt. IV).

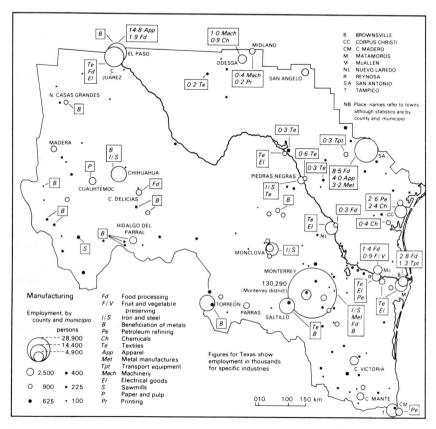

Fig. 20. Manufacturing

MANUFACTURING

With the exception of Monterrey, the heavy industrial and metallurgical base of the frontier, the Borderland towns generally have a prime function to serve a variable hinterland. Manufacturing is limited in scope, largely related to the availability of local raw materials or the needs of the nearby market (Nathan *et al.* 1968). Food-processing is widespread (Fig. 20) but for most products there is an inelastic demand and distance from major metropolitan markets is a deterrent to increasing production. Frequently it is only the first stages in processing that take place in the Borderlands, for meat, fruit, vegetables, grain, or fish and greater value is added elsewhere. Glass, cement, and petrochemicals are other resource-related industries, but regional linkages are limited and there have been few significant multiplier effects.

Non-ferrous metal refining, of copper, zinc, lead in particular, characterizes El Paso, several Chihuahua towns, and Monterrey. Iron and steel manufacture, since 1900 at Monterrey, and more recently, on a small scale, at Monclova and Piedras Negras (1944) was initially based on local coal (Rosita) and iron ores. It has led to major linked industries at Monterrey, in engineering, car assembly (Borgward, since the transfer of this firm from Germany in 1963), and agricultural machinery (Revel-Mouroz 1969). The apparel industry, on both sides of the Border, relates in part to a local raw material, cotton, and serves a local market, but it is also one of few examples of manufacturing attracted from outside the region. The attraction lay in the large reserve of unskilled or semi-skilled labour, notably women, with a very low level of union organization (9 per cent overall in El Paso in 1968). The apparel industry came to El Paso in the 1930s and grew rapidly in several Border towns in the 1950s, specializing in the output of blue jeans and western wear, later diversifying into women's and children's clothing. Even with low labour costs, contrasting sharply with those in New York, the site of several parent firms, the El Paso industry has faced difficulties in its distance from national markets, and also in even lower labour costs across the Rio Grande (Nathan *et al.* 1968). Under the International Garment Agreement and the 1978 Multifibre Agreement there has been some protection for US-based firms, but growing union troubles have rather offset this advantage. Finally, the garment trades pay low wages and contribute little to the regional economy, since there are virtually no multiplier effects. The more recently arrived electronic components industry is a similar case, with no multipliers, a low-wage system and almost entirely female jobs. The whole question of the controversial American 'in-bond' (*maquiladora*) plants in Mexican Border cities is discussed later (p. 219).

The sad truth is that the Borderlands are at the greatest disadvantage in just those industries which have contributed most to local development (Nathan *et al.* 1968). This is partly a factor of market distance, but also relates to the lack of local skills, a custom of not processing beyond the first stages, lack of local capital, and above all a dependence on cyclical manufacturers, susceptible to fashion change and economic depression, or inelasticity of prices. To these generalizations Monterrey is a triumphant exception. Since 1900 the city has developed into the second industrial base of Mexico, with a diversified range of growth manufacturing: steel and steel products, car assembly, electrical and electronics, heavy chemicals, and synthetic textiles, in addition to a spectrum of food-processing and consumer goods production. Twenty per cent of industrial output is sold abroad, with steel, glass, and machinery prominent in trade to the US. Many US firms have branches in Monterrey and there is also a considerable influx of technology and capital from north of the Border (Revel-Mouroz 1969, 187).

THE SERVICE FUNCTION

There are three aspects of this urban function: first, the adventitious effect of large-scale federal government spending on the US side of the Border; second, the service to the town population and thereafter to its hinterland; and third, the impact of tourism (p. 204). Within the hinterlands there is some overlapping in the competition among urban centres, but there is little evidence for a graduated, marketing hierarchy of towns (Unikel *et al.* 1976; Huff and DeAre 1974) on either the American or the Mexican sides of the Rio Grande. Between the paired cities on the Rio Grande there has grown an interdependence and complementarity, at times rudely shattered as the result of unilateral shifts in frontier policies. Torres (1976, 1406) has formulated a developmental model to interpret this interdependence. Economic stimulus in a US Border city attracts migrants, increases local economic activity, and earnings per capita. Initial needs are then met by US industry at large; but local industry, commerce, and services grow in proportion to the market. Demand then becomes diversified, especially for consumer goods, but also for further capital investment. A rising labour requirement stimulates migration from the adjacent Mexican city. Growing US earnings are increasingly spent in part across the Rio Grande, leading to labour-intensive services and recreation facilities there. Such job opportunities attract more immigrants from a greater distance, often greatly in excess of available employment and a marginal population of the unemployed comes into being south of the Rio Grande. Mexicans working in the US stimulate demand for retail goods there and a strong growth takes place in that sector. Because of these reciprocal influences each twin-city is larger than would be expected from its geographical setting, natural resource base, or location with respect to its own national markets.

US federal spending on the Border is mainly in defence-related establishments, though there is of course disseminated economic and social aid to communities under many federal welfare programmes. Defence spending is adventitious and though the multiplier effects on the local economy may be very substantial, such development is sensitively vulnerable to changes in defence policies, both in war and peace. There have always been garrisons on the US Rio Grande, since it became the international boundary, but two world wars led to the creation of very large military bases. In the mid-1960s almost 50,000 were employed around El Paso alone, at the military or air bases, and the White Sands nuclear-testing range. At Laredo the 150 ha site of a former air force base is now being developed for industrial use, while Del Rio still has the powerful economic underpinning of an active air base. The spending power earned on these bases has also been a valued contribution to the shops and recreational facilities in nearby Mexico.

The 'oasis' West is thinly-peopled and the towns of El Paso and C. Juárez are of a size out of all proportion for serving such a hinterland (Jeanjean and Revel-Mouroz 1975, 53–4). C. Juárez immediately services nine scattered, desert *municipios* with about 60,000 people in all. For retailing and wholesaling NE Chihuahua is the field of coverage, intersecting with the hinterland of C. Chihuahua. For higher banking services C. Juárez relies on C. Chihuahua, for university education (until very recently) and specialist hospital services on El Paso. Yet the Mexican city has a major international tourist function and in the American 'in-bond' plants it is also tied into the US economy. With more nodal communications El Paso is unambiguously a regional metropolis, though there are only 1.8 million people within a radius of 320 km, including Mexico. Seventy-two per cent of retailing is internal to the twin-cities. Although the wholesaling hinterland is limited even within western Texas, El Paso polarizes shopping from a radius of almost 200 km in Texas and New Mexico. Laredo serves its own county markets, but because there is no other city of more than 50,000 within 160 km in either the US or Mexico there is a widespread attraction of shoppers from almost as far as Monterrey to the south. Indeed, Laredo has a higher dollar value of sales per square metre of retail floor space than most stores in New York or Dallas (Sloan and West 1976, 457). The Brownsville–Matamoros twin-cities show similar interdependent functions (Dillman 1969, 96–8). Brownsville dominates the retail trade, controls access to foreign markets through its port, and is a major source of wage income for Mexicans; its commercial hinterland penetrates Mexico as far as Poza Rica, Torreón, and even San Luis Potosí. Matamoros, a cotton metropolis, spends 52 per cent of net income on foreign purchases and reciprocates by selling tourist services and both local and national products.

All Texan Border cities have a retailing hinterland deep into northern Mexico, trading in an arc between 180 and 360 degrees. Weekly or monthly shoppers may come from 240 km south of the Rio Grande, by bus, train, or car. In the eastern Borderlands San Antonio and Monterrey dominate, and the service provision in the Border cities, on both sides of the river, is weakened accordingly. The hinterlands of San Antonio and Monterrey overlap, the stronger service economy of the former complementing the more powerful industrial base of the latter. Both cities are important decision-taking centres, in the government, banking and insurance, and commercial sectors. Yet it is part of the overall weakness of the Borderlands as of all peripheries, and particularly true throughout manufacturing or the defence establishments that major decisions are always taken at a great distance, in the latter case usually in the federal capital cities. This is especially true for manufacturing in Mexico, substantially dependent upon the nationalized petroleum, steel-making, and fertilizer industries.

THE LIFE-WORLD

CULTURAL ATTITUDES AND PERCEPTIONS

The objective study of national character requires a study of the values that influence important aspects of behaviour.

R. Díaz-Guerrero, 1967

The (Texan) State is not just so many competing regions or counties but a whole cluster of subcultures held together with conscious effort, around symbols, dreams, and a sense of destiny.

L. Kennamer, 1969

Mexican culture along the Border comes to represent, in general terms, a loss of identity, the dubious mixture of two national life-styles (each at its worst), the deification of technology, and a craze for the new.

C. Monsiváis, 1978

How people live and work are objective realities. How they look upon their situation, how they regard and are regarded by others, what thoughts they may cherish and what actions they may take as a result are much more conjectural, but no less significant. Perceptions, attitudes, and beliefs condition the behavioural response, among individuals, but also within groups and at the aggregate level as between cultures (Hofstede 1980). Environmental, historical, cultural, and political influences play their part, but in frontier regions there is added a further, potentially discordant ingredient, national character. In the fluid interaction of life-worlds across the frontier national differences are apt to be exaggerated, worse still may be manipulated for political ends, leading to stereotyping and the creation of derogatory caricatures. Such debasement enters local folklore and, typically, disturbs relationships among frontier peoples, colours their attitudes both to particular transactional events and the general course of change. It adds further to the frictions of the power-political struggle, which is an inevitable feature at the frontier interface. Yet national differences also rest innately and deeply upon positive traits and values cherished by contrasting cultures, creative as well as destructive in the minds of men. A sense of heritage and a code of values are motivating forces in national, as well as in local society, often at their strongest when under the greatest threat. The overlapping of the North American and the Latin American lifeworlds along the Rio Grande prospectively offers a uniquely great challenge, for political domination in the most negative sense, for cross-cultural co-operation and harmony in the most positive manner.

To portray this frontier interaction as a polarization between two internally homogeneous, but externally discordant life-worlds is greatly to oversimplify a complex cultural situation. Even the notion of a cultural continuum from the heartland of English-speaking 'Middle America' to the core of Spanish-speaking Central Mexico has its limitations. The intermediate cultures, Anglo-Texan, Mexican-American (in the US), Border-Mexican (including the *norteño* sub-culture) represent distinct breaks and conglomerations of cultures, rather than a smooth transition of values or attributes. Furthermore, there is a good deal of support (Martínez P.D. 1971; Martínez O.J. 1977; Paredes, 1978) for the view that the Rio Grande frontier itself has led to a distinctive Border culture. This is most clearly so on the Mexican side, 'expanding into a vacuum where identity becomes rarified and lost' (Monsiváis 1978, 66) but, in a wider sense, the 'border effect' made people 'on one or both sides of the Border more different from either "core-culture patterns" than the core patterns were from each other' (Díaz Guerrero 1967, 88). Above all, there is general agreement that the Mexican-American, the *chicano*, represents a rich social diversity but an identifiable sub-culture and not simply a modal personality between Mexican and American ways of life.

The evolution of a Border culture is the product, over a lengthy period of time, of the extent, intensity, and nature of interaction among national or ethnic groups, on the one hand, counterbalanced in part by the forces towards segregation and separateness on the other. In this complex process the reality and the changing significance of the international boundary has played its part, always bearing in mind that the Spanish-Mexican *cultural* frontier has for centuries lain to the north of the Rio Grande (Fig. 21), and that, in some material respects, a US consumer-oriented frontier has perhaps moved south beyond Mexico City (Paredes 1978, 93). The wide range of transactions within the Borderlands is discussed later (Pt. III), but such specific contacts, over a long period, have been accompanied by a mutual diffusion of values in the transition zone between the societies (Díaz-Guerrero 1967, 79). 'Selective assimilation of positive aspects of the neighbouring culture can only produce better Mexicans, better Americans and better international relations' (Díaz-Guerrero 1978, 302), but, unfortunately, the history of Border relations has hitherto been much more negative. The contact of the Mexican with the technology and modern life-styles of the American has certainly increased the cosmopolitan nature of the Rio

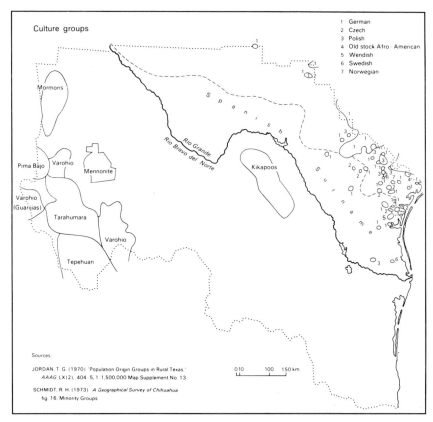

FIG. 21. Culture areas

Grande cities (Martínez 1977, 89), but on balance to the detriment of
the Mexican way of life. The cities south of the river clearly have
Mexican values, but these have increasingly been submerged in US
material culture, in food habits, clothing, use of domestic appliances,
leisure activities, spending habits, and career aspirations. The positive
impact of this has been greatest upon the wealthier or more educated,
but for the many there has been 'a loss of identity, the dubious mixture
of two national life-styles, the deification of technology, and a craze for
the new' (Monsiváis 1978, 67). At the polarized extreme, a poverty
culture has become deeply rooted in the slum *barrios* of the Mexican
Border cities, in which 'the individuals' concept of identity, moral
character, and world view are weak and disorganized' in a social
environment of decay, crime, and poverty. By comparison, the northward diffusion of Mexican cultural traits across the Rio Grande has had
no such dramatic effects. The Mexican-American culture in some ways
reflects the Mexican, while among the Anglos food habits or dress

customs are only marginal increments to the life-world. When people move or migrate acculturation in a new milieu becomes more complex than simply in the diffusion of customs, since elements of both the original and the adopted culture have to be accommodated. The rate of culture change then depends very much on opportunities for advancement (Díaz-Guerrero 1978, 303) and the negative aspects in the extent of segregation or discrimination which persists.

In South Texas physical segregation of culture groups has been a long-standing custom, with Anglo- and Mexican-neighbourhoods, visibly different in housing, social provision, available work but also in life-styles and community character. Residental segregation thus reflects social and economic as well as cultural distinctions. Table 4 shows the indices of residential segregation, by ethnic groups, in three major Borderlands cities.

Table 4. *Indices of residential segregation, 1960*

	0 = no segregation, 100 = total segregation					
	Anglo v. all others	Spanish surname v. Anglo	Negro v. Anglo	Spanish surname v. Negro	Spanish surname v. other non-white	Spanish surname foreign-born v. native-born
El Paso	52.9	52.9	79.2	59.5	52.8	17.9
Laredo	39.3	39.4	60.1	43.9	44.7	12.7
San Antonio	63.7	63.6	84.5	77.4	49.9	17.0

Source: Grebler *et al.* 1970, Table 12–1, 275.

To some extent related to ethnic preferences, segregation is also inescapably the outcome of income differentials, size of household, and the magnitude of the city. Since 1960 there has been some convergence in ethnic living standards and opportunities in life, and limited intermarrying has taken place in the Rio Grande towns. Discrimination has diminished in general, but much less so in rural or small-town Texas than in the larger urban areas. The international boundary, however, continues to act as an ethnic marker, limiting the northward equalizing flows of population which would otherwise take place. In short, though ethnicity is and long has been a prime reason for segregation, it is increasingly being diluted in favour of a separateness based upon economic or social status, reinforced by the outcome of political attitudes and prejudices. Certainly, among the poor, to think of cultural heritage may well seem a dispensable luxury.

The outcome of interaction may be positive, in steps towards acculturation, or negative, in a greater alienation between groups. In both cases, the sense of identity or of self-esteem is likely to be affected, one way or the other (Gecas 1973, 579). There may be a feeling of greater security and well-being in a reinforcement of identity, particularly under external threat. Indeed, the fate of those caught between two cultures, abandoning the one but still rejected by the other, the *pocho pachuco* of the Borderlands, is altogether unenviable, 'wedged between the pyramid and the skyscraper' (Paredes 1978, 93). Nationalism introduces an unstable and unpredictable element into such cross-cultural relationships and, at all times, it is much easier as a result to move towards confrontation and self-reinforcement than in the direction of co-operation or self-abnegation. The management of social, economic, cultural, or political tensions across an international boundary is thus a very delicate process, balancing adaptive moves towards lessening friction with reaction to maladaptive moves which exacerbate relationships. In dealing with such tensions, culture groups tend to show contrasting reactions: Americans, more positively, even aggressively in a competitive mood, the Mexican by tradition in more passive, resigned, even pessimistic frame of mind (Díaz-Guerrero 1978). This is not so for the wealthy Mexican *élite*.

Perceptions, attitudes, beliefs, and action on either side of the Rio Grande are much conditioned by the cultural legacies of history, yielding a sadly distorted set of stereotype images of both self and potential adversary. These images have been well summarized by Paredes (1978, 87–8): 'The Anglo's actively hostile stereotype of the Mexican is well known: he is dirty and greasy; he is treacherous, cruel and cowardly; thievery is his second nature; and he has always recognized the Anglo-Texan as his superior.' Conversely, to the Mexican 'the Anglo is cruel and treacherous if he can get you in his power, but he is easy to outwit because he is big and stupid'. The milder stereotype of the Anglo shows him to be

good-hearted but boorish; very rich, having made his money by cheating other people— for example cheating the Mexicans out of Texas; cagey and clannish, but so greedy and gullible that he can be tricked out of his money, or even his wife by appealing to his cupidity. In general, he is not really a bad fellow, even though he speaks funny Spanish and allows himself to be ruled by his women.

The corresponding stereotype of the Mexican suggests that he is 'a colourful and impractical character who speaks funny English; if old, he is a kind of Uncle Remus, full of antiquated and useless wisdom; if young, he loves flowers, music and a good time, but it is hard to get a good day's work out of him.' With the prevalence of such images in the popular mind there is little wonder that Border relationships and understanding have matured but slowly and painfully, whether along the Rio Grande, or more distantly among decision-takers in Washington or Mexico City.

THE TEXANS

Although South Texans have had surprisingly cosmopolitan origins (Fig. 21) with an enduring diversity of cultural traits, there is a deeply ingrained sense of Texan identity and a strong allegiance to their State as 'distinctive in the social fabric of the American nation' (Meinig 1969, 124). With the substantial inflows of migrants to Texan cities since the Second World War and the greater internal migration fluxes in response to urbanization and industrialization, there has been considerable convergence upon American norms of life-style. Such greater uniformity of the life-world has penetrated, but only slowly into rural South Texas and the frontier cities along the Rio Grande. The 'pragmatic American approach to life, the ideal of citizenship as a form of business and the belief in commerce as a builder of nationality' (Monsiváis 1978, 65) have been somewhat diluted on closer contact with the Mexican-American and Mexican life-worlds. Nevertheless, a more active style in coping with life's problems, a more competitive nature and an outlook that life is to be enjoyed rather than endured are said (Díaz-Guerrero 1978, 296) to be distinctive in Anglo-Texan cultural attitudes. This is an ideal of the struggle of the individual, whose worth is evaluated essentially in terms of the material success he achieves.

The Anglos' negative images of the Mexican have become deeply entrenched by the myths, the legends, and the realities of Texas history, from the Alamo and Goliad to the US–Mexican War and the century of Border troubles that followed. Derogatory names for the Mexican proliferated, with 'greaser' perhaps the least offensive and most current ever since 1836 (Monsiváis 1978, 79). Mexican attributes were derided as 'slow and lazy, overfriendly and liable to make sexual advances, unpunctual and irresponsible, polite but hypocritical, freely expressive but vulgar and with an intense, but pathological family concern' (Díaz-Guerrero 1978, 305). By tradition, Mexican-Americans in Texas were scarcely better regarded, 'a people without heroes, contributing nothing of cultural value to the Southwest and needing Anglo domination to make up for a lack of internal leadership' (view quoted in Stoddard 1973, 48). Such perniciously fallacious views were reflected in the 'American zeal for bettering people. The Latin should be . . . remade in the Anglo mould' (Madsen 1964, 12). Unfortunately, as Stoddard (1973, 39 et seq.) has pointed out, social scientists have all too often perpetuated similar erroneous stereotypes, in the cultural determinism of their folk-culture, value orientation, interethnic, and other socio-economic models of Mexican and Mexican-American cultural development.

Because South Texas is so diverse it would be unwise to generalize too far on attitudes. Personal encounters suggest that negative stereotypes linger longest and are at their most exaggerated in small-town mentality, and over vast rural tracts in which the non-Anglo is still held in a feudal, semi-caste situation (Grebler *et al.* 1970, 9). The irrigation farmer, more heavily dependent on Mexican workers, looks on them differently from the rancher, with his few skilled ranch-hands. The small business may employ undocumented aliens and many others benefit from their services, but this had rarely led to widespread benevolence, except in domestic situations. Professional folk and government servants mix liberally, countering discrimination whenever and wherever possible. Fortunately too there has been a generational change in attitudes, from the harder-line prejudices of older people on the Rio Grande to a somewhat more liberal, egalitarian society today. Ethnicity is perhaps less divisive in itself than the conditions of deprivation to which those of low ethnic status have for so long been condemned on both sides of the Border.

THE MEXICANS

Mexican society too is by no means uniform or monolithic. In particular, it is to be differentiated by class structure, the degree of American influence, the regional identity of the *norteños* around Monterrey, urban and rural differences, and certainly also in generational terms. Nevertheless, there are certain common cultural traits, often the reverse image of the values of traditional American society. Díaz-Guerrero (1967, xvi) contrasts the American socioculture, based on power as the main element in decision-taking, with the Mexican ethos, related to love rather than power, the decisions being reached in a passive affiliative manner. Mexicans thus tend to be 'obedient, affiliative,' interdependent, orderly, cooperative, not oriented towards self-achievement, and not self-initiated' (Díaz-Guerrero 1973, xvii). There is 'no sense of individual equality or of a search for individual power, but rather a defined hierarchical ordering of individuals within the family'. The use of Spanish, the sense of heritage, pride in Mexico, the extended family unit, attachment to the Catholic religion, and an innate conservatism from a rural past are important bonds in national as well as community cohesion. An acceptance that life is hard and demanding leads to attitudes that it is to be endured rather than enjoyed. Yet, in reality, there seems to be much more spontaneous enjoyment at all ages in Mexico than across the Border in Texas.

This identikit picture of the passive Mexican seems to contrast strongly with the commonly held image of *machismo*, projected as the essence of masculine virility or, better put, of male chauvinism (Paredes 1967). Such an aggressive stance defines the traditional male role in the Mexican family, but it is also an enactment of the myths and legends of a frontier past. *Machismo* became a violent expression of feeling in

Mexico at the time of the 1910 Revolution, following an upsurge of nationalist fervour, and yet also a sense of an inevitable, growing dependence on the US. Part of the *macho* feelings were directed against the Americans for Mexican resentment of the Anglo-Texan is very apparent at the Border, and this has long been the case. The two cultural communities have been almost equally inventive in insulting each other, with *yanqui blofero*, *gringo*, and *gabacho* some of the least offensive epithets for those north of the Rio Grande (Monsiváis 1978, 81). The intense resentment of Anglo attitudes to the Mexican in turn leads to chauvinistic defiance, in which there is more than a touch of sensed inferiority complex. Mexican attitudes to Americans (Paredes 1978, 304) see their high activity rates as neurotic behaviour, their directness as rude and aggressive, the sense of freedom leading to licence and sexual looseness, independent outlook as coldness, lack of expressiveness as stupidity, physical size as awkward, and self-assertiveness as pure egotism.

Within northern Mexico the *norteño* sub-culture around Monterrey has a special place (León-Portilla 1975). In one sense the Norte has a harsh environment, to which challenge there has been a most positive societal response in the exploitation of position and scarce local natural resources. Second, the influence of the US has been strongly felt, in investment, urbanization, and industrialization, creating the second most powerful economic base in Mexico. Whether genetically or culturally determined, or merely the effect of remoteness and independent development the people of the Monterrey region have played a vital role in economic growth, revolution, and reform. Its people have been 'proud, courageous, determined, industrious and adaptable with distinct attitudes and behaviour patterns'. As Díaz-Guerrero (1978, 302) put it 'I am quite sure that the people of the middle and even the lower classes in Monterrey are not conscious of how "Americanized" they have become in their life-styles and socio-economic characteristics, and all that this means concerning inter-personal, romantic and business relationships.'

Although Mexico has become steadily more urbanized, it retains many of the traits of an agrarian society. Table 5 on the class structure of Mexico in 1940 and 1960 (Rangel Contla 1970) shows the tiny élite apex of the social pyramid and the very broad base of workers; between lie the small proprietor and the limited number of the urban middle class (Ginneken 1978). The social, economic, and attitudinal differences among these classes are in some respects greater than those between Mexicans and the Americans north of the Rio Grande. In the northern Borderlands, the polarization of life between the towns and the rural areas is very pronounced. Some of the old-style *latifundistas*, in ranching country, or the owners of new *latifundias*, on irrigated land,

Table 5.   *Mexican class structure 1940, 1960*

	1940 (%)	1960 (%)
Bourgeois	1.3	0.9
Petty bourgeois	44.8	34.4
farmers	(12.3)	(13.9)
ejidatorios	(20.1)	(10.6)
others	(12.4)	(9.9)
Workers	53.9	64.7

Source: Rangel Contla 1970.

have capitalist organization and efficiency on the American scale. Below them the mass of small and medium-scale farmers suffer from endemic problems of scarce water resources, credit, commercial organization, and marketing. They and the *ejidatorios* commonly need to seek seasonal or part-time employment elsewhere, on other farms or in the towns. There they encounter the migrant landless labourers, who have provided most of the *braceros* in the past and quite a number of undocumented workers in more recent times. The great majority of rural people, 70 per cent of them at or below subsistence level, remain out of contact with the US life-world. Those who have been to that country experienced a depressed economic and social status, but, for many, were sustained in their ordeals by their ethnicity. Others fell short of their ambitions and have remained as slum-dwellers in the poverty culture of the Mexican Border city *barrios*.

In many ways the culture of the Mexican Border cities has come to resemble that of their American counterparts across the river. American customs, values, and practices have been diffused south-wards, while Mexican values have been transmitted in reverse, into the dominantly Mexican-American populations of parts of south Texas.

THE MEXICAN-AMERICANS (CHICANOS)

Consideration of this group immediately involves questions of definition, distribution, and cultural identity. The US 1970 census recorded 4.5 million persons of Mexican descent, some 50 per cent of all Hispanics; in the official estimates for 1978 the figures had risen to 7.2 millions and 60 per cent respectively (US Dept. Commerce 1978). The greatest concentrations of Mexican-Americans are still within the South-west, the original culture region within the US (Nostrand 1970; Meinig 1971), from which there has since been some diffusion, to the Middle West, the Pacific North-west, and Greater New York. The Mexican-American group is today mainly town-dwelling and internally very diverse, the product of a long and complex history. Some trace descent from Spanish settlers north of the Rio Grande, long before US Texas came into being, others have been one or more generations in the US, some have strong Indian traits, while yet others have only recently entered the country, whether legally or otherwise. Put differently, the majority rightly do not regard themselves as 'foreigners' in the US, but yet seek to sustain a valid ethnic and cultural identity within the cosmopolitan American nation (Dworkin 1965).

Casavantes (1969) identified the group as follows: sometime migrants from Mexico, with parents or relatives there; speak Spanish ('language loyalty') and have an accent when speaking English; Roman Catholic; possess darker skin, hair, and brown eyes; less than eight years' schooling if over twenty-five; and around one-third with annual incomes of less than $3,000. In terms of self-image there is still some confusion among Mexican-Americans, not surprising in a group which has undergone so many tensions while socializing within an alien and oppressive culture. The very name of the group arouses controversy, Mexican-American being the preferred term, but *chicano* coming into widespread use during the politically activist phase which began in the early 1960s. *Chicano*, a corruption of *mexicano*, tends to be identified in the minds of middle-class Mexican-Americans as associated with the radical culture coming out of the Border *barrios*, pointing up the rising significance of class polarization within a group supposedly oriented on the unifying concept of ethnicity (Stoddard 1973, 70).

Social distinctions reflect the different phases of acculturation in US society (Madsen 1964, 2): an initial transplant of a rural peasant from Mexico, the 'baseline' of the traditional Americanization process; second, a phase of alienation for many, caught between two cultures; and, third, a degree of incremental assimilation within US society, either functionally at a low material level for the masses, or by upward social mobility for the few. Grebler *et al.* (1970, 581 *et seq.*) stressed the great capacity of the Mexican-American for participation in US society, though admitting that in Texas this had been more constrained than in California, in the rural areas and small towns most notably so. Acculturation in recent times has come through: improved social relations, with school-friends and by intermarriage; a change in the family, the extended Mexican family now rare, the male role shifting from *machismo* and patriarchal domination to equality, while *compradrazgo* (the godfather bond) has now decreased in importance as a social tie; and by use of birth control. Nevertheless, many whites still regard the Mexican-American as 'imperfectly socialized' (Garza *et al* 1973, 16), if not incapable of assimilation, and his progress is constantly interpreted and monitored solely by the values and norms of the parent Anglo society. Conversely, many Mexican-Americans fear that assimilation can be achieved only at the expense of a loss of identity, and that would be too high a price to pay.

In the slum *barrios* on both sides of the Border the Mexican culture of poverty is still endemic, and the *chicano* life-style in Texas is then effectively a social cult for survival (Garza *et al.* 1973, 25). Recently it was said, (Moore 1970, 103) that the US lower Rio Grande town of Roma had *barrios* so little changed from the early twentieth century that it was a 'natural' location for a film on the peasant leader Zapata (1910). Given the deprived social and economic conditions in the *barrio* there has been little interaction with Anglos. Only the poorer jobs were available to the Mexican-American in South Texas and he has been steadily losing out in competition with short-term immigrants, legal or clandestine, for such scarce, low-paid, and exploited employment. In the *barrio* culture, however, social solidarity is an important defence mechanism: the extended family is stronger, male dominance more reassuring (to the man), and either fatalist resignation or political activism an outlet for the frustrations of discontent. Yet, a very encouraging sign, even from the *barrios* and the rural areas of South Texas some Mexican-American children have demonstrated high achievement goals (Garza *et al.* 1973, 46) though others (Kuvlevsky *et al.* 1971) argue otherwise. If validated, this is the surest passport to that upward social mobility which has been for so long denied to the majority of the Mexican-Americans.

Until the 1960s Mexican-Americans had been largely apolitical, even though persistently receiving second-class citizen treatment. Before 1920 constant violence on the Border had been projected back into racial discrimination against the Mexican-Americans. Political silence proved the wisest course and the logical outcome for an oppressed group fearful of *justicia* and afraid to vote. From 1920 to 1940 there was limited acculturation for Mexican-Americans, but they remained a depressed class, with restricted human rights. After 1940 embryonic political activism sought to change this state of affairs, even though 'racist' perceptions by the Anglos were giving way to 'cultural' recognition of the ethnic group (Grebler *et al.* 1970, 399). The American GI Forum 1950 and the Political Association of Spanish-speaking Organizations (PASSO), in the late 1950s, acted as pressure-groups for Mexican-American rights (Moore 1970, 137 *et seq.*) including the right to be fully participant in the political process. In South Texas the political struggle was initially focussed upon Crystal City (1963), where Mexican-American voters gained total control of the council, only to be denied by the dubious disqualification of some of their councilmen (Moore 1970, 34). Mexican-Americans have traditionally voted Democrat in south Texas, including 88 per cent of their voters as late as 1969. With the radical turbulence of the late 1960s, however, it is not surprising that an ethnic political party was founded, *La Raza Unida*, specifically to defend Mexican-American interests. First created in California in 1966 this party soon spread to Texas and was active in both local council and gubernatorial elections. In the November 1972 gubernatorial election, for example, the *Raza Unida* candidate, Ramsey Muñiz, polled 6.5 per cent of the votes. The subsequent white 'backlash' against *Raza Unida* in Border politics has been both sustained and sophisticated. The Democratic Party has regained some lost ground among Mexican-American voters, partly by taking into its fold some of the more talented activists, but the majority of the ethnic group who could vote seem largely disinclined to do so (Gutiérrez 1978). The spirit of local discrimination against them is by no means at an end, even though in 1970 (Moore 1970, 8) only 5 per cent of those questioned in San Antonio felt discriminated against, and 20 per cent said there was no discrimination at all.

With the American and the Mexican the Mexican-American completes the tricultural society of the Borderlands along the Rio Grande. Having considered the people, their work and social *milieu*, their perceptions, attitudes, beliefs, and actions as culture groups it is now time to look at the totality of economic and social transactions across the Rio Grande (Pt. II), as a prelude to an assessment of politics, policies, and planning in the Borderlands (Pt. III).

REFERENCES

PEOPLE AND PLACE

BEEGLE, J. A. *et al* (1960) 'Demographic characteristics of the US-Mexican Border', *Rur. Sociol.*, **25**, 1, 107–62.

BRADSHAW, P. S. and POSTON, D. L. (1971) 'Texas population in 1970', *Tex. Busin. Rev.*, **XLV**, 5.

BRIGGS, V. M. (1973) *Chicanos and rural poverty* (Baltimore: Johns Hopkins Univ. Press).

BROWNING, H. C. and FEINDT, W. (1968) 'Diferencias entre la población nativa y la migrante en Monterrey', *Demografía y Economía* **II**, 2, 183–204.

CABRERA, G. (1975) 'Migración y actividad económica en México', in P. Monbeig (ed.) 'Les migrations au Mexique *Cah. Amér. Lat.*, **12**, 2, 1–32.

GREENE, F. (1978) 'Analysis of major Mexican urban centres, 1960–1970', *Cornell Diss. in Plann.* (Ithaca, New York: Cornell Univ.).

GUTIÉRREZ DE MACGREGOR, M. T. and CARMEN VALVERDE, V. (1975) 'Evolution of the urban population in the arid zones of Mexico, 1900–1970', *Geogr. Rev.*, **65**, 2, 214–28.

GREENWOOD, M. J. (1978) 'An econometric model of internal migration and regional economic growth in Mexico', *J. reg. Sci.*, **18**, 1, 17–31.

MARGULIS, M. (1979) 'Crecimiento y migración en una ciudad de frontera: Estudio preliminar de Reynosa', *Simposio Nacional Sobre Estudios Fronterizos, El Colegio de México, Facultad de Filosofía y Letras de la UNAL* (Monterrey: N. León).

MARTÍNEZ, G. (1979) 'El crecimiento demográfico y los servicios públicos en las ciudades fronterizas', *Simposio Nacional sobre Estudios Fronterizos, El Colegio de México, Facultad de Filosofía y Letras de la UNAL* (Monterrey: N. León).

Morrison, P. C. (1963) 'Population changes in Mexico, 1950–1960' *Revista Geogr.*, **59,** 79–92.

Nathan, R. N. *et al.* (1968) *Industrial and employment potential of the US-Mexico Border*, US Dept. Commerce, Econ. Devel. Admin., Washington DC.

Reyes, S. T. (1974) 'El desempleo en México: características generales' *Comercio Exterior*, **XXXIV,** 7, 730–8.

Stoddard, E. R. (1978) 'Patterns of poverty along the US-Mexico Border', *El Paso Univ. of Texas, at El Paso, Center for Inter-Am. Stud. and Organization of US Border cities.*

Ugalde, A. (1974) *The urbanization process of a poor Mexican neighbourhood* (Austin: U. of Texas, Inst. Latin Am. Stud.).

Unikel, L. *et al.* (1976) *El desarrollo urbano de México*, El Colegio de México.

US Congress, House (1977) Jt. Econ. Com. *Hearings before the Sub-Committee on Inter-American economic relations*, 95th Congr., 1st sess.

Whetten, N. L. and Burnight, R. G. (1956) Internal migration in Mexico', *Rur. Sociol.*, **21,** 140–51.

THE BORDER ECONOMY

Bernstein, M. D. (1964) *The Mexican mining industry, 1890–1950 a study of the interaction of politics, economics and technology* (Albany: State Univ. New York).

Brent, M. D. and Sandidge, J. R. (1969) 'Uranium production in South-Central Texas', *Prof. Geogr.*, **XXI,** 1, 15–17.

Chevalier, F. (1967) *The ejido and political stability in Mexico*, (Oxford: OUP).

Dillman, C. D. (1969) 'Border town symbiosis along the lower Rio Grande as exemplified by the twin cities Brownsville, Texas, and Matamoros, Tamaulipas', *Rev. geogr.*, **71,** 93–113.

Fagen, R. R. and Nau, H. R. (1978) 'Mexican gas: the northern connection, *Latin Am. Program Wkg. Pap. 15* (Washington DC: Wilson Center, Smithsonian Institution).

Fernández y Fernández, R. (1971) 'La Ley Federal de Reforma Agraria', *Comercio Exterior*, **21,** 6, 503–16.

Ginneken, W. van (1978) *Socio-economic groups and income distribution in Mexico* (London: Croom Helm).

Grayson, G. W. (1978) 'Mexico and the United States: the natural gas controversy', *Inter-Am. Econ. Affairs*, **32,** 3, 3–27.

Holt Búttner, E. and Padilla y Sotelo, L. S. (1976) 'Análisis de la distribución de la población económicamente activa y por actividades económicas, a nivel municipal', *UNAM Annuar. de Geogr*, 16, 239–357.

Huff, D. L. and DeAre, D. R. (1974) *Principal interaction fields of Texas metropolitan centers*, Bur. Busin. Res. (Austin: Univ. Texas).

JeanJean, L. and Revel-Mouroz, J. (1972) *Villes de la frontière Méxique-Etats Unis: population et économie de deux villes jumelles, Ciudad Juárez-El Paso* (Paris: Inst. des Hautes Études de l'Amér. Latine).

Ladman, J. R. (1979) 'The economic interdependence of contiguous border cities: the twin city multiplier', *Ann. reg. Sci.*, **13,** 1, 23–38.

Martínez, O. (1978) *Border boom town: Ciudad Juárez since 1880*, (Austin: Univ. Texas Press).

Mexico, Sec. de Industria y Comercio, Subsec. de Comercio (1974) *Diagnóstico agropecuario de la franja fronteriza norte*, México DF.

Nathan, R. N. *et al.* (1968) *Industrial and employment potential of the US-Mexico Border* (Washington DC: US Dept. Commerce, Econ. Devel. Admin.)

Nguyen, D. T. and Martínez Saldívar, M. L. (1979) 'Pattern of agricultural growth in Mexican states 1960–71: a shift and share analysis', *Reg. Stud.*, **13,** 2, 161–79.

Nguyen, D. T. (1979) 'The effects of land reform on agricultural production, employment and income distribution: a statistical study of Mexican States, 1959–69',

Econ. J., **89,** 624–35.

REVEL-MOUROZ, J. (1969) 'Monterrey et le Nord-Est méxicain: croissance urbaine et organisation régionale', *Cah. d'outre-mer*, **22,** 86, 161–90.

SLOAN, J.W. & WEST, J.P. (1976) 'Community integration and Border policies among élites in two Border cities', *J. Inter-Am. Stud. & Wld. Affairs*, **18,** 4, 451–74.

STAVENHAGEN, R. (1966) 'Social aspects of agrarian structure in Mexico', *Soc. Res.*, 33, 463–85.

TORRES, O. E. (1976) 'Algunas observaciones sobre la economía de la frontera norte de México', *Comercio Exterior*, **XXVI,** 12, 1406–13.

UNIKEL, L. *et al* (1976) *El Desarrollo Urbano de México. Diagnóstico e Implicacionas Futuras* México DF: El Colegio de México).

US CONGRESS (1976) Senate Com. on Foreign Relations and Jt Econ. Com. of Congress, *Mexico's oil and gas policy: an analysis* (Washington DC: USGPO).

WEIGAND, K. (1977) 'Chicano-Wanderarbeiter in Südtexas', *Kieler Geogr. Schriften*, **47.**

THE LIFE-WORLD

CASAVANTES, E. J. (1969) *A new look at the attributes of the Mexican-American* (Albuquerque: SW Coop. Educ. Lab. Inc.).

DÍAZ-GUERRERO, R. (1967) *The psychology of the Mexican: culture and personality* (Austin: Univ. Texas Press).

DÍAZ-GUERRERO, R. (1978). 'Mexicans and Americans: Two worlds, one Border . . . and one observer', ch. 14 in S. R. Ross (ed.) *Views across the Border* (Albuquerque: Univ. New Mexico Press), 283–307.

DWORKIN, A. G. (1965) 'Stereotypes and self images held by native-born and foreign-born Mexican Americans', *Sociol. and Soc. Res.*, **49,** 214–24.

GARZA, R. O. DE LA, KRUSZEWSKI, Z. A. AND ARCINIEGA, T. A. (1973) *Chicanos and Native Americans: the territorial minorities*, Englewood Cliffs, N.J: Prentice Hall.

GECAS, V. (1973) 'Self-conceptions of migrant and settled Mexican Americans', *Soc. Sci. Q.*, **54,** 3, 579–95.

GREBLER, L., MOORE, J.W. & GUZMÁN, R. C. (1970) *The Mexican-American people: The nation's second largest minority* (New York: The Free Press).

GUTIÉRREZ, A. (1978) 'The politics of the Texas Border', ch. 6 in S. R. Ross (ed.) *Views across the Border* (Albuquerque: Univ. N. Mexico Press), 117–37.

HOFSTEDE, G. (1980) *Culture's consequences* (Beverly Hills, Cal.: Sage Publications).

KENNAMER, L. (1969) Introduction to D. Meinig *Imperial Texas*, (Austin: Univ. Texas Press).

KUVLEVSKY, W. P. *et al.* (1971) 'Status projections and ethnicity: a comparison of Mexican American, negro and Anglo youth', *J. Vocat. Behav.*, 1, 137–51.

LEÓN-PORTILLA, M. (1975) 'The *Norteño* variety of Mexican culture: an ethnohistorical approach' in E. H. Spicer and R. H. Thompson (eds.) *Plural society in the Southwest* (Albuquerque: Univ. New Mexico Press), 77–114.

MADSEN, W. (1964) *The Mexican Americans of South Texas* (Case studies in cultural anthropol.) (San Francisco: Rinehart, Holt & Wilson).

MARTÍNEZ, O. J. (1977) 'Chicanos and the Border cities: an interpretative essay', *Pacif. Hist. Rev.*, **46,** 85–106.

MARTÍNEZ, P. D. (1971) 'Ambiente sociocultural en la faja fronteriza mexicana', *Am. Indíg.*, **XXXI,** 2, 311–22.

MEINIG, D. W. (1969) *Imperial Texas* (Austin: Univ. Texas Press).

MEINIG, D. W. (1971) *Southwest: three peoples in geographic change, 1600–1970.* (New York: OUP).

MONSIVÁIS, C. (1978) 'The culture of the frontier: the Mexican side', ch. 3 in S. R. Ross (ed.) *Views across the Border* (Albuquerque: Univ. New Mexico Press), 50–67.

MOORE, J. W. (1970) *Mexican Americans* (Englewood Cliffs, N.J: Prentice Hall).

Nostrand, R. L. (1970) 'The Hispanic-American Borderland: delimitation of an American culture region', *Geogr. Rev.*, **60,** 638–61.

Paredes, A. (1967) 'Estados Unidos, México y el machismo', *J. Inter-Am. Stud.*, **9,** 65–84.

Paredes, A. (1978) 'The problem of identity in a changing culture' ch. 4 in S. R. Ross (ed.) *Views across the Border* (Albuquerque: Univ. New Mexico Press), 68–96.

Rangel Contla, J. C. (1970) 'La polarización de la estructura de clases en México', *Revta. mex. Sociol.*, **XXXII,** 2, 395–416.

Stoddard, E. R. (1973) *Mexican Americans* (New York: Random House).

US Dept. Commerce, Bureau of the Census (1978) *Persons of Spanish origin in the US,* Current Popn. Rep., Set P–20, 328.

PART III
Frontier Transactions

CHAPTER 4

Managing the Environment

In a semi-arid environment the basic natural resources of water, potentially fertile land, useful vegetation, or valuable soil bases are scarce, and the local ecology is in a perpetually fragile state. Not only scarcity but instability too is a problem. Flood may succeed drought, salinity pollute cultivable land, itself subject to sheet or gully erosion; soil fertility may quickly be lost and a vegetation cover, once removed, may never be restored. Even the air itself, in its very stability over the drier tracts, may be the more readily polluted, whilst the onset of summer storms and hurricanes in the lower Rio Grande create their own destructive hazards. The substantial peopling and economic development of the Rio Grande basin, on a rising tempo over the past hundred years, has increased the pressures upon such scarce resources, and the pursuit of economic growth has, ironically, threatened the environment ever more menacingly. Extending the ecosystems to man opens the prospect of disease or ill-health, environmentally generated, to add to the misfortunes he had already brought upon himself. In the past three decades urban sprawl, industrialization, and agribusiness have all sharpened the potential environmental conflicts.

In the face of such varied, substantial, and cumulative hazards co-operation, regulation, and conservation among human groups seem to be inescapable, but history shows that logic and the outcome have little in common, for predictable reasons (Utton 1973; Kennedy 1979). In the affluent society of the United States burgeoning federal legislation seeks to safeguard the environment, enforce minimum standards, and enact proper conservation of resources, but the realities may be somewhat different. States and local governments, are apt, jealously, to guard their responsibilities, and along the Rio Grande US Border communities, plagued by unemployment and slow growth, may set their environmental priorities lower. Furthermore, in a democratic, profit-oriented society the individual may successfully assert his rights against those of the community, while sectional interests will not be backward in advancing their exploitative claims, both within the political process and outside it.

In Mexico, still a developing country beset by a myriad social and economic problems, environmental issues, not surprisingly, are viewed in an altogether different light. It is a common complaint in most developing countries that they are subjected to unreasoning pressures by an affluent environmental lobby from abroad, from nations which can afford the 'luxuries' of sophisticated environmental programmes. To Mexicans poverty, unemployment, ill-health, and lack of development dominate the scene, the greatest of all polluters of the human condition. Mexico certainly has federal anti-pollution standards, though these may not always be observed in her Border cities, but jobs must take precedence in the claims on scarce financial resources. 'In the USA ecological concern means improving living standards; to those south of the Border it means life itself' (Lyon 1978, 337).

The struggle to conserve the fragile Border ecosystems thus starts from an unpropitious situation, with no clear consensus on either bank of the Rio Grande and all the more difficulty in developing international co-operation for the husbanding of inevitably scarce resources. The Boundary Waters Convention of 1906, for an equitable distribution of the waters of the upper Rio Grande (US Statutes 1906), and the 1944 Treaty for the utilization of the waters of the Colorado, Tijuana, and the (lower) Rio Grande (US Statutes 1944) were outstanding, if belated and only partial indications of what was both possible and mutually beneficial. The more limited organizations set up to manage and monitor Border air pollution (Busch 1978, 358) and Border health (Reiss 1978, 251) are further significant, if only recent and piecemeal achievements. Otherwise, a spectrum of ill-assorted and little co-ordinated federal, state, and local bodies for specific purposes on the US side faces a more centralized set of scarcely comparable, and certainly not compatible institutions in Mexico. Different remits, contrasts in legislative and executive powers, and a variety of areas over which jurisdiction is exercised underline the organizational problems endemic in any attempt to defend the Border environment in an integrated, effective manner. Lacking any comprehensive overview or co-ordinating body, for which no political will exists on either bank of the Rio Grande, and least of all in the transnational context, the conservation battle will continue to be fought on every side with a large measure of self-interest. All too often the interests of local communities conflict with the lofty idealism of environmental management schemes at federal level in both the US and Mexico. On the other hand, the cities facing each other across the Rio Grande have the liveliest concern for co-operation in face of the manifest and serious ecological problems affecting the daily lives of their citizens. The citizens too, at least in the US Border cities, are solidly behind environmental betterment. In El Paso, for example, 86 per cent of those polled expressed concern over air pollution, 78 per cent thought the government should do something about it, and 68 per cent were willing to pay higher taxes to abate pollution (Busch 1978, 356). South of the Rio Grande citizen commitment is less apparent. As Lyon (1978, 33) put it: 'We Mexicans cannot get excited over ecological problems which are the by-product of industrial development. We tend to look upon such questions as the most recent fad of a rich country seeking distraction from the real problems, such as nutrition, housing and public health.' Indeed, there is heavy criticism of the United States for its 'environmental pollution, tampering with the hydrological system and the dumping of waste on the continental shelf which are all destroying the ecosystem'.

International transactions on the environment of the Border concern access to, the use and misuse of shared resources. Of these water, the lifeblood of man, animals, and the land is incomparably the greatest, followed by air and then, briefly, considerations of health.

WATER MANAGEMENT

Neither the United States nor Mexico realized in 1848 (Treaty of Guadalupe Hidalgo) that their boundary river would prove to be grand only in its length, variable discharge, value of water and irrigable lands, disastrous floods, shifting channels, and attendant international confrontations.

RAY MUELLER 1975, 121

The international apportionment of the scarce and irregular water resources of the Rio Grande basin represents one of the most successful examples of bi-national co-operation, but the negotiations have had a complex history, and even the cumulative achievements have not been without a legacy of litigation and present dissatisfactions (Day 1970). The problems of a fair and equitable sharing have been bedevilled by differing legal frameworks, of principle and priority, not only as between the United States and Mexico, but also among the US States and authorities flanking the Rio Grande. Inevitably too, the uneven phases in the regulation of the river flow, by storage in reservoirs, changed the hydraulic efficiency of the channel in the downstream tracts (Mueller 1975, 117 *et seq.*). Offsetting a little the benefits of flood control, the river course became less stable within its banks, leading to disagreements and the need to redefine the principles of detailed configuration for the international riverline boundary (ch. 1). Attention here is focussed on water as a resource, for sharing, within a unified river basin, the problems which have arisen in its progressive allocation, policies to meet those problems, and the outcome of the application of those policies, at both international and national levels (Fig. 22).

THE WATER RESOURCE

Water scarcity and semi-aridity are keynotes in the climatic character of the international frontier tracts along the Rio Grande. Total precipitation is low, on average less than 25 cm per annum from El Paso to the river Conchos confluence, increasing to about 50 cm near the

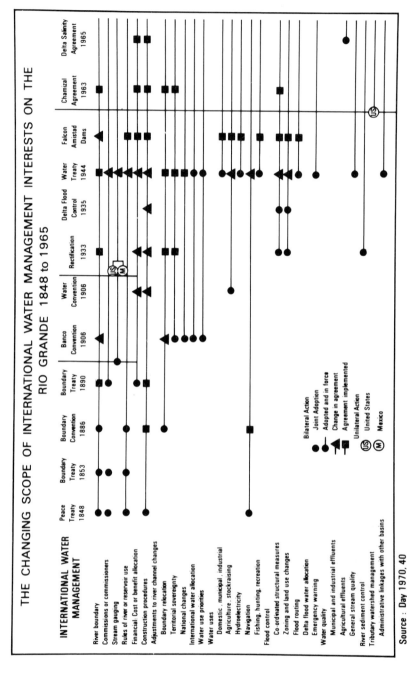

Source : Day 1970, 40

Fig. 22. International Water Management, Rio Grande, 1848–1965

Amistad reservoir, sustained to the head of the delta, then increasing to the Gulf coast. More importantly, even these low totals are threatened both by instability and year-to-year variation in volume and seasonal incidence on the one hand, and the considerable evaporation and water loss on the other. Of the yearly precipitation at El Paso, concentrated between May and October, some two-thirds is lost by evaporation at the time, while over the year the potential evaporation loss exceeds 250 cm. Droughts of several years are not uncommon in the El Paso–Juárez valley and even the scarce run-off of precipitation, on average less than 2.5 cm, is itself threatened by a minimal 60 per cent variation from year to year at El Paso, increasing to 80 per cent in many parts of the lower Rio Grande basin. Put rather differently, for Mexican stations, the water balance through the year is extremely precarious. At Chihuahua, for example, it is only in September that the normally expected precipitation equals the potential evapotranspiration; for all other months there is a deficit and this takes no account of the years in which the rains fail, as they not infrequently do. The situation is marginally better at Piedras Negras: November to February a surplus of precipitation, but a severe deficit throughout the summer growing season, even though in May and September this deficit is somewhat reduced. At Matamoros, on the delta, the water balance diagram is still irregular, in severe deficit in mid-summer, mitigated only a little by late spring rains, and in surplus fleetingly, first in September and then, more prominently, in December and January.

   Without the flow of the Rio Grande and its tributaries the prospects for settlement and commercial agriculture would have been bleak, confined to the better-watered slopes at higher altitudes well away from the river, in its Colorado headwaters, or the slopes of the Sierra Madres in Mexico. Fortunately, the heavier precipitation in these areas, 90 cm of snow for most years in the Colorado mountains and up to 75 cm in the Sierra Madre Occidental, nourish stream-flow which in earlier times sustained the Rio Grande, like a miniature Nile as President Jefferson called it, all the way to the Gulf of Mexico. It is this precious, uneven, unreliable, and turbulent flow which has been belatedly, but on the whole effectively managed for the benefit of Mexicans and Americans alike. Table 6 dramatically illustrates the reduction in stream-flow as a result of the progressive harnessing and management of the Rio Grande (Schroeder 1958, 328–9), the taming of the Rio Bravo, the 'wild' river in its Mexican title.

   In effect, the ponding back and increasing abstraction of water, mainly for irrigation purposes, has virtually broken up the Rio Grande river system into three detached sections with, at times, almost dry river-beds between: the main course down to El Paso; the section below Presidio, after the discharge of the Mexican Conchos tributary; and the

Table 6.   *Rio Grande, mean annual flow, 1884–1914, 1943–53*
           (in thousand acre-feet*)

	El Paso	Fort Quitman	Presidio	Del Rio	Laredo	Brownsville
1884–1914	1,000	1,000	2,000	3,500	4,000	5,000
1943–1953	500	100 (29)	750	1,600	2,500	200 (655)
	(1950–64 figures in brackets)					

Source: Schroeder 1958.
* 1,000 acre-feet = 1.23 million m³

Texan Pecos branch above the town of Pecos. Such an interrupted river course developed earlier from natural causes, but today the regulated flow has been carefully monitored and managed. Already in 1914 it was reported (US Congress 1914) that '. . . it [the Rio Grande] frequently goes dry, sometimes for two hundred miles, and in one year there was no water passed for eight months'. Another writer (Fergusson 1955, 3) observed that in many places it was 'not a river at all but only a wide strip of sand baking in the sun'.

Flooding too was a natural hazard to be contained. Upper-basin flooding was originally transmitted throughout the entire course, the product of spring snow-melt in the mountains of Colorado and New Mexico. Such flooding occurred from April to July and was on occasion augmented, even submerged, in the lower basin by summer floodwaters from both Mexican and American tributaries. Such summer floods in the lower course have indeed had the greatest destructive potential (Day 1970, 17–18). The Conchos basin in Mexico had a maximum rate of discharge (160,000 cu. ft, 4,530 m³ per sec) in the twenty-five years prior to the closing of the Elephant Butte dam in 1916, some seven times the then highest recorded flood in the mainstream section below El Paso. The Pecos river has registered 948,000 ft³ sec⁻¹ (26,845m³ sec⁻¹), the Devil's river 597,000 ft³sec⁻¹ (16,905 m³ sec⁻¹), while the maximum discharge in the Rio Grande at Del Rio was in a 1,140,000 ft³ sec⁻¹ (32,280 m³ sec⁻¹) wave-crest in June 1954. Downstream from Del Rio storm surges and flood peaks diminish, but below Falcon dam flooding may threaten the delta lands from the two Mexican tributaries: the Alamo 144,800 ft³ sec⁻¹ (4,100 m³ sec⁻¹) and the San Juan 353,000 ft³ sec⁻¹ (9,995 m³ sec⁻¹). Such floods still present a serious problem, with the need to divert peak storm discharges through the floodway systems artificially created for that purpose (see Fig. 8).

PRELUDE TO STRIFE

For some decades after the Rio Grande became the international boundary in the Treaty of Guadalupe Hidalgo the issue of sharing the common water resource lay almost totally dormant. The Treaty itself made no mention of irrigation, confining its provisions to the safeguarding of navigation, then a prime principle in the use of international watercourses. Since the banks of the Rio Grande were sparsely settled there seemed little need to allocate rights in the development of the river basin. Certainly there had been diversions for irrigation from as early as the mid-seventeenth century, at the Spanish missions around Juárez (Clark 1978, 71). The total irrigated area may have peaked at about 16,190 ha, though it was much diminished by 1800. In the mid-eighteenth century some 4,000 colonists settled upstream in New Mexico, but it was the advance of the United States frontier which gave rise to mounting pressures for development, and priority claims for sovereign use of that most precious asset, potential irrigation water. After the American Civil War there was a great influx of settlers into the San Luis valley of Colorado. To the 74,050 ha under irrigation in New Mexico in 1880 were added some ten years later, 121,400 irrigated hectares in Colorado (Hundley 1966, 19). About the same time the Southern Pacific railroad reached El Paso (1881), opening the prospect of new markets and increasing the demand for irrigation in the El Paso–Juárez valley.

Similarly, but posing a less serious prospect of strife, there had been piecemeal irrigation in the lower Rio Grande since the mid-eighteenth century, followed by an era of speculative commercial farming on both sides of the river. In 1870 George Brulay arrived and put 400 ha into cotton, later switching to sugar and irrigation farming; in 1883 John Closner established his holding which within twenty years had become 18,200 ha of rich farmland, irrigating a wide diversity of crops. In the early years of the twentieth century the first citrus plantations were set up and the arrival of the railway in 1904 gave further momentum to economic development (Hundley 1966, 30–1). Yet these early Texan entrepreneurs regarded the river waters as their own, and never filed claim to the resources they so freely plundered (Sandos 1980, 497).

THE UPPER VALLEY

Trouble between Mexicans and Americans first flared in the El Paso–Juárez valley. The salt riots of 1877 were followed by intermittent years of drought, at a time when the spreading acreage of irrigation and the growth of towns was stimulating the demand for increasingly scarce water resources. Texan farmers accused the Mexicans of damming the river and unilaterally diverting water 'in direct opposition to the rights of riparian owners (to an undiminished flow)'. This was a first expression of absolute property rights in water, strongly represented in Texan State laws, but an anachronism under the conditions of the semi-arid lands on the Rio Grande. The citizens of El Paso pressed for construction of an international dam some three miles upstream from the city, though without intending any formal commitment to sharing the waters with Mexico. Meanwhile, large-scale organization of irrigation lands began to replace the earlier scattered 'ditch' companies, each irrigating little more than one hundred American hectares. For example, the Rio Grande Irrigation and Land Company (1893), a British venture, planned 93,000 ha of ditchlands and a further 120,000 on the *mesa* (Clark 1978, 72). By this time the Mexicans were thoroughly alarmed. Land values on the Mexican bank had fallen, and the population was beginning to drain away as irrigation farming became steadily more problematical. A formal claim by the Mexicans, for thirty-five million dollars' compensation, was lodged with the US government, citing loss of water rights and, interestingly too, that American water diversions had impeded navigation on the Rio Grande. The Mexican loss of rights to water rested on historical grounds that they had been water users 'for hundreds of years before the inhabitants of Colorado and, according to the principles of civil law, prior claims take precedence'. The US authorities continued to assert a form of absolute sovereignty over the Rio Grande headwaters and their apportionment and, in particular, denied the Mexican claim to compensation for the interruption of navigation. This issue was complicated, even within American law. First, it was asserted that the primacy of navigation, the only principle of water use written into the foundation treaty of Guadalupe Hidalgo could not affect the right to dam the river, or abstract water upstream of the international section. Second, even though denying Mexican rights, the US Federal lawyers nevertheless sought to refuse American entrepreneurs the right to dam the river within the national section on the grounds that conservation of navigation was an issue for the Secretary for War and not for the civil authority. Furthermore, the Rio Grande was used for the rafting of logs and thus could technically be deemed navigable in at least one sense (Hundley 1966, 26), a right which ironically, might be denied internationally but at the same time safeguarded for national self-interest.

THE 1906 CONVENTION

The contest over sharing the waters of the upper Rio Grande had to be resolved and, in 1895, the International Boundary Commission (IBC) was asked to report on the situation with a view to an equitable allocation between the US and Mexico. The findings (IBC 1903) largely exonerated unilateral American water-users, but underlined that unless reservoir storage was introduced the prospects for irrigation agriculture in the El Paso–Juárez valley would become increasingly threatened. Indeed, there was already evidence that American farmers too were drifting away from the valley. The outcome was the US proposal (1905) to build a multi-purpose barrage reservoir at Elephant

Butte, initially contested by Mexico, which preferred an international site just above El Paso. In the event, the issues concerning equitable international allocation of waters were resolved by the 1906 Convention, on equitable distribution of the waters of the (upper) Rio Grande (US Statutes 1906). In the same year Texas and New Mexico water-users entered into agreement with the US Reclamation Service to construct the Rio Grande Project, an elaborate irrigation system in the vicinity of El Paso (Day 1975, 50; Stoddard 1979). The dam at Elephant Butte, completed in 1916, was an essential part of this project, before it also became the means of safeguarding at least some of the treaty-stipulated irrigation supply to Mexico. The 1906 Convention 'made arrangements' for Mexico to receive 60,000 acre-feet (74 million m^3) of water annually, in turn for the withdrawal of Mexican compensation claims on the US government. Deliveries of water were to be distributed seasonally according to an agreed schedule (Art. II), without cost to Mexico (Art. III). This allocation to Mexico was based on the estimated maximum land under irrigation there at the time of the Convention, and it has ever since been a considerable constraint on irrigation development south of the Rio Grande. Not only was the total volume of water to be supplied kept inflexible, but in the event even that limited volume has not been available in quite a number of years. Between 1938 and 1967, following completion of the American dam near El Paso, deliveries to Mexico fell below 60,000 acre-feet (74 million m^3) in fourteen of the twenty-nine years; indeed in the driest year only 6,650 acre-feet (8.2 million m^3) were delivered to Mexico. Further underlining the unequal outcome of the 1906 Convention, the United States unilaterally declared that in years of serious drought, low flow, or accidental failure of supply (Art. II) on the Rio Grande it would reserve the right to reduce allocation to Mexico, though on a basis proportionate to the reductions to be suffered by Texan water-users of the Rio Grande Project (Stoddard 1979, 48 *et seq.*) in the El Paso–Juárez valley. Even after the building of the supplementary storage reservoir at Caballo in 1938, to act as a holding area for water released from Elephant Butte during the generation of hydroelectric power, the supply to Mexico was no more assured. As late as 1978 (Nash 1978, 644) the US Secretary of State told the Mexican ambassador that there would be a diminished and delayed irrigation supply to Mexico, that the 1906 Convention could not be modified, but that strictly *ex-gratia* supplementary amounts might be made available by the US Commissioner.

The international water allocation was further complicated by litigation among the three American States (Colorado, New Mexico, and Texas) with an interest in the waters of the upper Rio Grande. In 1924 the Rio Grande Compact Commission was created to adjudicate on conflicting claims of these three internal riparian users, leading to a temporary Compact, allocating quotas in principle in 1929, more formally so in 1938, and put into operation in 1940 (Clark 1978, 74). This inter-State Compact still functions, annually considers water storage levels, and makes allocations to the constituent parties. A 790,000-acre-feet (97 million m^3) supply norm from Elephant Butte reservoir was agreed in 1940, but the discharge through Caballo dam was deficient in twenty-two of the first twenty-six years of operation (Day 1970, 54). By 1965 the cumulative deficit in Compact releases from project storage approached three years of stream-flow. Between 1952 and 1966, Colorado was in arrears 928,000 acre-feet (114 million m^3) to New Mexico, which was in turn 92,400 acre-feet (11 million m^3) in debt to Texas users (Stoddard 1979, 47). Although New Mexico and Texas jointly filed complaint against Colorado, in the US Supreme Court in 1966, for the continuing shortfall no decision was handed down in the hope of encouraging an administrative solution. Final figures, for end-December 1973, (Stoddard 1979, 64) showed that these inter-State debits had by then been considerably reduced.

An unexpected aspect of water storage, the provision and use of recreational facilities on Elephant Butte reservoir, threatens to have wide inter-State implications. Legislation to keep a minimum water level at Elephant Butte and Caballo reservoirs, in order to meet environmental demands for waterborne recreation, for the maintenance of fish stocks, and the aesthetics of a constant lake level, threatens to curtail the downstream water control functions which were the original purpose of the dams. As Stoddard (1979, 50) puts it, 'Downriver water needs are now subservient to the maintenance of minimum water levels in these two water-holding facilities and excessive floodwaters which might endanger lakeside enterprises would conceivably be turned loose at the peril of downstream interests rather than allowing high water levels to destroy a major recreation, leisure-oriented "complex".'

Sharing of waters in the upper Rio Grande has thus had a disproportionately unfavourable outcome for Mexico, tying her allocation to a long-outdated norm, itself dependent upon the beneficence of her more powerful neighbour whenever the flow was unilaterally declared to be inadequate for the annual supply of 60,000 acre-feet (74 million m^3). As population has built up in the Juárez area the pressures for more irrigated land, and greater provision of waters for domestic and industrial use have been relentless, but without avail or even prospect of amelioration either by a properly guaranteed, or even better an increased allocation.

THE LOWER VALLEY

In contrast to the upper Rio Grande valley, where American interests were paramount, the balance of power, in terms of water resources, in the lower course was much more in favour of Mexico, since around 70 per cent of aggregate stream-flow in the main river below Fort Quitman came from Mexican tributaries. Furthermore, these tributaries were the source of some of the most devastating floods, a major cause for concern among Texan farmers and citizens in the lower reaches and the delta. Development had initially been much much greater on the Texan banks, pumping water from the incised Rio Grande channel. Not surprisingly, in view of the one-sided international allocation of waters in the upper valley, the Mexican government proved intransigent in dealings with the Americans, standing firm on the doctrine 'Mexico should have all the water she needs (or will need) before the United States gets one drop' (Hundley 1966, 39). Equally unsurprisingly, the United States argued for an allocation based on existing land uses, evidently very much in her favour in view of more extended development. For almost the first three decades of the twentieth century Mexico was in a state of unrest, unable to counteract the increasing but unilateral abstraction of Rio Grande waters for the rapidly spreading irrigated farmlands of Texas. By the 1920s the Texans had usurped virtually all the low season flow (Sandos 1980, 501) and, though in principle opposed to any treaty which might reduce their unilateral act of possession, nevertheless accepted that the main course of the Rio Grande would need to be regulated by damming and reservoir storage. Such a scheme would unquestionably require Mexican co-operation (US Statutes 1924, 118).

Conscious of its national identity and rights, the Mexican government of President Calles determined to press ahead with major irrigation schemes on its Rio Grande tributaries (485,000 ha proposed, about half that realized). Under the National Irrigation Commission, created in 1926, dams were built on the Salado, the San Juan river and an irrigation network developed in the Conchos valley. The Texans became particularly alarmed, not only for what they saw as a threat to their legitimate water supplies, but even more because there had been a period of land speculation in the Texan delta, with settlers tempted in to farm land for which substantial additional supplies of water would be absolutely essential (Hundley 1966, 58). The Mexicans proved obdurate in the face of mounting US pressures, contenting themselves with the doctrine that 'priority and prescription (as argued by the Americans) are not established in international law'. Indeed Mexico, for her part, claimed exclusive rights to the waters of all her tributaries, and hinted that if she was to be persuaded to move from this stance it could only be by US concessions in the use of lower Colorado river waters in the west, where the Americans held a virtually monopolist position.

Succeeding the period 1913–30, described by Hundley (1966) as one of 'negotiation without compromise', there followed a phase of 'mounting crisis'. The IBC was already deeply involved in delta flood-control measures, since international *levée* building along the river had led to storm overflows flooding the Mexican area of the delta (Day 1970, 91). The Commissioners were agreed in principle on flood control, and an elaborate programme for the construction, operation, and maintenance of floodways and levels was to be undertaken. There was also to be international co-operation in the construction of two major river-diversion structures to regulate the overall delta storm surplus. This co-operation in the delta was necessitous, but even though there was co-ordination under the lower Rio Grande Flood Control Project (LRGFCP) (US Statutes 1935, 660) the wider question of sharing the lower-basin water resources remained unresolved. Indeed, under President Lázaro Cárdenas, there were even more grandiose schemes for land reform, including the putting 400,000 ha. of rich deltaic soil under cultivation and the construction of the massive El Azúcar dam, one of whose purposes was said to be 'to force the US to trade Colorado river water for Rio Grande water' (Hundley 1966, 94). The Retamal diversion canal, on Mexican soil, commenced in 1935–6, was to divert a sizeable proportion of the flow of the lower Rio Grande into the Mexican part of the delta. Although Roosevelt's Good Neighbour Policy had prepared the climate for fuller co-operation, manifestly for mutual self-interest, it did not prevent the Americans in 1939 from investigating a massive 271-km Valley Gravity Canal, entirely on US territory, with its own water storage projects. This was intended to impound and distribute 400,000 acre-feet (493 million m^3) of water otherwise lost to the Gulf. The fact that the intake to the canal was to be *upstream* from the Mexican Retamal diversion was not lost on the Mexicans. In a sense this 'checkmating' led both sides to the successful conclusion of the 1944 Treaty, for the utilization of the waters of the Colorado, Tijuana, and Rio Grande (US Statutes 1944).

The preliminary negotiations were from entrenched positions. The opening US bid was for all the waters of her own tributaries, plus one million acre-feet from Mexico, and also half the product of all springs and *arroyos*. Mexico would not accept the transfer of one million acre-feet (1.2 billion m^3), alleging that this would curtail her intended irrigation acreage expansion (Hundley 1966, 110). Her offer to the Americans was initially little more than one-quarter of the flow of Mexican tributaries 'reaching the Rio Grande', an uncertain proposition indeed, together with half the flow of springs and *arroyos*. An increase in the Mexican quota in the upper Rio Grande was also inserted as a bargaining counter, but consistently turned down by the US negotiators. The threat of the proposed US Valley Gravity canal still hung over the Mexicans, and, furthermore, the knowledge of their totally insecure position on the lower Colorado conditioned the kind of compromise they ultimately conceded. The Mexicans contested all American claims based on prior use and prescription in irrigated land already being farmed in the lower Rio Grande, arguing instead for an apportionment of waters based on 'land susceptible of being irrigated', of which they held a very considerable volume.

The Mexicans were clear that a trade-off between their hopeless position on the lower Colorado river and their negotiation from relative strength on the lower Rio Grande was a centrepiece of the 1944 Treaty. Day (1970, 137) quotes Oribe Alba, the Mexican Secretary to the Ministry of Water Resources, recommending the Treaty to the Mexican Senate:

without the Treaty we would only be able to irrigate about 778,000 acres [315,000 ha] in the tributaries of the Rio Grande. Moreover, it would be impossible to irrigate at all with Colorado river water, and very little by means of diversions from the Rio Grande channel. On the other hand, the Treaty will permit Mexico to irrigate 494,000 acres [200,000 ha] on the Colorado delta, 778,000 acres [315,000 ha] with water from the Rio Grande tributaries, and 605,000 acres [245, 000 ha] with water diverted from the main Rio Grande channel. This is a total of 1,877,000 acres [760,000 ha] and represents 1,099,000 acres [445,000 ha] more than Mexico could irrigate without the Treaty.

The US Commissioner on the International Boundary and Waters Commission (IBWC, the former IBC, renamed in 1944 to enforce the Treaty provisions) was equally adamant that there had been no trade-off between the Rio Grande and other basins. 'The settlement was entirely on the basis of each stream system. There is no connection in amounts, there is no connection in the physical situation or the geography.' Mexicans, perhaps more realistically, have continued to think otherwise.

THE 1944 TREATY AND ITS AFTERMATH

This Treaty (Fig. 23) made an almost equal allocation of surface waters between the US and Mexico in the lower Rio Grande (Day 1970, 138–40: Utton 1979); thereby Texas received more than the inflow of her tributaries would justify. The United States was allocated: all the waters contributing to the main stream by the principal US tributaries below Fort Quitman, though Texan share of the Pecos was determined by a New Mexico–Texas Interstate Compact (US Congress, Senate 1949); one-half of the flow in the main channel of the Rio Grande below the lowest major international storage dam (Falcon reservoir, 1953); one-third of the flow into the main channel from the principal Mexican tributaries above Salineno, Texas, guaranteed by Mexico to average at least 350,000 acre-feet (431 million m^3) per year over a five-year period, failing which deficiencies must be made up in the next five-year period;

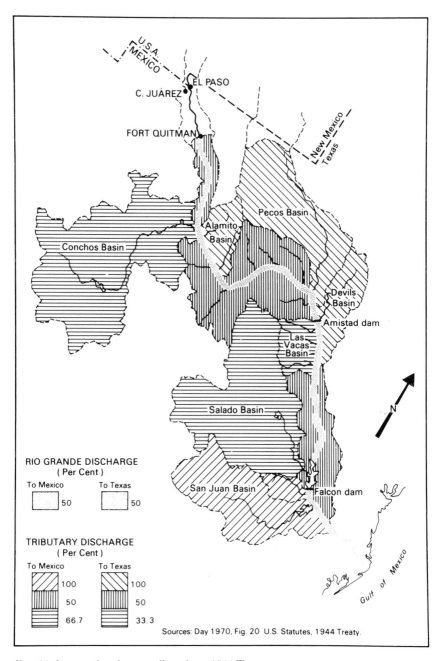

FIG. 23. International water allocations, 1944 Treaty

and one-half of all other waters flowing into the Rio Grande, except for the discharge of the Alamo and San Juan rivers and any return flow from irrigation on these two rivers. Mexico received all the waters of the Alamo and San Juan basins; two-thirds of the flow of Mexican tributaries above Salineno; and one-half of all other flows in the main channel of the Rio Grande.

The 1944 Treaty was considered far more equitable in Mexico than the 1906 Convention for the upper Rio Grande basin had been (Mexico, Sec. de Rel. Ext. 1947). Mexican water rights were clearly defined and a flexible water delivery schedule could be adjusted to changing crop needs. Nevertheless, there was opposition to the Treaty provisions from both sides of the Border. In Mexico, opponents emphasized the inconsistency of legal principle, in accepting divided absolute sovereignties on the Rio Grande, having acquiesced in the US right of prescription on the Colorado; the unconstitutional nature of assigning even part of Mexican waters, in principle wholly to be retained by the nation under the 1917 Constitution; and the general constraints laid upon the desirable scale and tempo of economic development in the northern frontier provinces, by virtue of the ceding of Mexican waters. In particular, exception was taken to two clauses: Art. 10(b), which exactly as in the 1906 Convention gave the Americans the right 'in the case of extraordinary drought or serious accident to the US irrigation system . . . to reduce the water supply to Mexico (from Falcon dam) in the same proportions as that for consumers in the USA'. Yet by Art. 4B(d) of the very same Treaty the Mexican government was obliged to compensate the American consumer over five years if the water allocation from the Mexican tributaries fell short of the minimum supply guaranteed to the USA (Sepúlveda 1978, 132–4). There was also concern lest the IBWC, created by the 1944 Treaty, with power to bind the two governments once agreement had been reached, should seek to assume supranational powers in its own right. In fact, this prospect has not materialized, although the organization has carried major responsibilities for the orderly development and use of a critical resource in a vast international region. These responsibilities have included: the supervision, carrying-out, and monitoring of water allocations; flood control and the maintenance of the Rio Grande as an international boundary; and in only a minor way, unfortunately, issues of water quality and sanitation (Dworsky 1978, 150). Neither the USA nor Mexico had the slightest intention of permitting supranational powers to be conferred on the IBWC.

An essential follow-up to the 1944 Treaty was the construction of international barrage reservoirs to control flooding, the long-term scourge of the delta, and to regulate the uneven flow of water throughout the seasons. Two such dams have been constructed: Falcon in 1953 and Amistad in 1968. Falcon dam is a multi-purpose project, basically for flood control and water storage, but with secondary hydro-power and recreation functions (Day 1970, 113 *et seq.*). Construction costs were shared between the US and Mexico in the proportions of reservoir storage capacity on national soil, namely 58.6 and 41.4 per cent respectively. Costs of power generation and its allocation were to be equally divided. In its prime functions of flood control and water storage Falcon dam has been an outstanding success. The highest flood for three hundred years, in 1954, was successfully contained and it has been estimated (Day 1970, 114) that within five years of its completion the dam had saved almost double its construction and power installation costs in preventing flood damage to Texan lands alone, and probably as much again in Mexico.

Falcon dam also achieved the predicted annual water yield of two million acre-feet in eight of the first twelve years of its operation, though the low flow in four years had significant economic and social effects in the lower Rio Grande valley and delta. As so often in multi-purpose barrage reservoirs, the hydroelectricity output has been disappointing. The scheduling of water releases to meet the needs of irrigators, the prime purpose of the dam, has little to do with the optimum generation of hydro-power. In only two of the first twelve years of its operation did the output of hydroelectric power achieve its predicted level, and indeed it is estimated that the power plants continue to operate at a loss to both the US and Mexico (Day 1970, 119). The recreational provision, initially seen as of little importance, has developed considerably during the 1970s, at both Falcon and Amistad, more particularly so at the latter. The question of the arbitration on minimum lake-levels, given different optima for the several water uses, has not yet assumed the stage of the problems faced at Elephant Butte (p. 120).

Amistad dam and reservoir, some twelve miles upstream from Del Rio-Ciudad Acuña, dates from 1968, located in *chaparral* country on the fringes of the Chihuahuan desert. It too fulfils a major flood-control and water-conservation role, with a maximum surface of 35,690 ha at flood-stage, some 22,250 ha of which lie within the US. The water-based recreation facilities are a major resource within the tourist planning of a semi-arid area. Sailing, fishing, camping, and the archaeological sites attract about one million visitors per annum on the American shore. Mexico's shore features a marina, beach, and tourist playground. It thus seems that here too, in time, recreation will figure as a priority in the determining of lake-levels to be maintained.

Since completion of the reservoirs, flooding has been abated and water delivery well regulated. Nevertheless, as under the 1906 Convention for the upper Rio Grande valley, the guarantee of water quotas has not been consistently honoured, in this case by the

Mexicans, in the upper valley by the Americans. In the first five-year cycle after completion of the Falcon dam (1953), the 350,000 acre-feet (431 million m^3) allotment to the US was in fact delivered; over the next five years there was a 16 per cent shortfall and this was not indemnified within the stipulated period (Day 1970, 141–2). One of the problems lay in the control over the countless diversion and pumping points below the Falcon dam. The detailed allocation of the national quota and the effective monitoring of the amounts abstracted proved to be an almost insuperable problem. On the Texan side a special Water Master represented most irrigation water users, controlling the hours, type, and amount of river pumping. In Mexico, the *Secretaría de Recursos Hidráulicos* (SRH) had a more unified, statutory responsibility. At the transnational level the IBWC had responsibilities for the supply, distribution, and monitoring of the allocations between the US and Mexico. In this sense it was a kind of arbitrator in disputes, but a body lacking overall enforcement powers. Its most significant achievement was the establishment of an accurate network of automatic stream gauges, with an efficient communications system disseminating the details of water availability and abstraction. Such an accurate system defines the volume of water passing from one recording point to the next, giving the total availability; thereby the waste of surplus water flowing unutilized to the Gulf could be limited and a proper check kept on lawful and equitable distribution at the times of greatest scarcity.

As so often in human affairs, the circumvention of such desirable regulation of a critical resource, in the international as well as national and local interests, is the result of individual initiatives, some legal, others quite the reverse. Texan water laws on the rights of riparian owners have remained unresolved. Some claimed to be the inheritors of rights to irrigation water conferred under original Spanish or Mexican land grants, though these were often obscure and not specifically stipulated; others asserted riparian rights to abstract a free resource, while in the 1960s the State sought to establish five priority classes of user (Day 1970, 213). With so many private pumps on the Texan shore, and something of a legislative anarchy on water rights, an unsatisfactory outcome was predictable. In Mexico, the federal water authority (SRH) had adequate laws and powers of control, more capable of enforcement since more than 90 per cent of the Mexican supply from Falcon dam was diverted by gravity flow at two points, reducing pumping by individuals to a minimum. Notwithstanding this, the supervisory powers within Mexico have at times been lax in enforcement and there have been many pinpricks of dispute concerned with citizens of each nation abstracting water illicitly, which should by rights have gone to riparian owners on the other bank (Day 1970, 142).

None of the legislation concerned with allocation of the waters of the

Rio Grande system made effective provision for, or even reference to, either the quality of the water to be supplied, or the problems and possibilities of using international underground aquifers, in supplementation of a scarce surface water resource.

INTERNATIONAL AQUIFERS

Effective river-basin management should cover water in all its forms: precipitation, surface flow, and underground storage in aquifers or the shallower water-table. All are genetically related within the hydrological cycle, and thus capable of ecologically sound use or misuse. The relationship between surface flow and groundwater is often complex, with the latter a more static resource, often building up over a very long period but capable of short-term drawdown or pollution, by extravagant or unilateral 'water-mining'. The history of groundwater usage in the Rio Grande basin has hitherto been of sporadic, largely unregulated, and uncoordinated measures unilaterally implemented.

Aquifers in the upper basin include the deep resources of the *bolsóns* in the basin-and-range province. Of these the Hueco *bolsón* (Day 1978) in the El Paso–Juárez valley is the most significant, in its resources, and in its international implications, since it lies astride the Border. In the drier limestone plateaux flanking the middle reaches of the Rio Grande there are localized aquifers, while there are abundant lenses of groundwater in the Gulf Coast sands of the coastal plain. The total available groundwater resources are not fully known, most having been individually prospected, by companies or water authorities. The prospects for co-ordinating abstraction by wells with the now reasonably regulated flow in the Rio Grande system remain poor, for any necessary legal framework for an effective management policy is essentially lacking. However, there is a mounting need for careful management of groundwater resources, as economic development takes place, surface flow continues to fall short of requirements, and the Border cities in particular have recourse to more drilling for the supply of their rising populations. Indeed, Texas is already among the heaviest users of groundwater throughout the United States. It is extremely desirable to work out an international policy for harmonious development of groundwater use, ahead of the acrimony, litigation, or confrontation which are otherwise likely as this scarce reserve risks depletion, pollution, or both misfortunes concurrently.

By and large, groundwaters have not been a general issue of international concern (Hayton 1978) and there are thus no well-tested precepts of international law to provide a framework for application within the Rio Grande system (United Nations 1975). The only useful bi-national comparison, but within an altogether different geographical milieu, is the 1960s agreement between the Soviet Union and Poland

(United Nations 1966), cited in Utton (1979, 101). This includes clauses relating to groundwaters 'intersected by the State frontier'. Lacking universal precepts for application, the alternative is to try for consensus and synthesis within a federal and State plurality, which already amounted to legal and institutional near-chaos.

In domestic US law there is something of a legal vacuum concerning groundwater and the practice of individual States is widely different (Utton 1979, 100 *et seq.*). In general it has been thought appropriate to treat groundwater as if it were an appurtenance of the land, or as a commodity which may be taken into ownership by the sinking of a well. Under Spanish and under English common law, which latter prevailed in Texas on this issue, the groundwater is the property of the super-adjacent landowner. He may draw water without restriction, even though this may draw down his neighbour's water-table. On the other hand, he may not pollute his neighbour's supply. This practice of absolute ownership has inevitably promoted 'wild-cat' and excessive exploitation of a fugitive resource, whereas security and flexibility should be the keynote of a socially aware and community minded system of abstraction. Just as in the attempted curtailment of riparian rights to surface water in the Texan lower Rio Grande so too the State has taken powers, under the Texan Water Code (1975), to designate underground water conservation districts and areas liable to subsidence by excessive groundwater abstraction (Day 1978, 170). Unfortunately, these powers were not exercised in the Hueco *bolsón* where they were most urgently needed. The good old Texan principle prevailed, of getting there 'firstest with the mostest'. As Hayton (1978, 203) put it 'We are still plagued (in the USA) with the spurious propositions about groundwater that were propagated by ingenuous (and ingenious) counsel, and became part of the common law doctrine estabished by uninformed judges.'

In Mexico, on the other hand, the situation is entirely different. Under the 1917 Constitution surface waters were vested in the nation, and in 1974 groundwater too was effectively nationalized. Though landowners are in *de facto* control of the exploitation of groundwaters the Water Resources Ministry (SRH) can regulate extraction and designate prohibited groundwater zones wherever the aquifer is endangered or existing water uses threatened (Utton 1979, 100; Day, 170). Mexicans see groundwater as 'a trump card for facilitating development . . . amenable to sovereign control by the Mexican government, exclusive, or nearly so, of US interference' (Mumme 1980, 43).

Co-operative arrangements have generally been lacking. The Inter-State Compact, of the type used between Texas, New Mexico, and Colorado on the upper Rio Grande (p. 119), has been widely tried for allocation of inter-State border streams and, since 1961, has become a framework for regulating access to and use of common groundwaters in several of the humid Eastern United States (Clark 1978, 156). In a minimal way on the US–Mexican Border, the IBWC has sponsored an agreement to limit pumping on an aquifer at Yuma, in the arid West. During the early 1970s it also sponsored water resource investigations in the transnational Hueco *bolsón*, and set up an international groundwater data exchange. Tentatively, some accord on US–Mexican shared groundwaters had been mooted as part of the Colorado river salinity agreement, but little came of it. Texans have proved tenaciously hostile to the idea of the IBWC being involved at all in groundwater questions (Day 1978, 176). The case as put states: the US Department of State does not have Congressional approval to enter into negotiations for a groundwater treaty; investigations towards such a treaty are thus illegal; both urban and rural Texans would be adversely affected; and, in any case, no prior consultations had taken place with all interested Texan parties.

In practical terms, the problems may be illustrated by referring to the Hueco *bolsón*, and the water supply difficulties of the El Paso–Juárez metropolitan area. Water pollution too is increasingly an intrusive and vexatious part of these problems. The Hueco *bolsón* (Day 1978) is the most massive groundwater resource in the upper Rio Grande, straddling the international boundary in the El Paso–Juárez valley. Its 2,745 metres of sediments are overlain by 23 to 30 m of Rio Grande alluvium, occasionally deepening to 76 metres. The aquifer contains about 10.6 million acre-feet (13 billion m^3) of water in Texas, 6.2 (7.6 billion m^3) in New Mexico, and 4 million acre-feet (5.4 billion m^3) below Mexico, recharged from the surrounding mountain massifs. The water in the *bolsón* is fresh to slightly saline, with an interface between the two qualities sustained by aquifer pressure (Hernández 1978, 7). Though there is no clear relationship to the quality of surface water in the Rio Grande the saline content of the most accessible reserves in the *bolsón* is increasing, particularly in the vicinity of El Paso (1938: 250 parts of salt per million; 1963: 470 parts) and C. Juárez, as the level of the water-table is drawn down. In 1959 when the Juárez well system was rehabilitated chemical and bacteriological contamination of the deep aquifer was clearly established (Burman and Cornish 1975, 468). Between 1903 and 1976 the water level fell 22 m below El Paso and 25 m under C. Juárez. Natural recharge rates for the aquifer (5 per cent per annum), failed to match depletion locally. The downward percolation of saline water already encounters the capillary upward movement of more contaminated supplies. The cones of depression in the aquifer spreading out from below the two major cities are now inducing drawdown across the international boundary, while the rapid proliferation of wells on the Texan side, under the Rio Grande Project (525 in 1966, 800 in 1976) is further distorting the contours of the water-table. At the same time friction is growing between Texans and Mexicans, with allegations of pollution spreading below the boundary line, to the detriment of nationals on the other side.

The growing international friction over water usage is, in one sense, an extension of the unequal US–Mexican apportionment of surface waters under the 1906 Convention, but it is also powered by deep-seated cultural differences and perceptions. The limitations to 60,000 acre-feet (74 million m^3) in the water supply for Mexico in the upper Rio Grande catered only for the diversions for irrigation already existing way back in the 1870s. As irrigation spread subsequently demand for water rose, but it was the 'urban explosion' in C. Juárez after the Second World War that escalated scarcity of water to dangerous social proportions. Ever since 1926 Juárez has been constrained to depend wholly on the deep aquifer for urban supplies, developing a centrally planned, close pattern of neighbourhood wells, since storage facilities were very limited. Water supply to the squatter settlements, on the barren fringes of the city, produced further difficulties and contamination.

No international agreement constrained the rights of either El Paso or C. Juárez to draw supplies from the aquifer. Unlike irrigation needs, urban users were regulated solely by the domestic laws of each nation (Day 1975, 457). Texan law had already produced difficult problems for El Paso, even before the frictions across the international boundary. The US part of the Hueco *bolsón* was inefficiently managed, since the US Army owned large areas and abstracted supplies unilaterally. El Paso municipality sought to secure the groundwater reserve under the city by ordinances limiting private wells, while purchasing lands in the *bolsón* to secure future supplies in the capacity of surface property-owner. Nevertheless, more distant supplies had to be sought in due course, and the proportion of its rapidly growing water demand which El Paso drew from the artesian basin fell from virtually all its needs up to 1955, down to 30 per cent in 1964 and only 13 per cent in 1972 (Day 1975, 468). Though the city considered using surface water from the Rio Grande as far back as 1920 it was not until the 1950s that an agreement with the Bureau of Reclamation permitted the domestic use of 'wild' water, surplus to irrigation requirements. Ciudad Juárez had no such option available, and its population was uncontrollably rising more rapidly.

Indeed, discontent on the Mexican side focussed also on what was looked on as the profligate use of a scarce resource by the Americans. Per capita water consumption in El Paso rose from about 100 US gallons (378 litres) per diem in 1930 to nearly 200 (757 litres) by 1970; by comparison, the 1960 and 1970 figures for Juárez were only about 50

US gallons (190 litres) and fairly stable. The summer peak water demand at El Paso was around 2,500 million US gallons (9.4 billion litres) a month, in Juárez, with its much larger population, scarcely more than 500 million US gallons (1.9 billion litres). Half the total use of water in El Paso was for lawn or garden irrigation and in domestic appliances, while Mexicans were threatened with domestic and industrial water shortages, both in the city and on the land. These contrasting consumptions of water reflect cultural differences, but given a long-standing sense of deprivation and unequal treatment in Mexican minds they add fuel to the fires of nationalism.

POLLUTION CONTROL

SURFACE WATER POLLUTION

The problem of pollution in the main Rio Grande channel is both local and seasonal. Although saline content is more or less universal it is not generally a serious threat, either to agriculture or even industrial uses. One tonne of salt per acre-foot (1,233 m³) at El Paso and 2.5 to 4 tonnes at Fort Quitman (Hernández 1978, 2) indicate the acceptable limits, for all plants at the lower level of impregnation, for salt-tolerant plants at the higher figure. Saline content varies seasonally, lower at high-flow periods, higher after the return of water from irrigated fields or during low-season flow. It is only at the upstream end of the delta that dangerous levels of salt content have been regularly experienced (Day 1970, 20). Seventy-five per cent of the total increase of salts below Falcon dam, an average of 14.1 tonnes per acre-foot (1,233 m³) was delivered into the Rio Grande by the Morillo drain, upstream from most Texan abstractors (Day 1970, 145). Additional pollution by chlorides and boron traces made the water unsuitable for the irrigation of citrus or other sensitive crops on the Texan shore. After litigation, Mexico agreed to use part of her share of waters from Falcon dam to flush salts through the main channel, store more water in irrigation reservoirs in the tributary system, and create a jointly financed 37 km channel to carry polluted saline waters to the Gulf. That such pollution added to coastal waters might create hazards for inshore fishing or that sewage effluent might be legally dumped into the new channel by either international partner was neither regulated by treaty provision, nor indeed in any way taken into account.

Industrial and urban effluents in large volume are unacceptably discharged into the Rio Grande, especially around El Paso–Juárez and from cities on both banks in the delta area. Once again, there is no international regulation by treaty and the IBWC is powerless to enforce good sanitary arrangements. The rapidity of urbanization on both banks in the past few decades has outstripped the provision of adequate treatment facilities, for either sewage or industrial effluents. As a result, biochemical oxygen demand (BOD), bacteria counts (coliform and fecal coliform), soluble ions, and sodium concentrations all rise to levels above United States stipulated limits. Mexican standards are different, and priorities for improvement of public water supply take precedence over the lesser urgency of sewage farms. Moreover, in C. Juárez, liquid wastes are carried by underground mains to the city outskirts and thence by open ditches to the irrigation fields (Applegate and Bath 1979, 26). El Paso, on the other hand, passes about 24.2 million US gallons (91 million litres) of liquid waste per diem through four treatment plants, all of which waste is then dumped in the Rio Grande.

Water pollution, both surface and underground, is thus an inescapable outcome of rapid population and economic growth. The nature of the regulated régime of the Rio Grande means overriding priority for irrigation needs, with pollution rising sharply at low-season flow. In recent years, the commercialization of agriculture has brought in greater use of fertilizers, herbicides, and pesticides, increasing the range and diffusion of a new set of pollutants; furthermore, in Mexico, the poisonous organochlorine compounds are still in use (Applegate and Bath 1979, 10). The chemical and organic pollution of the Rio Grande is thus of great concern to both international partners, but since there are no jointly agreed anti-pollution standards, no treaty stipulations on pollutions, and lax enforcement of even existing domestic standards the Rio Grande continues to be increasingly contaminated by heavy pollution loads (Day 1970, 149).

SOLID WASTE DISPOSAL

In this issue too there are major cultural differences. The American Rio Grande cities generate a vastly greater volume of waste per capita, estimated at an average of 3.1 kg per diem in 1980, rising perhaps to 4.4 kg by the year 2000. There is presently no problem in finding suitable dumping sites in the open *chaparral* country, but little of the refuse is biodegradable and recycling is rarely an economic policy. On the Mexican side materials for wasting are fewer, fewer are wasted, and a great deal of recycling takes place informally, by individuals. 'Consumer discards such as lumber, worn-out appliances, tyres and cardboard, for use in homes and small manufacturing concerns' (Applegate and Bath 1979, 6) are collected by Mexicans on both sides of the Border, and committed to frugal re-use. The profligacy of American waste is resented by many Mexicans, but is inescapably the outcome of greater affluence and the 'packaging' revolution.

AIR POLLUTION

Sensitivity to air pollution is a hallmark of developed western industrial societies. Developing nations have habitually accepted air pollution as an inevitable by-product of the industrialization they have so avidly sought. Facing each other across the Rio Grande, at markedly different levels of development, it is not surprising that Mexicans and Americans look on air pollution from contrasting viewpoints. The most inflammatory issues in Border air pollution arise where the residents of one country are affected, in health or well-being, by contamination passing over the international boundary. Air pollution comes from diverse sources: homes, mines, factories, farms, or vehicles. Several attempts have sought to quantify the emission from those manifold sources along the US–Mexican Border (Utton 1973; Shoults 1974; Applegate and Bath 1979), though most figures relate only to the US Border cities.

Table 7. *Air pollution, point sources, Texas Border cities (1970)*

	tonnes/annum
Sulphur oxides	256
Nitrogen oxides	34
Hydrocarbons	23
Carbon monoxide	112
Particulate matter	38

Source: Busch (1978, 353).

Sulphur oxides are the greatest pollutant, mainly from copper, lead, and zinc smelters. Particulates, a characteristic pollutant in dry, semi-arid air, include quarry dust, cement or asphalt, and dust stirred by agriculture or windblow. Carbon monoxide comes from vehicle fumes, or petroleum and petrochemical plants in the main; the latter are equally the principal source of hydrocarbons. Burning of domestic and industrial wastes, especially in the Mexican cities is a further, widespread air pollutant. In the early 1970s a Pan-American Health Organization (PAHO) study (Applegate and Bath 1978, 93) classified pollution sources for El Paso and C. Juárez separately. El Paso had eight major point emissions of pollutants: the copper, lead, zinc smelter; the municipal solid waste site; two cement plants; two petroleum refineries and two large brick-making plants. The line sources of emission were: unpaved streets and from some 227,000 registered vehicles, which are estimated to generate 122,000 tonnes of carbon monoxide per annum in El Paso county alone, compared with a total Border discharge of industrial hydrocarbons of no more than 123,100 tonnes. Very high levels of pollution from vehicles are found around the stationary queues of cars at the Border checkpoints, especially on a hot summer's day. C. Juárez is overall the more polluted city, from domestic and industrial smoke, a cement plant, hot mix asphalt, and the municipal refuse tip.

Table 8.   *Suspended particulate matter, El Paso and Cuidad Juárez, 1974*

Zone		Min. (μg/m^3)	Max. (μg/m^3)	Annual Mean
El Paso	commercial	31	423	139
	rural	20	879	102
	residential	31	249	110
C. Juárez	commercial	100	1480	342
	rural	31	257	86
	residential	57	671	107
(US primary ambient standard for particulates 75 μg/m^3 annual mean)				

Source: Applegate and Bath (1978, 94).

In 1972 joint air-quality monitoring was set up in the El Paso–Juárez airshed, covering a 80-km radius around these towns. This led to an increasing public awareness of pollution problems, at least on the American side of the Rio Grande (Busch 1978, 358). Sulphur dioxide and particulates were the most stringently monitored and much of the instrumentation and recording came from the United States. Curiously, during the tensions on the Border in 1976 the Mexican government refused to allow US trucks to collect air samples, and in return the US authorities temporarily suspended all co-operation—a good indication of the sensitivity of Border issues, even when a co-operative practice is manifestly to mutual continuing advantage.

On the other hand, the ASARCO smelter case at El Paso, in the early 1970s, clearly showed the altruistic aspect of international Border collaboration. The lead content of children's blood in Mexican settlements near the American smelter gave rise to concern. Although nine-tenths had acceptable levels of lead traces up to 30 μg/100 ml, this still left some eight thousand children, between one and nine years old, at higher risk levels (Barojas-Weber 1978, 102). The American company paid damages when the case of contamination was proven. Interestingly enough, it was the United States Public Health Service which conducted the enquiry in Mexico (Bath 1978, 194), resulting in a conviction against its own nationals.

BORDER HEALTH

The spread of disease or ill-health, whether in humans or in animals (Machado 1968), is no respector of international boundaries. The semi-arid climate is itself the medium for the diffusion of the environmentally derived pollutions already described, and the uneven incidence of air-borne or water-borne ill-health which results. The search for that 'state of complete mental, physical and social well-being', which defines health in the eyes of the World Health Organization is, however, largely determined by economic, social, and cultural differences. Reiss (1978, 242) sums up the contrasts between Mexican and US health problems: 'We Latin Americans are united . . . by a whole epidemiological panorama in which communicable and preventable diseases outnumber those which are not communicable. In the US degenerative and neoplastic diseases prevail, basically because up to now science has not been able to raise life expectancy to immortality' (Table 9). In other words, poverty, malnutrition, and lesser provision of health care south of the Rio Grande take their toll. Higher mortality and morbidity rates are characteristic, particularly among pre-school children. The management of cross-Border diffusion of ill-health thus requires: 'mechanisms for preventing the exporting of communicable diseases; prevention of environmental and social conditions brought about by diseases such as drug dependence north of the Border; and, lastly, the setting up of barriers against the migration of certain diseases and carriers (vectors) across the Border'. The sharp break in ecological conditions at the Rio Grande increases the risk of epidemiological diffusion, though it must constantly be borne in mind that the cultural Border lies well to the north of the river (see Fig. 5). The *chicanos*, Mexican-Americans in the United States, share traits from both cultures, but on balance they have recognizably severe health problems and a second-class health care delivery system within the US (Teller 1978, 261). Poverty among *chicanos* is often allied with a Mexican folk-health sub-culture, and a lack of information about or interest in a public health service, which may seem alien and, in any event, is often beyond their means.

Table 9. *Principal causes of death, Mexican provinces (1971), selected Texan border counties (1969–71)*

	specific mortality rate per 100,000	
	Mexican provinces†	5 Texan counties*
All causes	762	703
Influenza/pneumonia	92	32
Enteritis/diarrhoea	93	5
Tuberculosis	27	4
Cerebrovascular	29	90
Violent, incl. accidents	56	64
Heart	75	210
Malignant neoplasms	52	113

† Chihuahua, Coahuila, Nuevo León, Tamaulipas
* Cameron, Hidalgo, Maverick, Starr, Webb

Sources: Dirección General de Bioestadística; Texas Vital Statistics; Ross (1978, 245 and 263).

Health conditions in the Mexican cities along the Rio Grande are better than in the country at large, though considerably poorer than in the US communities on the other bank of the river. In their turn, the American cities on the Border compare unfavourably with the nation as a whole, in the incidence of disease and ill-health. This indicates a further anomaly in the bi-national contrasts at the Border interface. Mexican municipalities may show lower mortality rates and lower disease levels than for the nation, but this conceals some serious problems. Healthy young immigrants to the Border cities dilute the disease ratios and diminish the mortality figures, thus disguising the very much worse than average conditions in the squatters' *barrios*, or the congested urban slums. Furthermore, even though not on US scales of provision health care is more abundant in the larger cities, in marked contrast to deprivation in the countryside. There 'children die more quietly, without giving too much trouble' (Reiss 1978, 244). In general, though, the higher living standards overall for many in the cities raises their epidemiological status, in quantity if not in quality.

The data for Texan border counties on the Rio Grande outline a unique health region, with poor health status, by American standards, and one with a second-class medical care system for the ethnic immigrants (Teller 1978, 259). It is difficult to isolate the specific problems of ethnic groups within the total data, but sufficient is clear to confirm severe problems among *chicanos* and the importance of different cultural attitudes among them towards health care and practices (Weaver 1973). Crude death-rates for the five selected Texan counties (Table 9) are lower than for the State as a whole, perhaps reflecting the more youthful age structure on the Rio Grande. Yet death rates from infectious and parasitic diseases are nearly twice those of Texan whites generally and, for dysentery and amebiasis, twice those of whites and nearly four times those for blacks (Teller 1978, 262). Deaths from normally non-fatal diseases are higher along the Border, and also from ill-defined causes, a sure indication of low health care provision. The health risks in particular US Border cities came out most strikingly in data on children's illnesses. Screening of eligible child-welfare clients, in 1973–4, showed (Teller 1978, 266): higher than average lead in the blood, abnormal haemoglobin, throat and skin conditions at El Paso; and lung, heart, scalp, and musculoskeletal diseases in the lower Rio Grande valley.

The Border medical market shows two-way flows. Middle- and upper-class Mexicans frequently seek diagnostic, consultant, or hospital treatment in the better facilities in the US cities. Poorer *chicanos* may patronize the less expensive clinics (and dentists) along the streets just across the Border bridges into Mexico, if they do not remain outside health care altogether. In rural Mexico informal medicine may be widely practised by *curanderos* and others, but there is little evidence of this among the *chicanos* in Texas (Teller 1978, 274). For the moment, Border health co-operation across the Rio Grande is consultative only. The Mexican–American Border Health Association has a main purpose to stop infectious diseases passing across the international boundary. The Pan-American Health office is a further source of limited bi-national agreements (Reiss 1978, 251).

CONCLUSION

The environment of the Rio Grande thus poses serious problems to its residents, in the use of shared resources of water, good quality air, land, and the conditions for health and well-being. Such resources are often scarce, and their quality is increasingly threatened by the growth of population and the exploitation following upon economic growth. It is in the interests of both Mexicans and Americans that there should be further co-operation and better management than in the past. Yet different cultural perceptions, contrasting legal systems, and a clear distinction within decision-taking powers at local, State, or national level mean that progress on transnational organizations has been slow, partial and, on at least one occasion, bitterly contested. If relative strengths alone are to prevail then it is difficult for Mexico to reverse her traditional condition of dependency and much rests on the altruism or magnanimity of the better-funded, technologically more advanced United States. The sensitivities of Mexican nationalism, nevertheless, make further intrusions by the US into Mexican affairs, even to help solve endemic problems, liable to misinterpretation and misrepresentation. In the case of shared water resources, in 1906 and 1944, treaty allocations were made, to Mexico and to the US respectively but in neither treaty were all the important questions considered: water quality, groundwater resources, and pollution were ignored. Nor has the outcome of allocation, rigidly adhered to, proved altogether satisfactory. The allocations were frozen at a point in time, though development has continued and inequalities and lack of justice have resulted. Supranational management powers are not a realistic proposition for the forseeable future, given great national sensitivities on both banks of the Rio Grande. Notwithstanding this, the limited authority of the IBWC, the Border air pollution monitoring body, and the Border Health Association have real achievements to their credit. Yet the Border ecosystem continues to be fragile. If it is to be conserved in the interests of mankind, both political as well as ecologically sound policies will need to be put in hand, by both parties on a much wider scale than hitherto. Of this for the moment there is little indication, to the great detriment of many as a result.

REFERENCES

APPLEGATE, H. G. AND BATH, C. R. (1978) 'Air pollution along the United States-Mexican Border', *Nat. Resour. Jl.*, **18**, 1, 91–100.

BAROJAS-WEBER, L. H. (1978) 'Impacto del crecimiento en la calidad del aire en las comunidades fronterizas', *Nat. resour. Jl.*, **18**, 1, 101–9.

BATH, R. C. (1978) 'Alternative cooperative arrangements for managing transboundary air resources along the Border', *Nat. Resour. Jl.*, **18**, 1, 181–99.

BURMAN, B. G. AND CORNISH, T. G. (1975) 'Needed: a groundwater Treaty between the United States and Mexico', *Nat. Resour. Jl.*, **15**, 2, 385–404.

BUSCH, A. W. (1978) 'Environmental management: a basis for equitable resource allocation', ch. 17 in S. R. Ross (ed), *Views across the Border* (Albuquerque: Univ. of New Mexico Press), 338–60.

CLARK, J. W. (1978) 'The upper Rio Grande', *Nat. Resour. Jl.*, **18**, 1, 69–76.

CLARK, R. E. (1978) 'Institutional alternatives for managing groundwater resources: notes for a proposal', *Nat. Resour. Jl.*, **18**, 1, 153–61.

DAY, J. C. (1970) 'Managing the lower Rio Grande', *Univ. of Chicago, Dept. Geogr., Res. Pap.*, 125.

DAY, J. C. (1975) 'Urban water management of an International River: the case of El Paso-Cd. Juárez', *Nat. Resour. Jl.*, **15**, 3, 453–70.

DAY, J. C. (1978) 'International aquifer management: the Hueco Bolsón on the Rio Grande', *Nat. Resour. Jl.*, **18**, 1, 163–80.

DWORSKY, L. B. (1978) 'The management of water-land environmental resources at international boundary regions', *Nat. Resour. Jl.*, **18**, 1, 143–51.

FERGUSSON, H. (1955) *The Rio Grande* (New York).

HAYTON, R. D. (1978) 'Institutional alternatives for Mexico-US groundwater management', *Nat. Resour. Jl.*, **18**, 1, 201–12.

HERNÁNDEZ, J. W. (1978) 'Interrelationship of ground and surface water quality in the El Paso-Juárez and Mesilla valleys', *Nat. Resour. Jl.*, **18**, 1, 1–9.

HUNDLEY, N. Jr (1966) *Dividing the waters: A century of controversy between the United States and Mexico* (Berkeley: Univ. of California Press).

INTERNATIONAL BOUNDARY COMMISSION (1903) *Proc. of the International (Water) Boundary Commission, United States and Mexico, Treaties of 1884 and 1889: Equitable Distribution of the Waters of the Rio Grande*, Washington, 2 vols.

KENNEDY, W. C. (ed) (1979) 'Environmental problems along the Border', *Border State Univ. Consortium for Latin Am., occ. Pap.* 7

LYON, J. A. V. (1978) 'Ecology of the Border region, ch. 16 in S. R. Ross (ed) *Views across the Border* (Albuquerque: Univ. New Mexico Press), 333–37.

MACHADO, M. (1968) *An industry in crisis: Mexican–United States cooperation in the control of foot-and-mouth disease* (Berkeley: Univ. California Press).

MEXICO, Secretária de Relaciones Exteriores (1947) *El Tratado de Aguas Internacionales celebrado entre México y los Estados Unidos el 3 de Febrero de 1944: Antecedentes, consideraciones, y resoluciones del problema de los Aguas Internacionales*, Mexico, DF.

MUELLER, J. E. (1975) *Restless river, International Law and the behaviour of the Rio Grande* (El Paso: Texas Western Press).

MUMME, S. P. (1980) 'US-Mexican groundwater problems', *Jl. Inter-Am. & Wld Affairs*, **22**, 1, 31–55.

NASH, M. L. (1978) 'Contemporary practice of the United States relating to international law. International Waterways, Rio Grande', *Am. Jl. Inter. Law*, **72**, 3, 644.

REISS, R. L. (1978) 'Considerations on the health status along Mexico's northern Border', ch. 12 in S. R. Ross (ed) *Views across the Border* (Albuquerque: Univ. New Mexico Press), 241–55.

ROSS, S. R. (ed) (1978) *Views across the Border*, (Albuquerque: Univ. New Mexico Press).

SANDOS, J. A. (1980) 'International water control in the Lower Rio Grande basin', *Agric. Hist.*, **54**, 4, 490–501.

SCHROEDER, K. (1958) 'Der Rio Grande del Norte unter dem Einfluss der modernen Wasserwirtschaft', *Die Erde*, 3–4, 321–34.

SEPÚLVEDA, C. (1978) 'Instituciones para la solución de problemas de superficie entre México y los Estados Unidos', *Nat. Resour. Jl.*, **18**, 2, 131–41.

SHOULTS, J. M. (1974) 'Air pollution from US industrial sources along the US-Mexican Border', in H. G. Applegate and C. R. Bath (eds) *Air pollution along the US-Mexican Border*, (El Paso: Texas Western Press), 28–33.

STODDARD, E. R. (1979) 'A 3D perspective of water gate rip-offs along the Rio Grande' in W. C. Kennedy (ed) 'Environmental problems along the Border', *Border State Univ. Consortium Latin Am., occ. Pap. 7*, 38–71.

TELLER, C. H. (1978) 'Physical health status and health care utilization in the Texas Borderlands', ch. 13 in S. R. Ross (ed) *Views across the Border* (Albuquerque: Univ. New Mexico Press), 256-79.

UNITED NATIONS (1966) *Agreement concerning the use of water resources in frontier waters*, 17 July 1964, Poland–USSR, Treaty Series, 8054, 552 UNTS 188.

UNITED NATIONS (1975) *Management of International Water Resources: Institutional and Legal Aspects*, UN Dec. ST/ESA/5, 188.

US CONGRESS, HOUSE (1914) Committee on Foreign Affairs *United States Mexico Water Boundary*, Hearings, 63rd Cong., 2nd Sess. (Washington, DC: USGPO).

US CONGRESS, SENATE (1949) *Pecos River Compact*, Senate Doc., **109**, 81st Cong., 1st Sess. (Washington, DC: USGPO).

US STATUTES (1906) *Convention between the United States and Mexico for the equitable distribution of the waters of the Rio Grande for irrigation purposes*, **XXXIV**, 3, 2953–6.

US STATUTES (1924) '*An act providing for a study regarding the equitable use of the waters of the Rio Grande below Fort Quitman, Texas, in cooperation with the United States of Mexico*', **XXXIII**, 1, 118.

US STATUTES (1935) *An act providing for a study regarding the equitable use of the waters of the Rio Grande*, **49**, 1, 13 Aug., 660.

US STATUTES (1944) *Treaty for the utilization of the waters of the Colorado and Tijuana rivers and of the Rio Grande*, 3rd February **59**, 2, 1219–1267, 79th Cong., 1st Sess. (Washington, DC: USGPO).

UTTON, A. E. (1973) *Pollution and International Boundaries—United States-Mexican Environmental Problems* (Albuquerque: Univ. of New Mexico Press).

UTTON, A. E. (1979) 'Water problems and issues affecting United States-Mexico relations: policy options and alternatives', in W. C. Kennedy, (ed) 'Environmental problems along the Border', *Border State Univ. Consortium Latin Am., occ. Pap. 7*, 91–120.

WEAVER, J. L. (1973) 'Mexican American health care behaviour: a critical review of the literature', *Soc. Sci. Q.*, **54**, 85–102.

CHAPTER 5

The Alien Tide

A great haemorrhage of the frontiers.
WALTER MONDALE, 1977

Many of them [illegal aliens] have been law-abiding residents who are looking for a new life and are productive members of their community.
PRESIDENT JIMMY CARTER, 1977

We want to export commodities, not manpower . . . I want to emphasize that they [undocumented aliens] are not criminals and that a possibility of infringing immigration law does not entail a corresponding right to violate labour laws, much less human rights.'
PRESIDENT LÓPEZ-PORTILLO, 1977

Illegal Mexican migration is the most critical issue currently affecting relations between the US and Mexico. It is of considerably greater importance than illicit drug-traffic, prisoner exchange, Colorado river salinity, or other issues which have dominated discussions between the two countries for more than a decade.
W. A. CORNELIUS, 1977

Federal officials . . . could open up at least one million jobs for US citizens almost immediately by apprehending unauthorized workers.'
GENERAL CHAPMAN, former COMMISSIONER INS, 1976

The massive and continuing 'silent invasion' of the United States by undocumented Mexicans is perhaps the greatest illegal flow in world history, though understandably so since 'if they could, half the peoples of the world would walk to the United States in search of improvement' (Corwin 1973, 557). Its full dimensions may never be fully established, yet undocumented movement has already given rise to major and often bitterly contested controversies, persistently threatened to undermine good relations between the United States and its southern neighbour, and poses some of the most intractable problems of human rights, race, and ideology. The impact of such a scarcely controllable floodtide of migrants is complex and deep-seated, wide-ranging both structurally and spatially. Paradoxically, as in Victorian views on sex, illegal migration is something as widely to be deplored as it is universally accepted in practice. The Borderlands are the zone of transit for these movements and the impact has an especial severity there, though contributing also in some positive ways to the activities and culture on both sides of the Rio Grande (Camara 1979).

SCALE AND SIGNIFICANCE

Though uncertainty remains about the volume of undocumented immigration into the United States and the numbers living there at any one time, there is general agreement that numbers are substantial, more than half are from Mexico and the 1970s have seen an acceleration of illegal entries. In the late 1970s half-a-million illegal aliens were estimated to be entering the US annually (*Inter. Am. Econ. Affairs*, 1977). Furthermore, for Mexicans, undocumented entries have long dwarfed the numbers entering legally (Table 10). It is true that according to President Carter in 1977 at least sixty countries then contributed illegal migrants to the United States, but the Mexican proportion is always dominant, variously estimated between 50 and 60 per cent of the total (Teitelbaum 1980, 23). Between 1941 and 1970 6.8 million legal migrants entered the United States, but this number was almost matched by the numbers of undocumented Mexicans (6.6 millions) during the same period; Briggs (1974, 10) even calculated an excess of undocumented aliens. From an estimated total of 1.5 million illegal immigrants living in the US in 1970 (US Congress, Jt Econ. Com. 1977, 70) the figure had risen to 8.2 millions by 1975, according to one calculation (Lesko Associates 1975), including 5.2 million Mexicans. The Lesko figures are suspect in the eyes of many social scientists (Cornelius 1977, 1), but they have been extensively used for propaganda purposes against illegal migration. Other contemporary estimates range from as low as four or six millions (US Congress, House 1978a, 1; Teitelbaum 1980, 23) to as high as twelve millions in the United States at the present time. As Briggs (1978b, 517) put it, there is little conceptual difference among competing estimates, provided it is accepted, as it must be, that the volume is considerable, has been growing sharply, and bids fair to go on rising. This is not surprising, given the remarkable differentials in living conditions, employment opportunities, and wage levels in the two economies, and, not least, on the two sides of the Border. Whereas in 1920–30, 3 per cent of the Mexican population migrated to the US, this became 5 per cent 1950–9,

Table 10.   *US immigration, total and Mexicans 1931–77*

1,000s	Total legal (1)	Mexican legal (2)	(2) as % (1)	Deportable aliens located (3)	Deportable Mexicans located (4)	(4) as % (3)	Total deported (5)	Total required to depart (6)
1931–40	528	18	3	147	94	64	117	93
1941–50	1,035	59	5	1,377	1,295	94	110	1,470
1951–60	2,515	319	12	3,584	3,441	96	129	3,883
1961–70	3,321	443	13	1,608	995	62	96	1,334
1971–77	2,900	420	14	5,276	4,333	82	160	4,585*

* of 867,015 in 1977 alone, 818, 849 (94 per cent) were Mexicans
Sources: US Dept. Justice (INS) 1980, Table 23; Samora 1971, 46; Blejer *et al.* 1977, 329.

and has risen to between 8 and 10 per cent at the present time (Mumme 1978, 70). These rising percentages are even more significant when it is realized that the total Mexican population grew substantially over the same period.

An alternative method of assessing the scale of illegal migration is to use the Immigration and Naturalization Service (INS) figures of apprehensions, deportations, and voluntary departures. Detection of undocumented aliens varies according to changing US policies and the rigour with which they are implemented by the Border Patrol, or by Customs and Immigration officials. Given the huge flux of Border crossers (1955: 120 millions; 1965: 176 m; 1977: 266 m, including 156 m Mexicans) and the small size of the enforcement bodies, it is not to be wondered that detection rates of undocumented aliens are so low. In 1974 (US Congress, House, 563) General Chapman, former INS Commissioner, estimated that only one in three or four of those entering illegally or becoming illegal after entry were apprehended, though a high proportion of these were taken in the Border area. Deportation involves a cumbersome legal process with penalties for subsequent illegal re-entry. 'Voluntary' departure is a polite euphemism for the great majority of detected undocumented Mexicans who are returned by the INS to their home location in Mexico, without legal proceedings and without the risk of being prosecuted after subsequent re-entry to the United States. The hypocrisy of the latest category (Bustamante 1978b, 524) of 'deportation with honor' will be lost on no one.

The uneven relationship between undocumented Mexicans located and the current of both total and Mexican legal immigration into the US is clearly apparent; likewise the low ratio of legal Mexican to total legal immigrants and the high, though fluctuating, relationship between undocumented Mexican and total undocumented immigrant flows. The dramatic situation emerging in the 1970s is well illustrated by the scale of undocumented aliens located. At times of economic recession in the US, as in the late 1970s, concern over illegal migration is fanned into flame, an even more combustible subject when alarmist projections of present trends are made. General Chapman (US Congress, House 1974, 583) pessimistically forecast 'I think in four or five years it [the number of undocumented aliens] will double; in ten years again, when the figure might be thirty millions or thirteen per cent of the United States population.' In a Texan context, Corwin (1973) claimed that 'if an "open" frontier is established then in one or two generations half Texas will become a *chicano* Quebec' (*Comercio Exterior* 1978).

Massive migrations are not unusual in world history. Indeed, the expulsions of Europeans to North America as the Industrial Revolution progressed, and the later floodtide of peasants from Southern and

Eastern Europe, both enriched American society and became a part of her traditional welcoming heritage. Mass movements of workers in search of betterment have long been a feature of economic development, in response to the difference in employment potential between regions, and the centre–periphery contrasts within most States. Of course, the flow of human beings between two countries should theoretically be as unimpeded as the free movement of capital. It is possible to argue that migration from Mexico to the USA takes place within a unified labour market and is but one more step in the internal migration patterns within Mexico, from the less developed States into the Federal District and the northern States (Camara 1979). But impediments set in when frontiers are crossed (Marshall 1978). The flow is then monitored and often regulated, usually in the interests of citizens in the host country. Problems mount when labour migration is across contiguous landward boundaries between States with marked differences in living standards, culture, or development prospects. Trans-ocean flows of migrants from the New Commonwealth into Britain (Lawton 1977, 146–51) have given rise to social and economic issues of assimilation and acculturation, but given the ocean distance and the insular nature of Britain there is scarcely any illegal inflow. Within Latin America labour immigration from Bolivia, Paraguay, or Chile into Argentina, or from Colombia into Venezuela and Panama, is a form of equalizing flow in search of work or better jobs (US Congress, House 1977, 18). The contemporary illegal flow of migrants from China into Hong Kong (1980) highlights the deep economic and ideological divide there. The movement of undocumented Mexicans into the United States is a more massive version of all these migrations, with the more traumatic implications because of the juxtaposition of extremes in the two adjacent countries, extremes of wages, income, life-style, and culture. By comparison, the seasonal movement of several thousand French Canadians to harvest potatoes in northern Maine is a small-scale, well-regulated, and untroubled microcosm of the problems on the Rio Grande (US Congress, Senate 1969). Nor are deportations unique to the US–Mexican situation. With the sales decline in the car market in the 1970s, for example, Germany 'humanely' deported many tens of thousands of assembly-line workers back to Portugal, Yugoslavia, and Turkey (US Congress, House 1978c, 837). In this case too there was no territorial contiguity between the host country and those of its contracted 'guest-workers'.

The economic and social impact of trans-frontier migrations is often most sensitively felt in the areas near the international boundary and special provision is not uncommon in treaties or by statute to protect frontier workers (*frontaliers*, *grenzgänger*) commuting or moving seasonally into the adjacent borderlands (House 1980). Likewise, the interests of frontier citizens in the host country are conventionally safeguarded, often by some form of limitation on numbers, kinds, nature of employment, and periods of stay for immigrant workers and their dependants. Markedly unlike the US–Mexican Borderlands, in Western Europe the sending country is often given credit for the contributions immigrant workers pay into social or welfare funds. Outwards from the Borderlands there is a 'rippling' effect, ensuring that what seems at first sight a limited frontier or even a regional phenomenon may quickly spread to the utmost corners of the national space in the two countries involved.

US–MEXICAN ATTITUDES AND PERCEPTIONS

Apart from uncertainty on the dimensions of the undocumented migration flow from Mexico there is a wide, even diverging, spectrum of attitudes on the implications and impact of the movements and what, if anything, should or can be done about the situation, and by whom. Although it is possible to agree with Arellano (US Congress, House, 1977, 17) that 'until we [the US] are able to solve this problem [undocumented aliens] amicably and cooperatively with Mexico, it will be a festering sore which will adversely affect the totality of our relations with Mexico', it is far from the case that the two governments view the problem in the same light, or with a similar degree of priority. Nor do the governments each speak with a monolithic voice, unchanging through time, and then there are innumerable structural and sectoral interest groups and partisans, expressing varying prejudices or degrees of social concern, most notably in the United States. Even the myriad research workers investigating undocumented migration show a spectrum of widely differing interpretations and prescriptions.

At its simplest, the polar positions may be expressed as follows (US Congress, House 1978c, 820 *et seq.*):

(a) There is a rising tide of foreign workers, mostly Mexican; they come from a hopelessly underdeveloped and troubled country whose unbridled population growth has reached unmanageable proportions; this leads to a tide of illegal immigrants which threatens jobs, bleeds social services, and undermines the standard of living. Therefore the correct policies are: to stop migration by whatever means necessary, deport existing illegal migrants, introduce birth control in Mexico, and support economic growth in that country by a massive industrialization, to be financed by both US and other foreign capital. The interdictory aspects fail to heed the lesson of Vietnam: that the application of force, however sophisticated the theory of behaviour modification, cannot alone determine a people's behaviour (US Congress, House 1978a, 345).

(b) Alternatively, the US has in some measure been the cause of the problem: by interference in Mexico since the nineteenth century; in particular, by the intrusion of multinationals, producing growth without commensurate jobs and skewing income distribution still further; the illegals are honest folk looking for jobs and a better life; identification of the Mexicans as the cause of US unemployment is racist and a search for scapegoats, whereas capitalism is to blame; the problem will not be solved by placing an INS army at the Border, nor by increasing US involvement in the Mexican economy, nor by Washington/Mexico City bureaucrats.

At a deeper level, the alien tide has its roots in the underdeveloped and dependent condition of Mexico, its traumatic levels of under-employment and unemployment, great and even growing income disparities, discrimination in favour of cities in government funding, and its indebtedness to foreign capital and technology to promote development. In the US, on the other hand, there is an insatiable demand for cheap labour, cheapened still further by forces creating a docile, submissive workforce (Bustamante 1978b, 523). At all events, there is a marked asymmetry of power, with Mexico the dramatically weaker partner, vulnerable through its economic and technological dependence to decisions taken in Washington, or by the multinational corporations. At the same time, the penetration of values and con-sumption patterns from the rich United States weakens the Mexican sense of identity. Basic Mexican policies and even the political system must be seen to be acceptable to Washington (Ojeda *et al.* 1978, 306 *et seq.*)

American attitudes and perceptions are infinitely more diverse and formative at many different levels, both official and among private groups or individuals. Mexican views are the more monolithic and, in policy terms, more rigid, centralized, and bureaucratic. The numerous US Congressional Committees on Illegal Aliens heard witnesses from the entire spectrum, from almost hostile xenophobics to caring radicals. The Director of Americans for the Rights of Citizens (US Congress, House 1978c, 775) deplored the welfare burden of illegal immigrants, on schools, public hospitals, and the incidence of crime among this group in Los Angeles. This is in line with the view, held by journalists or political opportunists in the main, who see the issue as one of personal immorality by the immigrant, deserving of punishment and incar-ceration as a negative sanction (Stoddard 1978, 16). Such prejudicial views are buttressed by gross assertions (quoted in Bustamante 1977, 149) such as those of the Inner City Fund (1975) that illegal aliens 'represent a burden of US $13 billions per annum for the American taxpayer'. The Executive Council of the major US labour organization, AFL–CIO, has persistently sought stern measures to restrain illegal immigration as a threat to the jobs and living standards of American workers. The United Farmworkers branch of the AFL–CIO, on the other hand, has proved more humane and realistic, requesting an unconditional amnesty for all undocumented workers and their families (US Congress, House 1978a, 330). Some would see the negative aspects of US attitudes as responding to the deep structures of American history: 'Despite the principles of the American revolution and the US Constitution . . . during the 116 years between the Cherokee removal of 1838 and Operation Wetback (1954), power groups have always dealt with minorities, at times of crisis, in a manner involving forcible removal and almost always violation of constitutional rights' (Dr J. Sommers in US Congress, House 1978a, 353).

To liberal Americans, and Mexicans, the problem is one of under-employment in Mexico, reported as 37–45 per cent in 1970, and 62–68 per cent in farm labour (Alba-Hernández 1978, 471). Relentless deportations should be stopped, unconditional amnesties promoted, social benefits and civil rights should be guaranteed. Perhaps the *Washington Post* (13 November 1974) summed up a general feeling: 'It is hard to get the message back to the "teeming shore" [from the inscription on the Statue of Liberty] that those who were once welcome are now an intolerable burden.'

Official attitudes are necessarily tinged by greater political expediency. Faced with the operational problems of dealing with un-documented aliens, the Commissioners of the INS have traditionally followed hardline attitudes. General Chapman (US Congress, House 1974, 563) stressed that no fewer than one million jobs could be released for Americans by a more effective immigration enforcement pro-gramme, 190,000 of them in the US Border cities alone. At the same time, he forecast dire consequences if present illegal immigrant trends continued. His successor, Leonel Castillo (US Congress, House 1978a, 4–17), credited with the introduction of the term 'undocumented alien' in 1977, has taken a more sceptical, though still a protective, stance for his Service. He emphasized the difficulties of implementing any im-migration policies with scarce resources in the field. Policies of the US Congress and of President Carter are more fully reviewed later. For the moment, it should again be stressed that at times of economic recession attitudes harden. Though more liberal than the US Senate's attitude, President Carter's 1977 proposals on undocumented aliens (US Congress, House 1978a, 356 *et seq.*) still included more rigorous enforce-ment measures at the Border, sanctions on employers recruiting illegal workers, restrictions on migrants acquiring residential status in the US, and the introduction of limited five-year work permits. With their carefully defined and limited amnesty provisions, these proposals have failed to convince the US Congress and yet have aroused strong criticism from Mexico (Bustamante 1978b). Though vaguely mentioning co-operation with the Mexican government, the Carter proposals continue, wrongfully, to see undocumented aliens as essentially an internal American problem.

Perhaps surprisingly, the Mexican government only slightly acknowledges the issue, looking on illegal emigration as a temporary and reversible phenomenon, whose long-term impact is likely to be negligible (Mumme 1978, 74). Such emigration violates Mexican statutes, is said to 'siphon off valuable human capital', but at the same time certainly acts as a kind of safety-valve, given the rapid population growth and high levels of unemployment in Mexico. Migration is thus a bargaining weapon within the wider context of US–Mexican diplomatic strategies. Action by the Mexicans in the short-term is concerned to diminish exploitation and protect human rights, including the right to move freely, even for their undocumented citizens in the United States. Mexican policy is propounded at presidential level: 'emigration of Mexican workers disturbs the national conscience . . . we wish to export commodities, not national problems' (Pres. Luis Echeverria 1975); 'let us export commodities, not manpower' (Pres. López-Portillo 1977). Undocumented migration is not, however, a priority issue in Mexico, and most policy formulation on that subject is in reaction to American decisions rather than a search for solutions within Mexico itself. Nowhere is the voice of the 'wetback', the undocumented alien, to be heard. Perhaps the injustice inherent in Ruben Salazar's observation, shortly before his death in 1970, will suffice: 'There is no law against hiring wetbacks, only against being a wetback' (*Los Angeles Times*, 27 April 1970).

It might be expected that the great volume and diversity of academic research on undocumented aliens would be cooler, detached, and more objective. In fact, such writings cover almost as wide a spectrum as that of the politicians. Briggs (1974, 1975a, b, 1976, 1978a, b) highlights the 'shadow labour force' of individuals without rights in the US, an easy prey for exploitation, but he is even more concerned with the clear and present danger to the standards of living of all Americans with whom they compete for jobs, housing, and community services. The offer of labour in the US South-west is kept in surplus, wages low, and unionization retarded; the Mexican–Americans (*chicanos*) of the Border cities and countryside are the most seriously, adversely, and increasingly affected. Bustamante (1971, 1972, 1973, 1975, 1976a, b, 1977, 1978a, b, 1979), who earlier audaciously carried out fieldwork by becoming a 'wetback' himself, analyses the problem within two frameworks of exploitation. In the first place, in American eyes the undocumented alien is unfairly labelled and thus condemned as a social deviant, a central element in his subsequent exploitation within the moral spirit of American law-makers. Second, he is a commodity-migrant within the structural processes of a capitalist society whose traits and practices in the Borderlands are scarcely removed from those pilloried by Marx in the nineteenth century.

More recent American scholarship is at pains to balance the case against the undocumented alien by pointing up his limited drain on US resources and the positive contributions made to American society. North and Houston (1976) were among the first to establish that illegal workers pay more in taxes than they receive in social benefits, that they make minimal claims on schools, hospitals, or welfare services. Furthermore, the costs of their education and bringing-up have been borne in Mexico before they become fully-fledged workers in the US. Stoddard (1976, 1978) further indicates that pehaps 40 per cent of the Mexican aliens' wages are spent in the US and their hard work for minimum wages (or below) is an indirect subsidy to the US consumer. Nevertheless, the undocumented worker burdens local taxpayers with the cost of services used, however, sparingly, while enriching federal and State treasuries through deductions (Stoddard 1978, 18). Cornelius (1977) found no evidence that Mexican illegals take jobs away from native Americans and that, positively, the limited claims on welfare services were far outweighed by social security contributions and tax revenues.

THE HISTORY OF MEXICAN MIGRATION TO THE USA

A brief survey of migration phases puts the contemporary situation into context, underlines the deep-seated cultural attitudes often still prevalent, and offers a prelude to later critiques of policies adopted or to be preferred. Figure 24 and Table 10 illustrate the longer-term trends of Mexican migration to the US. They should be related to the trends of total population change discussed in chapter 3. Key elements in the interpretation of these fluctuating trends are the economic conditions in the United States, the onset of boom or depression, and the changes in immigration laws and practices which were the closely related result. Indeed, it has been argued that US immigration laws have been engineered to manipulate the manoeuvrability of labour power, controlling the relationship between capital and labour not only in the US but, more strikingly, in dependent nations such as Mexico (US Congress, House 1978a, 320 et seq.). More simply and cynically put, the United States has consistently welcomed Mexican immigrants as workers, but not as residents, least of all as citizens.

During the second half of the nineteenth century fewer than 30,000 Mexicans entered the US, most of them as seasonal harvest workers, cattlemen, or shepherds (Taylor 1934, 100 et seq.). The completion of railways across the Border and on its approaches in the 1880s offered

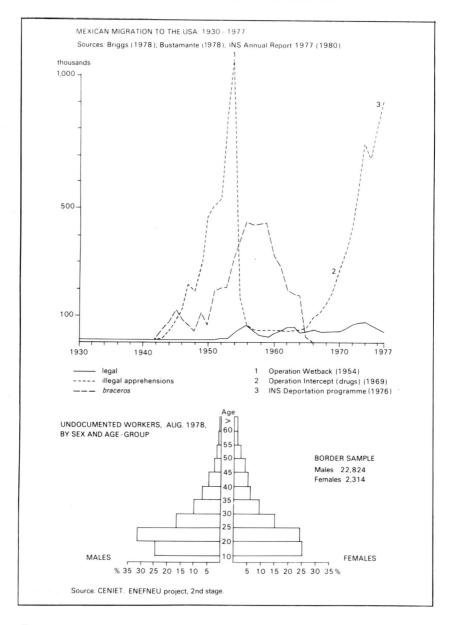

FIG. 24. Mexican migration to the USA, 1930–1977

work to migratory labour gangs and also increased personal mobility in the poverty-stricken, hitherto largely stagnant rural economy of northern Mexico. It was not until the twentieth century that numbers of Mexican immigrants became significant. It is true that the need for US guards on the Mexican border was recognized as early as 1903, but to keep out the Chinese! (Samora 1971, 34). Insecurity, for a decade after the Mexican Revolution of 1910, stimulated the exodus from that country, the banning of oriental immigrants opened oportunities for Mexicans, and both wartime shortages and the rising momentum of economic development in the American South-west increased the demand for labour: in the decade 1911–21 250,000 Mexicans entered the USA, and a further 459,000 during the next decade (Galarza 1964, 28). For the first thirty years of this century about 90 per cent of Mexicans stayed within the South-western USA.

The Burnett Law (1917) was the first to impose restrictions on the entry of Mexicans, with a head tax and tests for literacy (Martínez 1976, 100), but American wartime demand for labour caused its suspension until 1921. The National Origins Act of 1924 excluded Mexicans from quota restrictions, though provisions on literacy, contract labour, and the various fees required could be, and were, used to control the volume of Mexican entries (Samora 1971, 40). The creation of the Border Patrol in 1924 introduced the first official interdictory measures, but these were rudimentary and on a very small scale.

In the early 1930s the economic depression and the enactment of deportation measures reversed the flow: Mexican emigrants from the US came to exceed immigrants by a ratio of five to one. Over 200,000 aliens (mostly Mexicans) were deported between 1930 and 1940, in addition to several hundred thousand more who were forcibly 'repatriated' during that decade (Briggs 1975a, 6); US citizens of Mexican–American origin were often caught up and swept back over the Border on this tide. Injustice came not so much from a particular Border policy as that there was no consistent policy, and certainly none agreed with the Mexican government.

The beginnings of illegal migration to the US in the early 1940s coincided with labour shortages, on the land and in factories, during the wartime economy. Parallel with this, American agribusiness pressed its government to introduce a contract labour programme, initially refused by the federal authorities. The Mexican Labour Programme (1942) recruited *braceros* who were contracted exclusively for agricultural work. The programme was fitful until formally renewed in 1951 by Public Law 78, which continued until the end of 1964. Since then, in spite of pressures by American growers and a rather weak set of proposals by the Mexican government (US Congress, House 1978a 358 *et seq.*), there has been no renewal. As Fig. 24 shows, illegal migration took off very rapidly in the 1940s, in spite of a co-ordinated campaign by the Border Patrol in 1947. The period 1944–54 has been termed the 'wetback' decade, many of the wetbacks being former or would-be *braceros* (Samora 1971, 45). By illegal entry the labourer could save time, expense, and inconvenience, as well as the official and unofficial fees (Grebler *et al.* 1966, 32). The American employer, in his turn, could thereby circumvent the safeguards intended to protect the Mexican worker. In 1954 a major campaign, Operation Wetback, repatriated more than one million illegal Mexicans. Thenceforth, the scale of apprehensions fell away, though illegal entries are unlikely to have done so. It is, however, clear that from 1964, the *bracero* programme being terminated, the illegal flow again gathered momentum to its present disturbingly high levels of about half a million entries annually. Legal migration from Mexico, on the other hand, has been limited under the Immigration and Naturalization Act (1965). As part of the 120,000 to be allowed from the Western Hemisphere an annual quota of 40,000 Mexicans was decreed, since exceeded through the arrival of dependants, but in 1977 the Mexican quota was reduced to a derisory level of only 20,000. At the same time, post-Vietnam, a vigorous re-patriation programme was applied to undocumented workers. Never-theless, the alien tide has surged ahead and in the early 1980s is again presenting US policy-makers with a most serious challenge, at once ethical and moral, but a flow buttressed by economic pressures from American interest groups.

The problems arising from undocumented immigration are sharply focussed at the Border, and since almost two-thirds cross into Texas most severely felt there. No longer do most illegals stay only in the States along the American side, but rather diffuse throughout the United States (Álvarez 1967, 20). Yet there is a 'ponding-back' effect on the Mexican side of the Rio Grande and a further congestion in its cities as undocumented workers are 'voluntarily returned' to their homeland. In Texas the competition of legal and illegal Mexican immigrants with native *chicanos* is most acutely felt, and the employment or social welfare problems resulting are among the most severe in the United States today.

A TYPOLOGY OF MIGRANTS

The simplest dichotomy distinguishes legal from illegal migrants. In reality there is an overlap between the two categories: those who had been *braceros* (1942–64) not infrequently re-entered illegally, either during the programme or subsequently; conversely, those with previous experience as undetected illegals in the US often explored every avenue to re-enter as legal immigrants at a later date. Short-term immigrants, including seasonal workers (H-2), daily or weekly commuters for work (I-151) or shoppers (I-186) might exploit such a status to reside illicitly for longer periods. Legal and illegal migrants to the US have often contended for the same jobs, and both have competed with less privileged, underpaid American workers, most particularly in the Border area.

Legal migrants (Newton and Osborn 1979) have included the following categories: (a) *braceros*, or farmworkers, admitted as contract labour 1942–64; (b) quota immigrants, under successive Immigration Acts, including the 40,000 Mexicans and their dependants to be admitted under the 1965 Act; (c) seasonal workers (H-2 documentation); (d) 'green-carders' to work (I-151); and (e) shoppers, or 'white-carders' (I-186).

The *bracero* programme (Hancock 1959; Galarza 1964; Samora 1971), terminated for more than a decade, continues to colour attitudes and inflame prejudices in today's altogether different situation. Figure 24 shows the scale and rhythm of contract labour recruitment and the relationship of this massive, controlled movement to the accompanying tide of illegal 'wetbacks'. The *braceros* provided labour for the intensive cultivation needs of American agribusiness. As Bustamante (1974) put it, 'there was the deliberate creation of a reserve labour army by the manipulation of US immigration laws and their policing, which increased or diminished the capacity to arrest those in breach, according to the needs of entrepreneurs'. The *braceros* were recruited through government centres in Mexico, mainly 'unemployed or landless labourers of good moral character' (Hancock 1959, 64). Confined to farm work, they ranged as far north as Wyoming, following the successive harvestings. Until 1947 the Mexican government permitted no movement of *braceros* to Texas 'because of the cases of extreme, intolerable racial discrimination' (Scruggs 1963, 251). Illegal 'wetback' entry was difficult to prevent and growers in the US were not averse to exploiting these vulnerable illegal workers, 'anxious to please, willing to endure' (Galarza 1964, 30). There were periods of 'drying out' or legalizing 'wetbacks' (1947), but as soon as the demand for labour fell the Mexican workers were invariably rejected and repatriated in large numbers. Though it had fulfilled American needs, the *bracero* programme left scars which have never healed. At the peak, *braceros* were providing more than one-fifth of all the labour in intensive Southwestern agriculture (Galarza 1964, 94) but they were employed to do 'only the stoop labor that white Americans simply would not accept' (Galarza 1964, 89). E. Nelson's (1972) harrowing novel, *The Bracero*, indicted the growers, and both governments for the tragedies, human suffering, and misery of the peasants transported only to be grievously and inhumanely exploited in all too many cases. Yet the *bracero* programme has been described as the 'most effective foreign aid that the US could grant to its sister republic to the south' (Galarza 1964, 243). Indeed, the *braceros* have been compared with the migrant Italians at the turn of the century, who alternated seasonal labour in Argentina with a return home for the annual wheat harvest (Randall 1962, 75). As poor recompense for their labours 186,000 jobless *braceros* were returned to Mexico at the ending of the programme.

Quota Mexican immigrants share characteristics in common with other immigrants: preference for urban areas; a slightly higher proportion of women but a little younger age than the general American population. On the other hand there are differences: greater preference for the US South-west, relatives or friends already in the US, and a higher proportion of blue-collar workers (Briggs 1975a, 12). A 1973 sample of 821 legal immigrants (Alba-Hernández 1978, 474 *et seq.*) showed: 60 per cent with previous US residence, 50 per cent from towns of more than 20,000, only 10 per cent in farm work, mostly under thirty years old.

The legal migrants with the greatest impact on the Borderlands are the commuters to work in the US (I-151) or to shop there (I-186). It is the latter, particularly, who may use their status to work illicitly. Seasonal workers under the contract H-2 programme are few (30,000 in the USA in 1977) and only a few thousands are from Mexico, though in 1977 some 800 Mexican workers were admitted to Presidio, Texas, to harvest onions. This provoked the US labour unions who sued the INS for illegally permitting jobs to be taken from American workers; the Department of Labor, in dispute with the INS, in turn sued the employers for US $200,000 in back payments due to Mexican workers.

Figure 5 shows the distribution of Border commuters into the US along the Rio Grande, referred to as 'this generation's *braceros*' (in Briggs 1974, 15). The commuters to work (I-151) are residents of Mexico who have acquired permanent resident alien (immigrant) status, but have decided to live outside the US while working there. They have the right to move into the US to live, but choose not to do so (North 1970), perhaps in order not to disrupt the closely-knit Mexican family, or to enjoy cheaper living south of the Rio Grande. The green card (I-151) is thus little more than a work-permit. The conditions that the holder may not be unemployed for more than six months, be a strike-breaker, or use time living outside the US as eligibility for citizenship, are readily circumvented (US Congress, Jt Econ. Com. 1977, 176). Arguments for and against the system (Dillman 1970; Ericson 1970; Dillman and Gifford 1971a,b) are evenly balanced. *For*: needed by local employers; long-standing practice; if terminated, would add to housing and public costs in US; human rights; spend most of earnings in US; work at jobs US residents would not take; if they left, American women in work would be deprived of household help. *Against*: depress local wages and working conditions; higher rate of minimum wage violations; increase unemployment; often strike-breaking; enjoy best of both worlds; and prevent effective unionization of labour. Such international commuting has been accepted by the INS since the early 1930s and affects almost exclusively the US twin-towns along the Rio Grande. The commuters are an interesting control group against whom to assess the illegals who are often in competition with them, to indicate what might happen if a new non-immigrant worker programme was to be brought in, and to monitor generally the Border labour market (North 1970, A-3, 4).

The 'white-carders' (I-186) are an unknown but substantial quantity of Mexican Border residents who visit the US towns along the Rio Grande, often regularly for shopping. Since 1965 these cards have been valid for only five years and could be used for a stay of not more than seventy-two hours. Previously, movement was limited to 150 miles (240 km) from the Border, now reduced to twenty-five miles without special permission; with an SW434 permit the stay may be increased to fourteen or fifteen days and movement permitted anywhere within the four Border US states. Again the provisions are easily circumvented. A white-carder may go beyond the 40 km and mail the card back to Mexico. If apprehended, he claims to be an illegal entrant, accepts voluntary departure, is returned to Mexico, collects his white card and re-enters the US to continue the cycle (US Congress, Jt Econ. Com. 1977, 177). In El Paso some 3,000 white cards a month were issued in 1970 and several hundreds withdrawn; some 75,000 residents of C. Juárez had such cards (Samora 1971, 22). At a rough estimate in 1978 there were 5,000 illegal aliens with full-time domestic jobs in El Paso, while during a bus strike that year more than 21,000 Mexicans a day walked every morning across the two bridges.

Illegal migrants are undocumented, more difficult to categorize or to assess. Though Mexicans are vastly dominant in such movements, there has been a disturbing trend in the 1970s for entries from further afield, from Colombia, Ecuador, and even through smuggling rings organized in South-east Asia (US Congress, House 1978a, 9). Estimates of numbers of Mexicans have already been referred to; here their characteristics and behaviour are under review. Certainly these differ in some respects from those of legal migrants, especially in a higher ratio of single males. The stereotype of the undocumented worker is that he is male, single, under thirty, from an unskilled rural background, with poor education, speaking little English (Briggs 1975b, 357). He is thus often regarded as a poor illiterate peasant, the product of rural misery and subsistence agriculture under semi-feudal conditions in an underdeveloped country. Yet 'he sees little or no social stigma attached to his illegal status. If he is apprehended and deported it is bad luck; if successful, especially after multiple re-entries to the US, he improves prestige among his peers' (Blejer *et al.* 1977, 329). Changes in the structure of undocumented migrants are, however, setting in: the percentage of apprehended illegals who had been farmworkers in Mexico fell from 65 per cent in 1940, to 54 per cent in 1960 (Frisbie 1975, 6) and from 57 per cent in 1972 to 47 per cent in 1975 (Comisión Inter-secretarial 1972; North and Houston 1976; Bustamante 1977, 162). One-third of illegals who had had jobs in America were estimated to have been working in agriculture, one-third in manufacturing and construction, and one-third in service jobs (Briggs 1975a, 13). Greenwood and Ladman (1977) found that recent undocumented migrants were coming from higher income areas as well as the poorer parts of Mexico, while Fogel (1975) confirmed that the growth in employment of illegals was now taking place largely outside the agri-cultural sector. Jobs taken were mostly unskilled, but within a wide diversity of forms of employment, in non-durable goods as well as in primary metal manufacture, the construction industry, food-serving, and the transport industry. On the United States side of the Rio Grande the textile and apparel industries in most Border towns exercised a particular attraction. In a sample of 919 recent illegal migrants (Cornelius 1977, 9) the mostly frequently held jobs had been: agricultural field labourer, dishwasher or waiter, and unskilled con-struction worker. The matching of Mexican labour to the needs of the secondary labour market was close and, by providing elastic increments to such a labour force, this was held to sustain low wage-levels and increased the power of employers to exploit their workers (Fogel 1975, 45).

Among 6,261 undocumented Mexicans returned by the US authorities back across the Rio Grande in August 1978 (García 1979, Table 2) only 241 were women; of the males, 25 per cent were 15–19, 28 per cent 20–24, and 16 per cent 25–29 years of age.

Undocumented aliens have traditionally come from five of the poorer States in Mexico (US Congress, House 1978a, 133): Guanajuato, Chihuahua, Michoacán, Zacatecas, and Jalisco. Ever since 1969 immigrants from these States have regularly provided more than half the INS apprehensions, mostly from rural areas, though C. Juárez in Chihuahua was a most notable exception. As the 1976 devaluation of the peso worked through, and travel costs have risen generally, there has been a greater concentration of undocumented workers from Mexican Border States immediately contiguous to the USA. The pat-terns on Figs. 11 and 12 certainly include some of the major un-documented migrant flows passing over into the US, and demonstrate a general gravity-model type of flow for such movements. Indeed, Greenwood and Ladman (1977, 157) found a very significant distance-decay effect in illegal migration currents. Figure 25 shows that Mexican State of origin of some 22,822 undocumented males 'deported' from the US in August 1978 (García 1979, Table 8). The general pattern of

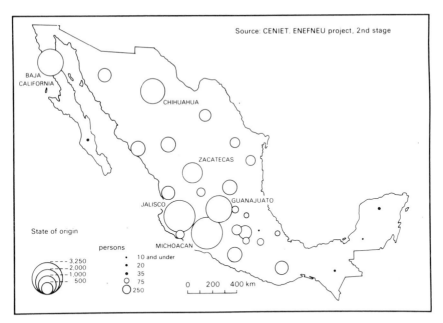

Source: CENIET. ENEFNEU project, 2nd stage

FIG. 25. Source areas of repatriated undocumented Mexicans, August 1978

concentration on the poorer States of the Central Highlands is confirmed, while Baja California Norte is now an even more significant frontier source area than the traditional Chihuahua. Twenty-four per cent crossed the Rio Grande frontier on their outward journey and 18 per cent came back that way. More than three-quarters of the sample with origins in the Border States, from Chihuahua to Tamaulipas, crossed into Texas; from interior States between one-quarter and one-third did so (Durango 37, Guanajuato 36, Zacatecas 26 per cent). Similarly, there is a diffusion of illegals into the interior of the USA. The most favoured destinations in 1977 were Southern California, Chicago, and Texas, in that order (Cornelius 1977, 7). California offers many farm jobs to those lacking resources to move further north; Texas, on the other hand, has lower wage rates and greater restrictions on the unionization of labour. With a diverse economy and higher potential earnings Chicago is the traditional Mecca for those with the funds to travel that far north. The poorer migrants have to settle for the smaller towns or the countryside nearer the Border, even though overall migration is increasingly directed towards larger urban centres.

The undocumented alien is for the most part a temporary or 'shuttle' migrant. Hence the alarmist projections based on a cumulative total for such movements over a number of years are likely to be notoriously wide of the mark. North and Houston (1976) found that just over half those apprehended by the INS had been in the US for fewer than twelve months, while 71 per cent had remained for shorter than four months on their initial trip; more than one-third were unemployed when caught (Briggs 1976, 120). This quicker return to Mexico contrasts with experience in the 1920s (Gamio 1930), when stays of several years by illegal entrants were not uncommon. The most recent evidence, from the sample of 'deported' Mexican male migrants (García 1979, Table 1), showed that 40 per cent had been apprehended in the US within twenty-four hours of entry, a further 7 per cent during the second day; thereafter, the possibility of being taken fell away, but only 13 per cent had been in the US for more than eighty-four days. These figures are for the entire US–Mexican Border. For the Rio Grande frontier they were, respectively, 28 per cent, 7 per cent, and 19 per cent of longer-stayers. These results contrast with those of North and Houston, perhaps because they are based on a very much larger samples and record more faithfully short-term moves. Sixty per cent of the males had made only one illegal entry to the US in the preceding year, compared to 85 per cent of females; for two entries, 21 and 7 per cent, and for three, 8 and 2 per cent respectively. At the more turbulent extreme, about 2 per cent of males had had more than eleven illegal migrations in the year. Three-quarters of those interviewed by Cornelius (1977, 8) preferred to 'continue living in Mexico and working in the US from time to time'. Cultural, community, and family ties proved most enduring. 'To be sure there are smugglers and dope peddlers and prostitutes and every other undesirable element that trickles through with these people, but basically the mass are good, hard, solid working people that want to make more money in two months than they can do all year in Mexico, and then go back and take care of their families' (Pellerzi in US Congress, House 1974, 465). Perhaps the ultimate epitaph on the illegal migrant is 'he probably moves from poverty to greater poverty and, whatever his experience, the economic and financial benefit for Mexico, for his family, and for himself, is small. Those who benefit are those who employ him or smuggle him' (Samora 1971, 105).

THE SMUGGLING OF ALIENS

The US Border Patrol was set up in 1924, with only sixty men, to prevent illegal entry, monitor Border crossings, trace and apprehend undocumented aliens. At El Paso a defensive strategy in depth was early adopted. There were river guards to apprehend at the moment of illegal entry, mounted men to pursue, and men to open and inspect freight cars before any left the Border and all passenger trains. Further inspectors were stationed at strategic points along the highways and railways leading north (watching also for Chinese (*sic*) travelling on foot) (US Dept. Labor 1923, 18–19). Although methods of detection have become increasingly sophisticated, the Patrol has always had to operate with a derisorily small number of men (1,350 and 1974, of whom only 200 are on patrol during any eight-hour spell), spread across 1,860 miles (3,000 km) of the entire US–Mexican Border frontier. The INS has consistently taken the view that 'the prevention of illegal entries . . . is more difficult, requires more ingenuity, more men and equipment, but is, in the long run, more economical and humane than the expulsion process' (US Dept. Justice 1955, 14). Under President Carter's 1977 proposals the strength of the Patrol was to be doubled, and an Anti-smuggling Task Force was set up in the following year. The means of interdiction and surveillance are limited: in and near the major settlements or athwart the major known entry routes a 3.5 metre chain fence has been erected (The 'tortilla'curtain', Stoddard et al. 1979), not without vocal opposition from the Mexican side and even from American employers. Those who cut or climb the fence are alambristas (or wire-jumpers), in contrast to the mojados (wetbacks) who have traditionally swum or waded across the river. Nowhere does the Rio Grande afford a major obstacle, and over many stretches in the middle and upper reaches it is conveniently fordable for most of the year. In El Paso it is only a short dash from the river into the relative security of the Mexican-American barrio. The riverline, the fence, and their immediate hinterlands are monitored by sophisticated sensing devices, backed up by mobile ground and air patrols. Sensing devices include infra-red sensors, seismic recorders, magnetic and optical viewing techniques, monitored from control points. Over the entire US–Mexican Border, however, it is estimated (US Congress, House 1974, 580) that not more than 250 km of the 3,000 km are effectively controlled by devices of any kind. Low-flying, single-engined aircraft track those who are mostly on foot through the most inhospitable country, though increasingly helicopters are used on night patrols. The pilots are trained to look for 'sign-cutting' and fly low enough to detect footprints in the sand of the daily prepared drag-strip on most accessible urban entry corridors (US Congress, House 1978b, 4). Additionally, there are mobile checkpoints on the major highways leading north. Nevertheless, it has been said (Pellerzi in US Congress, House 1974, 64) that to control the Border effectively would 'need the entire National Guard of five or six States on full-time duty'.

Samora (1971, 72 et seq.) referred to the game in which the illegal aliens (pollos or chickens) and those who smuggle them (polleros–chicken hawks) seek to outwit the immigration authorities; in this they are aided by the coyotes who include lawyers, forgers of documents, and contact men on the ground. The whole procedure is fraught with danger since the Border Patrol has its informants among the smugglers and spies in

the Border towns. Many illegal aliens cross individually or in small
groups, but most have at least fleeting contact with organized smuggling (Selzer 1979). More informal arrangements are often made with
arrangers (*pagadores, enganchadores*) in public parks or squares of the
Mexican Border cities. The would-be migrant is congregated with
perhaps five or ten others to await a Border crossing. A guide then leads
the group across the river or through the fence, usually at dusk to give
maximum darkness for movement, to a motel or low-grade hotel (drop-
house) on the American shore. When the motel room is full the smuggler backs a van, or perhaps a camper, up to the door, loads up and
heads north. Suspected smugglers' vans are often followed by the INS
Agents up into the Middle West or even to the Atlantic coast. In a case on
14 February 1978 (Selzer 1979, 8) a van was traced from the Border at
Laredo as far as Champagne, Illinois before the arrests were made, in
order to flush out the network and trace its payoffs.

Corruption (Operation Cleansweep in the INS in 1972), extortion,
and tragedy are never far away. Illegal aliens are often crammed into
hidden compartments, possibly under a load of vegetables or wood,
kept there in suffocating conditions often for hours on end. Deaths
under such conditions are not unknown and the reckless driving of
smugglers pursued by INS agents has led to other fatalities; in February
1979, for example, the charred bodies of two aliens were found in the
trunk of a car which crashed when pursued through South Texas.
Death or severe injury has occurred on the Santa Fé and Southern
Pacific railway bridges at El Paso as immigrants fell at night when
confronted by Border Patrol officers. The undocumented aliens, often
poor and little educated, are also preyed upon by those they think are
helping them. Apart from absconding with the fees for crossing without
fulfilling the task, it is not uncommon for extortionate charges to be
levied. Early in 1977 six aliens paid $1,000 each to be transported from
Eagle Pass, Texas, to Houston; the lowest fees recorded for the smuggled Border crossing are generally around $300 per capita, though
Cornelius (1977, 6) mentioned $150–220 for those in his sample. The fee
varies too according to the distance to destination. Poorer illegal
migrants have to stay in the Border area to look for jobs and are thus
more readily apprehended. Bribes at all stages, the traditional *mordida*
of Mexico, add to the costs, and strong-arm tactics or threats against
families ensure that fees and bribes are forthcoming and are not
delayed. The smuggling of children, secretly held in Los Angeles on one
occasion, led to extortionate demands for additional fees before the
illegal alien parents could obtain their release. If not a slave trade, the
smuggling of undocumented aliens comes very close to it. The smuggling rings are highly organized, often involved in other aspects of vice
along the Border. Their tentacles often reach deep into Latin America

and, on occasion, even to South-east Asia (US Congress, House 1978a, 9). They exploit the illegal alien, offer no safeguard, and treat him extortionately and often inhumanely into the bargain. The alternative of crossing alone or informally carries greater risks of detection and, outside the towns, of death by exhaustion or famine in the desert wilderness (Samora 1971, 76).

In a sample of 919 undocumented workers, Cornelius (1977, 6) found that almost two-thirds had entered the US by swimming the Rio Grande, 27 per cent by wire-jumping in California, and 7 per cent on foot across the deserts; only 5 per cent had been 'visa-abusers'. About one-third had used the services of professional smugglers, and approximately the same number had never been apprehended by the INS, though they had entered the US on several occasions. Samora's figures (1971, 87) suggest that among 493 apprehended, 53 per cent were for the first time, 21 per cent for a second, 10 per cent for a third, and the remainder more frequently. The risk of apprehension decreases substantially with each successive illegal re-entry. Of those who are caught and then accept 'voluntary departure' to Mexico about one-third attempt re-entry within a few days and they are often successful.

Most aliens smuggled into West Texas, and they contain a high proportion with urban experience, head for Chicago with its large community of undocumented Mexicans; others work in the grain belt of the Middle West. Through the lower Rio Grande the Atlantic seaboard is often the preferred destination (Selzer 1979, 8), and in this sector there is a higher proportion of poorer peasants among the intruders. Increasingly, the trend is for smuggled aliens to seek work in city industry (53 per cent) rather than on farms or ranches (31 per cent).

The US immigration authorities have been accused (Saunders and Leonard 1951, 82) of 'allowing enough [undocumented labour] in to permit work to be done rapidly and cheaply, but sending out enough to prevent overcrowding'. This 'balance-wheel' function of the Border Patrol in particular is reflected in the alternation of severe policing of the Border, large-scale apprehensions and deportations or voluntary departures, with periods in which the urgent demands for immigrant labour in the US have led to a more routine observing of immigration policies. More recently, the rise of unemployment in the late 1970s in the US ushered in a more rigorous appraisal of the role in it of un-documented aliens, though there is no proof of a causal connection between the two (Bustamante 1977, 149). The peak deportations of the early 1930s, 1954 (Operation Wetback) and 1976 stand out, and the sophistication of the departure system has developed considerably. There are two detention centres in Texas (Samora 1971, 5), where 100–300 aliens per diem are processed to check for felonies or depor-tation. If 'voluntary departure' is accepted by the alien he is expelled within two days, usually taken by bus to the frontier and thence, by contract with Mexican bus operators, to his declared home. In 1976 the so-called 'champagne flights' on commercial airlines (Bustamante 1977, 163) were briefly brought in to repatriate Mexicans living south of a line from Mazatlán to Tampico. This deliberate distancing of the expelled alien, at considerable cost, was designed to make re-entry more difficult. In practice it was open to abuse: many claimed residence in the Mexican Border towns, for easier re-entry, others bribed the bus driver to permit them to leave long before arriving home, or even to allow them to return by the same bus. Such 'directed' movement within Mexico, at the behest of a foreign power, offends directly against the provisions of the Mexican Constitution which guarantees the freedom of citizens to migrate without let or hindrance (Mumme 1978, 73). At the same time, it is an offence for a Mexican national to take work abroad without authorization of the Ministry of the Interior (ch. 2, Art. III, Mexican General Law on Population, 1973) though this provision is rarely enforced.

REASONS FOR MIGRATION

Research evidence suggests that the motivation behind migration to the US is complex and in some respects conflicting. A balance between sets of push and pull factors tips in favour of a decision to go or stay. At the level of the individual there is a natural desire to improve living standards, incomes, and obtain better health, prestige and security (Arroyo-Alejandre 1979, 204). Given that many would-be migrants have very imperfect knowledge of opportunities in the US and probably hear exaggerated tales about prospects, decisions on migration may not be well founded. In the mass the countless individual decisions are merged, to be set within the economic, social, and political context of differentials between the two countries. The reasons for movement in the mass are then hypothesized from the analysis and interrelationship of push–pull factors. In this sense the interpretation differs little in principle from analysis of internal Mexican migrations (Downing 1979), though the gradients of living standards and prospects are steeper in the direction of the US, and the international boundary is a clear but variable impediment to an otherwise unified bi-national labour market.

There is general agreement among researchers on the primacy of economic motives for migration, whether these are loaded more heavily on the push or the pull sides of the equation (Blejer *et al.* 1977, 335; Jenkins 1977, 179). Indeed, some econometric models (Greenwood and Ladman 1977) evaluate migration levels as a calculated reaction to changes in the economic character of areas of origin and destination.

Such an interpretation seems to discount the effects of the international boundary, which nevertheless remains a variously impermeable membrane. Perhaps not surprisingly, it was an American economist (Briggs 1975a,b) who laid particular stress on the pull variables: the economic gradient, the strong labour demand, cultural affinities (in the American South-west), lax immigration policies, and the lure of the 'promised land'. By comparison, he found the push variables less determining: 'safety-valve' for surplus population, need for foreign exchange, existence of unemployment and poverty. Support for pull factors has also come from Lillydahl and Balli-González (1979), with the finding, from a sophisticated econometric model, that opportunity for employment in the US was the most important variable in the migration equation. Jenkins (1977, 183 *et seq.*), on the other hand, from a regression analysis of those taking farm jobs initially, found that few pull variables worked as predicted, whereas all push variables worked in favour of movement, for both legal and illegal migrants. Evidently, complex interrelationships between push and pull factors are involved, and these are likely to be differently interpreted by legal and illegal migrants. If effective bilateral policies on migration are to be worked out and applied with international harmony, it is important to determine how far action within Mexico is an essential priority for success.

The attraction of the US labour market cannot be denied. It is possible to earn more in one to three months there than in one year in Mexico (US Congress, House 1977, 18; Cornelius 1977, 6). Alba-Hernández (1976, 174) found that about one-half of his sample 821 legal migrants to the US gave the prospect of work and a better salary, with improved living conditions, as the reason underlying the decision to migrate. Samora (1971) and Jenkins (1977, 180) confirm the importance of the lure of work, better paid and more steady employment. Though Jenkins (p. 186) found that fluctuations in wage-levels in US agriculture were not reflected commensurately by changes in migrant flows, least of all for illegals, this conclusion was confounded in an econometric analysis by Frisbie (1975, 11). Cornelius (1977, 3) recorded that three-quarters of his sample of 919 illegal migrants cited the need to increase earnings as their principal motivation; only 7 per cent mentioned lack of work at home. Furthermore, when asked why the US was preferred to Mexico City, as a destination, higher wages were given as the reason. This was also true for those who had not yet migrated to the US but intended to do so. In 1977 (*Inter-Am. Econ. Affairs*, 1977, 96) it was estimated that rather more than half the illegal aliens in US employment received between $2.50 and $4.49 an hour, with an additional 10 per cent getting more. The effects of the 1976 devaluation of the peso had increased the income benefits of migration, initially by 50 per cent. From such evidence it is argued that even if conditions in

Mexico were to improve dramatically, the lure of the US labour market would still polarize migrant flows.

On balance, however, the weight of recent research stresses the push elements of conditions in Mexico: 'Migration is the failure of roots' (Galarza 1964, 17). Cornelius (1977) admitted the strength of push elements: unemployment and underemployment at 30 per cent or more in rural areas, the lack not only of jobs but of well-paid jobs; the environmental hazards of small-scale farming; an excess of population and its continuing rapid growth. Frisbie (1975) stressed the predominance of push factors in illegal migration of farmworkers. Changes in Mexican farm wages, agricultural productivity, and commodity prices were inversely correlated with the rate of illegal movements across the Border. Demographic pressures and structural changes in agriculture are widely judged responsible for mass movements off the land towards Mexico City or the Border. Greenwood and Ladman (1977, 157), rather surprisingly, found no significant correlation between migration and unemployment at the place left by the migrant. Yet Bustamante (1977, 160) reported that 79 per cent of a sample of 919 undocumented workers had been without a job at the time they left Jalisco in Mexico. Unikel et al. (1973, 47) found population growth and increased farm productivity to be the major explanatory variables in such migration, with a high outward movement even from areas of the most modern agriculture. Although demographic pressures were greater on the communal farms or *ejidos* there was, anomalously, less migration from thence: less integration into market economy, physical isolation, lack of contacts generally. Jenkins (1977, 184–6) confirmed these findings, stressing that the exodus was not due to a scarcity of land for farming, so often alleged, but to structural changes in agriculture, creating a landless proletariat and a decline in the rate of growth of *ejidos*. Arroyo-Alejandre (1979) pointed to the problems of *minifundia* and the capital reorganization of farming as the major reasons for destabilizing the rural population. Alba-Hernández (1976, 1978) widened the argument by citing the uprooting and ferment of mobility also among semi-skilled workers in the towns, as the result of modernization in production and consequent economies of labour. As he put it (p. 472) 'The strategy of modernization followed by Mexico since World War II uprooted a large proportion of the population and separated them from traditional means of satisfying necessities, without providing institutional mechanisms to guarantee minimum economic security.' The real guilty parties behind the alien tide then include the rate of economic growth and accompanying inflation in Mexico, the economy of labour by commercialization of farming, concentration in industry, influence on rapid population growth, but without a commensurate increase in jobs, least of all in those which might be taken by a largely unskilled labour force.

THE IMPACT OF MIGRATION

Reference has already been made to the colouring of attitudes, for good or ill, especially those concerning illegal (undocumented) immigrants to the US, and the diverse, often conflicting research evidence which may be adduced for or against a particular opinion. The impact of the migrants is both structural, upon economy and society, and spatial in its incidence. Effects are to be felt in both the dispatching and receiving countries and the impact is in some respects at its most severe in the Border region. North and LeBel (1978, 3) suggest three options to describe the Border impact: an economic gain for employers through cheap labour; enhanced unemployment among those with whom immigrants compete; or a negative impact on wages and working conditions.

Briggs (1975a,b,c; 1978a,b) accentuated the ill-effects of illegal entries. The US labour force is disrupted, by a 'shadow labour force' which is felt but seldom seen; wages are depressed and citizens must either work and live as the illegals do, or leave the job or the area. Illegals are exploited by employers, most notably in rural areas, and this has indirectly provoked the great urbanward movement of native *chicanos* since the 1940s. *Chicanos* remaining in the rural areas are often forced to join the long-distance seasonal harvesting drift northwards (Weigand 1977; also Stoddard 1978, 19) because the Border labour market is overrun by illegals. Unionization at the work-place is impeded by the employers' use of the immigrants in strike-breaking, or exploitation of the docile, vulnerable illegal labour. In the towns the *barrios* are overcrowded and the illegal competes even more stridently with the *chicano* there, not only for jobs but also for low-cost housing, welfare, school places, or public health facilities. In support of his case Briggs (1976, 122) refers specifically to the impact on South Texas: unemployment rates consistently higher than the State or national levels; the two poorest national metropolitan areas (SMSAs) in per capita income; widespread minimum federal wages paid; poorest counties in Texas; drop-out rates from school high; unions largely absent; food stamps and welfare payments high. In other words, 'Poor Mexicans make poor *chicanos* poorer.'

Cornelius (1977) deploys the counter-arguments, disputing at the outset that because unemployment in the US is high there must be a causal connection with the level of immigration. He further contends that the jobs taken by illegals involve 'dirty, physically punishing tasks, low wages, long hours, generally poor working conditions, low job security and little chance of advancement' (p. 9). Even in the urban sector Cornelius found no evidence of serious job displacement of Americans by illegal aliens. Illegals were usually an addition to the secondary labour market, in jobs that Mexican-Americans and blacks habitually shunned (Cárdenas 1976). Where illegals have been deported from such jobs in the Border areas these have been taken by commuters (legal short-term immigrants) from Mexico rather than by local US residents (Villalpando *et al.* 1977). Also on the positive side, Cornelius (p. 12) estabished that Mexican illegals made 'amazingly little use of social welfare services, and that the cost of the services they do use is far outweighed by their contributions to social security and taxes'. Stoddard (1978, 17) adds that 40 per cent (60 to 70 per cent, Cornelius 1977, 15) of the earnings of the illegal alien is spent in the US, while his hard work for low wages indirectly subsidizes the American consumer.

In a sample of illegal aliens, Cornelius (1977) found the following: 919 in total, of whom 509 had a job before apprehension (85 per cent paid by cheque); of those paid by cheque (433): 74 per cent had had tax deductions and 66 per cent social security deductions; of the 919: only 1 per cent had had children in school, 3 per cent had claimed welfare, and 7 per cent medical care (reported in US Congress, House 1978a, 109).

The beneficial effect of immigrant remittances to Mexico has been an under-researched theme. Gamio (1930) established the volume at that time (1919: 5 m pesos; 1927: 16.7 m pesos) and how it fluctuated with the seasonal migration patterns. Cornelius (1977, 14) estimated total remittances from immigrants at more than US $3 billions per annum, considerably more important in total to Mexico than the income from tourism. Income from US employment is crucial for the support of the immigrant's family (an average of four dependants) in Mexico and, on his return home, for establishment and progress in his community. Alternatively put, the volume of remittances equalled one-tenth of the 1977 Mexican Federal budget or twice the Mexican trade deficit with the USA. Money remitted to the rural areas is particularly beneficial, though admittedly it makes only a small contribution to a more equal distribution of wealth in Mexico (Lillydahl and Gassler 1979, 102). It is doubtful it the process of illegal migration really provides a significant escape valve for Mexico's burgeoning surplus population, though it doubtless offers relief at the margin.

Summing up the profit-and-loss account for the two countries, Samora (1971, 4) claimed: for the USA—cheap labour, spending by aliens (including taxes contributed), employment of officials; losses by the USA—costs of administering control measures, impacts on the labour market and on public welfare spending; for Mexico—relief of unemployment, remittances; losses by Mexico—people uprooted and displaced, Mexican Border cities overrun, with vast social costs, education and training of migrants lost to the home country.

POLICY MEASURES AND THEIR EFFECTIVENESS

Given the wide differences of view on the nature of the problem of illegal immigration, its motivations, and the differential impact on origins and destinations, it is not surprising that policies formulated and solutions proposed are no less varied, even contradictory. In the first place, different cultural values are involved on either side of the Border. As Max Weber put it, rationality is culturally bounded when it refers to substantive issues affecting a culture, and mass migration is surely one such issue (Bustamante 1977, 171). Thus US and Mexican perspectiveness are likely to have different starting-points and contexts, different priorities and perceptions of the problem. Not only that but, within the US at least, there are varied interests and pressure groups capable of influencing decision-takers and the course of political policies. It is thus no surprise to find that American policy on illegal migration and what should be done about it has always presented a disjointed amalgam of strong economic interests compounded by benign neglect on the part of political leaders. This is inevitably a prescription for prejudiced action, fuelled by a deliberate undermining of any policy which might offend powerful sectional interests. During the 1970s the onset of economic depression sharpened the will for protective measures by the US, though issues of human rights constantly intruded to mitigate the severity of unilateral action. The disagreement is rather about which basic rights should have precedence over which other basic rights (Teitelbaum 1980). Bustamante (1972, 715) pilloried the innate contradictions in US policy on illegal immigrants: condemned as deviants, and yet eagerly sought as labour; penalized for their status, but the employer escapes scot-free; surveillance by enforcement agency, but only according to the needs and dictates of the labour market.

The Mexican government, on the other hand, has been reluctant to place the migration issue in the forefront of national policies, perhaps in case such prominence should be taken as a sign of national failure. Nevertheless, the treatment of Mexican citizens in the US has become a burning emotional issue which has forced its way into the national conscience (Mumme 1978). It has, furthermore, become a bargaining tool in the complex set of contemporary US–Mexican relationships. Indeed, the way in which illegal migration has been conceptualized has governed the solutions and policies which have been advanced (Stoddard 1978, 24).

The ambivalence at the heart of present US policies is well illustrated by the difference of view between Briggs (1975a,b, 1978a,b) and Marshall (1978), on the one hand, and Cornelius (1977) on the other. Briggs represents a line of argument with interdiction and protection in the ascendant. A fuller certification of immigrant workers is required, to which Marshall would add the need for a counterfeit-proof identity card and a policy of gearing legal immigration closely to the changing needs of the labour market; the immunity of employers from prosecution for knowingly taking in illegal workers should be ended; the INS should have more help and the inflow of illegals thus better contained; and there should not be an amnesty for illegal aliens already in the USA (Marshall favoured a partial amnesty). It is true that Briggs also counselled 'special impact' funds for the relief of certain regions and cities with a large immigrant population and he also laid stress on the need to aid development of Mexico and its northern Border region in particular.

Quite to the contrary, Cornelius felt that there should be a moratorium on fresh unilateral attempts by the US to restrict immigration. This would but treat the symptoms and not the disease; moreover, the 'social unrest caused by massive deportations could do more damage to US security than aliens do to the US economy'. In any case, additional restrictive measures would probably be minimally effective, since the attraction of work in the US would continue to persuade the Mexican that the risk of apprehension was less than the certainty of unemployment or underemployment and continuing low living-standards by remaining at home. Cornelius favoured increasing the legal quota for Mexican immigrants and introducing a six-month temporary worker visa which, unlike the former *bracero* programme, would not bind a worker to a particular employer. He favoured an amnesty for illegals in the US since 1972, but also saw that the Mexican government should be encouraged to decentralize family planning, and provide for small-scale, labour-intensive rural industries as a most cost-effective action to help stabilize the ferment among the rural population.

On 4 August 1977, President Carter put forward to Congress specific proposals, a mixture of both 'carrot and stick'. First, there was to be a doubling of the Border Patrol for more effective law enforcement, a measure which some critics have regarded as likely to increase violence on the Border (Vellano in US Congress, House 1978a, 357) and to risk massive resultant damage to human rights. The argument by Grayson (1977) that 'closing the Border escape valve will force the Mexican government to confront difficult questions about Mexican economic development' may amount to no more than dangerously wishful thinking. A second provision was for fines on employers knowingly using illegal aliens. This has been one of the most intractable issues for a long time. Nine States, including California, have already enacted such legislation, but the provisos are either largely ignored or applied only with laxity. Texan legislators have resolutely rejected such proposals. As far back as 1952 (US Congress 1952, 8 USC, section 1324) Texas introduced an amendment to federal legislation on 'concealing, harbouring or shielding [illegal immigrants]' by causing to be added 'provided, however, that for the purposes of this section employment . . . shall not be deemed to constitute harbouring'. More recently, the proposed Texas Bill HB 816 to penalize employers of illegal aliens was decisively rejected, even though it intended exemptions for the majority, farmers or ranchers, and those hiring domestic servants. The concept of penalizing employers has also been strongly resisted by *chicanos*, fearing that they in turn would be affected, since employers would not take risks on the identity of genuine Mexican-Americans. It has also been said (*Comercio Exterior* 1978) that such penalties ignore the fact that there is a high continuing demand for undocumented labour and the concept is founded on the false assumption already mentioned, that US workers are displaced by the illegals.

Proposals for the legalization of status for illegal immigrants take the form of a conditional and limited amnesty. Permanent residential status would be conferred on those living continuously in the US since 1970. This might cover 500–700,000, though some would have difficulty proving continued residence. Temporary resident alien status would be available for those entering 1970 to 1 January 1977. They would be allowed five years' residence if they could prove date of entry, would not be allowed to bring in dependants, nor be entitled to social services, though ironically they would be paying contributions and taxes. Perhaps 2–3½ millions would come under this provision. Those entering illegally since 1 January 1977 would be subject to immediate deportation and further illegal immigration would be restrained. Some claim that millions would be unable to prove that they were not in the deportable category and would fear to come forward on that account. *Chicanos* opposed these new status proposals, believing that temporary resident status would create a new class of sub-citizen while many others would remain 'underground' rather than take the risks of being deported. Early evidence (US Congress, House 1978c, 778) suggested, ironically, that the prospective amnesty provisions might indeed attract more illegal immigrations to the US. A Border Patrol spokesman at Laredo commented 'A lot of the ones we're catching tell us they came in because they heard of the amnesty and figured they had to get here to take advantage of it.'

The Carter proposals contained statements of general intent to provide aid to countries sending undocumented aliens, but it has been argued that the social and economic pressures on Mexico might be dramatically increased thereby. In Mexico the Carter plan was seen as a yielding to internal US political pressures rather than a considered response to the facts of the situation (Bustamante 1978b, 525). In spite of the US government's assertion that Mexico agreed with the policy, the government of that country maintained a strongly negative attitude, while the mass of the Mexican urban population continued largely ignorant of the problem. Alternative Mexican proposals included a weak and almost covert suggestion for a new *bracero* programme, to help relieve rural unemployment (US Congress, House 1978a, 359 *et seq.*). Such new *braceros* would have wages and living conditions below the average and would not be bound to particular employers, a weakness in the 1942–64 scheme. A new contract labour scheme was opposed by all US labour interests, not least because the Mexican worker would be both exploited by the employer and yet abused by those with whom he was possibly competing. Furthermore, a new *bracero* programme would become an inducement to migration, provoke an oversupply of labour and institutionalize an underclass (US Congress, House 1978a, 154).

During 1978, the Committee on the Judiciary (US Congress, House 1978b) recommended a package including stronger enforcement measures against undocumented immigrants, economic disincentives (penalties for employers, temporary worker documentation) and, on the positive side, co-operation with Mexico. Such co-operation would be long-term, both in direct financing and also through incentives for investment in agriculture and labour-intensive industry. Translating such an intended bi-national programme into a strategy for action meets immediate difficulties, not the least of which is the sensitivity of the Mexican government to aid which smacks of dependency for Mexico, and to which political strings might be thought to be attached. The priorities for such aid come up against competing objectives: promoting national economic growth in Mexico indicates traditional investment in manufacturing or commercial agriculture and in infrastructure; contributing to a reduction of out-migration from Mexico indicates priority for disseminated rural investment, in small-scale labour-intensive activities. During the early 1970s the World Bank aided the Mexican government in promoting an integrated rural development programme, to bring more of the poor into the market economy, expand agricultural output beyond subsistence, improve income distribution, and encourage greater social stability (US Congress, House 1977, 30 *et seq.*). Rain-fed agriculture, typical of many of the dry Border tracts of northern Mexico, and industrialization in rural areas would both prove intractable problems in any development programme. There is some considerable doubt if these rural programmes will seriously contribute to a solution of the illegal immigration question (R. Dungan in US Congress, House 1977, 39).

Bustamante (1976 in US Congress, House 1978a, 362 *et seq.*) proposed a more practical attempt to reduce rural out-migration. Labour-intensive 'units of production' for processing farm produce, would be established in areas from which migrants are traditionally coming. These units would be privately owned and would give preference in jobs to those rural dwellers with no record of apprehension in the US. Financing would be by the Mexican government and the products would be bought by the US for its foreign aid programme. There would thus be no competition with the American farmer and US labour interests should welcome such redirection of undocumented workers to more stable jobs in Mexico. The proposals have been criticized: even the international agencies involved would be tied to the US State Department; by requiring workers to show a clean bill of health the INS would have a voice in interior Mexico; being locked into US foreign aid programmes would identify Mexico with US foreign policy; instead of the more desirable amnesty, a modulated but enforced repatriation of undocumented workers would take place.

Ultimate easement of the undocumented alien problem, or dilemma as it has been called (Briggs 1978a, 222) will certainly need to involve bi-national, probably even international action. Reduction of the gap in economic opportunity between the US and Mexico must be an ultimate but long-term objective. For the moment there is a bilateral impasse as each national system produces different sets of perceptions and responses (Mumme 1978, 68), with a very disordered and unprogressive outcome. In a practical sense, groups and organizations should be brought together, in the short-term, on a local and regional basis on both sides of the Border, to analyse the situation and prepare co-operative action programmes. Agricultural employment in the Borderlands is likely to be only a short-term palliative, since large-scale organization and concentration of land ownership had already produced a landless proletariat in both countries, thus adding to the migrant streams and aggravating the illegal alien problem. Unless an effective set of proposals is defined and implemented, the situation is likely to become rapidly worse. Bustamante (1978b) forecast that the harder US line on undocumented workers in the late 1970s would lead to a massive, enforced ebb-tide of migrants to Mexico, with many ending up in the already congested Border cities just south of the Rio Grande. This southward flow of returned undocumented workers would encounter the strong, continuing, northward flow of would-be immigrants to the US, to produce an explosive situation. The increasing social disorder thus provoked might well strengthen the hand of authoritarian elements in the army and government of Mexico. Such an outcome would not be contained south of the Rio Grande but spill over on to the US side, further embittering US–Mexican relations. The scale and urgency of the problem cannot be denied. As Briggs (1978a, 222) put it:

> unless coupled with a massive foreign aid programme by the US . . . hundreds of
> thousands are going to suffer, no matter what is done or not done. Without such
> assistance, the steps proposed that call for more restrictive Border policies mean that
> many of the would-be illegal Mexican aliens are condemned to lives of squalor. On the
> other hand, if the prevailing situation is allowed to continue, thousands of [US] citizen
> workers, mostly *chicanos* at present, will continue to work under deteriorating conditions
> in a generally surplus labour market.

Among the many problems focussed at the Border, the transit of
illegal aliens, and their impact on economy and society in the towns on
either bank of the Rio Grande, is the most serious in its magnitude and
implications. The international boundary interrupts a bi-national, contiguous labour market. Though it may be argued that the flow of human
beings between two countries should be as natural and unimpeded as
the flow of capital, this is to ignore the power of cultural differences,
sense of heritage and complex self-interest which motivate political
forces. These forces in the US currently influence the role of the international boundary in the direction of closure, or at the least more
deliberate restriction of movement even for those masses seeking a
better life under conditions of human dignity. In a poll in 1980, 91 per
cent of Americans responding wanted an all-out effort to stop illegal
entries into the US (Teitelbaum 1980, 21). In all this surely too the
undocumented workers themselves have a right to be heard, unless the
'silent exodus' is to continue as a mute witness to inhuman market
forces and the chauvinistic or uncaring attitudes of two contending
governments.

REFERENCES

ALBA-HERNÁNDEZ, F. (1976) 'Exodo silenciosco: la emigración de trabajadores
   mexicanos a Estados Unidos', *Foro Internacional*, **XVII**, 2 (66), 152–79.
ALBA-HERNÁNDEZ, F. (1978) 'Industrialización sustitutiva y migración internacional:
   el caso de México', *Foro Internacional*, **XVIII**, 3 (71), 464–79.
ÁLVAREZ, J. H. (1967) 'Perfil demográfico de la inmigración a los Estados Unidos
   1910–50', *Demografía y Economía*, **I**, 1, 18–39.
ARROYO-ALEJANDRE, J. (1979) 'Synthesis of some relevant ideas on Mexican migration
   to the US: a research proposal', ch. 14 in B. W. Poulson and T. N. Osborn (eds.)
   US-Mexico economic relations (Boulder, Col.: Westview Press), 201–13.
BLEJER, M. I., JOHNSON, H. G. and PORZECANSKI, A. C. (1977) 'Un análisis de los
   determinantes económicos de la migración mexicana legal e ilegal hacia los
   Estados Unidos' *Demografía y Economía*, **XI**, 33, 326–39.
BRIGGS, V. M. (1974) 'The Mexico–US Border: public policy and chicano welfare',
   Stud. in Human Resource Dev., **2**, Bur. Busin. Res. (Austin, Univ. Texas).
BRIGGS, V. M. (1975a) 'Mexican migration and the US labor market: a mounting issue
   of the seventies', *Stud. in Human Resource Dev.*, **3**, Bur. Busin. Res. (Austin, Univ.
   Texas).

Briggs, V. M. (1975b) 'Mexican workers in the US labor market. A contemporary dilemma', *Int. Labor Rev.*, **112,** 5, 351–68.

Briggs, V. M. (1975c) 'Illegal aliens: the need for more restrictive Border policy', *Soc. Sci. Q.*, **56,** 3, 477–84.

Briggs, V. M. (1976) 'Illegal immigration and the American labor force: the use of 'soft' data for analysis', *Am. Behavioral Scentist,* **19,** 3, 351–63. Reprinted as ch. 6 in W. B. Littrell and G. Sjoberg (eds.) *Current issues in social policy* (Beverly Hills, Sage Publications), 113–25.

Briggs, V. M. (1978a) 'Labor market aspects of Mexican migration to the United States in the 1970s', ch. 10 in S. R. Ross (ed.) *Views across the Border* (Albuquerque: Univ. New Mexico Press), 204–21.

Briggs, V. M. (1978b) 'La confrontación del chicano con el inmigrante mexicano', *Foro Internacional,* **XVIII,** 3 (71), 514–21.

Bustamante, J. A. (1971) ' "Don Chano". Autobiografía de un emigrante mexicano', *Revta mex. Sociol.*, **XXXIII,** 2, 333–74.

Bustamante, J. A. (1972) 'The "Wetback" as deviant: an application of labeling theory', *Am. J. Sociol.*, **77,** 4, 706–18.

Bustamante, J. A. (1973) 'El espalda mojada: informe de un observador participante', *Revta mex. cienc. política,* **71,** Jan.–Mar., 81–107.

Bustamante, J. A. (1975) 'Espaldas mojadas: materia prima para la expansión del capital norteamericano', *Cuad. Cent. Estud. Sociológicos,* **9,** México D.F., El Colegio de México. Reprinted in P. Monbeig 'Les migrations au Mexique', *Cah. Am. Latines,* **12,** 2, 275–314.

Bustamante, J. A. (1976a) *More on the impact of the undocumented immigration from Mexico on the US-Mexico economies: preliminary findings and suggestions for bi-lateral cooperation.* Paper presented to the 46th Annual Conference of the Southern Economic Association, Atlanta, Georgia, 17–19 Nov. 1976.

Bustamante, J. A. (1976b) 'Structural and ideological conditions of undocumented Mexican immigration to the United States', ch. 8 in W. B. Littrell and G. Sjoberg (eds.) *Current issues in social policy* (Beverly Hills: Sage Publications), 145–57.

Bustamante, J. A. (1977) 'Undocumented immigration from Mexico: research report', *Int. Migration Rev.*, **11,** 2, 149–77.

Bustamante, J. A. (1978a) 'Commodity migrants: structural analysis of Mexican immigration to the United States', ch. 9 in S. R. Ross (ed.) *Views across the Border* (Albuquerque: Univ. New Mexico Press), 183–203.

Bustamante, J. A. (1978b) 'Las propuestas de política migratoria en los Estados Unidos y sus repercusiones en México', *Foro Internacional,* **XVIII,** 3 (71), 522–30.

Bustamante, J. A. (1979) 'Facts and perceptions of undocumented migration from Mexico', ch. 11 in B. W. Poulson and T. N. Osborn (eds.) *US-Mexico economic relations* (Boulder, Col.: Westview Press), 171–82.

Camara, F. (1979) 'Differential migration streams, economic growth and socio-cultural changes in Mexican Border cities', ch. 6 in F. Camara and R. van Kemper, (eds.) *Migration across frontiers: Mexico and the US, Inst. Mesoamer. Stud.* III (Albany: State Univ. New York), 101–26.

Cárdenas, G. (1976) 'Public data on Mexican immigration into the United States: a critical evaluation', ch. 7 in W. B. Littrell and G. Sjoberg (eds.) *Current issues in social policy* (Beverly Hills: Sage Publications), 127–44.

Comercio Exterior (1974) 'Braceros: la corriente alterna', *Comercio Exterior,* **XXIV,** 11, 1127–9.

Comercio Exterior (1978) 'Los ilegales mexicanos, legado de la historia y presión de la economía, *Comercio Exterior,* **XXVIII,** 7, 798–805.

Comisión Intersecretarial para el Estudio de los Problemas de la Corriente

MIGRATORIA DE TRABAJADORES MEXICANOS A LOS ESTADOS UNIDOS (1972) *Informes de la encuesta* (Mexico, DF: Secretaría de Relaciones Exteriores).

CORNELIUS, W. A. (1977) *Illegal Mexican migration to the United States: a summary of research findings and policy implications*, Monograph Ser. on Migration and Dev., Center of International Stud., M.I.T., Cambridge, Mass.

CORWIN, A. F. (1973) 'Causes of Mexican emigration to the United States: a summary view', *Perspect. Am. Hist.*, **7**, 557–635.

DILLMAN, C. D. (1970) 'Commuter workers and free-zone industry along the Mexican-US border', *Proc. Ass. Am. Geogr.*, **2**, 48–51.

DILLMAN, E. G. and GIFFORD, A. S. (1971a) 'The non-resident commuter: arguments for', *El Paso econ. Rev.*, **VIII**, 5.

DILLMAN, E. G. and GIFFORD, A. S. (1971b) 'The Green Card commuter: arguments against', *El Paso econ. Rev.*, **VIII**, 4.

DOWNING, T. E. (1979) 'Explaining migration in Mexico and elsewhere', ch. 10 in F. Camara and R. van Kemper (eds.) *Migration across frontiers: Mexico and the US, Inst. Mesoamerican Stud.*, III, Albany, State Univ., New York, 159–67.

ERICSON, A. S. (1970) 'The impact of commuters on the Mexican-American border area'. *Monthly Labor Rev.*, **93**, 18–27.

FOGEL, W. A. (1975) 'Immigrant Mexicans and the US work force', *Mon. Labor Rev.*, **98**, 5, 44–6.

FRISBIE, P. (1975) 'Illegal migration from Mexico to the United States: a longitudinal analysis', *Int. Migration Rev.*, **9**, 1, 3–13.

GALARZA, E. (1964) *Merchants of labor: the Mexican Bracero story* (Charlotte, N.C. and Santa Barbara, Cal.: McNally & Loflin).

GAMIO, M. (1930) *Mexican immigration to the United States* (Chicago: Univ. Chicago Press).

GARCÍA, G. M. (1979) *La encuesta nacional de emigración a la frontera norte del país y a los Estados Unidos: descripción del proyecto y hallazgos de la segunda etapa (Agosto 1978)*, (México DF: Secretaría del Trabajo y Previsión Social, Centro Nacional de Información y Estadísticas).

GRAYSON, G. W. (1977–8) 'Mexico's opportunity: the oil boom', *Foreign Policy*, **29**, 65–89.

GREBLER, L., NEWMAN, P., and WYSE, R. (1966) 'Mexican immigration to the United States: the record and its implications', *Advance Rep. 2, Mexican-American Study Project, Division of Research, Graduate School of Business Administration, Univ. California Los Angeles.*

GREENWOOD, M. J. AND LADMAN, J. R. (1977) 'Economía de la movilidad geográfica de la mano de obra en México', *Demografía y Economía*, **XI**, 32, 155–66.

HANCOCK, R. H. (1959) *The role of the bracero in the economic and culture dynamics of Mexico: a case study of Chihuahua* (Stanford, Conn.: Hispanic Am. Soc.).

HOUSE, J. W. (1980) 'The frontier zone: a conceptual problem for policy-makers', *Int. Pol. Sci. Rev.*, **1**, 4, 456–77.

INNER CITY FUND, INC. (1975) *Report of preliminary findings to the INS*, 4 Dec. *Inter Am. Econ. Affairs* (1977) 'government documents: data on the illegal aliens problem', **31**, 1, 95–6.

JENKINS, J. C. (1977) 'Push/pull in recent migration to the U.S.', *Int. Migration Rev.*, **11**, 2, 178–89.

LAWTON, R. (1977) 'People and work', ch. 2 in J. W. House (ed.) *The UK space: resources, environment and the future* (London: Weidenfeld & Nicolson), 146–51.

LESKO ASSOCIATES (1975) *Final report. Basic data and guidance required to implement a major illegal alien study during fiscal year 1976*, in partial fulfilment of Contract no. CO-16-75.

LILLYDAHL, J. and BALLI-GONZÁLEZ, F. (1979) 'A macro-model of Mexican migration to the US', ch. 12 in B. W. Poulson and T. N. Osborn (eds.) *US-Mexico economic relations* (Boulder, Col.: Westview Press), 183–91.

LILLYDAHL, J. H. and GASSLER, R. S. (1979) 'A theoretical model of remittances sent to Mexico', ch. 7 in B. W. Poulson and T. N. Osborn (eds.) *US-Mexico economic relations* (Boulder, Col.: Westview Press), 89–104.

Los Angeles Times, 27 April 1970

MARSHALL, F. R. (1978) 'Economic factors influencing the international migration of workers', ch. 8 in S. R. Ross (ed.) *Views across the Border* (Albuquerque: Univ. New Mexico Press), 163–82.

MARTINEZ, V. S. (1976) 'Illegal immigration and the labor force: a historical and legal view', ch. 5 in W. B. Littrell and G. Sjoberg (eds.) *Current issues in social policy* (Beverly Hills: Sage Pubs.), 97–112.

MUMME, S. P. (1978) 'Mexican politics and the prospects for emigration policy: a policy perspective', *Inter-Am. econ. Affairs*, **32**, 1, 67–94.

NELSON, E. (1972) *The bracero* (Berkeley, Cal.: Thorp Springs Press).

NEWTON, J. R. and OSBORN, T. N. (1979) 'A profile of legal migration to the United States', ch. 18 in B. W. Poulson and T. N. Osborn (eds.) *US-Mexico economic relations* (Boulder, Col.: Westview Press), 261–72.

NORTH, D. S. (1970) *The border crossers: people who live in Mexico and work in the United States*, Washington DC, Trans-century Corporation. Reprinted in US Senate Hearings on Border Commuter Labor Problems, 91st Congress, 21 May 1969, 2194–2527 (Pt 5A).

NORTH, D. S. and HOUSTON, M. F. (1976) *The characteristics and role of illegal aliens in the US labor market*, unpubl. Research Rept., Employ. and Train. Admin., US Dept. Labor.

NORTH, D. S. and LEBEL, A. (1978) 'Manpower and immigration policies in the United States', *Special Rept. 20, National Commission for Manpower Policy*, Washington DC.

OJEDA, M., DEL VILLAR, S. I., and BUSTAMANTE, J. A. (1978) 'México-Estados Unidos: cuestiones clave', *Foro Internacional*, **XIX**, 2 (74), 303–25.

RANDALL, L. (1962) 'Labor migration and Mexican economic development', *Soc. econ. Stud.*, **11**, 1, 73–9.

ROSS, S. R. (ed.) (1978) *Views across the Border: the United States and Mexico*, (Albuquerque: Univ. New Mexico Press).

SAMORA, J. (1971) *Los mojados: the Wetback story* (Notre Dame, Ind.: Univ. Notre Dame Press).

SAUNDERS, L. and LEONARD, O. E. (1951) *The Wetback in the Lower Rio Grande valley of Texas*, Austin: Univ. Texas Press.

SCRUGGS, O. M. (1963) 'Texas and the Bracero Program, 1942–47', *Pacif. Hist. Rev.*, **XXXII**, 3, 251–64.

SELZER, W. H. (1979) 'Alien smuggling—an enterprising business', *INS Reporter*, **27**, 5, 5–9.

STODDARD, E. R. (1976) 'A conceptual analysis of the 'alien invasion': institutionalized support of illegal Mexican aliens in the U.S.', *Int. Migration Rev.*, **10**, 2, 157–85.

STODDARD, E. R. (1978) *Selected impacts of Mexican migration on the US-Mexico Border*. Paper presented to a State Department Select Panel on Border Problems, Washington DC.

STODDARD, E. R., MARTÍNEZ, O. J., and LASSO, M. A. M. (1979) *El Paso-C. Juárez relations and the 'Tortilla curtain'* (El Paso, Texas: El Paso Council on the Arts and Humanities).

TAYLOR, P. S. (1934) *An American-Mexican frontier. Nueces County, Texas* (New York, Russell & Russell).

TEITELBAUM, M. S. (1980) 'Right versus might: immigration and refugee policy in the

US', *Foreign Affairs*, **59**, 1, 21–59.

UNIKEL, L., RUÍZ CHIAPETTO, C., and LAZCANO, O. (1973) 'Factores de rechazo en la migración rural en México, 1950–1960', *Demografía y Economía*, **VII**, 1, 24–57.

US CONGRESS, HOUSE (1974) Committee on Government Operations *Immigration and Naturalization Service Regional Office operations, part 5*, Hearings before Subcomm. on Legal and Monetary Affairs, 93rd Congr. 2nd Sess., Washington DC, USGPO.

US CONGRESS, HOUSE (1977) Committee on Banking, Finance and Urban Affairs, *Development lending and illegal immigration*, Hearing before Subcomm. on International Development Institutions and Finance, 95th Congr. 1st Sess., Washington DC, USGPO.

US CONGRESS, HOUSE (1978a) Committee on Appropriations, *Departments of State, Justice and Commerce, the Judiciary and related agencies appropriations. Undocumented aliens*, Hearing before the Subcomm. on State, Justice, Commerce and the Judiciary Appropriations, 95th Congr., 2nd Sess., Washington DC, USGPO.

US CONGRESS, HOUSE (1978b) Committee on the Judiciary, *Illegal immigration and US-Mexican border control. Analysis and recommendations*, 95th Congr., 2nd Sess., Washington DC, USGPO.

US CONGRESS, HOUSE (1978c) Committee on Appropriations, *Depts. of State, Justice and Commerce, the Judiciary and related agencies, appropriations for 1979, part 8*, 95th Congr., 2nd Sess., Washington DC, USGPO.

US CONGRESS, JOINT ECONOMIC COMMITTEE (1977) *Recent developments in Mexico and their economic implications for the United States*, Hearings before the Subcomm. on Inter-American Economic Relationships, 95th Congr., 1st Sess., Washington DC, USGPO.

US CONGRESS, SENATE (1969) Committee on Labor and Public Welfare *Migrant and seasonal labor powerlessness, part 5-B, Border commuter labor problem*, Hearings before Subcomm. on Migratory Labor, 91st Congr., 1st & 2nd Sess., Washington DC, USGPO.

US DEPT. JUSTICE (1955) Immigration and Naturalization Service, *Annual Report*, Washington DC, USGPO.

US DEPT. JUSTICE (1980) Immigration and Naturalization Service, *1977 Annual Report*, Washington DC, USGPO.

US DEPT. LABOR (1923) Commissioner General of Immigration *Annual Report*, Washington DC, USGPO.

VILLALPANDO, M. V. *et al.* (1977) *A study of the socioeconomic impact of illegal aliens on the County of San Diego* (San Diego, Cal.: Human Resources Agency).

Washington Post, 13 Nov. 1934

WEIGAND, K. (1977) 'Chicano-Wanderarbeiter in Südtexas', *Kieler Geogr. Schriften*, **47**.

CHAPTER 6

Illegal Transactions

A SMUGGLER'S PARADISE?

It has always been a smuggler's paradise. But now the illegal flow of people, drugs and contraband caches of everything from computer parts to *tequila*-tranquillized parrots has reached unprecedented volumes going in both directions. Efforts to control that flow have been increasingly feeble. The legal traffic in people and goods has turned it [the US–Mexican Border] into the world's busiest boundary, and it is unique for nowhere else on the globe do two nations, representing, in effect the so-called Third World and the First World, confront each other so abruptly and openly. A flood of Mexican aliens, heroin, *marijuana*, manufactured goods, plant and animal pests flow into the USA. A floodtide of smuggled consumer goods, arms and luxury items that are debilitating their nation's feeble economy and hurting its social stability, flows into Mexico.

Latin American Press Reports, April 1977.

In the short-run better enforcement will have to be done, but you simply cannot seal the Border. In the long-run, the US cannot afford to wall itself off from the poor people of the world.

RAY MARSHALL, Secretary of Labor, 1977.

These two quotations highlight the problem and pose the dilemma of US–Mexican economic relations across the Rio Grande. The problem is nowhere greater and the dilemma nowhere more acute than in the twin US–Mexican cities, the transit ports of entry, indissolubly locked together in the artificial conditions of the Border economy. Given the vastly different economies and cultures of the US and Mexico, the extreme inequalities in their degrees of development, and the different range and severity of their economic and social problems, it was inevitable that relations between them would be uniquely open to exploitation, and that it would be Mexico's role to be exploited. The dilemma is that while the United States should seek to keep open its Border to enable under-privileged Mexico to take advantage of complementary trade on favourable terms, the opportunities for illicit trading and exchange of all kinds—to benefit from the vast potential of the United States as supplier and market—necessarily requires appropriate, sophisticated, and growing measures of Border control by the US. Though illicit dealings are mostly northward across the Rio Grande there is also a not inconsiderable, though differently structured, southward flow in return.

The illegal transactions are collectively immense, most notably so in alien workers and in the drugs traffic, which are treated separately in this account. The southward flow of weapons is closely related to the needs of rural insurgents, drug plant growers and drug traffickers in Mexico, and is considered in that context. The flow of American clients to call-girls and prostitutes in the Mexican Border cities is lucrative enough and of such large scale as to influence significantly local municipal revenues. It merits separate condemnation within the broader social pathology of the Rio Grande.

This introductory view explores simply the variegation and change among smaller items of the Border smuggling economy. It is an illicit process very sensitive to shifts in demand. 'You ask your smuggler to get you a hairdryer, a stereo set, a Colt-45 automatic, an electric toothbrush or a new pair of shoes,' suggested one informant. This is the province of the small-scale smuggler, the *fayaquero*. Tariff walls against US consumer goods are high and there are many prohibitions on imports to protect 'infant' industries in Mexico. Many consumer goods enter Mexican Border towns daily as commuters or shoppers return over the Rio Grande bridges. Within this flood there operates the horde of small smugglers, hoping to escape detection or, if caught, to buy or bribe (*mordida*) their way out of trouble. The *contrabandistas* are larger-scale entrepreneurs, dealing in the regular supply of major consumer durables, or perhaps in machinery and components for which there is a long waiting-list in Mexico, or where prices may be double or more than the US equivalent. The 1965 American federal restrictions on liquor imports in their turn led to the 'Rum run', for getting *tequila* and rum into the USA (Demaris 1970, 108). A list of preferred items for smuggling northwards over the Rio Grande included: mercury, silver, watch movements, jewellery, pre-Columban artifacts, diamonds, bullion, pornography, and parrots (Demaris 1970, 112). Illegal aliens and drugs, of course, outstandingly held pride of place and were a specialized, highly organized volume traffic in each case.

The trade in parrots, from Central America, is a curious but profitable operation, with immense potential hazards for the US poultry industry. These parrots may carry Newcastle disease, communicable to domestic poultry. In 1972 one smuggled parrot cost poultry farmers in southern California twelve million chickens and turkeys, and it required $25 millions of government money to eradicate the disease. Yet the demand for parrots through pet shops continues unabated.

Pricing differentials on either side of the Border may change the structure of commodities being smuggled. In 1977 consignments of coffee appeared for the first time, moving into the USA. Two trailers from C. Juárez were seized at the Border checkpoint, containing 63 tonnes of coffee worth $295,000 in the US, but little more than half of that sum in Mexico.

Traffic in stolen US cars or lorries has long been a profitable, mobile, and easily transferable source of income for smugglers. Mexican law forbids its citizens, or Americans residing in Mexico, to drive a car registered in the US or bearing American licence plates. Mexican citizens are furthermore not permitted to own a US auto newer than four years old. Nevertheless, there is a ready market for illicit imports of stolen cars or lorries, with US pick-up trucks a widely preferred item. Indeed, in some of the more remote areas of the Big Bend country of the middle Rio Grande, the 'currency' demanded in exchange for Mexican narcotics was often in the form of stolen US vehicles.

Smuggling is highly profitable to its entrepreneurs and has brought undoubted income 'spin-offs' to Border communities on both sides of the Rio Grande. The smuggler may claim to be operating at the margins of a normal commercial trading system, frustrated by artificially high tariff barriers, or quota restrictions on the logical flows and interchange of products and commodities. Nevertheless, it is a process, on the scale practised, that is damaging to a country's economy, certainly at the local and regional scale, frustrates the collection of revenues and taxes, alters buying power, and produces distortions in trading balances. Certainly, it has had damaging effects on attempts by either the US or the Mexican governments to rehabilitate or develop the economies of their problem Border regions on the Rio Grande.

POPPY POLITICS

Trafficking in heroin has been described by the head of the US Federal Drugs Enforcement Administration (DEA) as 'the greatest threat to American society' (US Congress, Senate 1978a, 193). Indeed, in the 1970s, the narcotics traffic has rapidly become the most important aspect of US–Mexican relations. During the past ten years Mexico dramatically replaced Turkey and the defunct French Connection as the main source of illicit heroin smuggled into the United States, adding a potentially lethal stream to the rising volume of high potency *marijuana* traditionally sent northward across the Border from the Mexican Sierra Madre. With Americans in the late 1970s estimated to be spending each year as much money on heroin and other drugs as the US Government spent per annum on the Vietnam war (US$27 billions), drug trafficking is both the greatest untaxed and the most lucrative industry in the world. It thrives in a world of peasant growers, cottage and *barrio* operators, Mafia circles, and rich tycoons. With around 50,000 registered heroin addicts in the USA and perhaps ten times that number on the road to addiction (Craig 1978, 107), culminating in a peak of 650,000 in 1978, together with some fifteen million regular or casual *marijuana* users, the potentials of the US market are immense. It is to serve this vast and lucrative market that a complex web of dope trails has been organized from and through Mexico into the USA, trails riddled with vice and crime, the most sordid and dangerous of all Border transactions. The volume of drug trafficking grows, its value escalates even more rapidly and the efforts of both the US and the Mexican governments are directed to stopping the cultivation and processing of drug raw materials, and suppressing the traffic and marketing of the refined products. The drugs trade flourishes within other Border smuggling, of people, arms, commodities, but it also has an evil, burgeoning life of its own. The profits are 'laundered' into countless enterprises both legitimate—in landholdings, hotels, shopping arcades—also illicit—in brothels, gaming casinos, sex-shops and night-clubs, and in sustaining the hierarchy of criminals all down the social scale along the dope trails. These trails cross the Border at innumerable points, but originate and penetrate deeply into both countries. New York still has the greatest concentration of addicts, but the diffusion centres are now Chicago, Los Angeles, New York, and San Antonio (Texas) in that order of significance. Border communities are manifestly affected, both by the vice and crime which flourish, but ironically too in the beneficent effects of the re-investment of such 'wages of sin'.

Mexico too has a serious problem of drug addiction. The use of native hallucinogens (*peyote* seed; *hongo*, the hallucinogetic mushroom) has long been widespread in the countryside. Today, however, the problem is most acute in the towns, and is indeed perhaps a very product of rapid urbanization, rootlessness, and poverty. In 1978 some 10,000 heroin/opium addicts were said to be under treatment in Mexico (Craig 1978, 111), while the rapid growth of *marijuana* smoking was seen as yet another undesirable cultural transplant from the US. Psychotropic drugs (amphetamines and barbiturates) represented an increasingly serious problem with confiscations during 1978 three times those of the preceding year (Craig 1980, 362). Inhalants (glues, solvents) were widely used on a disturbing scale among the teenage populations of the cities and *barrios*.

A TYPOLOGY OF DRUGS

The narcotic drug scene in the US is dominated by the opium alkaloid *diacetyl morphine*, commonly known as heroin. The Federal Bureau of Narcotics (becoming the DEA in 1973) said that for 93 per cent of all recorded addicts heroin was the drug of choice (Fernández 1977, 126). Heroin is a semi-synthetic derivative of the opium poppy, which grows remarkably well in the thin, dry air of the Sierra Madre Occidental. The harvested poppy's seed-pod yields a milky-white sap which is chemically reduced, via the raw opium state (*negra*) to the natural alkaloid, morphine, often in many small, crude, and widely scattered laboratories. Such a reduction, to around one-tenth of the original weight, is followed by treatment with acetic acid. This converts to heroin, with triple the potency of morphine. At all stages along the road to final marketing the product or semi-product is liberally and substantially adulterated by countless worthless substances (US Congress, Senate 1977a, 738).

Marijuana (*mota* in Mexico) is a product of the Indian hemp plant (*cannabis sativa*), capable of widespread and year-round cultivation in the Mexican uplands. When sun-dried, the plant looks and even smells rather like wilted alfalfa, but beneath that scent is a more pungent odour, with something of the tang of tobacco (Becker *et al.* 1972, 414). Substantially less valuable than heroin, *marijuana* nevertheless offers a lucrative, if bulky traffic, less readily concealed and necessarily moving in larger volume, by sea, road, and air.

Cocaine, a nerve stimulant, is derived from the dried leaves of an Andean plant (*coca*). The traffic in cocaine is long-distance and small in scale when compared with heroin transiting through Mexico from Peru, Bolivia, Colombia, and even Buenos Aires ('The Cocaine Express') en route to the United States. The greater proportion of this flow takes place across the Border into California, rather than across the Rio Grande. During the 1970s the drugs traffic became diversified into psychotropic substances, mainly barbiturates and amphetamines (US Congress, Senate 1974). In powder form or as pills or tablets (Mexican 'reds'—*secobarbitol*; 'black beauties'—amphetamines) these drugs are often diverted from normal commerce, either brought out but re-imported into the USA, or manufactured in Mexico. In 1971 eight million illicit amphetamine tablets from Mexico were confiscated in the US, in 1973 twenty-six million. In the mid-1970s it was estimated that group violators in Mexico had ordered enough amphetamine powder from Europe to make fifty million tablets. Raids on laboratories in Monterrey revealed a close network of connections to smaller laboratories at Piedras Negras and C. Acuña on the Rio Grande (US Congress, Senate 1974, 153).

THE CHANGING GEOGRAPHY OF DRUGS

Opium/heroin production in Mexico is of long-standing. It was intro-duced by Chinese labourers in the late nineteenth century, initially rooted in Mexico City but later diffused to cultivation areas in Sonora and Sinaloa provinces. Production was traditionally for home con-sumption but during the First World War the traffic spread to the USA, following Chinese migrants into California. In the inter-war years the flow of drugs from Mexico abated but rose again in the Second World War, when supplies from Europe were cut off. Already in 1948 the first 'search and destroy' missions were carried out (*La Gran Campaña*) by

Mexican federal troops to control cultivation in the North-western provinces (Craig 1978, 108). The extensive common border with the US and the large volume of crossings provided ready access to the then limited crude opium supplies of the Sierra Madre. During the Second World War several New York-based narcotics rings, including members of the infamous '107th Street mob', established contacts with opium sources in Mexico and arranged for the smuggling of considerable quantities of that drug and its derivatives. Underworld chemists, operating makeshift laboratories in apartment houses or lofts in New York City, produced an exceptionally good grade of heroin which brought very high prices (Gaffney 1969). Nevertheless, Mexico had become traditionally known as the source of 'brown' heroin and traffickers for a purer product turned back to Europe in post-war years.

After the war, Turkey was soon re-established as the principal source of opium for the legitimate pharmaceutical industry in Europe and North America, but also once again became a major supplier of illicit opium for the international heroin trade, through the notorious French Connection. White heroin was made in sophisticated laboratories in Marseilles, using opium gum from illicit Turkish poppies. The French Connection produced the world's most wanted heroin, a fine white powder up to 98 per cent in purity. As long as it was available most addicts in the USA would accept nothing less. White heroin dominated the markets of the East coast, and only a trickle of Mexican brown heroin passed across into the US South-west. Mexican traders were then somewhat contemptuously dismissed as 'boot and shoe' operators because the amount they smuggled in was so small it was readily carried in footwear.

It was not, however, until the late 1960s that the alienated, 'turned-on', drugs-based youth culture really gripped the United States. In 1965 there were 18,815 arrests for *marijuana* possession, in 1970 188,682, and in 1974 450,000 (US Congress, Senate 1977a, 141). The traffic in heroin reached serious proportions and international action was directed to its limitation, since suppression was out of the question, certainly for the foreseeable future. As a DEA spokesman put it, 'We know we can't stamp it out. That's why we never use the expression "War against drugs". It suggests something that might be won or lost.' In 1972 Turkey banned opium gum production (US Congress, Senate 1978a, 193), then developed a straw poppy method of crushing the pods, making conversion to heroin more difficult (US Congress, House 1977, 272). Under pressure from the Nixon administration, and in view of the rising number of heroin addicts in France (perhaps 200 in 1966, 20–30,000 officially admitted by 1972), the French government tracked down and eliminated the illegal heroin laboratories in Marseilles. Furthermore, laws were passed permitting microscopic examination of drug traffickers' finances. 'Suddenly the traders were losing their houses, their restaurants, Mercedes-Benz cars, and yachts. Their sons were jerked out of College and their girl-friends were back pounding the beat' (*Latin Am. Press Repts. 1977*). The French Connection was broken, at least for a time. The most recent evidence (*Sunday Times*) suggests that in its place there has grown an Italian Connection, with French gangsters back in business in alarming partnership with the Sicilian Mafia, to supply the vast bulk of the No. 4 grade heroin now available in the USA. Ironically indeed, the rise of the Mexican heroin trade and the powerful wealthy gangs it has given rise to were the outcome of the very success of the US campaign to stop the trade in white heroin from Turkey through France. Though there is some dispute as to the exact proportion of US heroin coming from Mexico it is universally accepted to be substantial, and has been growing: 1969, 15 per cent; 1971, 20 per cent; 1974, 70 per cent; 1975, 90 per cent of source identifications (US Congress, Senate 1977a, 128); and in 1976 (US Congress, House 1977, 272) 67–75 per cent. Not surprisingly, in view of its volume and bulk, almost 90 per cent of smuggled high-potency *marijuana* consumed in the US during most of the 1970s passed across the US–Mexican Border. The latest data (Craig 1980, 358) suggests a dramatic downward shift in the importance of Mexican traffic in drugs to the USA. Mexican brown heroin supplied only 50 per cent of the US market in 1978 and, even more spectacularly, *marijuana* from south of the Rio Grande provided only 20 per cent of American needs in the same year. Colombia had replaced Mexico for *marijuana*.

MEXICAN SOURCE AREAS AND SUPPLY ROUTES

Though the opium poppy and the *marijuana* plant could be grown over very wide areas, their cultivation today is limited to many scattered, inaccessible sites in the Sierra Madre Occidental the so-called 'Zone 6' or the *triángulo crítico* (Craig 1980, 349) (Fig 26). After rather more than a decade of increasingly active and sophisticated 'search and destroy' missions, by the Mexican federal forces, discussed later, concealment of the cultivation plots has become no less elaborate. The drugs plants are intermingled with the normal food crops, often in the same fields. Other sites are remote, in tracts at the end of tortuous trails through virtually impenetrable thorns and brambles. The cultivators are almost invariably peasants, friendly in town on market day, sullen or aggressive to any suspected intruder in the mountains—'*No hay paso por aquí*'. For all its risks, the opium poppy can earn the cultivator ten to twenty times the value of any legal crop. With less work and worry, crop after crop of *marijuana* can provide five to ten times what corn or beans would pay him (Becker *et al.* 1972, 415). Furthermore, there is security in the remoteness of growing areas and the drugs traffic is a dazzlingly

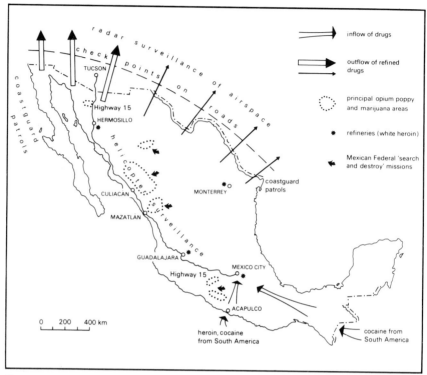

Fig. 26. The political geography of drugs

attractive alternative to grinding poverty in a mountain countryside turbulent with guerrilla activities, land seizure, *caciquismo*, and rural unrest.

From the poppy fields the dope trail to the Border winds down countless mule-tracks to the dropping-points, where the middleman takes over the increasingly precious cargo. Most movement is by night on prearranged patterns. The *negra* (blackened raw opium), cooked from the white, milky sap of the scored poppy-heads, is carried in cans or market bags, and ten kilograms would be a big buy for any middle-man. *Marijuana* may be pressed into gunny sacks or compacted by hydraulic jacks into one-kilogram bricks. The middlemen are not in-frequently relatives of the farmers who had earlier moved to the towns, or they may be the outermost employees of the trafficking rings stretch-ing deep into the USA.

The task of the middleman is to move the opium to the refineries concealed in northern Mexican towns, and the *marijuana* to warehouses where full vehicle loads may be made up. The risks at this stage are those of 'hide and seek', to get past the Mexican truck inspection stations on approaches to the towns. False-bottomed cars and lorries, or specially built road-tankers are needed for the more bulky *marijuana*. Opium is more readily concealed within or under lorry loads, in the boots of cars, or on the person. Many middlemen remain small-scale operators, perhaps with a small, legitimate business as a sideline: taxi-operators, lorry-drivers, shopkeepers, or bus-owners. In the town laboratories the opium is refined to heroin, usually bypassing the morphine stage, and emerges as No. 3 Mexican brown smoking heroin.

From the refinery in Mexico to the market in the USA the drugs pass through a complete network of operators. At every stop the value of the heroin rises dramatically, its bulk is broken down, and each package becomes more liberally adulterated. *Marijuana* initially does not change bulk and must continue to be moved in substantial loads, never less than one ton in commercial operations. Nevertheless, for landward crossings of the Border, the *marijuana* is usually in the form of hydraulically compressed 'bricks'. One-pound sizes have been popular on the run into Texas, for ease of concealment in vehicles, and 'manicured' pot is not uncommon crossing the Rio Grande, i.e. adulterated by the stalks and other plants. The Border crossing is the most perilous phase of the journey, a constant 'cat-and-mouse' game between the Customs and the smuggler. As a Customs official put it verbally:

Drugs come through in every conceivable hiding-place. Cocaine, heroin, and opium worth thousands of dollars even in small amounts, are easily hidden in clothing, suitcases, briefcases, women's handbags. Drugs are put into balloons which are swallowed or tucked into body cavities. Packages have been found in freshly baked bread, in sealed food-cans, inside the plaster statues that tourists bring back with them. Smugglers conceal drugs in hollow shoe heels, diapers, and dolls. Cripples hobble across the Border with drugs in hollow crutches; one man had a secret compartment in his artificial leg. They build double doors, double roofs, false beds in trucks and campers. They put drugs in gas tanks, under dashboards, inside tyres, behind headlights. We even found ten pounds of heroin welded into the drive-shaft of a truck.

The major drop trail is along the Pacific flank, using Mexican highway 15 into California and Arizona. A further major trail converges on El Paso, while Starr County in the Lower Rio Grande has gained notoriety as an active drugs pipeline for both heroin and *marijuana* (US Congress, Senate 1977b, 1448). Press reports of the mid-1970s spoke of the great increase of wealth in Starr County, Texas, from the illegal drugs trade, with an estimated $500 million worth passing through each year (perhaps 7.5 tonnes of *marijuana* and 5 kg of heroin per week) and offering a lucrative livelihood to perhaps one-third of the local population, either directly or indirectly. Much of the traffic was reported to be across the Rio Grande in inner tubes, on rafts or in small boats, some of it waded across at low water, under the watchful eyes of well-paid armed guards. The local smuggling rings were said to be organized by a dozen or so Mexican-American families, in Mafia-like groups, families tightly knit socially within a wall of silence. From Starr County a major *marijuana* trail led northwards, beyond the screens of highway checkpoints, to Falfurrias on US highway 281. As so often in settlements benefiting from the traffic in drugs, most folk locally were worried that the law seemed powerless to do anything in the face of the appearance of sudden, unexplained riches in an otherwise impoverished community.

Ojinaga, across from Presidio, Texas, was indicated as one of the most active centres for illegal narcotics (*Latin Am. Press Repts.* 1977). Four-wheeled drive and other vehicles were stolen in the US and used in barter for drugs across the Border into Brewster County. Gunrunning and gun smuggling were reported to be rife in the same area. Santa Elena, in the remote wastelands opposite the Big Bend country, is another known transit point for *marijuana* in exchange for stolen vehicles or guns, with pick-up trucks said to be 'a particularly valued commodity'.

The journey over the Rio Grande is no doubt the most hazardous part of the dope trail, but motivated by the uniquely high potential profits for all concerned, there is no shortage of willing participants. There are many small operators, 'mules', who will carry small consignments of drugs regularly, often by night but not infrequently in blatant fashion by daylight. They may cross the Border fence, wade the river, or push packages through the fence to known collecting-points. It is mostly these 'mules' who are caught and prosecuted, but inevitably they return, others readily take their places and the considerable risk undertaken is reflected in the price and the profit; adding to these illicit profits by denouncing the customer to the authorities is also by no means unknown. Some operators may even guarantee delivery of *marijuana* by the kilo or heroin by the ounce to the very door-step in US Border cities. Green-card commuters too (p. 154) have been known to carry small quantities of brown heroin on a regular basis across the Border bridges into Texas.

The smuggling of drugs in vehicles represents the bulk of the traffic, with perhaps only 40 per cent of land traffic passing across by other means between the checkpoints on the Rio Grande. The volume and regularity of movements by vehicles requires more substantial organization, on both sides of the Border. According to the INS three-quarters of *marijuana* seizures take place at highway checks in the US well back from the Rio Grande (US Congress, House 1974, 135). Some smuggling organizations are based in the Mexican Border cities, including the Juárez base of that legendary post-war 'dope queen of the Border', *La Nacha* (Demaris 1970, 141). Others are in the production business, with a network of laboratories, but using couriers to cross the Border. Some of the largest operators control the drugs pipeline from source to destination: the Herrera group based in Durango had links right through to the market in Chicago (US Congress, Senate 1978b, 201). Indeed, a key element in the DEA strategy to break the drugs rings has lain in 'shadowing' suspected vehicles on the long haul from border checkpoint to the Midwest or the Eastern seaboard cities.

During the 1970s, however, a new dimension for the drugs traffic has appeared, in the large-scale use of private single-engined aircraft to pass over the Border. As a Senate witness put it (US Congress, Senate 1978b, 177):

Only six years ago most narcotics smuggling came through the landward borders; today Customs estimate that twenty-seven to thirty aircraft loaded with marijuana fly into the US each day, mostly across the Mexican Border. By embracing modern techniques of air freighting, the smugglers have shown that the sky above the Border is even more porous than the Border itself.

Aerial photos have revealed 1,500 clandestine airstrips in Mexico used to fly drugs to towns along the Border; half these airstrips are in the mountains east of Culiacán, a major centre for opium poppy cultivation (*Latin Am. Press Repts.*, 7 March 1977).

Using small single or twin-engined aircraft, the airborne smugglers fly fast and low, landing in the USA on abandoned military strips, deserted county roads, and even dry river beds. With light loads a low altitude air-drop may suffice, making detection additionally difficult. A single flight with a few hundred pounds of *marijuana* may net $70,000; even bigger money may be made flying in hard drugs.... The ratio of automobile to aerial smuggling varies. When pressure is put on auto traffic, air traffic picks up (Becker *et al.* 1972, 430–5).

Such air traffic is highly organized, with regular schedules, met by lorry or car at the landing-point. Not all flights touch down only short distances across the Border, but the risks of detection increase with longer journeys since no flight-plans are filed and radar screening is well developed. Some flights are sponsored by larger-scale entrepreneurs, but others are 'flight-by-night operations by amateurs lured by visions of easy money' (Becker *et al.* 1972, 434). There is a growing tendency for a two-way smuggling traffic, back-hauling refrigerators, television sets, or electrical components before returning north with an even more lucrative cargo of drugs. Most pilots in the illicit trade are American, not all are adequately trained; during 1975 102 smuggling aircraft crashed on US soil (US Congress, Senate 1976, 1038). The dealers to whom they hand over are usually young, including College students, though there is really no typical dealer profile.

Widely disseminated and frequent aerial smuggling is difficult to counter effectively. Radar tracking and aerial interception account for perhaps fewer seizures than the feedback from undercover agents who penetrate the drugs network, or even as the result of reports from citizens who detect unusual night-time air activity in the more remote areas. Short of more sophisticated devices and an army of watchers, airborne smuggling on a sizeable scale will persist. Once again the policy ultimately is so to increase the risk that fewer operators will be prepared to face the prospect; of this, in 1981, there is as yet little sign.

To complement the scanning of the landward Border and the airspace above it, both the US Coastguard and the Mexicans have regular seaborne patrols off the California coast and in the Gulf of Mexico. Police, Customs, and the Navy are used to intercept flotillas of small craft seeking to slip through the screen to off-load at an American coastal rendezvous, or tranship to a US craft for the run in-shore. In tactical manoeuvring, the problems of enforcing maritime sovereignty in coastal waters, and the limited right of search on the high seas, are exploited to the full by the traffickers.

A brief word on profits in the drugs trade may help to underline why it is so widespread, so lucrative, so complex, and so hard to combat. The peasant cultivator of *marijuana* gains five to ten times the value of his normal crop, for opium poppies ten to twenty times as much. The price approximately doubles for delivery of raw opium at the refinery. From the refinery, with an 80 to 90 per cent pure heroin, the value rapidly escalates along the dope trail. Even in the late 1960s (Demaris 1970, 124) a kilogram cost $10–12,000 at the refinery, and during its complicated journey to the American market was liberally adulterated, to perhaps thiry times its original volume; the principal adulterants were sugar, instant coffee, and cocoa. The mark-up in price per adulterated kilo in 1977 (US Congress, Senate 1977a, 144) was reported to be: 300 per cent at the point of importation, 100 per cent when consignments were broken down to individual kilograms, 145 per cent for the man dealing at the level of an ounce (30 g), 114 per cent to the middleman or pusher, 124 per cent to the street dealer, and a final 50 per cent to the seller or 'juggler'. The unfortunate addict in the late 1960s paid $5 a shot for what was often no more than 3 per cent heroin. One estimate (Demaris 1970, 124) puts the gross earnings on one kilo of heroin at all stages of its movement as high as $640,000. In 1980 (*Sunday Times*) the New York *wholesale* price for No. 4 grade heroin was reported to be $246,750 a kilo. Cocaine was being dealt in at $140,000 a kilo ($400–600 an ounce) in Mexico in the mid-1970s, with US prices today likely to exceed those for heroin. Not for nothing is cocaine termed the rich man's drug of choice. *Marijuana* profits may be less, but the volume sold is infinitely greater. From an initial price of $50–85 a kilo, depending on the variable effectiveness of law enforcement, $450 a kilo is likely to be exacted on landing in the USA. The final estimated price at the point of delivery (*Daily Telegraph*, 7 August 1980) would be around $4,400 a kilo in the British market, with 1,000 reefers per kilo; in US terms this value is likely to be greatly underestimated. It is true that a delivered price in New York in 1971 (Becker *et al.* 1972) was mentioned as low as $1,650 per kilo, but much has happened since then. Furthermore, *marijuana* too is commonly adulterated. 'It gets lighter when it dries out, and it is thus often soaked in water, wine, soda or even human urine. Perfume and wax are often added to disguise the definitive odour' (Becker *et al.* 1972, 450). Poisoning by *paraquat* is mentioned later.

The economics of the drugs trade spirals with inflation and according to the entrepreneur's assessment of risks, but in the heroin traffic the street dosage price remains remarkably stable. It is the heroin content in the dose that deteriorates, as an inverse corollary of rising prices. Indeed, a crude barometer of the success of preventative measures is the general level of heroin purity in the retail trade; in 1968, 6.4 per cent; in 1970, 9.6 per cent; in September 1977, 5.0 per cent (US Congress, Senate 1978a, 198; US Congress, Senate 1976, 1126).

COUNTER-MEASURES AND US–MEXICAN POLICIES

As so often in international relations across the Rio Grande there is a history of unco-ordinated, unilateral measures, belatedly so on the part of the Mexican authorities. It was only during the 1970s, when the scale and seriousness of the drugs menace threatened both countries, that co-operation became a keynote of policy, even then not without suspicions and sensitivities by both parties.

Throughout the 1960s, US policy attempted more effective inter-diction measures against drugs crossing the Border from Mexico, but it was early recognized that physical exclusion of drugs was an even more difficult task than the repression of illegal aliens. In 1969, Attorney-General John Mitchell's Task Force I was constituted to 'move against the source of drugs' (US Congress, Senate 1975, 96). In September of that year Operation Intercept was launched, 'the nation's largest peacetime search and seizure operation by civil authorities'. It rep-resented one all-out attempt to halt the inflow of *marijuana*, then the major problem, but it was in some ways a classic example of economic blackmail 'to get the Mexicans to come around and really start doing something about dope' (Craig 1978, 109). The massive hold-ups at the Border checkpoints led to diplomatic incidents, and within three weeks the programme was renamed Operation Co-operation, a face-saving bi-national arrangement. This ill-tempered experience at least con-vinced the Americans that no effective solutions could be envisaged, unless their Mexican neighbours were equally concerned and, more-over, were given the massive financial and technical help that would be required. In the meantime, it was clear that a major reorganization of the campaign was essential on the US side of the Border. A 'bureau-cratic Border war' was spoken of among the American agencies (US Congress, House 1974, 1): Reorganization Plan 2 established the Drugs Enforcement Administration (DEA) in the Department of Justice

(1973), created at El Paso the Inter-Agency Drug Intelligence Center for the South-west (1978), and set up a Customs Patrol to supplement the long-standing Border Patrol of the INS. The latter Patrol had uniquely been responsible for enforcement problems in the country between the ports of entry. In the early 1970s CADPIN, a computer-based Customs Automated Data Processing Intelligence Network was set up at 160 locations throughout the USA. This computer was later linked to that of the FBI at the National Crime Information Center. The Command Intelligence Center established at El Paso (US Congress, Senate 1978a, 204) was to co-ordinate the efforts of the DEA, Customs, INS, Federal Aviation Administration, and Coastguard.

A US air interdiction centre was also set up, with twenty-four light aircraft for the DEA and eighteen for the INS. Furthermore, a comprehensive Texas 'Strike Force' was established in 1977 to aid thirty-three special agents in the field. Initially, one helicopter was based at Laredo, but this was supplemented by small fixed-wing planes which were less conspicuous. Tactical interdiction units were set up, linking ground and air, and these enjoyed considerable initial success (Table 11). Table 12 sets these figures within the total of nation-wide drug seizures.

The figures tend to confirm the observation by an American narcotics

Table 11.   Marijuana *seizures, US checkpoints on Mexican Border, 1973–4*

	1973 (kg)	%	1974 (kg)	%
Special agents	59,719	78	—	
Tactical interdiction units	—		126,605	73
Ports of entry	16,734	22	46,828	27
	76,453	100	173,433	100

Table 12.   *US grand total drug removals, 1971, 1974*

	1971	1974
In kilograms		
Opium	21	15
Heroin	528	245
Cocaine	358	673
Marijuana	86,414	397,955
In dosage units		
Hallucinogens	3.6m	3.3m
Depressants	319,506	539,858
Stimulants	10.3m	8.8m
Other dangerous drugs	6.3m	24.8m
Methadone	36,468	4,543

Source: US Congress, House 1974, pp. 119 and 165.

agent in Mexico City: 'We have to stop drugs before they get into the States. Once they enter the United States they are distributed so fast that it's like opening up a pillow and scattering the feathers in a high wind.'

Mexican laws on narcotics and *marijuana* are similar to those of the USA, but in Mexico these are administered only federally, and there is no counterpart to the legal responsibilities of the States in the USA. Nor has Mexico developed legislation on stimulants, depressants, or hallucinogenic drugs (US Congress, Senate 1969). Nevertheless, under Article 195 of the *Código Penal* the use or possession of hard drugs is a severe criminal offence, 'an offence against health', and Mexico has been a signatory to every important international treaty on drugs. Law enforcement on drugs in Mexico is under the *Procuraduría*, or State Attorney's office, co-ordinating the Army, the State, and local law enforcement bodies. The 1948 *Gran Campaña* in the Mexican Northwest has already been referred to (p. 181). It involved laborious 'search and destroy' missions on foot, by federal troops, aided later by federal judicial police (MFJP). *Marijuana* plots rather than opium poppies were the target in the early days. Plots were burned or crops trampled, but it was a hazardous business and, for many peasant-recruited soldiers, a most uncongenial task. Unless the operation was to degenerate into a political cosmetic entirely new methods and resources needed to be mobilized. Plots were expertly concealed, cultivation spread like wildfire and, in the early 1970s, the opium poppy became the lucrative crop of choice. Remoteness and the vast areas to be reconnoitred regularly enforced the use of aircraft. So too did the realization that the police and even federal troops were increasingly likely to meet resistance by force of arms. Nor could burning and trampling of the discovered crops match the growing scale of the task. Herbicides and defoliants came under consideration but parallels with Vietnam rested uneasily in Mexican minds. In the early 1960s the US provided the first aircraft and spares. As a result, there was a dramatic increase in the areas of opium poppies destroyed: 139,000 m² in 1960–1; 3.8 Mm² in 1961–2 (Craig 1978, 109). Yet the problem of interdiction grew to be increasingly unmanageable. The number of opium or *marijuana* fields spotted in a day would take six to eight months to destroy; to destroy an 8-hectare field might take thirty men seven days. In 1970–1 the US delivered three fixed-wing aircraft and five helicopters, and in the next year or so a further eight helicopters (US Congress, Senate 1977a, 539; see also US Dept. State 1973). Pilot training for Mexicans was funded in the USA and, in 1974, American expertise in multispectral analysis of aerial photographs was passed to the Mexicans (US Dept. State 1974). In the following year mobile interdiction systems for roadblocks were transferred by treaty (US Dept. State 1975).

Bolstered by American technical aid and equipment, Mexican anti-drugs strategy was first to halt the cultivation and processing of opium poppies, *marijuana* and psychotropic drugs, and, secondly, to disrupt domestic and international traffic flows (Craig 1978, 115). Operation Condor I was launched in 1976 and continued for two years. At the outset 20,000 opium poppy fields were said to exist; the truth was probably nearer double that amount. At its height 10,000 troops were employed, together with 250 federal narcotics agents, plus planes, helicopters, and patrol boats. Vietnam-style spraying from the air with herbicides was concentrated in the first few months of the year; 2-4D *paraquat* and gramoxone were used for spraying *marijuana* fields, while *paraquat* also defoliated the opium plots (Craig 1980, 353). Troops and police were in the mountains throughout the year, but were concentrated in follow-up operations in the early spring. Further fields were burned and growers were arrested. Many fields were promptly replanted and had to be resprayed to control a second crop even in the same season.

Table 13 shows the impressive results of the Mexican anti-drugs campaign even before Operation Condor, in terms of plots destroyed, drugs seized, vehicles confiscated, and violators arrested. Nevertheless, the successes were limited and talk of eradication was wildly premature. As one rural mayor put it 'we've got 1,500 square miles of wilderness to

Table 13.   *Mexican anti-drugs campaign, 1973–6*

	1973–4	1974–5	1975–6
Marijuana			
Plots destroyed	8,112	6,762	16,686
Area (km²)	19.9	20.8	56.1
Opium poppy			
Plots destroyed	6,540	13,580	21,405
Area (m²)	17.7m	44.9m	58.1m
Drug seizures (kg)			
Opium	193.7	880.1	676.6
Morphine	0.6	6.9	4.4
Heroin	129.4	452.2	292.5
Cocaine	146.9	255.3	214.5
Vehicles seized			
Cars/trucks	880	758	828
Planes	27	41	77
Persons detained			
Mexican	2,751	2,524	4,021
Foreign	415	228	378
Rings disrupted			16

Source: *Procuraduría General de la República Mexicana*, reported in Craig (1978, 120).

cover. Our police force is six men with three old M-1 rifles among them'
(Craig 1980, 354). In the second year of operation 64,750 km² were
sprayed, but follow-up forces remained remarkably thin on the ground.
There is some evidence that there was a lack of commitment to an
'anti-drug' role by the army, even that there was corruption and
connivance with the growers, most especially among the NCOs and
men of the federal forces, some at least of whom were similar in outlook
and background to the peasants they were hunting. Furthermore, the
risks of armed conflict with growers and traffickers found even the
military at a disadvantage locally. The exchange of drugs for guns from
across the Rio Grande had brought in some of the most modern light
automatic weapons from American National Guard armouries. Indeed,
in the first few months of Operation Condor 234 rifles and automatic
weapons and 438 pistols were captured by the Mexican federal forces.
Sixteen were killed on the government side, including fourteen soldiers
and two DEA agents. Later it was estimated that as many as one
hundred of the security forces had been lost, by ground fire or cables
strung across the valleys (Craig 1980, 353). There were disturbing
reports (US Congress, Senate 1977a, 573), denied by the Mexicans,
that there were sizeable mountain tracts which were effectively 'no-go'
areas for the anti-drug forces, whether or not they were supported by
military strength.

The arrest of either Mexican or American nationals for drug offences
in the neighbouring country inevitably led to diplomatic incidents and
issues. Extradition was rarely possible, in either direction, but under
Operation Janus Mexican attorneys could hear evidence against their
nationals who had been major heroin traffickers in the US and then
prosecute those who had fled back to the presumed security of their own
country. The case of American prisoners in Mexican jails was also a
vexatious question. By mid-1977 some 600 US citizens were in Mexican
prisons. The majority were convicted of the possession of dangerous
drugs, with no pre-trial bond for 'crimes against health' under the
Mexican penal code. Criminal proceedings take about eight months,
with sentences and convictions from two to nine years for possession
and three to twelve years for trafficking in drugs (Becker et al. 1972,
424). During 1976 there was a formal exchange of prisoners and this has
continued in succeeding years, though the returning Americans usually
had to serve out their sentences in home-based prisons.

The 1980s will see the anti-drugs campaign stepped up, with even
more sophisticated devices and, probably, heavier investment in manpower and equipment. Yet there may be technical limits. It was
reported by an American narcotics officer in Mexico that 'the fields are
often so small that they (the guys from NASA) have been unable to
train their computers to understand what a poppy is at close range. It

simply hasn't been able to follow the command "find poppies"!' (Craig 1980, 362). There continues to be a basic dilemma: the price of enhanced success lies in an increased US involvement in the Mexican effort, but national sensitivity makes this altogether unacceptable. The widespread use of defoliant chemicals, with echoes of Vietnam, has aroused considerable public opposition in Mexico. The indiscriminate nature of their application has inevitably damaged food crops as well as drug plants, and that they have to be used at all shows how serious the problem of drugs has become. The Mexican public appears not to wish to know. Already in the 1977 Trizo campaign in Mexico the government required the participation of the United States DEA to be withdrawn, as offensive to the Mexican people (US Congress, Senate 1978a, 216). Spraying with 2-4D *paraquat*, for eradicating *marijuana* and the opium poppy, has had poisonous side-effects. The *marijuana* plants wither in forty-eight hours but growers usually manage to harvest them before they die. Once dried and compacted into bricks, the crop enters commerce in the normal way in spite of the poisonous contamination, which can be lethal to the eventual pot smoker. In 1978 it was estimated that one-fifth of the *marijuana* then circulating in the US had been contaminated by *paraquat*.

The jointly developed US–Mexican advanced poppy detector system now uses electro-optical techniques (US Congress, Senate 1978a, 218; US Dept. State 1976), a sound intelligence base for a more effective 'search and destroy' effort. What must remain in doubt, and balance the equation eventually in favour of the grower or the trafficker, is the depth of the official commitment to the anti-drugs campaign. The peasants have resorted to fresh ruses for concealment, and have countered the risks of having their acreage confiscated by often tilling their drug plots on government-owned land (Craig 1978, 128). The drugs traffic is highly organized and the major entrepreneurs shelter effectively behind the countless small operators, who esteem the risks of the trade well compensated for by the undoubted profits. Sixteen drug rings were broken in 1975–6 (Table 13), but the octopus quickly grows more tentacles and the Mexican Connection remains unbroken.

The impact of the traffic in drugs on the communities on either side of the Rio Grande is hard to evaluate, but the multiplier effects are substantial and must be growing. By one report (Demaris 1970, 143) some of the finest hotels, restaurants, and brothels on the Border are owned by narcotics smugglers. According to another (US Congress, Senate 1977b, 1448), profits on narcotics through Starr County, Texas, are invested in lands and businesses, particularly in vast landholdings on the Mexican side, owned by blood relatives and used as 'staging-posts' on the drugs pipeline. One particular impact on the Border cities has arisen from the traffic in exchange of US weapons for imported drugs. Burglaries from US residents, hold-ups of sporting-goods stores, and raids on National Guard armouries have become too frequent (US Congress, House 1975, 76). Not surprisingly, when an M16 rifle fetched $1,000–1,200 in Mexico in the mid-1970s, the price of one ounce of heroin.

Once more in US–Mexican relations, as in the case of illegal migrants, the problem of the traffic in drugs sets a vast US market potential against a large-scale supply source south of the Border, wealth against poverty, sophisticated technology and organization against peasant cunning and endurance. Perhaps it is only by the eradication of rural poverty in Mexico that both the traffic in migrants and in drugs will eventually be diminished. For the foreseeable future such a hope can be little more than a pious incantation.

THE WAGES OF SIN

Yet another flagrant example of the gross exploitation of Border Mexican society by its richer northern neighbour is the well-established, rife, and flourishing industry of prostitution. The description of the Border as 'a pleasure strip measurably oriented to *gringos* with low libidinal thresholds' (Demaris 1970, 4), the target of a 'volatile stream of puritans in search of sin' dramatically but truthfully under-lines but the latest phase of a long-standing trait of low life on the Rio Grande. The supply and demand sides of this particular equation in social pathology are well balanced, and the magnitudes on each side are substantial. Organized prostitution is illegal in both the US and Mexico, but, like illegal migrants or drugs, it is a highly profitable operation for the entrepreneurs. Moreover, it is not only the practitioners and their controllers who profit. One estimate (McNamara 1971), for C. Juárez, showed that the civic revenue from prostitution amounted to one million US dollars per annum, or half the total city income. Border cities on the frontier with California could probably show an even better return. Most recently, changing attitudes to drugs and sex on the US side of the Border have diminished the flow in search of vice across the Rio Grande. 'Topless and bottomless bars, blue movies, and sexual permissiveness have stolen the thunder of night life that once made C. Juárez a mecca for fun-seekers from throughout the world' (Martínez, 1975, 126).

The supply side of prostitution may be a function of demand, but it is also a damning indictment of social conditions in rural and urban Mexico. The drift of young men and women off the land in search of better-paid jobs, even jobs at all, and a higher standard of living with the hope of better prospects, inexorably leads to disillusionment and despair for the vast majority, as they but add to the already teeming

stock of the urban poor. This is a function of the rate of population
growth, compounded in the Mexican cities along the Rio Grande, by
the 'ponding-back' of the floodtide of those seeking to enter the US, or at
least to profit by living, and hopefully working, in close proximity to the
American 'way of life'. The provision of work in Mexican Border cities
cannot possibly measure up to the demand for jobs. Unemployment is
endemic and while men are driven into the most menial occupations,
the alternative for many women has been life on the streets. Though this
may be one of the inevitable outcomes of a drift by individuals to the
city, there is evidence too of an organized trade in women and girls.
Advertising for maids may lead to the offer of a very different job on
arrival; prisons too are said to be fertile recruiting grounds for brothels,
while there is more than a suggestion of 'white slaving' rings based upon
at least one Mexican Border city (Demaris 1970, 15).

Prostitution has a particularly well-assured place in any culture
which, ironically, places a high value on the purity of the family and
idealistically extols the virtues of womanhood. On the Rio Grande there
are also exceptional circumstances boosting the demand. Traditionally,
the larger US Border towns on the river have had permanent, at times
sizeable, military garrisons. No less traditionally, the soldiers and air-
men have regularly sought sexual outlets south of the Border. The
longer-term tendency to station US black troops on or near the
Mexican Border added in the past to an already very turbulent social
issue, provoking the notorious incidents in Brownsville already fifty
years ago (Fernández 1977, 128). Both during the Second World War
and the Vietnam war the Border army training-camps and air bases
were considerably enlarged. The movement across the Rio Grande in
search of pleasure reached an unprecedented peak in the 1960s, at a
time when the population of the Mexican Border towns was expanding
at its most rapid rate and unemployment was exploding. The closing of
bases in the 1970s and the rundown of US Border garrisons was in some
measure offset by the growth of the tourist industry, a fresh source of
short-term clients. The 'image' of the Border as a violent, vice and
crime-ridden society was overdrawn no doubt, and there was even less
truth in the assumption that the permissive society began at the
Mexican Border checkpoint. Nevertheless, tourists and the convention
industry have bolstered the large and variegated call-girl and prostitution industry on the Rio Grande, and ensured its continuing
proliferation and success.

The *zona roja*, or the *zona de tolerancia*, is a feature of most Latin
American cities, and those on the Rio Grande are no exception. At
times the *zona* is compact and almost a self-sufficient commercial unit,
with shops, night clubs, clinics, and medical facilities. At Reynosa it is
protected by a wall and a moat-like irrigation ditch. In the larger cities,

or those closest to the major American bases, the *zona* is more differentiated. That in C. Acuña is said to be the 'largest and toughest *zona* on the Rio Grande'. In C. Juárez the high-class call-girl area is 'on the side-streets, some twelve blocks or so along Avenida Juárez; the more ordinary brothels in Calle Mariscal' (Demaris 1970, 14). The high-class brothels are said to be linked into the narcotics trade. Below this level there is a progressive degeneration and degradation, almost through a social caste structure, down to the slum brothels. Demaris (1970, 10) mentions one between Mier and Nuevo Guerrero, with its appalling conditions, peopled by rejects from other Border brothels. 'Ageing at 21, old at 25 and by 35 years at the end of the line' sums up the tragedies of these 'slums of despair'.

Prostitution has its place in the widely diverse pleasure industry of the Border. It is a large-scale, lucrative, and profitable activity, attracted to and stabilized on the Rio Grande by the sudden cultural, social, even moral break assumed to exist when passing from the United States into Mexico. It is an industry with ramifications into many aspects of the Border economy, with both illicit and legal multiplier effects. The municipal revenues of Mexican Border cities ironically derive a significant contribution from the 'wages of sin'. Put cynically, prostitution does also provide work in cities with a great dearth of jobs for women, but it achieves this at an unacceptable cost in human terms, of misery, degradation, and ill-health. The Mexican Border Development Programme (PRONAF) and the Border Industrialization Programme (BIP) (see chapter 7) seek to provide jobs for women as well as for men, and improve the living environment, thus reducing the need for women and girls to resort to the streets for a livelihood. In this aspect of national policy, too, the scale of the social problem is such that new female job provision lags far behind demand and, in some respects, has itself led to an aggravated exodus of women and girls from the countryside.

A singular, more innocent sidelight on relations between the sexes relates to the relaxed divorce laws in Chihuahua, enacted as far back as 1931. Like Reno, C. Juárez flourished for a time as a 'mail-order' divorce centre, and the destination of the 'divorce-run' flights from New York through El Paso, locally known as the 'Freedom-riders' special' (Demaris 1970, 33). In March 1971, however, a new Mexican Federal law limited divorces to Mexicans or permanent resident aliens. C. Juárez reportedly 'lost a sizeable sum in multiplier spending as a result' (Martínez, 1975, 126).

REFERENCES

BECKER, J. *et al.* (1972) 'The dope trail', *Contemp. Drug Probl.*, **1**, 413–52.

CRAIG, R. B. (1978) 'La Campaña permanente: Mexico's antidrug campaign', *J. Inter-Am. Stud. Wld. Affairs*, **20,** 2, 107–31.

DEMARIS, O. (1970) *Poso del Mundo: inside the Mexican-American border from Tijuana to Matamoros* (Boston, Mass.: Little, Brown & Co.).

FERNÁNDEZ, R. A. (1977) *The United States-Mexico Border. A politico-economic profile* (Notre Dame, Ind.: Notre Dame Univ. Press).

GAFFNEY, G. H. (1969) 'Narcotic drugs, their origin and routes of traffic', ch. 6 in J. R. Wittenborn *et al.* (eds.) *Drugs and Youth, Rutgers Symposium on Drug Abuse, Rutgers Univ. 1968* (Springfield, Ill.: Charles C. Thomas), 55–61.

Latin American Press Reports (1977) Latin Am. Centre, Univ. Texas at Austin.

McNAMARA, P. H. (1971) 'Prostitution along the US-Mexico Border: a survey', in E. R. Stoddard (ed.) 'Prostitution and illicit drug traffic on the US-Mexican Border', *Border-State Univ. Consortium Latin Am. Res., occ Pap. 2*, El Paso, Tex.

MARTÍNEZ, O. J. (1975) *Border boom town: C. Juárez since 1848* (Austin: Univ. Texas Press).

Sunday Times, 27 July 1980.

US CONGRESS HOUSE (1974) Committee on Government Operations, *Law enforcement on the Southwest border* (Review of Reorganization Plan no. 2 of 1973 and related developments), 93rd Congr., 2nd Sess., Washington DC, USGPO.

US CONGRESS, HOUSE (1975–6) Committee on Armed Services, *Thefts and losses of military weapons, ammunition and explosives*, Hearings before Subcomm. on Investigations 94th Congr., 1st and 2nd Sess., Washington DC, USGPO.

US CONGRESS, HOUSE (1977) Committee on Commissions and Temporary Committees, *Oversight hearings on narcotics abuse and current federal and international narcotics control effort*, 94th Congr., 2nd Sess., Washington DC, USGPO.

US CONGRESS, SENATE (1969) Committee on the Judiciary, *Narcotics legislation*, Hearings before Subcomm. to Investigate Juvenile Delinquency, 91st Congr., 1st Sess., Washington DC, USGPO.

US CONGRESS, SENATE (1974) Committee on the Judiciary, *Psychotropic Substances Act 1973*, Hearing before Subcomm. on Juvenile Delinquency, 93rd Congr., 2nd Sess., Washington DC, USGPO.

US CONGRESS, SENATE (1975) Committee on the Judiciary, *Poppy Politics*, vol. 2, Hearings before Subcomm. on Juvenile Delinquency, 94th Congr., 1st Sess., Washington DC, USGPO.

US CONGRESS, SENATE (1976) Committee on Governmental Affairs, *Federal drug enforcement, part 5*, Hearings before Permanent Subcomm. on Investigations, 94th Congr., 2nd Sess., Washington DC, USGPO.

US CONGRESS, SENATE (1977a) Committee on the Judiciary, *Global connection: heroin entrepreneurs*, vol. 1, Hearings before Subcomm. on Juvenile Delinquency, 94th Congr., 2nd Sess., Washington DC, USGPO.

US CONGRESS, SENATE (1977b) Committee on Governmental Affairs, *Federal drug enforcement, part 6*, Hearings before Permanent Subcomm. on Investigations, 95th Congr., 1st Sess., Washington DC, USGPO.

US CONGRESS, SENATE (1978a) Committee on the Judiciary, *Department of Justice budget authorization*, 95th Congr., 2nd Sess., Washington DC, USGPO.

US CONGRESS, SENATE (1978b) Committee on Appropriations, *Treasury, Postal Service and general government appropriations for FY79 part 2*, 95th Congr., 2nd Sess., Washington DC, USGPO.

US DEPARTMENT OF STATE (1973) *TIAS 7906*, 3 Dec. 1973, **25,** pt. 2.

US DEPARTMENT OF STATE (1974) *TIAS 7863*, 10 June 1974, **25,** pt. 2.

US DEPARTMENT OF STATE (1975) *TIAS 8041*, 24 Feb. 1975, **26,** pt. 1.

US DEPARTMENT OF STATE (1976) *TIAS 8294*, 4 Feb. 1976, **26,** pt. 2.

CHAPTER 7

The Border Market

We cannot accept that it is impossible to conquer the Border market. The same power of workers and entrepreneurs, who have shown the world what we can achieve, with the strong support and guidance of the government, must achieve the economic conquest of the frontier.

SECRETARIO DE HACIENDA Y CRÉDITO PÚBLICO, May 1971

The flux of transactions across the Rio Grande reflects the overall trading patterns of the two nations, but the interaction between the Border communities is more complex than simply a microcosm of such inter-State relations. Trade on the national scale is markedly asymmetrical (Table 14), intensifying differences and magnifying problems in the frontier zone. To the United States Mexico is a minor trading partner, with less than 5 per cent of American trade; to Mexico the United States remains, as it has long been, the dominant buyer-and-supplier (70 per cent of total trade in 1980), in spite of recent Mexican policies to diversify the country's markets. Indeed, the inclusion of Mexico in the General Preferences system (GPS) of the US in 1976, as part of a programme to aid Third World countries, grants some preferential tariffs to Mexico among others; 950 Mexican items now enter the US free of tariffs, though sixty-one products will be subject to full tariff rates, because of exclusionary clauses. Unfortunately, these latter items include textiles and certain foodstuffs and represent over 25 per cent of current Mexican exports to the USA.

Table 14. *Mexican–US trade and frontier transactions, 1965–79*

	% imports from USA	% exports to USA	Frontier transactions of Mexico ($USm)				Tourism ($USm)			
			Income	Expend.	Bal.	Coefficient of retention	Income	Expend.	Bal.	Coefficient of retention
1965	65.7	57.5	499	295	+204	40.9	274	119	+155	56.7
1970	61.5	70.0	892	563	+329	36.9	415	192	+223	53.9
1975	62.8*	61.9*	1,578	1,160	+418	26.5	800	445	+314	39.2
1979	71.5*	68.6*	2,981	2,516	+465	15.6	1,429	692	+737	51.6

* excluding *maquiladora* operations
Source: Banco de México, SA.

The asymmetry of trade is indicated also by its structure and by its net impact upon the Mexican economy. During the period since 1960 the proportion of foodstuffs and raw materials, other than petroleum, in Mexican exports to the US has been falling, and that of manufactured goods, particularly machinery and transport equipment, has been rising (Ramírez 1978). In spite of this degree of convergence in structure the overall Mexican deficit has been growing, both in absolute and in proportionate terms. In frontier transactions generally, though there has been an increase in Mexican net income, 1965–79, the coefficient of retention of US dollars earned has been falling steadily, and even in the case of net tourist receipts the coefficient of retention, though substantial, has obstinately failed to improve. The general verdict then must be one of economic drainage towards the USA, posing an increasingly acute problem for Mexican policy-makers anxious to protect their economy and retain control over its destiny.

Nowhere is this issue more acute than in the Border communities along the Rio Grande. Coefficients of retention of US trade dollars vary widely by individual Mexican cities, but virtually without exception they have been declining in recent years. In 1970, Rio Bravo showed 65 per cent retention, Acuña 59 per cent, and Matamoros 57 per cent. Nuevo Laredo on the other hand had only a weak 25 per cent retention (México Sec. Indust. Comercio 1972). Fortunately, there was a much higher level of retention of the US tourist dollar, with some 57 per cent of total Mexican tourist receipts accruing to all northern Border cities..

The international boundary is to a limited extent a permeable, even a porous membrane (Sloan and West 1976, 451), while in other respects it acts as a finite barrier, defining and constraining the nature and volume of transactional flows. National screens at the Border seek to protect the local labour market from oversupply and competition, prevent the overburdening of social or welfare services, and keep out undesirables. In terms of goods, local products are to be safeguarded, revenues acquired through tariffs on imports, unnecessary luxury imports limited, and the import of dangerous substances prevented (Price 1971). In operating such Border screens tensions in the frontier zone are inescapable. In social interaction among frontier communities the very measure of intensity of communication gives greater potential for instability, just as the range of interaction provides grounds for enhanced social conflict (Bustamante 1979, 471). Yet in the cities on the Rio Grande, remote from the major centres of economic and social activity even within their own State or Province, there has developed a symbiotic interdependence (Stoddard and West 1977, 8), in which the frontier zone itself has become an interlinked, contiguous economic system. Within such a system are reflected, and at times magnified, the general frictions of international trading. Given such a prospectively disruptive situation it is not surprising that the Border cities have sought ways and means of mitigating their hardships by closer collaboration for mutual advantage. Such co-operation, however, has had to be set within a framework of wider national policies which, though no doubt good for the nation, have often had an altogether undesirable impact at the Border.

The degree of economic interdependence between the Mexican Rio Grande cities and their US counterparts (p. 251) is on a scale rarely found along any other world frontier, and, furthermore, it has been growing steadily. As an El Paso witness put it to an Immigration Commission hearing:

The Commission may question our concern for the welfare of the Mexican city at Juárez, or why this estimated fifty million dollars in wages should not be earned by US citizens. Aside from the fact that these people are our very good friends, the drawing of an arbitrary line through 750,000 people does not separate them culturally, socially and most of all economically. Because it is estimated that eighty-five per cent of all the wages earned by commuters in the El Paso area are spent in El Paso we have a selfish interest (US Congress, House 1968, 147).

Or, to quote an influential citizen of Laredo: 'We'd be a cow town without good relations across the river' (Sloan and West 1976, 462).

The commercial relationships between the US and Mexican cities on the Rio Grande are concerned primarily with retailing and tourism. Wholesaling of American goods in Mexico is tightly restricted and the extension of US services across the Border is effectively prohibited.

RETAILING

Table 15 illustrates the two-way flow of shopping purchases, modified on the basis of a field sample enquiry in El Paso and Laredo in 1978.

The range, quality, and price of goods usually favours the American retailer, except for those items which are distinctively Mexican in character and, on that account, are competitive from within Mexico. The main streets of the US Border cities are thronged with Mexican daily shoppers or commuters purchasing items to take back across the Rio Grande. On the streets leading to the river in El Paso the cheaper stores vie with second-hand clothing shops, saloons, and junk-merchants competing for the mass Mexican trade. In the main shopping areas speciality shops and the larger department stores serve the Mexican middle-class as well as local residents, while a growing number of modern shopping malls on the American side act as magnets for buyers from a wide area of northern Mexico. The policies of the Mexican government to offset their consumer flow to the US are referred to later. For some decades American competitiveness has been increasingly dominant, binding together the economy of the US and Mexican Border towns.

The hinterlands (p. 93) served by retailers in the Rio Grande cities are often remarkably widespread (Huff and DeAre 1974).

Table 15.   *A complementary shopping list*

Buy in Mexico	Buy in US
Services, including	Manufactured goods,
Entertainment	Clothing, including second-hand
Medical, especially for Mexican-Americans	Cars
	Car parts
Dental, particularly appliances	Consumer durables, washing
Some car repairs	machines, refrigerators
Legal	Electrical goods and appliances
Haircuts	Canned goods
Staples	
Sugar, rice, most vegetables, fruit, beef	Poultry, eggs, salt, bread, processed milk, margarine
Bottled beverages	
Spirits	Spirits
Beer	
Soft drinks	
Furniture	
Prescription drugs	Cigarettes
Tourist items: arts and crafts; clothing; records	

Sources: D. S. North (1970) *The Border Crossers*, 39; fieldwork

Although the Border retail market is inextricably interwoven, it is still highly sensitive to currency fluctuations and to shifting national policies. For about one hundred years there has been a cumulative devaluation of the Mexican peso against the US dollar. The sharpest devaluations occurred in the late 1890s, the 1930s, in 1954 and, most dramatically, in September 1976 (Martínez 1977). In all cases there was short-term dislocation of the Border economy, sharp rises in unemployment, poverty, aggravated inflation, and a withering of trading contacts, lasting variably from a few months to a year before adjustments could be made to the new situation. South of the Rio Grande the cost of imported commodities increased and the standard of living fell as US demand forced up prices even in Mexico. The economic stagnation in northern Mexico from the 1890s' devaluation lasted through the effects of the 1910 Revolution to the boom of the 1920s, inspired by Prohibition in the US. The Depression of the 1930s and its peso devaluation had a similar traumatic impact, inducing unemployment, poverty, and bankruptcy on both the US and the Mexican shores of the Rio Grande. Large numbers of poor Mexican-Americans regularly crossed the river to buy essentials in the Mexican Border cities, contributing to inflation in Mexico and causing US officials to seek authorization to remove from the relief rolls any who spent welfare dollars outside the country. A further devaluation of the peso in 1954 virtually brought Border trade to a standstill. By this time the Mexican

PLATE 7. Del Rio. South Main Street

PLATE 8. C. Acuña. Main shopping street

government was envisaging the protective policies for the northern Border which came into effect in the 1960s and 1970s. From an initial loss of perhaps 30 to 40 per cent of their retail trade, El Paso traders recovered their prosperity as the Mexican Border experienced a population boom and a rapid increase in consumer purchasing power.

The 1976 devaluation was the most considerable, from 12.5 to 20 pesos to the dollar, and the short-term impact was correspondingly severe (Stoddard and West 1977), though it was uneven among individual towns and cities along the Rio Grande. Inflation in Mexico was rampant (22 per cent per annum in 1974), but the US Border cities were also undergoing a recession with rising unemployment levels, at a time when the sharp Mexican devaluation struck home. Lacking diversity in an economic structure which had been increasingly geared to the needs of Mexican consumers the impact caused an abrupt downturn in local US revenues and bridge tolls, as well as creating a rising need for unemployment and welfare relief. Eagle Pass, Laredo, Hidalgo, and Brownsville were the most seriously affected. With a resident population of about 1,500 but a daytime visitation by thousands of transients Hidalgo was stopped in its tracks, while the downtown areas of Laredo and Brownsville, serving pedestrian traffic from Mexico, were economically devastated. McAllen further upstream was prospering at the time of devaluation and had a unique supplementary revenue from the 'snow-birds', annual migrants from the Northern winter in search of Southern sun. El Paso initially experienced a loss of 50 per cent of retail trade, aggravating an already serious unemployment level (20–25 per cent at the peak). Small businesses were the most directly affected, with clothing shops the principal sufferers. The buyers' market spread across into Mexico. At the PRONAF shopping centre in C. Juárez it was reported: 'We have to have sales and mark our produce down by thirty per cent. We give our customers free soft drinks, coffee, and tea and even good brandy. And still they come and insult us by making us prove our silver is sterling and our turquoise is real by using a flame test!' Like El Paso, however, Del Rio had a large nearby armed forces camp and, with tourism from Mexico, weathered the storm better. Within a year the Border economy had readjusted, though some economic scars still remain. In Feb. 1982 the peso was again devalued, by 30 per cent.

TOURISM

To a beleaguered Mexican Border economy tourism was hailed as a panacea, but like all glittering prospects has somewhat flattered to deceive. 'It is an infinite resource, renewable and unlimited' claimed the Secretary for Tourism, but it is unlikely to be as cheap and prolific a source of income as in the past' (Stansfield 1980, 227). The volume of tourism has certainly progressed (Bryan 1957), and by the mid-1960s income from tourism equalled 60 per cent of Mexican exports by value. Though there had been fluctuations during the 1970s, by 1979 tourism constituted almost 9 per cent of Mexican national income (Table 16). Moreover, during the 1970s the incidence of tourism had become all-year-round, with balance of traffic between the seasons. The numbers flying into Mexico form a rising proportion of tourist traffic (60 per cent in 1979), with no impact on the overflowing Border economy. On the other hand, this potential loss is vastly more than offset by the formidable day-traffic of American citizens across the Rio Grande. This traffic is concealed within global figures of Texas Border bridge-crossings (1977) at 81 millions, of whom 50 millions were US citizens. For the El Paso bridges the figures were respectively 28 and 16 millions; at Laredo 11 and 7 millions.

Table 16.   *Tourists visiting Mexico (residential stays), 1930–79*

	1930	1939	1947	1960	1970	1979
	23,769	127,822	239,756	690,693	1,984,307	4,135,000
1979		Mean expend. $US		(per diem)	Mean stay (days)	
by air	2,496,000	447		47.7		9.4
land	1,639,000	190		16.7		11.4
	1st	2nd		3rd		4th quarter
by air	716,000	602,000		570,000		609,000
land	352,000	413,000		407,000		467,000

Source: Banco de México.

The economic and social impact of tourism is territorially highly selective, and variable over the years, in response to general economic conditions, shifting consumer tastes, and the degree of success of advertising and government policy. Certainly there is enhancement of foreign exchange earnings, though the counterflow of Mexican tourists to the US (now rising ever more sharply) reduces the net takings to little more than one-half. Employment opportunities are expanded, and throughout Mexico 750,000 people are directly involved in the tourist industry, while some 3.75 millions are dependent upon its prosperity. Yet many of the jobs in hotels, catering, or curio shops are temporary and ill-paid; moreover, there are fewer openings for men who form the bulk of the unemployed on the Border. Also on the positive side it is argued that the multiplier effects from tourism, especially the social spin-off, create 'demonstration benefits' to add quality to life (Jud 1974, 20). Potentially, tourism may help to stimulate the local economy in rural

PLATE 9.   Laredo. International bridge, from US customs post

PLATE 10.   Rio Grande, looking across to Laredo from the Mexican shore; new shopping mall on the left

PLATE 11. Matamoros. Mexican Customs post and Border traffic

PLATE 12. Brownsville. Rio Grande and International bridge. Possible *mojados* below the bridge

areas, but of this there is no sign on the Rio Grande. Even the re-creational activities around the Amistad Dam are an integral part of the economic structure of the nearby towns, and of little or no benefit to the Mexican peasantry.

On the debit side, the high social costs of tourism affect local culture and the pleasure, if not vice-oriented intentions of visitors have traditionally created an undesirable social climate (p. 102). In the Mexican towns on the Rio Grande 80 per cent of American tourists failed to stay overnight, but came for 'a day of horse-racing, bull-fights, *margaritas* and a car-boot full of shopping'. The image carried by the visitors has much to do with an unflattering, more turbulent historical heritage, violent, sinful, free-loading, and forgettable. It has been the talk of the Mexican federal planners to try to change this image, substituting order, folk-culture, and cleanliness in its place. The task has still far to go.

COMMERCIAL DEVELOPMENT POLICIES

The domination of the Borderlands by US traders led to protective measures by the Mexican government on behalf of its citizens and entrepreneurs. Such policies showed a degree of ambivalence, however, since the Mexicans were at all times anxious to benefit from the 'spread' effects of the more vigorous economy and affluent life north of the Rio Grande, while seeking a measure of control on the adverse 'backwash' implications from a lesser degree of provision or competitiveness. The US government, on the other hand, on principle remained aloof from the commercial market, concerning itself from time to time simply with tariff modifications, or the relief of local unemployment by piecemeal Economic Development Administration (EDA) measures after 1965.

Between 1885 and 1905 a *zona libre* ('Free Zone') was reconstituted on the Mexican side (p. 57), to a depth of 20 kilometres (12 miles), within which there was effectively duty-free movement of goods. American merchants claimed that such privileges gave Mexican competitors an unfair advantage, aggravated by the increasingly lucrative trade in smuggling (Stoddard *et al.* 1979, 6). The Free Zone was abolished under President Porfirio Díaz, the result of both internal and external pressures, but such a policy was reintroduced with more limited application during the 1930s. Free zones were defined on the Californian Border and *perímetros* (duty-free frontier enclaves) facing Arizona, and along the Border with Guatemala; the Mexican cities along the Rio Grande enjoyed no such benefits before the 1960s.

The serious unemployment in Mexican Border cities, following upon the termination of the *bracero* farmworker programme and the contemporaneous floodtide of immigrants from the Mexican countryside, created a politically explosive social situation during the 1960s. To meet the deepening crisis the National Frontier Programme (*Programa Nacional Fronterizo*) was launched in 1961 (Chávez 1961), with wide-ranging initial objectives, to 'create a gigantic continental shop window' (Dillman 1970, 501). The frontier zone for this policy was once again defined as 20 kilometres in depth and, in effect, the full Mexican customs boundary was moved to this southern limit. The tariff schedules even at that limit were closely geared to the protection of the interior market for domestic products: 5 per cent on raw materials, 5–10 per cent on capital goods, 50 per cent on consumer items, and 100 per cent on luxury goods.

The three elements of the PRONAF were: the regeneration of the Border cities, diversification of both the local agricultural and indus-trial economies, and the beautification of the Mexican Border entry points. The latter achievement is indeed very striking in architectural terms and the casual visitor may be forgiven for assuming that it is rather the Mexican end of the Border bridges that is the gateway to the affluent society. A general urban 'clean-up' programme was set in motion, but priority seems to have been given to new civic buildings, tourist hotels, and the face-lifting of only the main streets leading from the Border into Mexico (Fouts 1973, 4). Moreover, the largest cities were the major beneficiaries of a policy designed both to promote tourism and to foster consumer spending by the Mexicans on their own side of the Border, rather than in the US twin-cities across the Rio Grande. By 1970 there was clear evidence of achievement, though it was concentrated and often verged on the grandiose. In C. Juárez, for example, a new race-track was built, a *charro* (rodeo) ring created, a major new shopping complex for tourists located on the edge of town, a country club, stores and restaurants subsidized, and a Museum of Art and History set up (Gifford 1969). Less progress was made in offsetting the magnetic attraction of the US retail centres and voices were raised against a programme overtly intended to influence American visitors, rather than addressing itself to the rampant social ills of the rundown and overcrowded Border cities. As a Mexican put it: 'The federal government always launches the construction of grandiose projects . . . It is more important to plan on paving streets and providing water and electricity.' Some even claimed the 'PRONAF was not intended to solve local problems', but rather to 'negotiate diplomatic understandings, to indulge business interests on both sides of the Border, and to obtain the funds necessary to pay the price of the country's political stability' (Ugalde 1978, 112).

Also under the 1961 PRONAF policy there was a remission of some duty on goods imported by local entrepreneurs and on sales of indus-trial goods made by Mexican residents within the 20-kilometre frontier zone. Furthermore, to promote two-way trade between the Mexican interior and her Border cities 25 per cent of air, rail, and sea freight costs could be remitted (México, Sec. de Industria y Comercio 1972).

Overall, success had been but partial and, in 1971, a more ambitious programme was put into operation, to 'achieve the economic conquest of the frontier' (Santisteban 1979, 37). The objectives had changed little: to integrate the Border towns more tightly into the Mexican economy, relieve unemployment, and stabilize the Mexican consumer within his local retail market. But the measures adopted were more complex and comprehensive (Urquidi and Villarreal 1975, 169). A new government commission was created (*Comisión Coordinadora del Programa Nacional de Desarrollo de las Franjas Fronterizas y Zonas Libres*) to co-ordinate the programmes, and the economic development committees established earlier in each Border town became the agents for the issue of permits and advice on development proposals. The measures ranged from improved facilities for the temporary import of goods and aid to establishments serving the Border zones; reduction or remission of federal taxes on sales in those zones; continuance of the freight subsidies mentioned above, with prospective increase from 25 to 50 per cent of charges; stimulus to the development of *maquiladora* manufacturing plants; and extension of the free importation of machinery and equip-ment needed by them.

The development programme for the retail sector was seen as especially important. The expansion of custom-built commercial centres was encouraged by ten-year subsidies and tax remissions on the import of essential foreign goods and equipment needed for the estab-lishment and operation of the centres. The capital behind such centres had to be Mexican, or in exceptional cases with a majority Mexican shareholding, imported goods for sale to local consumers had to be priced as on the US side of the Border, and at least 50 per cent of sales had to be of national products (Duret 1979). This latter provision led to a proliferation of curio and souvenir shops, arts and crafts centres, to serve the needs of the American tourists. An ingenious provision to keep the Mexican consumer from crossing the Rio Grande to shop was the programme of so-called lure items (*artículos ganchos*). These items were imported free of tax for sale in the Mexican frontier zone, but had to be priced at or below the US price (Basulto Ortega 1978). Quotas for both products and points of sale were laid down. Such imports increased rapidly during the 1970s, in spite of the unstable economic climate. In 1974–5 alone the sales volume of lure items increased by 39 per cent, while that of products of Mexican national origin fell by 21 per cent.

Although the programme of lure items was intended to staunch the loss of retail custom to the US Rio Grande cities it had certain adverse effects. Nor did it effectively diminish the retailing dominance of the US

Border towns, whose shops continued to have more varied and substantial stocks and were no less price-competitive. Furthermore, banking credits were more freely available to US retailers, at low interest
levels, for acquisition and holding of stock. Indeed, the lure items
programme added to Mexican dependence on the US, enhanced the
attractiveness of southbound smuggling for items in considerable and
steady demand, and drove many local Mexican products out of the
Border markets (Urquidi and Villarreal 1975, 171).

   Through the 1970s the unequal struggle with nearby US competitors
was pursued, with additional legislation to buttress the Mexican Border
economy. In 1974 Decrees were formulated to give fiscal aid for small and
medium-sized Mexican firms setting up in the 20-kilometre frontier
zone (Diario Oficial 1974). Initially, such firms had to have less than
five million pesos capital (raised to twenty-five millions in 1976) and be
100 per cent Mexican owned. Essentially, this was a policy of creating a
national counterpart to the implanted *maquiladora* firms, and it had
modest success. By December 1978 there were 184 aided firms, employing almost 5,000; seventy-four were in C. Juárez, twenty-seven in
Reynosa, twenty-four in Nuevo Laredo, twenty in Matamoros, and
seventeen in Piedras Negras. In a sense, this policy aimed to provide
a more balanced Border economy under Mexican control, with local
industrial entrepreneurs enjoying benefits similar to those of
merchants, shopkeepers, and hotel or restaurant owners. The outcome
was a greater local supply of Mexican products, ranging from clothing
to typewriters, electric motors, preserved fruits, and fruit juices. The
freight subsidies for products from the interior of Mexico and destined
for the Border markets were sustained, and the frontier zone continued
to be defined as a 20-kilometre strip.

   The involvement of the Mexican government in the Border market
has thus become cumulatively more significant, but in many respects,
in its impact, it was little more than a minor increment in the growth
process, ultimately powerless in the face of US dominance from across
the Rio Grande. Most recently, the underlying growth-pole philosophy
has been taken a stage further. Industrial decentralization is to favour
designated localities throughout Mexico, for the rational distribution of
industry and population. The new bonanza of abundant petroleum and
natural gas will be used to promote more balanced national economic
development. To succeed on the Rio Grande these policies will need to
integrate the disparate strands of industrial development with those of
commercial expansion, presently vulnerably divided and both inescapably fragile. National policies for greater industrial self-sufficiency
will need to be more actively presented. The enhancement of commercial policies to secure the Border market for Mexicans should go
hand in hand with a more effective persuasion of producers in central

Mexico to compete with their US rivals for the custom of the Rio
Grande cities. Presently they all too often prefer the high profit margins
of the protected internal metropolitan market.

Finally, although economic growth for the Mexican Border must be a
high priority, since new job provision is an essential ingredient towards
meeting rising unemployment and continuing population expansion,
such a policy must be more clearly tempered by social justice. To some
extent the city revenues, swollen by the proceeds of the tourist trade and
the American-owned in-bond plants, can provide for the needs of the
poor, but more deliberate attention to the problems of the *barrios* will
be needed if the turbulent social discontent is to be contained.

BORDER INDUSTRIALIZATION POLICIES

One of the most dramatic and unusual elements of the townscape of
Mexican Border cities on the Rio Grande is the peripheral location of
recently established manufacturing plants, almost exclusively branches
of American parent firms (Fig. 27). These plants would certainly not be
located there had the Rio Grande not acted as a line of sovereign
division, between States, economies, and cultures. Such an international interface posed special opportunities, but also alerted sensitivities on both sides, sharpened by the extreme inequalities between
the neighbours on either bank. As has been seen, the Mexican government has traditionally been protectionist for its Border communities.
Already in the 1917 Constitution, foreigners in Mexico were forbidden
to own property, including factories, within 100 km of the landward
frontiers and 50 km of the coast (Baerresen 1971, 55), and this interdiction still holds good. However, in 1965 a Border Industrialization
Programme (BIP), *Programa Industrial Fronterizo* (PIF), was launched by
the Mexican government, to become the driving force behind a set of
legislative measures for combating the serious economic and social
problems of the northern Border cities. It was in response to the
profit-making opportunities offered by the BIP that American firms,
many of them multinationals, established manufacturing capacity in
the Mexican cities on the Rio Grande. There have been shifts in official
policies, even within such a short time since the original Mexican
programme was formulated, and the dominating US economy has
fluctuated between prosperity and depression, but the cumulative
effects of the BIP are there for all to see: in December 1979, there were
570 plants under the programme along the entire US–Mexican Border,
employing 120,000 people; in June 1978, 165 plants in the Mexican Rio
Grande cities provided just over 53,000 jobs, which would not otherwise
have been available.

Nevertheless, even with such impressive short-term achievements the BIP continues to be a hotly debated issue, with protagonists and opponents on both sides of the Border. This process of Border industrialization involved the most developed economy in the world, on the one hand, and a classic developing country on the other. Inevitably, industrialization would be interpreted initially in global rather than local terms, and ideologically as well as in the practical or pragmatic terms of economics. From the point of view of this study, it is rather the differential impact on the Border itself, for good and ill, in the eyes of both Americans and Mexicans, that is principally at stake.

It is indeed tempting to set Border industrialization within the context of an unequal struggle between the developing and the developed world, the so-called North–South conflict. The sharpness of inequalities is nowhere greater than on the US–Mexican Border. All the classical models for growth and development may be brought into play in analysing so disparate a situation. The price of such ill-located, ill-balanced, and dependent industrial location may be said to be the sacrifice of development for growth, of equity in the interests of efficiency, and efficiency for the foreigner at the expense of the Mexican national. Not surprisingly, the evils of dependency are to be the lot of the Mexican Border cities, with the multinational firm cast as the villain of the piece (Fernández 1977, 131–2). Somewhat magnanimously the American view stresses interdependence (Jova 1975, 4) to mutual Mexican and American advantage, in commercial transactions, as in business and finance. A cooler Mexican look (Santisteban 1979; König 1979) sets out to balance the arguments for and against the BIP within the framework of cost–benefit analysis.

There can be little argument on the relevance of interpretations of the centre–periphery models for both countries and for the fortunes of their respective Border citizens. At the macro-scale, the US represents the centre and Mexico the periphery, in which case the polarizing flows of labour are northwards and those of capital, more selectively and exploitatively, southwards across the Rio Grande. Such an economic 'drainage' towards the centre created the long-standing dependency by Mexico on the USA. Prior to 1945 an international division of labour, based on natural comparative advantage, limited Mexico substantially to primary production. Since the Second World War Mexican government policy has been to break out of such a 'neocolonialist' stronghold, first by developing an import-substitution policy for industrial development (1950–70), and from 1970 onwards a policy more difficult of realization, the promotion of manufactured exports (Fernández 1977, 133). Under this latest phase an uneasy co-existence has developed between free market thinking and restrictive government practice, with foreign capital welcome but only under increasing surveillance and guidance. At the level of the Border, the cities of both countries are markedly peripheral within their national space, and marginal too in terms of their social and economic structure (US Dept. Commerce 1968; Méx. Sec. Indust. Com. 1974). The twin impediments of distant location and defective structure have led to particular forms of dependency locally across the Rio Grande, but, notably too, have transformed some of the bonds of Border dependency into the advantages of a mutual symbiosis (Torres 1976, 1406). The economies and social structure of American and Mexican Border cities, and their hinterlands, have already been shown to be distinctively different, and in a measure complementary. The paradox too has been remarked upon, whereby the American settlements are more affluent, more diversified, and have a materially better living environment than their Mexican counterparts, yet it is the US tract along the Rio Grande that is looked upon as one of the most serious problem areas of that nation. By contrast, the northern Mexican Border cities are by no means the most underprivileged nationally, in spite of their remote location and poverty of natural resources. Their problems are certainly serious and widespread, but so too are their potentials, in such close proximity to the US as supplier and market. Lest it be thought that the Border situation on the Rio Grande is inevitably and permanently to be at the expense of Mexico, the comment of a Swiss businessman might be recalled (Montoya 1971, 321: 'You have problems from being neighbours of the richest country of the world? Give me 100 metres of this frontier and you will see what I can do.'

ANTECEDENTS OF THE MEXICAN BIP

The earliest interventions by the Mexican government to protect and stimulate the northern Border economy date back to the Free Zone concept of the mid-nineteenth century (Fernández 1977, 76–80). The concept lapsed but was revived in the 1930s, though not for the frontier with Texas. The guiding purpose at that time was to accept its dependency on the United States, but to mitigate some of the evils of such a long-term relationship, while profiting to the full from the potentials offered. Federal Material Betterment Boards (*Juntas Federales de Mejoras Materiales* (JFMM)) were set up to promote civic improvements and public services in the Border towns, financed by a small percentage taken from local customs receipts (Evans 1972, 5). On the Californian flank of the US–Mexican Border Free Trade Zones (*zonas libres*) were estabished in Tijuana and Ensenada (1933), and in Baja California and western Sonora in 1939. In the latter year, small duty-free enclaves (*perímetros libres*) were created in Nogales and Agua Prieta. The principle of admitting duty-free US goods into these defined and restricted Border zones was a precursor of the later, more specialized BIP policy for the entire Border. Such earlier, duty-free privileges in the twentieth century were not extended to the Mexican Rio Grande cities, even though their economic and social problems were among the most acute. It is, of course, possible to argue that the relaxed attitude of the Mexican government towards collecting import duties from Border zone residents was little more than a recognition of the difficulty of enforcing them in the first place (Evans 1975, 2).

At the onset of the 1960s the accent in Mexican policies for the Border still lay heavily upon the development of the cities as service centres rather than as seats for manufacturing. The PRONAF programme 1961 (*Programa Nacional Fronterizo*) was intended to enhance the living environment of the Border cities, with a view to attracting foreign tourists, as well as improving the locally often deplorable social conditions. A giant government-sponsored Development Bank was to finance Border reception stations, hotels, shopping plazas, municipal buildings, and street improvements. The sudden cutting of the migrant worker (*bracero*) programme by the US authorities in 1964 followed upon the most rapid population growth in the Border cities. As a result, the ebb-tide of returning *braceros* (200,000 unemployed, Santisteban 1979, 2) met the swelling northward flow of rural migrants seeking work on the Border. More would be required from the Mexican authorities than a cosmetic face-lift for the Border, however spectacular such a 'shop-window' operation was intended to become.

THE BORDER INDUSTRIALIZATION PROGRAMME 1965 (PROGRAMA INDUSTRIAL FRONTERIZO)

Although the BIP was a unilateral Mexican policy it was and it remains a calculated response to opportunities offered by the changing industrial structure of the US. Soon after the Second World War it became apparent that all highly industrialized countries would have increasing difficulties in containing production costs, most notably labour costs, in that widening range of manufactures which were open to increasing international competition from low labour-cost countries. During the early 1960s this led to a wave of investment by US firms in 'offshore' production facilities in Puerto Rico, Korea, Taiwan, the Philippines, and Singapore. With the exception of Puerto Rico these countries lay distant across the Pacific and, in some cases, political instability was a perennial risk and there were threats to foreign capital to be reckoned with. Yet for an increasing number of American firms 'offshore' operations were said to be the only way to compete even in their own market with foreign-made goods, quite apart from sustaining US competitiveness in third-party countries. Aware that US companies were migrating to reduce operating costs, the Mexican government decided to establish a programme to attract such firms to Mexican northern Border cities. Labour-intensive imports into the US had grown from about one billion dollars in 1965 to three billions by 1969. In the latter year Mexico was getting only 2 per cent, compared with 55 per cent for Asia and 28 per cent of such trade for Europe. Thus the potential for Mexico to profit from the fast-growing demand for US 'offshore' facilities seemed immense, and on the very door-step.

From a Mexican standpoint the advantages of a successful BIP development were clear. It was likely to be one of few opportunities to create new jobs in an area of chronically rampant unemployment and heavy demographic pressure; in the short-term it would bring in much-needed foreign exchange to improve the balance of payments. The multiplier effects might be considerable: first-time training for industrial workers and native managers; diversification of the Border economy; establishment of satellite firms and businesses (transport, contracting, retailing, accountancy, commercial, banking, insurance); development of industrial linkages through Mexican auxiliaries, supplying raw materials or intermediate products; and an enhancement of Mexican fiscal revenues and the tax base (Bustamante 1975, 185; Newman 1979, 290).

To the US entrepreneur the advantages seemed equally positive (Newman 1979, 289). These included an ample supply of low-cost and committed labour, with initially at least little or no union organization; proximity to the US market; lower costs and ease of communications; rapid transit across the US–Mexican Border; Mexican political stability; possibility of 100 per cent equity ownership of the 'offshore' operation by the US manufacturer (1977 Regulation), except for textile manufacturers; and a possibility for US managers and skilled workers to live in the US Border cities and commute to work in Mexico.

The necessary catalysts to launch the BIP were twofold. The Mexican legislation permitted import into Mexico, free of duty, for all necessary machinery, equipment, raw materials, and components to be used in an 'offshore' plant. The only limiting requirement was that the entirety of production from the plant must be exported from Mexico, unless it substituted an imported good. At least 90 per cent of the labour force had to be Mexican nationals (McClelland 1979, 5), and there were stipulations on minimum wages and conditions of work. The Mexicans termed the US 'offshore' plants either 'in-bond' plants or, more commonly, *maquiladoras*. (The Spanish term *maquila*, in its original usage, referred to the portion of flour retained by the miller as payment for grinding someone else's grain.) In 1972 the definition of *maquiladora* was enlarged to include also industrial plant, already operating to serve the Mexican market, but which developed an export function, providing that the direct cost of the exported product should not exceed 40 per cent of total production (Urquidi and Villareal 1978, 157). The term 'in-bond' refers to the bond (*fianza*) which had to be deposited by the

US firm, determining the maximum of items permitted free entry at any one time. Revolving bonds were for sureties for materials assembled or processed; single-entry bonds were guaranteed for machinery and other capital goods (Dillman 1976, 140). Beginning in 1971, firms could pledge some of their Mexican assets to guarantee items usually covered by single-entry bonds (Baerresen 1971, 70–1). By 1973 bonding costs had been reduced considerably to encourage more US firms to enter under the BIP scheme.

A peculiar set of US Tariff Code provisions (USTS 806.30/807.00, Tariff Classification Act 1962) makes possible the shipment of US-manufactured components abroad for assembly or processing, with import duties having to be paid only on the value added to their finished or semi-finished product when reimported to the USA. Components may not be altered, except for lubrication or painting, but they may be integrated with others, e.g. condensers into radio sets, the sewing-together of clothing parts cut on the US side of the Border (Hunt 1970, 305). Schedule 807.00 covers, among other items, motor-vehicle components, semi-conductors and parts, TV sets and components; 806.30 concerns principally steel and other metal mill products, electronic and electrical articles, metallic vehicle parts. Textile products, including apparel, were similarly benefited, but only within the overall limiting quota on imports on Mexican textiles.

Table 17. *Imports from Mexico under Tariff Schedules 806.30 and 807.00; and textile products, 1978*

806.30	$USm	807.00	$USm	Textile products	$USm
Semi-conductors	18.5	TV receivers, parts	385.6	Brassières	28.4
Vehicle wheels	9.6	Electrical circuit		Women's and girls'	
		equipment	88.3	blouses	22.5
Other motor		Motor vehicle parts	80.9	Women's and girls'	
vehicle parts	4.3			slacks and shorts	22.1
Capacitors	3.3	Semi-conductors	58.5	Others	84.2
Internal combus-		Electric motors,			
tion engines	2.8	generators	56.9		
Materials handling					
equipment parts	1.6	Capacitors	54.1		
		Electrical conductors	51.6		

Source: US International Trade Commission (1979).

In its simplest form the BIP is a Mexican attempt to gain national advantage from the growing US 'offshore' operations. On one hand, it represents a somewhat uneasy alliance between Mexican labour and US technology or managerial enterprise; on the other a potential contest between the Mexican government and US multinational firms. It has led to the concept of the twin plant, or alternatively the dual plant

(Fig. 27). A twin-plant operation in the adjacent US Border city includes all support functions to the 'in-bond' plant on the Mexican side; it includes the assembly or processing of components and/or similar manufacturing operations. A dual plant refers to a limited 'staging' operation on the US side, to maximize efficiency in the Mexican counterpart across the Border bridges. For example, as between the twin or dual plants in Brownsville, Texas, and those in Matamoros across the Rio Grande, there is a clear division of function. The relevant Brownsville plant has the following role: goods inventory, incoming inspection, materials control, technical support, reworking, distribution–communication centre, and management advice; it also undertakes low-volume, short-run production. The Matamoros plant functions as the labour-intensive materials turnover operation, with high-volume, long-run work. In other words, assembly requiring labour-intensive use is completed on the Mexican side, while machining, capital-intensive production, and operations with no Customs advantage remain within the USA.

GROWTH AND CHANGE IN THE BIP

The most remarkable feature about the BIP is the rapidity of growth and proliferation of US plants locating in the towns on the Mexican side of the Border. In 1965 there were only twelve BIP plants on the entire Border, employing 3,087; in 1974 455 plants, with 75,977 employees; and in 1979 570 plants, providing no fewer than 120,000 jobs. There had nevertheless been a very sharp downturn in activity and closure of plants during the recession of the mid-1970s. At the outset, the same kind of comment on the BIP is appropriate as when assessing the contribution of government location of industry policies to the economic health of the British Assisted Areas (House 1978, 31). The volume of employment attained is sizeable and, without the govern-ment location policy, the jobs would not have come. Nevertheless, the BIP proportion of total employment (15.6 per cent of active population in 1970), even of industrial employment (30 per cent in 1970, Urquidi and Villareal 1975) on the Border is relatively low and the programme has by no means achieved a transformation of the local economy. It has, however, contributed a useful diversification and laid some of the foundations for a later industrial expansion.

Though originally, back in 1966, BIP plants could be established only within a 20 km Border zone (see Fig. 5), this was extended in March 1971 to the previously prohibited 50 km coastal zone, and, by Decree in November 1972, BIP plants could thereafter be established in principle anywhere in Mexico (*Comercio Exterior* 1978, 409). There remained an official power of veto on location if the proposed site was in an unduly congested or concentrated industrial city. Even though foreigners may still not own property within 100 km of the Border or 50 km of the coasts, a system of trusteeships has been estabished (1971), whereby Mexican credit institutions may purchase real estate in trust for renting to foreigners under ten-year, or even thirty-year contracts (Fouts 1973, 5). With this greater security on the site and buildings for his plant, together with the 1977 permission for foreigners (other than textile manufacturers) to own 100 per cent of the equity capital of BIP plants, the US entrepreneur was the more likely to favour Mexico than its more distant Far Eastern potential competitors. Interestingly enough the Mexican government counterbalanced its favours to US firms in some measure by an April 1971 Executive Order permitting Mexican manufacturers to recover the full Federal sales tax on their products if sold within the northern Border cities. Furthermore, a 25 per cent discount on air, sea, and rail freight rates was offered, rising to 50 per cent in some cases, on domestic manufactures shipped to the Border. Finally, to strengthen small and medium-scale Mexican industry, Decrees of March 1974 gave fiscal stimuli to such native firms in the 20 km (12.5 mile) northern Border zone. There could be 100 per cent exemption on import duties on machinery and equipment and 60 per cent on raw materials, parts, or assembly items, for firms which had 100 per cent Mexican capital (*El Mercado de Valores* 1974); the textile product industries are also excluded from this provision. The Mexican government remains fully committed to the BIP and in October 1977 fresh 'rules of the game' for *maquiladoras* in Mexico were published in the Official Gazette. A new Commission was created to stimulate the introduction of such plants (*Comisión Intersecretarial para el Fomento de la Industria Maquiladora*) and the Secretariat for National Patrimony and Industrial Development was given a co-ordinating responsibility for the BIP, in the place of previous fragmented ministerial jurisdictions.

In September 1979 the 531 BIP plants (88 per cent located in Border cities) included: 197 in the electrical-electronics industry; 134 in textiles, garments, and shoes; 38 in transport machinery; 32 in furniture; 13 in foodstuffs; 19 in services, and 98 in other manufacturing. The service plants were mainly coupon counters for US supermarkets needing to make claims on manufacturers. The types of plant essentially represent those industries with the lowest overall US Customs tariffs, not more than 25 per cent of the value of reimported items, and with a labour cost amounting to 50 per cent or more of the product (Dillman 1976, 143). About 75 per cent of all BIP employees were women and young girls, certainly not what was intended when the BIP was set up originally, to relieve mass male unemployment.

THE BIP ON THE RIO GRANDE

Table 18 shows the changing distribution of plants along the Mexican

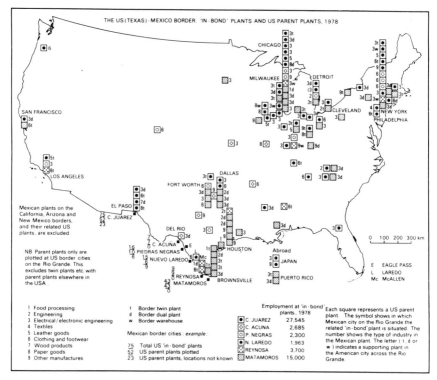

FIG. 27. United States 'in-bond' (*maquiladora*) plants, 1978

Table 18.   *BIP plants and labour force, Mexican Rio Grande cities, 1971–8*

	1971 Plants	Employees	1973 Plants	Employees	1978 Plants	Employees
C. Juárez	52	5,617	61	11,500	75	27,545
C. Acuña	2	818	5	250	7	2,685
Piedras Negras	7	1,594	14	3,487	16	2,300
Nuevo Laredo	24	4,055	19	5,335	15	1,963
Reynosa	2	181	15 ⎫	890	9	3,700
Rio Bravo	1	90	1 ⎭			—
Matamoros	34	3,373	49	6,200	43	15,000
	122	15,728	164	27,662	165	53,193
% Total US–Mexican Border	59	55	42	47	40	62

Sources: Sec. de Industria y Comercio (1971); Dillman (1976); Newman (1979).

side of the Rio Grande, their volume of employment, and the proportionate signficance of plants and jobs within the totals for the entire US–Mexican Border. Rapid but uneven and vulnerable evolution is apparent, even within such a short, but meteoric time-span. Piedras Negras and Nuevo Laredo had had the most fluctuating fortunes. Nuevo Laredo had one of the larger and more spectacular early electronic plants, Transitron, to employ 1,500 electronic assemblers; the US twin plant across the river had only seventy-five employees. A home-based plant of the same firm in Kansas City lost 45 per cent of its work-force about the time the BIP plant was opened. On the other hand, when the Mexican plant later had work stoppages, employment and overtime shot up in Kansas City (US Congress, Senate 1969, 2760). Transitron no longer figures in the list of BIP firms in Nuevo Laredo (El Paso Chamber of Commerce 1978).

Table 19.   *Industry groups, Mexican Rio Grande cities, 1978*

No. of BIP plants	Ciudad Juárez	Ciudad Acuña	Piedras Negras	Nuevo Laredo	Reynosa/ Rio Bravo	Matamoros	Rio Grande cities
1 Food processing	1	—	1	1	1	4	8
2 Engineering	2	—	3	2	2	5	14
3 Elec./electronic eng.	40	3	5	5	2	25	80
4 Textiles	4	—	—	1	—	—	5
5 Leather goods	4	—	—	—	—	1	5
6 Clothing and footwear	10	1	5	4	3	2	25
7 Wood products	6	—	—	—	—	—	6
8 Paper goods	3	1	—	—	—	1	5
9 Other manufactures	5	2	2	2	1	5	17
Total	75	7	16	15	9	43	165
Non-BIP plants	74	No inf.	13	24	27	20	158

Sources: El Paso Chamber of Commerce (1978); *El Mercado de Valores* (1979a).

The predominance of the electrical and electronic engineering industries is clearly apparent (Table 19), with clothing and footwear in second place. Apart from the two major groups the accent is on diversity, both in structural and in spatial terms. Overall, there is little representation of fast-growth manufacturers, though electrical and electronic engineering may be said to have been a major exception until recently. Most labour-intensive industries tend to be directly linked to the final consumer and are consequently liable to be recession-prone, particularly so in the clothing and footwear trades. It is these latter trades which had been based in US Border cities, notably El Paso, prior to the creation of the BIP (US Dept. Commerce 1968). Most other forms of BIP manufacturing, other than food-processing at Matamoros, had little previous relationship either to local resources or products traditionally made in Border cities on either side of the Rio Grande.

A new trend of the late 1970s has been the creation of 'Little Detroits', branch plants supplying car components for General Motors and the Chrysler Corporation. General Motors has three plants in C. Juárez and one in Matamoros, turning out wiring harnesses, seat covers, radios, instrument panel padding, and electrical controls. Chrysler opened a 9,290 sq m assembly plant at C. Juárez in 1979, for making wiring harnesses. A second Chrysler plant, in Piedras Negras, produces shock-absorbers. In happier times for the car industry these would have been notable additions of strength for the BIP, but in 1980 the car industry in the USA was among the most recession-prone.

Initially, most BIP plants were small and often located in temporary, inner-city premises. The ventures were then more speculative and risk-bearing capital was kept to a minimum. Within a few years, however, custom-built plants were being built, particularly for the multinational electrical and electronic firms, and the concept of the industrial park was adopted. C. Juárez (two), Matamoros (two), and Reynosa were the first on the Rio Grande (1973), but all Border cities set up industrial parks shortly thereafter (Dillman 1976, 142), to reap the advantages of grouped factory sites, on greenfield locations with centralized services.

Figure 27 shows the location of the US parent plants/firms related to the BIP plants in the Mexican cities on the Rio Grande. The most prominent feature is the concentration of US parents in the traditional manufacturing belt, from the Atlantic coast to the Middle West. New York (seventeen) and Chicago-Milwaukee (eighteen) are nodes within the belt, the former containing more clothing firms, the latter a high proportion of electrical/electronic manufacturing parents. There is then a scatter of parent firms through the manufacturing belt and southwards. Texas (fourteen in Rio Grande cities, twenty-one else-where in the State) has the greatest single State concentration of parent firms, particularly related to the Brownsville–Matamoros BIP operation. The Texas-based firms are in a wider variety of manufactures than those based in the north-eastern manufacturing belt. Only six US parents are to be found on the West Coast, confirming the lack of what Dillman (1976, 145) termed the 'cross-over' tendency, of linkages between the Rio Grande plants and the West Coast economy. Clearly the BIP linkages with the West Coast are more directly and substantially served from plants facing California, Arizona, and New Mexico.

THE IMPACT OF THE BIP

On the one hand there are the orders of magnitude, which speak largely for themselves; on the other the sets of opinions, attitudes, and prejudices which contribute no less to an evaluation of public policies. It is convenient to deal first with the spectrum of US views, before coming to the more complex, certainly more controversial assessments by the Mexicans.

US viewpoints

The views of entrepreneurs, organized labour, and the US government need to be clearly differentiated. The impact, for good or ill, on the US Rio Grande cities is a further specific issue.

American entrepreneurs profiting from the BIP are a variegated lot. The greater proportion are multinational companies, constantly evaluating the Mexican Border operation against 'offshore' alternatives in the Far East, the Caribbean, and elsewhere. The Mexican Border is perhaps especially favourable for the 'offshore' operation of the smaller or medium-scale US manufacturer, notably so if the items produced are also heavy and bulky. He has fewer options than the multinationals and may otherwise have to close altogether in the US in the face of rising production costs. Low labour-costs and lower total transfer costs to market, including US Customs treatment, are the greatest merits of the Mexican BIP. Labour costs must be seen in terms of wage rates, productivity, level of skill, turnover and recruitment potential, and union organization, together with the restrictions and requirements laid on the entrepreneur by the Mexican government. In the early years of the BIP Mexican wages were from one-third to one-sixth of comparable US rates, certainly not as low as the one-tenth character-istic of Far Eastern competitors. The proximity of Mexico to the USA helped to offset the higher direct labour costs by lower transfer costs, but the Mexican government already enforced minimum wage rates in all cities and stipulated that US firms in the BIP must pay wages 50 per cent above the local minimum (Briggs 1974, 23). The deepening US recession, 1973–5, forced a cutback in all 'offshore' operations, and plants on the Mexican Border were no exception. Inflation in Mexico accelerated alarmingly and, in monetary terms, wages followed suit, increasing by two-thirds between 1973 and 1975. The direct Mexican labour cost was then uniformly up to around one-third US levels, whereas in the Far East in comparable operations the figure remained at one-tenth. Successive devaluations of the Mexican peso, in the late summer of 1976, halved the payroll costs of US manufacturers operat-ing twin plants, but this differential was eroded as the result of more active labour organizations in the BIP plants, and the requirement by the Mexican government that the US firms contribute directly to welfare and the social wage (Mexican federal taxes on value-added, 5 per cent payroll tax for workers' housing fund (INFANOVIT) and one per cent for education, Dillman 1976, 148; holiday pay, cultural, and sports provision, Tansik and Tapia 1971, 333). In the late 1970s, US wage rates rose sharply, and Far Eastern rates proportionately more rapidly than those of Mexico and the Caribbean. Mexico has thus kept a competitive edge, except in the manufacture of very lightweight components with a very high labour impact, in which the Far East remains dominant (Watanabe 1974, 43).

Mexican labour proved to be productive in relation to its cost, and in comparable industrial operations has frequently matched, or even surpassed, the productivity of its US counterpart. Figures of 80 to 140 per cent of US productivity levels have been reported, varying according to the type of operation (Hunt 1970). Even where Mexican workers functioned less productively lower labour costs per unit were said to have offset diminished productivity (Dillman 1976, 143). For small and medium-sized firms the substitution of Mexican labour for the alternative of heavy capital investment in the USA frequently enabled such firms to remain competitive, at least for the time being. Furthermore, old machinery could be transferred to the Mexican Border plant and still remain profitable, when such less efficient technology was more than matched by lower labour costs. Additionally, savings on Mexican labour costs could be used to offset higher US distribution costs, or similar labour savings fund larger stock inventories carried inside the USA.

The labour cost advantage of Mexico remains the staple asset of the BIP, so much so that US plants in the BIP are often producing for American exports to third-party countries, the so-called 'springboard effect'. For example, television tuners are sold to Japan, colour television sets to Venezuela, and chain-saws to Europe, all from US components assembled in Mexico. Moreover, inflation and rising wage-levels have encouraged other industrial countries to enter the Mexican BIP. Japan plans to set up plants in six of the nine largest Mexican Border cities, while already in C. Juárez a Belgian firm manufactures clothing, shipping the entire output back to the home country. Taiwan and South Korea are also interested in producing textiles and electronics at several locations on the Border (McClelland 1979, 8).

Lower total transfer costs into the US market are the second major, and widely recognized, advantage of Mexico over all other 'offshore' competitors. This is not only a matter of lowest freight charges and quicker timing, but also the greater ease of total communications within a twin-plant operation.

US labour organizations only belatedly became antagonistic to 'offshore' operations by US firms, and to the Mexican Border operation in particular. Fernández (1977, 147) attributes this surprising state of affairs, 'the most dangerous "loophole" to minimum wage legislation in the US', as the inevitable outcome of the role organized American labour has played as 'a willing partner in the US government's international adventures. Thus organized labour is left in the paradoxical situation of standing up for imperialism and its necessary foreign policy.' Nevertheless, the American unions are in no doubt where they stand today. As the AFL–CIO Director for Arizona (Calderón 1973, 14) put it, 'It is the old story of North American capitalists exploiting the foreign workers by starvation wages.' The central objection is to so-called 'runaway' US plants (Duncan 1976), relocating in search of cheaper and unorganized labour. In practice, the Mexican government will not accept US firms intending to close down all home-based production, the true 'runaway' plants (*Comercio Exterior* 1971, 304). This process first began *within* the US as the garment trades, for example, set up new plants in Southern cities rather than adding further jobs in Greater New York. The earlier relocation of cotton manufacturing capacity from New England to the Piedmont States is a further, larger-scale and even better-known example. The additional ingredient in an 'offshore' operation is the artificial benefit conferred by the US Tariff Code provisions of items 806.30 and 807.00 (p. 217). As a Congressman put it:

A growing number of firms has used 807.00 to establish assembly plants abroad and thus avoid high US labor costs . . . which results in unemployment here and the possibility that other industries will follow suit to compete with the same margin of profit. This is particularly true of Mexico where a policy of trade development has been accepted as an extension of the Good Neighbour Policy (Tansik and Tapia 1971, 332).

The US unions now argue that the 120,000 jobs created in Mexico by the BIP represent jobs lost to American workers. The degree of truth in this statement is hard to establish. The effects of items 806.30 and 807.00 on the US economy have been constantly under review, and every year there are a few Bills before Congress seeking modification or outright elimination of the two articles. Official reports (US Tariff Commission 1970; US Congress, House 1976; US International Trade Commission 1979) tend to discount exaggerated fears of domestic job loss and, indeed, find the 'offshore' operations supportive of significant employment in the US, both directly and in the form of a return multiplier effect. The Flagstaff Institute's defence of the Tariff provisions claimed that their repeal would: (i) endanger 50,000 US jobs supplying components for assembly and/or processing abroad; (ii) threaten trade with less-developed countries; and (iii) damage the interests of US consumers who have benefited from the cheaper re-imported durables which 'offshore' plants make possible.

US Border communities also have shown some of these more positive economic impacts. From evidence at Brownsville–Matamoros (Garribay 1977, 101–2), one new job in the US was created for every ten in Mexican Border plants. Mitchell (1977) indicated that the 330 million dollar investment in the C. Juárez BIP plants had produced almost 30,000 jobs in that city and 780 jobs in the US twin-city of El

Paso. The American Industrial Development Council (Dorcy 1980) more optimistically claimed that, nationally, every *maquiladora* employee generated one to 2.5 jobs somewhere in the US. The creation of the one billion dollars value-added, the basis of tax on BIP goods re-entering the US in 1979, generated 2.1 billion dollars in US-made semi-processed goods. A recent survey of most of the BIP plants in C. Juárez (Mitchell 1978) showed that no fewer than 432 US companies in thirty-one States were directly supplying raw materials and components to the Juárez plants. The economic symbiosis with twin or dual plants in the US Rio Grande partner city has already been commented upon. There is also general agreement that Mexican BIP workers spend 40–80 per cent of their after-tax income in the adjacent American retail centres. Even where shopping plazas have been built on the Mexican side, to prevent this 'drainage' across the Border, most of the goods on the shelves are stamped 'Made in USA'.

Finally, on a more negative note, the BIP has had some unwanted side-effects on employment in the US Rio Grande cities (US Dept. Commerce 1968). The clothing industry in El Paso, for example, is affected by lower-cost competitors in the Mexican cities. Not all US firms have a twin-plant operation and there is the problem of labour recruitment. Previously, Mexican commuters were employed in large numbers; today they may have alternative jobs in their own Border cities. Labour unions have difficulties organizing workers in the US factories, partly because there is such a high labour turnover and no tradition of 'union shops', but also because of the more tolerant attitudes of labour to control in the BIP plants. According to Briggs (1974, 26) it is the *chicanos* on the Rio Grande who are the sufferers, since they are competing with Mexicans living more cheaply at home, and who have accepted working conditions below those of American standards.

Mexican viewpoints

The 'love–hate' relationship of Mexicans with the USA is well demonstrated in their spectrum of views on the BIP. Governmental and official attitudes in Mexico tend to extol the virtues of their brainchild, the BIP. Indeed, there is every intention of expanding the programme, though with an increasing set of safeguards for its better integration with the Mexican economy and other government policies on location of industry. At the outset of his term of office in 1976, President López-Portillo set several goals for the BIP during the following six years: to create 175,000 new jobs; increase the programme's exports by more than one billion dollars; enhance the proportion of Mexican materials used by Border plants to three billion pesos by 1982; promote the manufacture in Mexico of products currently imported by twin plants;

and stimulate increased national and foreign investment in Border industries. Such a programme of expansion, amounting virtually to 'more of the same', implies an underwriting of the benefits and a discounting of the costs incurred for Mexico by the BIP to this point in time.

Radical political viewpoints (Fernández 1973, 1977; Bustamante 1975; Calderón 1973; *Comercio Exterior* 1978) bring powerful critiques to bear on the BIP, systematically exposing its shortcomings in the light of professed objectives. However, the analysis is all too frequently set within a predetermined ideological framework of dependency, or neocolonialist exploitation by capitalism in the form of foreign multi-national firms, and little merit is acknowledged for a programme which has nevertheless introduced major and positive changes into the Border economy. Fernández (1977, 146) sums up an adverse criticism of the BIP as follows:

It has had a composite unsubstantial employment record, and it may have, in the long run, reinforced the elements causing unemployment. It has produced an undistinguished record of personal income, and has not been directed to relief of the specific structural characteristics of the unemployed population of the area. Its contribution to the development of the Mexican 'human capital' can best be described as nil, and the dollar inflow emanating from the programme is not clearly ascertainable. Finally, various sets of provisions protect BIP from almost any kind of taxation by the host country.

The radical viewpoint reflects strongly held intellectual and political views within Mexico and offers a penetrating and reasoned antidote to the blandness of official policy. Mexican economists (Santisteban 1979; König 1979) have adopted a more detached stance, seeking to assess and contrast the costs and the benefits of the BIP, taking account of political as well as directly economic factors.

The relief of chronic unemployment and underemployment, and the provision of new jobs for the rapidly growing population of the Mexican Border cities, was the principal objective of the BIP. This, then, must be the starting point in any balanced evaluation of its achievements. Mexican statistics on unemployment are neither readily available nor always reliable. The volume of jobs provided by the BIP (120,000 along the entire Border, more than 53,000 on the Rio Grande (1978–9)) must have had some effect on those previously without work, but certainly did not diminish the unemployed by anything like a commensurate amount. For this there are several reasons. Those taken on by the BIP plants were mostly young women—65 to 90 per cent of the BIP labour force according to the particular plant. Most of these had not previously been in work (König 1979, 16), but the unemployment problem at the Border concerned young men and male heads of households. In this sense, the BIP was 'no more than a palliative conceived by a govern-

ment faced with a crisis of underemployment, but incapable or un-
willing to implement the structural changes necessary' (*Comercio
Exterior* 1978, 413). Certainly, the BIP cannot be said to have made
serious inroads into the Border unemployment problem. In many
respects, it offered least to those most in need of jobs: the unskilled rural
folk flocking into the towns, or the dispossessed *braceros* returning from
the US. Indeed and ironically, there are those (Fernández 1977, 141;
König 1979, 16) who argue that the BIP may indeed have contributed
at times to the local unemployment problem. The vulnerability of BIP
plants to the US trade cycle and the consequent turnover of firms on the
Border has periodically added to the reservoir of the unemployed those
who previously had not worked but now sought alternative jobs. This
has been particularly true for young women who have found the conditions of factory working very much to their taste. The instability of
branch plants in marginal localities is a world-wide phenomenon, and
likewise their early closure as the 'bell-wether' of an approaching
depression. As a result, the labour force in such plants is perennially at
risk in what has been called 'the typical slash and burn procedure of
capitalist enterprise in backward countries' (Fernández 1977, 142), or,
one might cynically add, also in the marginal regions of even developed
countries like the UK.

A second criterion is the returns to labour in the form of personal
incomes and conditions of work. To this must be added the associated
public social costs and the extent to which these are offset by BIP firms'
contributions. Although the BIP laid down the minimum wage-levels
plus 50 per cent as required for all BIP plants, and increasingly constrained firms to contribute to the social wage, it has been commented
(Santisteban 1979, 36) that in this as in other respects transnational
capital imposed its own rules of the game. First, BIP firms were
officially permitted to pay only half the minimum wage to those in
training and the period for training allowed has been known to exceed
six months! Second, at the time of the 1974–5 depression BIP firms
exacted further concessions on the use of labour from the Mexican
government: *statutory* lengthening of the training period; power to
reduce the working week arbitrarily; authority to dismiss workers without indemnification; and contracting of apprentices below the
minimum salary level (Santisteban 1979, 35).

Nevertheless, the aggregate contribution of personal incomes to the
Mexican Border economy has been sizeable and decidedly a positive
factor. For 30 per cent of BIP operatives the industrial wage was the
only source of income, for a further 15 per cent it represented less than
30 per cent, and in no case was greater than 50 per cent of household
income (König 1979, 18).

The majority of BIP workers are women and young girls, seventeen to twenty-three years old for the most part, and 85 per cent are unmarried. This is the type of labour preferred for the manually dextrous, but repetitive and monotonous assembly or processing operations. Those born or brought up in the towns are given priority in recruitment and the BIP jobs have considerable local prestige. Women workers wish to keep this new life-style, but it can produce social problems. The daughter may well be the main provider for the family, the father being unemployed, or earning less (Baerresen 1971, 34). Social tensions build up in a local culture which still cherishes traditional taboos for its women. As one informant put it, 'They are destroying Mexican family life along the Border. Up to a few years ago Mexican women did not work outside the home after they were married. Now you see many wives working while the husbands are unemployed' (US Congress, Senate 1969, 2762). The freedom which a working life offers women has had unintended effects. Marriage is often postponed, since many husbands still might not allow wives to work, there are few bachelors with a similar level of prosperity, and many factory personnel officers discriminate against married women, in a 'buyer's' labour market.

Little contribution seems to have been made by the BIP to the social costs created by the steady streams of rural migrants towards the Border. Indeed, there is evidence (König 1979, 19) that personnel managers of BIP plants also tend to discriminate against migrants; of those migrants employed most came as children of parents driven from the rural areas.

It was also intended that the BIP should lead to a 'technological transfer' from the US, particularly in that conventional need of all developing countries (Sharpston 1975), the training and implementation of a factory-skilled labour force. Primarily, unskilled Mexican labour has been used in simple, disaggregated, repetitive operations, at times using equipment considered obsolete in the USA. For example, the assembly work on the semi-conductor has been described as 'intensive, fastidious and repetitive, requiring little capital and little training' (Minian 1978, 141). An alternative case concerns the training for making brassières: 'All are given a dexterity test which judges agility of fingers as well as mental reaction concerning sewing. Testing is based on elapsed time and varies from operation to operation in the bra-making procedure, which involves twenty-two separate steps on a sewing-machine' (Fernández 1977, 141). When skills have been required, the skilled workers or technicians have been brought in from other parts of Mexico, or from the US. The demand for these scarce skilled Mexican workers or professional men denudes indigenous industry to supply plants in the BIP.

The contribution of the BIP to the Mexican balance of payments and the need for foreign exchange is complex, and only a few variables can be measured (Table 20). During the 1970s, the BIP financed 7.8 per cent of the 1970 Mexican commercial deficit on international trans- actions, but as much as 15.0 per cent by 1977. The contribution of the BIP to specifically frontier transactions must have reduced in some measure the growing deficit for Mexico, indicated by a fall in the 'coefficient of retention' (the percentage value of each dollar import retained in Mexico) from 42.2 cents in 1955, and 37.3 per cent in 1965 to 27.0 per cent in 1977 (Santisteban 1979, Table 4). The coefficient of retention would have been higher as a result of the BIP, but for the loss of foreign exchange by the spending of Mexican workers' incomes in the US Border cities, and second, the use of transfer pricing by US BIP firms to reduce their declared profits within Mexico to the benefit of the American parent's profitability (Santisteban 1979, 31).

Table 20.   *Re-exports by BIP plants 1970–9*

	Valued-added re-exported ($m)	% total Mexican manuf. exports	Components imported ($m)	% total Mexican manuf. imports
1970	81.0	18.2	—	—
1974	443.4	23.6	554.7	10.5
1979	1,027.2	25.3	1,070.0	9.0

Sources: Santisteban (1979); Banco de México (1979).

Two manifest weaknesses of the BIP have been, first, the failure to produce significant multiplier effects within either the Border or the national economy and, second, lack of success in integrating with other public policies for the location and development of industry elsewhere in Mexico. Indeed, it has been argued that the BIP is both contrary to sound national growth policy and, furthermore, represents a flagrant contradiction of Mexico's own traditional Border development strategy (Briggs 1974, 365; Fernández 1977, 146). Border policy had tradition- ally been directed to reducing economic dependency on the US, and the 1961 PRONAF scheme was a further tentative step in that direction. The BIP, on the other hand, succeeded only in the measure that linkages with the US were developed and strengthened. Containment of the 'northern colossus' has thus been weakened, decision-taking on growth and investment transferred outside Mexico, and ties with the rest of that country have languished.

In terms of the creation of associated industries, or an enhanced contribution to the Mexican national market, the multiplier effects of the BIP have been negligible. Only 1.5 per cent of raw materials or consumables for the BIP plants originate within Mexico (Santisteban

1979, 30), and the totality of production must be exported. Indeed, the customs advantages of US Tariff schedules 806.30 and 807.00 would be lost if this were not so. Linkages with other Mexican firms on the Border are minimal and the BIP plants operate effectively within their own detached enclaves, an outlying section of the US economy rather than an integral part of Mexico. Almost all avenues for 'spread' effects have been blocked by legislation (Fouts 1973, 17).

It is true that the northern Border is remote from Mexico City and that it has always had poor and expensive communications with the metropolis. The official transport subsidies for Mexican firms on the Border have already been mentioned, but true integration policy is still little more than a pious intention on the part of the government. It is also the case that there has long existed a policy of reducing the industrial concentration and polarization on the national capital in an attempt to correct a disturbing and escalating centre–periphery imbalance. It is tempting, but would be erroneous, to look on the BIP as a considered and integral part of such a coherent programme to redistribute the benefits of growth. The truth is that until the late 1970s (*El Mercado de Valores* 1979b) there had been no overall industrial structure plan for Mexico, and spatial elements had been notoriously lacking, even in the fragmentary and unco-ordinated projects of State or Federal agencies (Lavell 1972, 360).

PROSPECTS FOR THE BIP

Prior to the 1980 world recession there was widespread optimism and a declared official intention to stimulate further growth of Mexican BIP plants. The number of such plants was expected to grow by 50 per cent between 1980 and 1982, creating 70,000 more jobs (Dorcy 1980). The degree of strength in the US economy was seen as the determining factor in any expanded programme, though the disturbingly high rate of inflation in Mexico potentially threatened the labour-cost advantage on which the BIP depends. The Mexican government devalued the peso in Feb. 1982 (30 per cent) to sustain this advantage, though the recently discovered large reserves of petroleum and natural gas could in time put upward pressure on the value of the peso (McClelland 1979, 9).

Mexican policy on the BIP has become more positive. The first priority is to see that the 'in-bond' plants consume more Mexican raw materials. Presently, inputs are limited to labour, electric power, and some other services. Increased consumption of Mexican raw materials would add to local production of intermediate manufactured goods. Several BIP firms have recently sought permission to sell up to 30 per cent of their output within Mexico, and there are even one or two cases where a *maquiladora* firm has ceased to be such and become part of the national industry. A second Mexican objective is the so-called 'industrial branch' policy. This is an attempt to diversify BIP plants away from traditional light manufactures such as electrical or electronic products, apparel or toys into more stable items such as heavy industrial products, the manufacture of capital goods, or car parts and industrial equipment (Newman 1979, 295). International activity will be directed to attracting US firms in these branches, with the hope that they more readily integrate with time into planned Mexican industrial development, while still fulfilling their export function, but an export function less dependent on the vagaries of the US consumer markets.

Third, the Mexican government wants to spread the location of new BIP plants away from the Border and into the interior of the country. In 1978 only thirty-seven of the 453 BIP plants were located away from the Border, though this had been legally permissible since 1972. Firms which began operating at the Border have sometimes moved into the interior when they expanded. Lower wage-levels and occasionally higher government incentives have both been attractions of the interior.

On balance, the BIP has been and continues to be beneficial to Mexico, most notably so in its generation of revenues and personal incomes, but there have manifestly been both economic and social costs as well as benefits. The contribution of the BIP plants is marginal at the level of the national economy and can do little to change the widespread problems of Mexican society. The programme is nevertheless a striking indication of the North–South dialogue, currently in high fashion in the Western world, but here translated into practical terms of mutual investment and focussed at the international Border.

REFERENCES
THE BORDER MARKET

BANCO DE MÉXICO SA (1979) *Indicadoras Económicas,* México DF.

BASULTO ORTEGA, J. D. (1978) *Importancia del programa de artículos de consumo fronterizo (artículos ganchos) en el desarrollo económico de la franja fronteriza norte del\país* Thesis, Univ. Nac. Aut. Méx., Méx. DF

BRYAN, W. M. (1957) *A geographic study of the tourist industry of Mexico,* Unpub. Master's diss., Oklahoma State Univ.

BUSTAMANTE, J. A. (1979) 'El estudio de la zona fronteriza México-Estados-Unidos', *Foro Internacional,* **XIX,** 3, 471–516.

CHAVEZ, A. (1961) *Programa Nacional Fronterizo* (México DF: Pronaf Press).

DIARIO OFICIAL (1974) *Decreto Presidencial,* 12 marzo.

DILLMAN, C. D. (1970) 'Urban growth along Mexico's Northern border and the Mexican National Border Program', *J. Dev. Areas,* **4,** 487–507.

DURET, M. L. (1979) 'Acciones para la integración comercial fronteriza', *Comercio y Desarrollo,* **1,** 6, 62–3.

FOUTS, S. C. (1973) *Mexican Border industrialization: an analogy and a comment,* Austin, Texas, Inst. Latin Am. Stud.

GIFFORD, A. S. (1969) 'Programa Nacional Fronterizo', *El Paso econ. Rev.,* **VI,** 1.

HUFF, D. L. and DEARE, D. R. (1974) *Principal interaction fields of Texas Metropolitan Centers*, Bur. Busin. Res. (Austin, Univ. Texas).

JUD, C. D. (1974) 'Tourism and economic growth in Mexico since 1950', *Inter.-Am. econ. Affairs*, **28**, 1, 19–43.

MARTÍNEZ, O.J. (1977) *The peso devaluation and the Border: some historical observations.* Unpub. manuscript, UT El Paso.

MÉXICO, SEC.DE INDUSTRIA Y COMERCIO (1972) *Estudio del desarrollo comercial de la frontera norte*, México DF.

MÉXICO, SEC. DE HACIENDA Y CRÉDITO PÚBLICO (1971) *Reunión Nacional Tripartita*, in Santisteban, J.L.F. (1979) q.v.

NORTH, D.S. (1970) *The Border Crossers* (Trans-century Corpn: Washington DC).

PRICE, J. A. (1971) 'International border screens and smuggling', in E. R. Stoddard, (ed.) *Prostitution and illicit drug traffic on the US-Mexican Border, Border-State Univ. Consortium Latin Am. Res., occ Pap. 2*, El Paso, Texas.

RAMÍREZ, O. R. (1978) 'Medición del comercio intraindustrial entre México y Estados-Unidos', *Comercio Exterior*, **28**, 10, 1243–62.

SANTISTEBAN, J. L. F. (1979) 'Algunas consideraciones sobre los programas de indus-trialización y de comercialización fronteriza, sus efectos y perspectivos', *Simposio Nacional sobre Estudios Fronterizos El Colegio de México*, Monterrey, Nuevo León.

SLOAN, J. W. and WEST, J. P. (1976) 'Community integration and border policies among élites in two Border cities', *J. Inter-Am. Stud. Wld. Affairs*, **18**, 4, 451–74.

STANFIELD, D. E. (1980) 'The Mexican tourist industry', *Bk. London S. Am. Rev.*, **14**, IV, 226–32.

STODDARD, E. R., MARTÍNEZ, O. J., and LASSO, M. A. M. (1979) *El Paso-Ciudad Juárez relations and the 'tortilla curtain': A study of local adaptation to Federal border policies*. El Paso, Texas.

STODDARD, E. R. and WEST, J. P. (1977) *The impact of Mexico's 'peso' devaluation on selected US Border cities* (Tuscon: SW Borderlands Consultants. Organization of US Border cities and EDA-).

UGALDE, A. (1978) 'Regional political processes and Mexican politics on the Border', ch. 5 in S. R. Ross, (ed.) *Views Across the Border* (Albuquerque: Univ. New Mexico Press), 97–116.

US CONGRESS, HOUSE (1968) Judiciary Committee *Western Hemisphere Immigration*, Hearings, Pt. I.

BORDER INDUSTRIALIZATION POLICIES

BAERRESEN, D. W. (1971) *The Border Industrialization Programme of Mexico*, Stud. in Internat. Devel. and Econ., Center for International Busin., Los Angeles, California (Lexington, Mass.: Heath Lexington).

BANCO DE MÉXICO, *Indicadores Socioeconómicos*, Mexico City.

BRIGGS, V. M. (1974) 'The Mexico-US Border: public policy and chicano welfare', *Stud. in Human Resource Dev.*, **2**, Bureau of Business Res. (Austin: Univ. Texas).

BUSTAMANTE, J. A. (1975) 'El programa fronterizo de maquiladoras: observaciones para una evaluación', *Foro Internacional*, **XVI**, 2, 183–204.

CALDERÓN, L. V. (1973) 'La industria maquiladora extranjera in México: mal necesario de una sociedad subdesarrollada', *Conferencia sobre relaciones economicas entre Mexico y los Estados-Unidos*, (Austin: Univ. Texas).

Comercio Exterior (1971) 'Fragmentos del informe de la Comisión de Aranceles de Estados Unidos sobre las industrias maquiladoras', **XXI**, 4, 292–308.

Comercio Exterior (1978) 'La industria maquiladora: evolución reciente y perspectivas', **XXVIII**, 4, 407–14.

DILLMAN, C. D. (1976) 'Maquiladoras in Mexico's northern border communities and the border industrialization program', *Tijdschr. econ. soc. Geogr.*, **67**, 3, 138–50.

DORCY, J. D. (1980) 'Maquiladoras: the best of two worlds', *The News*, Mexico City, 19–21 February.

DUNCAN, C. (1976) 'The runaway shop and the Mexican Border Industrialization program', *SW Econ. and Soc.*, **2**, Oct.–Nov., 4–25.

El Mercado de Valores (1974) 'De utilidad nacional, las pequeñas y medianas industrias de la frontera', **XXXIV**, 12, 338–40.

El Mercado de Valores (1979a) 'Facilidades a la industria fronteriza' **XXXIX**, 8, 132.

El Mercado de Valores (1979b) 'Estimulos a la descentralización hacia nuevos polos de desarrollo industrial', **XXIX**, 2, 19–20.

EL PASO CHAMBER OF COMMERCE (1978) *US/Mexico Border city twin plants*, El Paso, Texas.

EVANS, J. S. (1972) 'Mexican border development and its impact upon the United States', *SE Lat. Americanist*, **XVI**, 1, 4–10.

EVANS, J. S. (1975) 'The use of incentives for the development of Mexico's northern border zone', *El Paso econ. Rev.*, **XIII**, 9, 1–4.

FERNÁNDEZ, R. A. (1973) 'El Programa industrial fronterizo', *Rev. Radical Pol. Econ.*, Ann Arbor, Michigan, 59–79.

FERNÁNDEZ, R. A. (1977) *The United States-Mexico Border: a politico economic profile* (Notre Dame, Ind.: Univ. Notre Dame Press).

FOUTS, S. C. (1973) *op. cit.*

GARRIBAY, L. (1977) *The BIP of Mexico: a case study of the Matamoros Tamaulipas experience*, unpublished M.S. thesis, Austin, Univ. Texas.

HOUSE, J. W. (ed.) (1978) *The UK Space: resources, environment and the future* (London: Weidenfeld & Nicolson).

HUNT, L. H. (1970) 'Desarrollo industrial en la frontera mexicana', *Comercio Exterior*, **XX**, 4, 304–9.

JOVA, J. J. (1975) 'The US-Mexico Conference on Border industrialization', *El Paso econ. Rev.*, **XII**, 5, 1–4.

KÖNIG, W. (1979) 'Efectos de la actividad maquiladora fronteriza en la sociedad mexicana', *Simposia Nacional sobre Estudios Fronterizos, El Colegio de México–Facultad de Filosofía y Letras de la UNAL*, (Monterrey: N. León).

LAVELL, A. M. (1972) 'Regional industrialization in Mexico: some policy considerations', *Reg. Stud.*, **6**, 343–62.

McCLELLAND, E. L. (1979) 'U.S.-Mexico border industry back on fast-growth track', *Federal Reserve Bank of Dallas, Voice*, 3–9 July.

MÉXICO, SEC. DE INDUSTRIA Y COMERCIO (1974) *Indicadores socioeconómicos de la zona fronteriza Norte*, Mexico City.

MINIAN, I. (1978) 'Progreso técnico e internacionalización del proceso productivo. El caso de la industria maquiladora de típo electrónica', *Cuadernos del CIDE*, **1**, Mexico City.

MITCHELL, J. A. (1977) *Preliminary report on the impact of Mexico's twin-plant industry along the US-Mexican Border* (El Paso: Organization US Border Cities).

MITCHELL, J. A. (1978) *A case study of the 'in-bond' industry*, Tucson, Arizona.

MONTOYA, E. M. (1971) 'Hacia una política realista de desarrollo fronterizo', *Comercio Exterior*, **XXI**, 4, 318–21.

NEWMAN, J. L. (1979) 'Mexico's maquiladora program', *Business in Mexico* (Mexico City: Am. Ch. Comm. in Mexico).

SANTISTEBAN, J. L. F. (1979) *op. cit.*

SHARPSTON, M. N. (1975) 'International subcontracting', *Oxf. econ. Pap.* (New Ser.), **27**, 1, 94–135.

TANSIK, D. A. and TAPIA, S. H. (1971) 'Los problemas de las plantas gemelas en la frontera mexicana', *Comercio Exterior*, **XXI**, 4, 331–5.

TORRES, O. E. (1976) 'Algunas observaciones sobre la economía de la Frontera Norte de México, *Comercio Exterior*, **XXVI**, 12, 1406–13.

US Congress, House (1976) Sub-Committee on Trade, Submission by Flagstaff Institute, *Why we must keep 806.30 and 807.00*, Washington DC, USGPO.

US Congress, Senate (1969) Committee on Labor and Public Welfare, *Migrant and seasonal labor powerlessness, part 5-B, Border commuter labor problem*, Hearings before Subcomm. on Migratory Labor, 91st Congr., 1st and 2nd Sess., Washington DC, USGPO.

US Dept. Commerce (1968) Economic Development Administration, *Industrial and employment potential of the US-Mexico Border*, Rept. prepared by Robert R. Nathan Associates Inc., Washington DC, USGPO.

US International Trade Commission (1979) *Import of goods into the US under Tariff Schedules 806.30 and 807.00*, Washington DC, USGPO.

US Tariff Commission (1979) 'Economic factors affecting the use of items 807.00 and 806.30 of the Tariff Schedules of the United States', *TC Publication 339*, Washington DC, USGPO.

Urquidi, V. L. and Villarreal, S. M. (1975) 'Importancia económica de la zona fronteriza del Norte de México', *Foro Internacional*, **XVI**, 2, 149–74.

Watanabe, S. (1974) 'Constraints on labour-intensive export industries in Mexico', *Internat. Lab. Rev.*, **109**, 23–45.

PART IV

The Political Imperative

CHAPTER 8

Political Structures

At the final stage of assessment, the complexity of Border transactions must be set within the political framework of each country, through which power is exercised, decisions are made, policies formulated, and plans implemented. The nature of government at all levels, its role and significance in the life of the nation, and the structure of the political system are altogether contrasting as between the United States and Mexico. Thus each merits briefly a separate consideration before proceeding to an evaluation of contemporary international relations across the Rio Grande. Unlike the great diversity of economic and social transactions and fluxes political culture has always proved to be a much more intractable export. 'To Americans it is inconceivable and certainly undesirable for the Mexican system to exert an influence on their democracy. Consequently, it is their belief that the influence exerted by the United States on Mexican politics is invariably benign, as any negative elements that might exist (corruption, violence, Tammany Hall bossism) magically remain north of the Border' (Ugalde 1978, 98). The ignorance, even arrogance which this viewpoint implies, has fuelled the persistent misunderstandings which have bedevilled international politics on the Rio Grande, to the perpetual disadvantage of Border communities on both banks.

Political culture includes the Constitution, and the nature of power allocated to the legislative, executive, and judicial arms of government. Apart from interaction between these structural elements of authority, there is the reality of pressures brought to bear through the political parties in the parliamentary system and their relationship, in turn, to the realities of power within the community at large. The political process operates too at different territorial levels, federal, State (or Province), and local. At each level there is interaction through the allocation and exercise of governmental powers, certainly also in party political terms and through the interlocking levels of bureaucracies and agencies. Given this complexity and latent dynamism within each country, it is to be expected that there will be sluggishness, contradictions, and tensions when the interactions become international. In the international system of relationships it is convenient to identify federal to federal, State to Province, and city to city exchanges independently, though in reality these overlap, interlock, and not infrequently result in mutual recriminations. A state of affairs in which the lowest tier, the Rio Grande municipalities, are almost invariably the losers, but then many so-called Border problems may not be specifically Border probems at all (Clement 1979, 395).

THE UNITED STATES (TEXAS) POLITICAL SYSTEM

Both the United States and Mexico are constitutionally federal republics, but there is a great difference in the allocation of powers between the centre and the regions. The reality of power in the US federal system has shifted from an initial co-ordinate form of federalism, with almost equality of powers between the federal centre and the States, to the contemporary mould of co-operative federalism, in which a federal–State partnership provides the keynote, with the latter characteristically acting as the agency for the former in many social and economic fields. Since the Second World War, and most notably after the mid-1960s, the US federal role has proliferated in area development, housing and urban aid, social welfare, employment policy, and minority rights questions. Nevertheless, the diversity and strength of State viewpoints is solidly safeguarded, in the first instance by direct representation in the two Houses of Congress, the States like Texas with a larger population having a proportionately weighted voting strength in the House of Representatives. Second, the operation of federal agencies in a State is a co-operative venture and, though many federal aid programmes go directly to the local level, they usually do so on the advice and with the consent of the State.

The US political system has been characterized as proceeding, for the most part, by a form of disjointed incrementalism, in which political pressures are adjusted to in a gradualist manner, with pragmatism and self-interest, for groups or individuals, seen as cardinal virtues of the American ethos. The two-party system, each representing a broad 'political church', reinforces the system of checks and balances, not always in the direction of democracy, but with local or State interests always very much in mind. Given the traditional dominance by the conservative wing of the Democratic Party in the American South, the voting strength of Texas, and the individualistic identity of its political culture (Dickens 1972; Gutiérrez 1978) it is logical to anticipate that the State has perceptibly and regularly, though not dramatically moved the federal–State power equation in the direction of Texan advantage.

Within Texas the spirit of local democracy is strong, even in opposition to the occasional merits of bureaucratic efficiency. Most municipalities operate under home rule charters, with considerable powers over land use, adjacent unincorporated areas, programme development, and administration. By contrast, Texan counties (Murphy 1933) are substantially unable to control development, assume programme responsibilities, or provide the necessary services.

This has led to many special-purpose districts in unincorporated localities (ACIR 1973, 298). Politically speaking (Nimmo and Oden 1971), Texas has long been a Democratic Party State with a powerful party machine penetrating down to local level. Nowhere has this been more true than in the Rio Grande Border counties, where landowning and city élites have for long effectively controlled both the economy and the political process, even throughout a dual-ethnic society. The establishment and significance of the Mexican-American ethnic party, *La Raza Unida*, has already been discussed (p. 105), but its influence on the Border during the 1970s diminished with incorporation of many of its influentials into the Democratic Party machine (Gutiérrez 1978, 127 *et seq.*). Here and there in particuar communities the Mexican-American voice and vote are significant, if not determining (Garza 1974), but there is a long tradition, yet to be set aside, of the Spanish-surname majority not participating in the political process.

The Democractic Party machine either controls local politics, or sees to it that a minimum number of potential adversary voters goes to the polls (Gutiérrez 1978, 131). Election judges, clerks, and poll-watchers are chosen by the party and, in neighbourhoods where illiteracy is high, the voter will often ask for help from the judge. Mobilization of the vote for an opposition party faces immense difficulties, in which apathy, fear, mistrust, or the belief that the democratic process has little to offer vie with each other. Gutiérrez (1978, 133–4) saw only three possibilities for 'raising political consciousness among ethnic voters: spreading from small groups to a wider constituency, by discussion; reacting forcefully to some unfavourable event; or by setting up a local organization and working slowly over time'. Meanwhile, between one-half and three-quarters of the eligible electorate along the Texan Border do not choose to vote. If such masses could be mobilized 'the shock waves could be felt long distances from the thirteen-county area' (Gutiérrez 1978, 135).

To be effective in tackling economic and social problems political power must be executed through policies and planning bodies. In Texas this involves responsibilities shared between State organizations and federal agencies, with the State acting in the allocation of an important part of federal funding. Multi-county planning did not begin until 1966, to 'provide a focal point for co-ordinating policies, programmes, and plans of State agencies and local government entities' (ACIR 1973, 298). A 'wall-to-wall' system of regional councils resulted, and an additional network of twenty-one State planning regions was formulated during 1968. In the Rio Grande valley the regional councils, five in number, fortunately coincided with the State planning regions, but this harmony was disturbed by different areal designations for soil and water conservation, economic development, and some federal agency units. The regional councils are responsible for: county, city and special agency integration; co-operation in regional planning, though only in an advisory capacity for member governments; and receiving and expending funds from local, State or federal sources. In 1969 the regional councils became recognized as political subdivisions of the State of Texas, and the Upper Rio Grande, Middle Rio Grande (part of the Alamo district), South Texas, and Lower Rio Grande Valley were designated Economic Development Districts (EDDs), under the Public Works and Economic Development Act of 1965. As such they participate in housing planning and aid programmes, health and criminal justice planning and, in two cases, act additionally as regional manpower agencies. The regional councils are also heavily involved in the provision of services to member local governments. Though there is some dissatisfaction with the federal funding for sponsoring and supporting regional councils, this form of planning body represents a stable compromise between voluntary action and general purpose government. As such it is a concept well in touch with the political climate and culture on the Rio Grande.

In August 1977 a Title V Regional Commission was designated under the Public works and Economic Development Act (1965) to cover thirty-six counties in four States (twenty-four in Texas) on the South-west Border; further parts of New Mexico were added in October 1979 (see Fig. 5). The South-west Border Regional Commission (SWBRC) is a deliberate federal-multi-State co-partnership, with a federal co-chairman, to analyse regional economic problems and to develop overall strategies for enhancing economic growth in lagging regions. The Commission is required to 'assess the needs of the region via an inventory of resources and deficiencies, develop long- and short-range regional economic plans, initiate legislation regarding economic development, assist economic development districts within the region, and provide a forum for consideration of the problems of the region' (Clement 1979, 390). In these roles the Commission is a formal mechanism for federal inter-State decision-taking, but the component States are not bound to accept or implement the planning findings. A comprehensive development plan for the South-west Border (SW Border Reg. Comm. 1979) was adopted in February 1980, focussing on four main subject areas: employment and income; infrastructure development; bi-national co-operation with Mexico; and natural resources development. The plan serves as a guide for public and private investment in the region, as well as for determining Commission funding. As a component State, Texas formulated its own investment plan for the respective Border counties and the four State plans then became the building blocks for the Commission's regional plan. In this manner the primacy of State interest has been protected.

In the US Rio Grande cities community decision-making is

dominated by a small élite of businessmen and politicians (D'Antonio and Form 1959), with the former often more socially mobile and better educated than the latter. At El Paso (D'Antonio and Form 1965, 25) the Anglo business group, including many small and medium-scale proprietors, has been in effective control since the 1950s. In political terms, the city has been firmly in Democratic hands, though with very little intervention by either State or national committees of the party. Nevertheless, there is a strong opposition newspaper and the large Mexican-American population has its vocal champions, as it might well have, given the economic and social conditions of deprivation under which many live. Businessmen and politicians in El Paso are substantially in agreement on the problems the community faces and such conflicts as there may be usually centre on different coalitions of business and political influentials (D'Antonio and Form 1959, 814). At Laredo (Sloan and West 1976, 454) the 'political machine' dominates civic affairs and council government. The 'Independent Club' is an influential caucus and there is also a tradition of personal power, illustrated by the re-election of J. C. ('Pepe') Martin to a sixth four-year term of office in 1974. In all American cities there is also a more diffuse expression of citizen powers, through protest or pressure groups, but also surfacing in numerous community voluntary associations. In the US 'many programmes involving social or technological change are initiated, legitimated, and even completed with private resources, without any positive sanctions or financial assistance from formal government authorities' (Stoddard 1969, 480).

Given the many common problems faced by the US Rio Grande cities it was logical that they should organize to defend their interests and explore ways out of their difficulties. In February 1976 the Organization of US Border cities (OUSBC) was set up by the mayors for these purposes and to offer a united front to the federal government. Based at El Paso the OUSBC has pursued the following tasks: 'the ordering of priority among Border problems; dissemination of information on federal funding and economic development aid; unification of efforts on industrial development, tourism and trade' (Clement 1979, 389). Although there is overlap of functions with the SWBRC the OUSBC continues to function.

Academic bodies concerned to aid in solving Border problems include the Border States Universities Consortium for Latin America (founded 1969) and the Association of Borderlands Scholars (1976), created under the inspiration of E. R. Stoddard of the University of Texas at El Paso.

It is at the Border that some of the markedly differing interests of locals and the federal government are most sharply focussed. The international boundary is a federal and State jurisdictional line, con-

trolled and monitored in the national and not primarily in the local
interest. Hence what is good for the larger community may not at all be
so for the local. In any case there is an unresolved problem of the
multiplicity of federal bodies with Border responsibilities, loosely co-
ordinated, at times overlapping and even antagonistic. The traditional
pragmatic *ad hoc* approach of individual agencies to common problems
of major concern has proved to be woefully obsolete in today's complicated Border environment. The Immigration and Naturalization
Service (INS) with its Border Patrol (under the US Department of
Justice), the US Customs, the Department of Agriculture, the Drugs
Enforcement Administration (DEA), the Department of Trans-
portation (US Coastguard), the Department of State, the Federal
Aviation Administration, and the US Air Force (for surveillance) are
the principal federal agencies concerned with the Border. The scarcely
manageable problems of mass undocumented-worker entries (ch. 5)
and the growing drugs traffic (ch. 6) put the spotlight on long-standing
inter-agency conflict (US Congress, House 1974, 1) and, in 1978, led to
a Command Intelligence Center being established at El Paso (US
Congress, Senate 1978, 204) to deal with the more urgent issues of
co-ordination. Yet the wider question of agency responsibilities goes to
the very heart of political culture in a complex, sophisticated society
such as the US. The agencies are weakened through the process of
democratic checks and balances, or by the power-political struggle in
Washington DC. As political administrations change the weight of
direct government intervention may shift and the priorities among
agencies, or even their continuing existence may be threatened. This
flux in political powers and decision-taking takes place remote from the
Border, and largely without regard to the immediate concerns of those
who live on the Rio Grande.

THE MEXICAN POLITICAL SYSTEM

The Mexican federal structure is a form of organic or integrated federalism, in which the regions, over a long period, have simply become
administrative agencies of the centre. It is true that, in 1977, laws were
passed theoretically decentralizing Mexican public administration and
notionally giving greater powers to the States, while also in the urban
and industrial planning legislation of 1978–9 (México, Pres. de la
República 1978; México, Sec. de Patrimonio 1979) there was a clear
intention to decentralize in order to promote both greater efficiency and
equity. However, the decentralization intended is still effectively that of
the federal presence to the States and municipalities, rather than a true
deconcentration from the monolithic power pyramid, based on the
ruling party, *Partido Revolucionario Institucional* (PRI), with an almost

omnipotent President at its apex.

To appreciate the political realities of Mexican government it is important to look more closely at Presidential power and the role of the ruling party, setting these within the political culture of Mexico. The operation of the political system at federal, State, and local levels can then be focussed on its implications for the Rio Grande communities and the northern frontier zone, and on the national approach to relations with the United States.

Mexican politics are founded upon the contradictory legacy of the Revolution, and the ideologies and institutions which have taken root in its aftermath continue to be strongly conditioned by that underlying truth (Fagen 1977, 692). The revolutionary tradition is based on 'ideals and heroes, a historical synthesis focussed upon the identity of a people and the basis of the existing national order' (Padgett 1971, 59). *Mexicanidad*, the quality of being Mexican, is the unifying symbol and the mainstay of the revolutionary political coalition. Political culture is founded on the persistence of authoritarian relationships on the concept of *machismo*, a belief in strength, virility, and the need to eliminate weakness, on *maño*, the ability 'to formulate stratagems and fathom the motives of others', and on *chingar*, the element of violence, sense of guilt, and capacity to censure others. The cult of the *cacique*, the born leader at all levels in society, from the President's palace to the Border *barrio*, is complemented by the *camarilla*, a concept of social solidarity, even of co-optation and political nepotism.

Through time, the revolutionary fervour has been transmuted into more practical channels. The military and the clergy have been removed from political power, peace and internal stability have been assured, and economic progress or social welfare have become the operational goals (Padgett 1971, 59). To some (Womack 1970) the revolutionary ideals have been betrayed in the process and 'the promised revolution of social justice has been subordinated to élite power and aggrandizement'. Others (Smith 1977, 147) interpret a growing clash between political and business élites, since 'politicians want growth and change within a capitalist framework, but not on behalf of the capitalist class'. In any event, the government is deeply involved in a thoroughly mixed, not to say scrambled economy, and State corporations, *paraestatales*, are powerful throughout key sectors of industry.

It is scarcely to be wondered at, in the face of such a ferment of change, that the political system should be monolithic, centralized, and bureaucratic. Opinions differ both on the scale and limits of Presidential power and also the role and nature of the PRI party. Mumme (1978, 76) refers to 'a Presidentially-dominated corporate, authoritarian State'; Valadés (1970, 100) sees the President as immune from public accountability . . . responsible only to a handful of Kingmakers and *camarillas* who help him to ignore the needs of society whilst pretending to do otherwise'. Needleman and Needleman (1969), on the other hand, interpret the Presidency as more of an institution, in which the personal powers are conferred for six years (*sexenio*) and are not renewable. Though he can determine policies the President needs the support of Congress and the States if he is to be successful in implementing them. In the complicated task of managing a turbulent, rapidly developing country he further needs to mobilize geographically based support and to channel the energies of countless interest groups. From the Presidentially formulated goals policy develops incrementally through a complex bureaucratic administrative system. In these tasks the role of the PRI is fundamental and all pervasive.

Originally the National Revolutionary Party, since its formation in 1929 the PRI has never lost a presidential, gubernatorial, or senatorial election. The perpetuation of power is ensured by political centralization, and the PRI legitimizes this perpetuation of power via the electoral process (Ugalde 1970, 181). 'The PRI and the government form a single instrumentality of rule, but the party serves the government in ways which require separate institutional ideas. It functions as recruiter, broker and integrator for executive and governmental institutions' (Fagen and Tuohy 1972, 29). Political scientists are divided on a true assessment of the PRI. To some (Brandenburg 1964; Purcell 1973; Stevens 1974) it is essentially authoritarian and little more than an appendage of government; to others (Scott 1964; Vernon 1965; Padgett 1971) it is an aggregate or a coalition of interests, with an internal spectrum of political ideology as diverse as within any European parliament. Though the PRI is widely criticized, it is strongly supported.

The National Assembly is the most authoritative organ of the party, but extra-parliamentary power lies through the National Council and the National Executive Committee (CEN). Surrounding the central structure of the PRI, and penetrating down to the masses and to the most local government, there are three broad membership sectors: labour (CTM), agrarian (CNC), and popular (CNOP). Each is organized at *municipio* level and is represented also at the levels of the State and nation. Membership of the labour and agrarian groups is mandatory but the more diverse popular sector is permissive. Progressively, the popular sector has expanded, proliferating action groups, and, with a large professional membership, has come to dominate in the councils of the PRI (Johnson 1978, 82). Within the PRI groups, at all levels, there is an informal system of *camarillas* or political cliques, in which influence is spread and 'the struggle for power, advancement and the symbolic and material rewards of office' takes place (Fagen and

Tuohy 1972, 23).

Although penetrating throughout society, the power of the PRI should not be overestimated. 'If it had been all-powerful Mexico would have become a workers' State long ago' (Needleman and Needleman, 1969, 1033). Nevertheless, party officials dominate the government, and the party apparatus is in touch with the entire populace. It offers a channel for advancement, and this inevitably means a move towards the metropolitan centre, thus weakening the voice of peripheral areas such as the northern frontier. The PRI has become as bureaucratic and unwieldy as the government itself, with whose own ministerial bureau-crats it frequently finds itself in opposition. 'Bossism, opportunism, favouritism and careerism' (Needler 1971, 13) become rampant in what has been unkindly called *la cosa nuestra*. Opposition to the PRI itself comes principally from two sources, and both are stronger on the northern frontier: official opposition political parties and special-interest pressure groups. The 1963 Electoral Reform Law encouraged the formation and development of opposition parties. Of these, the National Action Party (*Partido Acción Nacional* (PAN)) is the most influential, a conservative grouping with a Christian Democratic tradition, going back to its founding in 1939. The task of opposition parties is extremely difficult. Some are registered, others are not, while bureaucratic impediments to party organization are legion. Not-withstanding this, the opposition parties are believed to poll well in the cities, including the Rio Grande towns, though electoral data are invariably hard to come by. The ruling party further weakens the opposition by a policy of co-optation of their influentials into its ranks, and by an ability to demonstrate and endow the 'spoils of office', which the opposition will never forseeably enjoy.

Ames (1970) sought to analyse the basis of support for Mexico's dominant party. He found that the higher the level of urbanization in a State the lower the percentage vote for the PRI; that the PRI always did well on a high turn-out; that federal spending was highest in States with a slightly lower PRI vote; and, directly to our purpose, that the presence of the US Border had little or no detectable effects on the level of support for the PRI at the *State* level (0.045 regression coefficient for direction of vote, −0.113 for the voter turn-out). An analysis of regres-sion residuals in the same study (Ames 1970, 165) showed that for States facing Texas there was a higher percentage level of PRI votes than the level of urbanization would suggest. This evidence then sug-gests that the effect of the US Border, reflected in a lower PRI vote, is upon the Mexican twin-city and is *not* diffused through the surrounding State.

In the Mexican hierarchical system of government there are some so-called free municipalities, but they are financially indigent and wholly dependent upon State governments. The *municipio* is a fixed form of organization, regardless of its urban or rural character (Cárdenas 1963, 34), with local taxation powers but, increasingly, its councils are at the beck and call of the State governor. Except in Chihuahua State the governor may dismiss municipal councils more or less at will, and in many cases State governments may actually be disinvesting *municipios* (Fagen and Tuohy 1972, 23). The State is responsible for the education service, hospitals, the security services, the courts, tourism, and the offices of agriculture and public works (Ugalde 1970, 122), but even at that level the federal government power is all-important. Less than 10 per cent of Treasury revenues pass to the States and there is total federal control of all major development projects in both urban and rural areas. The dependence of the States is total, in the economic, political, and military fields. The hierarchical government chain is well summed up in the words of a State governor (Fagen and Tuohy 1972, 22): 'The federal government screws me, and I screw the *municipios*.'

The Mexican Rio Grande cities are substantial, remote from the capital, in close proximity to the US with which they have important trade connections, and have traditionally nurtured a provincial, even a revolutionary spirit. The powerful *caudillo* or the *cacique* of the Borderlands past is a diminishing species, but there are still reputations to be made from successfully opposing federal authority, most particularly so when local interests and the federal intention do not harmonize. Yet the power élite in C. Juárez is generally, 'synonymous with formal government positions . . . and no civic programme can be initiated or have any chances of success without explicit or implicit sanctions from officials in command of government resources' (Stoddard 1969, 480). Though businessmen seemed influential in the local community their interests were often different from and even antagonistic to those of officials 'whose eyes were turned inwards to Mexico City and were trained upon national revolutionary ideology' (D'Antonio and Form, 1959, 814). At Nuevo Laredo the identity between party and local government was even closer (Sloan and West 1976, 454): the municipal president and six councilmen are elected for three-year, non-renewable terms and the council seats are apportioned among the three wings of the PRI (agrarian, labour, popular). This was in striking contrast to C. Juárez where, under Mayor Porvenir, PAN had enjoyed successes and the business influence in the community had thereby been increased, though only for a limited period against the federal centre.

Mexican federal agencies are prestigious and almost offer an alternative power pyramid to the conventional structure from *municipio* to Mexico City. The ministries concerned with agriculture, irrigation, mining, commercial and industrial development, and transport are of fundamental importance in regional development. Apart from these diverse ministerial responsibilities, funded from the Treasury, there is a proliferation of semi-nationalized corporations (*paraestatales*), including PEMEX, the national petroleum monopoly, and the fertilizer corporation (*Guanos y Fertilizantes*), both highly profitable and with a significant role in the economy of the northern frontier provinces. Eighteen other *paraestatales* exist, ranging from the Federal Electricity Commission to the railways, a national airline and CONASUP (*Compañía Nacional de Subsistencias Populares*), a major loss-making welfare organization concerned with the subsidy of basic goods for low-income families (Johnson 1978, 119). All these powerful, well-funded organizations have access directly to the national government. Their policies and actions may virtually control local economies, as does PEMEX at Reynosa, but there is virtually no local accountability.

Along the Rio Grande there are Mexican equivalents of the US frontier agencies, but they are more centrally controlled, fewer in number, and with much less of an overlap in their responsibilities. By popular reputation there is more corruption, in the taking of bribes, *la mordida*, at all levels in the boundary administration. The special frontier-zone development policies within Mexico have already been considered: the National Border Programme, PRONAF (1961), for economic and social revitalization of the Border cities, and the Border Industrialization Programme (BIP), in 1965, to strengthen the Border economy and accommodate US 'in-bond' (*maquiladora*) plants. In the late 1970s a much more comprehensive and co-ordinated policy of economic planning related Border policies more effectively to the Mexican national economy, while the emphasis upon decentralization from the Central Plateau and the capital city promised supplementation of the work of the Border Commission.

In June 1977 the Co-ordinating Commission of the National Programme for the Borders and Free Zone (*Comisión Coordinadora del Programa Nacional de Desarrollo de las Franjas Fronterizas y Zonas Libres*) was created, with responsibility for plans and programmes for all Border areas. This reinforced the National Commission for Regional Development (*Comisión Nacional de Desarrollo Regional*) established two years earlier (*El Trimestre Económico*, 1975), with a remit to stimulate national decentralization of economic activities, create more balanced development and greater equity in income distribution. This was seen as a means of strengthening Mexican federalism, by better co-ordination of federal, State, and municipal policies, with a novel feature, an appeal directly to the citizenry for consultation and participation. Priority is to be given to making new jobs available, especially in rural areas adjacent to under-utilized natural resources, with important implications for the northern frontier provinces. Under Article V of the Commission there will be recommendations from federal agencies directly to the Economic and Social Development Committees already established at local government level.

Two further nation-wide plans will affect the Rio Grande provinces: the National Urban Development Plan (PNDU, *Plan Nacional de Desarrollo Urbano*) of 19 May 1980, and the National Industrial Development Plan (PNDI, *Plan Nacional de Desarrollo Industrial*), of March 1979. The PNDU is a scheme for managing urban growth and change, by differential public investments to stimulate growth in some centres, and complementary policies of restraint on excessive self-reinforcing urbanization (*Comercio Exterior* 1978). Together with the Industrial Plan it is concerned to rationalize the distribution of population and activities over the national space, to promote integral and balanced urban development, and to improve the quality of urban living. The growth of metropoli is to be slowed, regional cities and medium-sized towns stimulated, and urbanization promoted in certain priority rural zones.

C. Juárez is designated within a priority zone, but for consolidation and regulation of growth, since there is an acute shortage of equipment and infrastructure and a serious constraint in the lack of adequate water or land for urban development. As a regional city, the Monterrey metropolitan area is expected to grow to a population of 2.4 millions in 1982 and 6.7 millions by the end of the century. Growth is to be limited by public policy, since further urbanization costs are likely to be disproportionately high; there are already diseconomies of scale and a disorderly urban spread and sprawl is taking place. The growth of Torreón is to be stimulated, to stabilize the economy of La Laguna, and Saltillo too is programmed to develop. Monclova, the steel town, and the Rio Grande cities of Nuevo Laredo, Matamoros, and Reynosa are to be consolidated, with an orderly development taking place without pressures for further growth. The only priority rural zone on the northern frontier is the Tarahumara Indian country in the highlands of the Sierra Madre Occidental.

The PNDI (México, Sec. de Patrimonio 1979) is an indicative, i.e. not compulsory, plan for translating economic growth into effective development through the medium of selective industrialization. Petroleum is projected as the pivot of national economic development, with mean annual growth rates in the GDP of 7.1 per cent in 1979, rising to 10.6 per cent in 1982. Six hundred thousand jobs per annum will be needed, or 2.4 millions over the four years of the Plan. The scheme is one for stimulating manufacturing for export, passing beyond the import substitution phase and there are priority zones for development, corresponding to those of the PNDU, the Urban Development Plan.

POLITICAL INTERACTION ACROSS THE RIO GRANDE

The political culture, the forms of government, and the distribution of power at differential levels in the territorial hierarchy have been seen to be very different on the two sides of the US–Mexican Border. It now remains to consider the interaction between the two political systems, starting with relationships between twin-cities on the Rio Grande, then touching on the limited State to State 'provincial' contacts, and finally considering federal to federal exchanges.

THE BORDER TWIN-CITIES

There is widespread recognition on the Rio Grande that the twin-cities are inescapably interdependent (Gildersleeve 1978). They share many common problems of poverty, high unemployment, a lack of growth industry, an inadequate tax base, insufficient public services, and a rising crime rate. Though there are many national controls on the free flow of goods, labour, and capital in the Border market the twin-city economy has developed in a very complementary manner. The US city offers many jobs to commuters, is important in retailing to Mexican consumers, and has many specialized commercial and professional services; the Mexican city accommodates US 'in-bond' plants, is a tourist and recreation centre, and offers many lower-level retail and professional services. This close relationship is very sensitive to policy changes affecting the 'permeable membrane' of the international boundary. In this sense, the twin-cities are both geographically very isolated and most vulnerable to the caprices of external decision-takers. It is widely held on the Rio Grande that 'it is difficult for people who do not live in a Border city to understand the problems of the Border' (Sloan and West 1977, 274). As a former city attorney put it, 'we live dangerously here in Laredo. We are subjected to floods, drought, the Mexican government and the US government' (Sloan and West 1976, 463). As a result, Border officials must seek to 'minimize adherence to the rules, regulations, and policies of the respective governments, in order to maximize co-ordinative efforts at the local level'. Only the federal governments have the powers to take decisions, make treaties or agreements, down even to small-scale issues affecting the international boundary. For that reason the process of interaction between the twin-cities is carried on through personal understandings between their élites, long regarded as binding, or by informal, but unsigned agreements. As one Eagle Pass official put it, referring to his Piedras Negras counterpart: 'Listen, I've known him for twenty-five years. I see him every day. There are all kinds of informal understandings between us.'

In such transnational contacts the Border city élites play an important part. Their differing cultural backgrounds have already been considered, the contrasting balance between business and political interests, and the national political setting within which they operate. The next step concerns their perceptions of each other, the attitudes adopted to changing events, and the actions and reactions which have resulted. Though bound together by common problems these are not necessarily viewed with the same priority ordering, nor are solutions proposed always seen as equally beneficial to both sides. Asymmetry too comes into the relationships. Whereas all those questioned among the US élites, except those at Del Rio, thought their city economy was dependent upon its Mexican twin, none of the Mexican élites felt the same way about their US counterpart (Sloan and West 1977, 274). Though pragmatism was the order of the day in approaching common problems the Mexican élites were usually less specific, talking generally about a range of understandings, whereas US attitudes focussed more sharply on commerce, physical planning, tourism, and public safety as negotiable issues.

The difference between the élites of the twin-cities is highlighted at El Paso–C. Juárez (Stoddard 1969, 480):

> The C. Juárez élite have, for the most part, been educated in American schools, can speak English well, and understand how the American system works. They have endeavoured to make strong friends on the US side of the Border, and they look to the US as a source of ideals, values and ideas, in addition to any economic benefits which might accrue from Border tourism or related activity. The El Paso influentials did not look to Mexico for new values, social contacts, intellectual challenges or new ideas.

They 'recognized the importance of being good neighbours and were willing to help C. Juárez develop into a more vital community. In general, they did not speak Spanish well; they had very few close friends in C. Juárez and they visited there rather infrequently. In short, they had worked out a *modus vivendi* with the city but had not internalized much of Mexican culture' (D'Antonio and Form 1965, 218). Stoddard (1969, 481) concluded that 'when successful bicultural relations occur (between the Border élites) it is because the Mexican influentials have deferred to the values and informal demands of the American influentials on a near unilateral basis'.

Nevertheless, the élite communications network in the Rio Grande cities involves numerous, complex, and friendly contacts. Apart from official contacts there are many social, professional, and business contact patterns, and the sharing of information sources is widespread (Sloan and West 1976, 452): 'we are able to get together on a social basis and, through this, we can meet people and work out problems that might arise in matters pertaining to municipal business' (Laredo city official). The increasing number of Mexican-Americans in posts as local US politicians or city officials has often facilitated closer contacts across the Rio Grande and has promoted a better understanding between twin-cities. The frequency of cross-Border visits on official business varied, according to city, from one-half to 90 per cent visiting at least once a month. Business in the Border communities had closer and more frequent contacts.

Civic co-operation across the Border is firmly based upon mutual necessities. Public safety figures prominently, notably in the first instance with police co-operation in law enforcement and the return of stolen property. Mexican police are occasionally trained in the nearby US city, and the American police loan equipment, and may offer specialized help (Sloan and West 1977, 278). Mutual protection against fires has seen both US and Mexican fire-engines cross the Border on several occasions every year in all Border cities. In public health, too, there is close co-operation in control measures for tuberculosis, venereal disease, rabies, and mosquito spraying. Air and water pollution monitoring and control are other important fields of co-operation. Information on communicable diseases is freely exchanged and there is some sharing of medical and dental facilities, on a paying basis. Natural disaster relief, and immigration or customs controls remain entirely federal responsibilities.

On the other hand, there is little official co-operation among the Border cities on city planning matters, housing programmes, the labour market, road building, or revenue raising (Sloan and West 1976, 468). Within the communities at large, there is considerable social inter-action, at the time of fairs, conventions, parades, public holidays, or ceremonial activities. Stoddard (1969, 481) takes a slightly jaundiced view on this:

It appears that the vast majority of 'Cultural Understanding Week' and 'Good Neighbour' programmes are conducted as a façade to hide the social and cultural processes across the Border, which Americans do not understand and are even less concerned about; whilst their Mexican counterparts accept the superficial show with tongue-in-cheek, understanding the Anglo's necessity for self-deception better even than he understands it himself.

The level of transnational co-operation within twin-cities on the Rio Grande varies, according to geographical proximity, degree of economic interdependence, extent of contacts socially and profes-sionally, and the nature of the local heritage and customs. Laredo–Nuevo Laredo and Brownsville–Matamoros have shown the highest level of interdependence, Del Rio–C. Acuña the least (Sloan and West 1977, 271). Between Del Rio and Acuña contacts are indeed limited. There is more frequent turnover of US officials and there are fewer *chicanos* among them, different bureaucratic norms apply, and the US city is oriented towards Laughlin Air Force base and Lake Amistad rather than in the direction of its rather distant Mexican neighbour. Deservedly or otherwise, C. Acuña has a reputation of being one of the more socially turbulent towns along the entire Rio Grande.

The durability of twin-city co-operation is from time to time severely tested by particular dramatic events. Stoddard (1979) refers to one such incident, the construction of a more elaborate Border fence by the American INS, to deter smuggling and illegal immigration. The fence design, made public in October 1978, aroused strong local opposition: local influentials in C. Juárez opposed the fence by a six-to-one ratio and even in El Paso there was a seven-to-three ratio against this so-called 'tortilla curtain'. National policies thus did not reflect Border needs or perceptions, nor did they anticipate the diplomatic embarrassments which would arise from the fence project. During the crisis, 'local informal communications maintained a high level of local stability between the two Border communities, while the international storm raged overhead' (p. 41).

STATE TO STATE (PROVINCIAL LEVEL) CONTACTS

Since neither Texas nor the adjacent Mexican States may sign treaties or enter into agreements this intermediate level of interaction remains limited. Committees may be set up to co-ordinate matters of mutual concern and the Texas Good Neighbour Commission has been active in promoting trade, cultural exchanges, and friendship with Mexico. For the most part, however, State interests must be promoted through the domestic federal system, and disputes across the Border must be tackled in the same indirect manner.

FEDERAL SYSTEM INTERACTION

Federal authorities in the US and Mexico have interacted at the diplomatic level across the Rio Grande for more than one hundred and fifty years. During that long period the issues have changed, priorities have shifted, but there has been a long-sustained American domination in the asymmetry of power-political relationships. The functioning of local contacts along the Rio Grande has sought, by informal means, to enhance the permeability of the international boundary, and to mitigate any adverse local impacts and spin-offs from diplomatic decisions taken in far-off federal capitals. Some federal bodies have sought to increase the openness of the boundary, for trade and commerce; others have sought, conversely, to plug leaks in the Border by customs and immigration surveillance (Stoddard 1980, 12). Such federal policies have only indirectly and secondarily been concerned with the problems of residents on the Rio Grande, problems still imperfectly appreciated at the federal level in either country. Wherever and whenever the national interest conflicts with the local interest it is the latter which must suffer.

The spectrum of Border problems looks different through American and Mexican eyes. To the United States the priority issues are control, or better still regulation, of undocumented worker inflow; the drugs traffic; and the safeguarding of American interests in Mexico (the 'in-bond' plants; patents; and multinational investments). The Mexicans see greater importance in access to and control of water resources, including groundwater supplies; the Border and national balance of payments; access of workers to the US (including Border commuters); control of smuggling, in both directions; and the regulation of American fishing rights in the Gulf of Mexico (Ugalde 1978, 106). With such a range of delicate problems and given the differences in priorities it is not surprising that the interacting federal bureaucracies have been sluggish and *ad hoc* and, above all, cautious in their dealings with each other. Some problems, including that of undocumented workers, may not be solvable within the foreseeable future and, in that case, trade-offs in unsolved problems between the two powers may offer the only way out. Other problems may be ameliorated in a step-by-step progression, while yet others, such as trade and tariffs, are part of the developed–developing world relationships and can only be dealt with in that much wider international context.

There is a problem in defining what is a Border problem. Few are entirely indigenous or unique to the Rio Grande cities and counties; indeed all have ramifications extending at times far beyond. Clement (1979, 395) defines a Border problem as 'one directly concerned with the political/economic boundary or linked with the enforcement of laws regarding trans-Border flows'. A much wider second category includes issues which are simultaneously of concern to Border residents and distant decision-takers, matters relating to environmental management, mass transit or law enforcement in the wider sense. These correspond to many of the issues Stoddard (1980, 5) identifies as those of shared resources and quality control, and also include the day-to-day transactions across the international boundary by local residents. A final category of problems includes those intractable questions that arise from the sharp social and economic interface between a rich and a much poorer nation. Mass northward migration and distortions in the labour market, smuggling of selected, lucrative commodities in both directions, and the polarization of trade and retailing according to price and quality differentials on either side of the Border are among the major outcomes. The benefits and costs of policies which seek to regulate and mitigate some of these problems are not equally shared, either structurally in society, or territorially as between the Border cities, the States and the national communities. The Rio Grande city administrations, in particular, feel that traditionally they have borne more of the costs and enjoyed fewer of the benefits arising from their vulnerable situation.

Stoddard (1980, 17) makes four points on this state of affairs: (i) the federal level of policy-making in both countries is often out of touch with local Border realities and generally unacquainted with the informal and integrative systems through which daily activity is co-ordinated there; (ii) in both countries the political view of Border communities is weak at the federal centre; (iii) successful resolution of Border problems at the diplomatic level has 'usually obscured their latent and often negative consequences for Border communities and residents'; and (iv) in the absence of some regionally responsive (international) body informal networks and understandings will continue as the only means of survival in the frontier zone across the Rio Grande.

Attempts to create regionally responsive bodies in the past have promised more than they subsequently delivered. Presidents of the two countries have met regularly, not infrequently at the Border, and joint ventures have occasionally been set up as a result. In 1966 CODAF, the US–Mexican Commission for Border Development and Friendship, was established to seek ways of raising living standards and improving relations along the frontier. Within four years CODAF had been dissolved, for political reasons and as the result of a change in national administrations (Martínez 1976, 3). In 1976 Presidents Carter and López-Portillo set up a Consultative Mechanism which, in the following year, gave rise to a Border sub-group to study and co-operate, on managing and solving common economic and social problems. The setting up of the US SW Border Regional Commission in 1977 (p. 242). and a Mexican counterpart, the Co-ordinating Commission of the National Programme for the Borders and Free Zones, in the same year (p. 249), offered a fresh range of possibilities. Though both seek limited bi-national co-operation it would be unwise to assume that either will be granted more than information or consultative powers in relation to the international neighbour. It will be entirely within the verdict of history if all decision-making continues to be centralized in Washington DC and México City DF, whether or not this may be to the detriment of the dwellers on both banks of the Rio Grande.

REFERENCES

ADVISORY COMMISSION ON IINTERGOVERNMENTAL RELATIONS (1973) *Regional Governance. Promise and performance*, Substate Regionalism and the Federal System, vol. II, Case Studies, ACIR, A-41 Washington DC.

AMES, B. (1970) 'Bases of support for Mexico's dominant party', *Am. pol. Sci. rev.*, **64**, 153–67.

BRANDENBURG, F. (1964) *The making of modern Mexico* (Englewood Cliffs, N.J.: Prentice-Hall).

CÁRDENAS, L. (1963) 'The municipality of Northern Mexico', *SW Stud.*, **I** (El Paso: Texas Western College Press).

CLEMENT, N. (1979) 'Institutional response to recent Border problems: survey and analysis', ch. 28 in B. W. Poulson & T. N. Osborn (eds.) *US-Mexico economic relations* (Boulder, Colorado: Westview Special Stud.)

COMERCIO EXTERIOR (1978) 'Un plan para desconcentrar y urbanizar', **28,** 10, 1197–1203.

D'ANTONIO, W. V. and FORM, W. H. (1959) 'Integration and cleavage among influentials in the two border cities influence systems', *Am. Sociol. Rev.*, **24,** 6, 804–14.

D'ANTONIO, W. V. (1965) *Influentials in two Border cities* (Notre Dame: Univ. Notre Dame Press).

DICKENS, E. L. (1972) *The politics and government of Texas* (Huntsville, Texas).

El Trimestre Económico (1975) 'Decreto que crea la Comisión Nacional de Desarrollo Regional (México)', **XLII,** 3, 167, 731–4.

FAGEN, R. R. (1977) 'The realities of US-Mexican relations', *Foreign Affairs,* **55,** 4, 685–700.

FAGEN, R. R. and TUOHY, W. S. (1972) *Politics and privilege in a Mexican city* (Stanford Calif.: Stanford Univ. Press).

GARZA, R. O. DE LA (1974) 'Voting patterns in 'bi-cultural' El Paso: A contextual analysis of *Chicano* voting behavior', *Aztlán,* **5,** 235–60.

GILDERSLEEVE, C. R. (1978) *The international Border city: urban spatial organization in a context of two cultures along the US–Mexico boundary* (Lincoln: Univ. Nebraska, Ph.D. diss.).

GUTIÉRREZ, A. (1978) 'The politics of the Texas border: an historical overview and some contemporary directions', ch. 6 in S. R. Ross (ed.) *Views across the Border* (Albuquerque: Univ. New Mexico Press), 117–40.

JOHNSON, K. F. (1978) *Mexican Democracy: a critical view* (New York: Praeger).

MARTÍNEZ, O. J. (1976) 'Border relations: a brief comment', *El Paso econ. rev.,* **XIII,** 3.

MÉXICO, PRESIDENCIA DE LA REPÚBLICA (1978) 'Plan Nacional de Desarrollo Urbano', *El Gobierno Mexicano,* **14,** 44–9.

MÉXICO, SEC. DE PATRIMONIO Y FOMENTO INDUSTRIAL (1979) *Plan Nacional de Desarrollo Industrial, 1979–82*, México, DF.

MUMME, S. P. (1978) 'Mexican politics and the prospects for emigration policy: a policy perspective', *Int. Am. econ. Affairs,* **32,** 1, 67–94.

MURPHY, W. C. (1933) *County government and administration in Texas* (Austin: Univ. Texas Press), Bull. 3324.

NEEDLEMAN, C. and NEEDLEMAN, M. (1969) 'Who rules Mexico? A critique of some current views on the Mexican political process', *Jl. Politics,* **31,** 1011–34.

NEEDLER, M. C. (1971) *Politics and society in Mexico* (Albuquerque: Univ. New Mexico Press).

NIMMO, D. D. and ODEN, W. (1971) *The Texas political system* (Englewood Cliffs, N.J.: Prentice Hall).

PADGETT, L. V. (1971) *The Mexican political system* (Boston, Mass.: Houghton Mifflin).

PURCELL, S. K. (1973) 'Decision-making in an authoritarian régime', *World Politics,* **XXVI,** 1, 28–54.

SCOTT, R. E. (1964) *Mexican government in transition,* (Urbana: Univ. Illinois Press).

SLOAN, J. W. and WEST, J. P. (1976) 'Community integration and border politics among élites in two Border cities', *Jl. Int.-Am. Stud. Wld. Affairs,* **18,** 4, 451–74.

SLOAN, J. W. and WEST, J. P. (1977) 'The role of informal policy-making in US-Mexico Border cities', *Soc. Sci. Q.,* **58** (Sept.), 270–82.

SMITH, P. H. (1977) 'Does Mexico have a power élite?' in J. L. Reyna & R. S. Weinert (eds.) *Authoritarianism in Mexico*, Inter-Amer. Pol. Ser. 2, Philadelphia, 129–51.

SOUTH-WEST BORDER REGIONAL COMMISSION (1979) *Annual Report*, Washington DC.

STEVENS, E. P. (1974) *Protest and response in Mexico* (Cambridge, Mass.: MIT Press).

STODDARD, E. R. (1969) 'The US-Mexican Border as a research laboratory', *Jl. Int.-Am. Stud. Wld. Affairs*, **XI,** 477–88.

STODDARD, E. R. (1979) *El Paso-C. Juárez and the 'tortilla curtain': a study of local adaptation to federal Border policies* (El Paso: Univ. Texas El Paso Press).

STODDARD, E. R. (1980) *US-Mexico diplomacy, its latent consequences in the Borderlands* (El Paso: Univ. Texas at El Paso).

UGALDE, A. (1970) *Power and conflict in a Mexican community: a study of political integration* (Albuquerque: Univ. New Mexico Press).

UGALDE, A. (1978) 'Regional political processes and Mexican politics on the Border', ch. 5 in S. R. Ross (ed.) *Views across the Border*, (Albuquerque: Univ. New Mexico Press), 97–116.

US CONGRESS, HOUSE (1974) Committee on Government Operations, *Immigration and Naturalization Service regional office operations*, pt. 5, Hearings before Subcomm. on Legal and Monetary Affairs, 93rd Congr., 2nd Sess., Washington DC, USGPO.

US CONGRESS, SENATE (1978) Committee on Appropriations, *Depts. of State, Justice and Comm., the Judiciary and related agencies appropriations, Undocumented Aliens*, Hearings, 95th Congr., 2nd Sess., Washington DC, USGPO.

VALADÉS, J. C. (1970) *El presidente de México en 1970* (México: Editores Mexicanos Unidos).

VERNON, R. (1965) *The dilemma of Mexico's development* (Cambridge, Mass.: Harvard Univ. Press).

WOMACK, J. (1970) 'The spoils of the Mexican Revolution', *Foreign Affairs*, **48,** 4, 677–87.

CHAPTER 9

In Conclusion

A LOOK AHEAD

A better, more rational future for this geographical area must dignify the disappearance of the present economic elements of unity, i.e. the disappearance of imperialism.

R. A. FERNÁNDEZ, 1977, 157

Let us bind the two countries in a continual demonstration of common purpose, common hope, common confidence and common friendship.

PRESIDENT JIMMY CARTER, 1977

In the harsh and remote environment of the Rio Grande frontier, continuing interdependence is the keynote for further development, and even maybe for long-term survival. Scarce natural resources will continue to be shared, their contamination or exhaustion is at risk, and there are always climatic hazards in the offing. The complex range of frontier transactions binds the Border communities, through commerce; the flows of goods and services; the transfer of technology; direct and indirect investment; mobile labour; and in tourism, or communications linkages. The problems which arise may be peculiarly acute on the Border, but they are not unique to that area. Nor are they likely to be solved with the interests of Rio Grande residents seen as paramount. National interest at the federal level of diplomacy will have pride of place, and even so the notion of any 'special relationship', as in the past with Mexico, is increasingly out of favour in an age of global relationships. Issues like trade, immigration, energy, or capital flows have multilateral implications and are likely to be negotiated, with a degree of evenhandedness elsewhere in the hemisphere and the Third and Fourth worlds' (Fagen 1977, 700).

As problems continue to unfold they will be tackled from two very different negotiating stances, as befits the contrasting dilemmas facing the US and Mexico (US Congress 1977, 8 *et seq.*). The US has to decide between allowing more Mexicans in to form a cheap labour pool, or 'closing' the frontier to limit immigration; and between the wish to expand exports to Mexico, but yet to restrict imports from that country; the national interest to have a healthy, politically stable neighbour, and the desire to perpetuate and benefit from Mexico's continuing dependence; and acceptance of the failure of the Alliance for Progress and the idea of a new Marshall Plan. Mexican dilemmas are no less acute: to seek labour-intensive industries to absorb the unemployed, or capital-intensive industries to maximize economic growth; to accept or reject further US involvement in the Mexican economy; to diversify trading partners, or continue to rely mainly upon the US; to maximize food production or to pursue less productive land reform; and to seek a more open US frontier, or to try to keep young Mexicans at home.

Resolution of these dilemmas is a matter for domestic decisions, but inevitably even there linkages between issues and trade-offs come into question. In the bi-national arena the negotiations are fuelled by national self-interest and the degree to which either partner has effective bargaining leverage. In the first place, the political actors on the international stage have different powers and status. Within American decision-taking the executive and the legislature have the greatest authority, but on all the issues of concern on the Rio Grande key roles may be played by the judiciary, regulatory bodies, intelligence agencies, State governments, the mass media, or 'special interest' groups. The general ethos in international negotiations, through the State Department, is to deal with each issue separately, broken down where possible into its technical elements (Grayson 1980, 432). The Mexican style, under an authoritarian President, has been described as 'closet diplomacy'. There is a preference for individual contacts at the highest level with US officials, in sharp contrast to the fragmented, incrementalist approach favoured by American bureaucrats. Mexicans also prefer 'total package' negotiations rather than piecemeal consideration of issues.

The US has always had a strong self-interest in aiding Mexico, and this will undoubtedly grow with the crucial importance of the recently discovered vast reserves of oil and natural gas in Mexico. Mexico has long been of great strategic importance as an adjacent neighbour in the western hemisphere, while her population size and aggregate economy imply a considerable and growing market for US goods and investment. At the very least the US should avoid being a 'bad neighbour'. Even though the social problems may be acute there must be 'no large-scale deportations of undocumented aliens, no yielding to protectionist tendencies further restricting Mexican access to US markets, no insisting on full implementation of IMF austerity programmes, and no punitive measures against Mexico' (for her foreign policy attitudes) (Fagen 1977, 698). 'Fortunately, Mexico has now (1982) passed beyond the austerity phase of IMF plans and has embarked on a long-range strategy designed to turn herself into a major industrial economy by the end of the century. On the positive side, US concessions to Mexico, in trade, finance, or the transfer of technology would seem more appropriate today, since Mexican bargaining leverage has been greatly enhanced by the oil finds. Indeed, the US National Security Council has gone on record suggesting specific concessions to include admission of large numbers of Mexican migrants (Grayson 1980, 452).

This immediately raised doubts on the merits of the trade-off for oil, in view of the possible impacts on the job security and well-being of American workers.

The process of bi-national linkage-bargaining and leverage among oustanding issues is likely to be complex and slow-moving. As has been said (Truett and Truett 1980, 84), 'If it had not been for the recent Mexican oil discoveries, delay would have been the name of the game.' The linkage approach to bargaining assigns weights to particular issues, to determine their value in a trade-off situation. 'How many barrels of crude oil to balance the entry of say two hundred un-documented workers, or how many tonnes of tomatoes imported at a reduced tariff to justify a twenty-year supply contract for Mexican natural gas?' (Grayson 1980, 432–3). The current world recession imposes its own constraints and imperatives, in the national interest, on both sides of the Border. Mexico has declined to join GATT and the USA, as recently as 1979, has proved reluctant to modify the General System of (Trade) Preferences (GSP) in Mexico's favour. Nevertheless, the US–Mexican working groups of the Consultative Mechanism, initially three in 1977, now eleven in number, will be preparing the ground for later bilateral negotiations from knowledge, rather than from relative strengths alone.

MEXICAN OIL AND NATURAL GAS

The recent large-scale discoveries of oil and natural gas in Mexico have transformed the bargaining situation with the US decidedly to Mexico's advantage (Mancke 1980; Ronfeldt 1980). Even conflicting statements on the available reserves have been used as bargaining counters. On 1 September 1980 proved petroleum reserves totalled 60,126 million barrels, probable reserves 38,042 million barrels, and potential reserves 250,000 million barrels (López-Portillo 1980). There is still some uncertainty about these figures. It is said that natural gas is included, about 35 per cent of reserves, that recoverable quantities may have been exaggerated, and that some 'probable' reserves may have been put in the 'proven' category (Grayson 1980, 430). Yet, even so, the scale of this natural resource is prodigious, almost at Saudi Arabian levels of potential. It is clearly of the first order of political importance.

Negotiations with the US for the supply of Mexican oil or natural gas well illustrate the complex bargaining process, and the possibility of trade-offs. Mexico has a technical need to sell natural gas. It is found with oil and 'must be injected, consumed at home or exported to prevent loss through "flaring"' (Grayson 1980, 440); otherwise, oil production itself may be restricted. Within the US, opinion is divided on a natural gas deal with Mexico. The Senators and Representatives from six States, including Texas, negotiated with PEMEX in a very positive manner; yet the Midwestern States in particular were opposed to an agreement. In the early stages of negotiation, in 1977, there was a total breakdown since the US refused to pay the price required by the Mexicans ($2.60 per 28m^3, of gas). In retaliation President López-Portillo decreed that the gas pipeline to Texas should stop 75 miles south of the Rio Grande.

In the late 1970s and early 1980s the Mexican negotiating posture had hardened. Compared with OPEC members Mexico is in a stronger domestic position: her oil resources are nationalized and she is not 'in-bond' to the transnational oil corporations, while the quality of her crude, and proximity to western hemisphere markets, both justify a premium price. Crude oil is to be exported in the short-term to provide the financing and technology for national economic growth, but the Mexican government is determined to serve the greatest diversity of overseas customers to limit dependence on the US (Grayson 1980, 448). The Cactus field to Reynosa (Rio Grande) pipeline has been agreed, but only surplus natural gas will be permitted to flow north and then only at a Mexican-determined price. During 1980, twelve countries entered into agreements to buy Mexican oil, so that from a US predominance of 85 per cent of exports in 1978 there was a planned fall to only 60–66 per cent in 1980. By the mid-1980s Mexican oil exports should reach 1.8 to 2.5 million barrels per day, but even if two-thirds of this went to the US it would meet only 12–15 per cent of total American requirements.

The impact of oil and natural gas exploitation on the course of Mexican development needs to be assessed with caution. Fagen (1977, 698) has claimed that

Oil may allow Mexico to slip away from the IMF but not from the facts of history . . . It may give breathing space . . . for Mexico's hard-pressed politicians. But oil by itself cannot respond to peasant demands for land; nor can it create hundreds of thousands of new jobs a year; nor can it keep millions of Mexicans from crossing the Border; nor make rapid inroads on redressing a distribution of income that is one of the most unequal in the world; nor reduce public and private corruption; nor deal with the human and social problems generated by a population that doubles in size every twenty years . . . It may postpone or soften the sharpening of the contradictions inherent in the Mexican development model. It cannot solve them.

The Mexican Rio Grande Border cities will benefit directly from oil and natural gas. Pipelines for natural gas already link the production fields with C. Chihuahua, Monclova, Nuevo Laredo, and Matamoros, while there have been important natural gas finds at Sabinas (N. León) and at two places in the State of Coahuila. The risk, however, continues to be that the fruits of national economic expansion in Mexico will be polarized away from the Border, notwithstanding the good intentions inherent in the National Plans for Industries or the Cities.

Finally, there is one intriguing new ingredient in US–Mexican relations across the Rio Grande, the playing of the *chicano* card. The adverse effects on *chicano* workers in US Border cities, even throughout Texas, by the 'unfair' competition from undocumented Mexican immigrants gives *chicanos* a stake of self-interest in Border problems. Their political awareness during the 1970s, and a growing sense of cultural identity with a Mexican past, has belatedly led *chicano* leaders to seek a greater voice in shaping policies with Mexico. Although 'internally divided, with disagreement on strategies and objectives, low educational and income levels, and with limited political experience' (Grayson 1980, 444) they have had some successes. *Chicano* leaders were received by the Mexican President and a *Chicano*–Mexican Commission has been set up. This is a fresh reminder that the Rio Grande Borderlands are abundantly the home of a tri-cultural society, undergoing shifts in political and cultural power away from an Anglo-American domination.

To move from dependency, through interdependence, to a true symbiosis across the Rio Grande will take a considerable time and even greater political goodwill, if the sense of the past is to be set aside and equality replace subservience in Mexican–US relationships. There are those (Mumme 1978; Clement 1979, 398) who are pessimistic on the outcome: 'Changes (in the development strategies of both countries) are unlikely to occur in the near future and will probably take place only as a product of changes in the global economic system. Until then, incremental changes will dominate and probably lead to increased structural problems for the Mexican economy in the long run.' More optimistically, 'this complementarity (of economic interests) . . . replete with linkage opportunities, further illuminates a growing coincidence of interests that means that neither country will again have to approach the other with hat in hand' (Grayson 1980, 435).

After almost two centuries of discord, the people of three Borderlands cultures are now poised for a more stable, prosperous, and harmonious relationship. The potential for such manifest international benefits has already been well demonstrated, at the local scale, by the countless folk who have lived, loved, and laboured on both banks of the Rio Grande.

EPILOGUE

In reflecting on the findings of the study some thoughts may be shared on the efficacy of the methodology used, the relationships to relevant theoretical frameworks, and the contributions from other disciplines to frontier studies. Above all, the degree to which the input–output transactional flow model of the frontier system is capable of general application needs some comment. The relationship of the riverline as a topic or problem in international law is a separate but related issue.

CRITIQUE OF THE MODEL

There is an urgent need both for more empirical and comparative studies of a dynamic nature for frontier situations, whether these involve confrontational or co-operative relationships, and for a more coherent set of theoretical frames within which to study such situations. The operational model developed for the Rio Grande seems readily capable of being transferred and applied in other frontier studies, provided its potentials and limitations are appreciated. It satisfied as a coherent general thinking framework for the totality of inter-State relations at various spatial, structural, and temporal scale-levels. It is flexible enough to be used in the analysis of particular events or in forecasting the outcome of alternative scenarios for the future in the frontier zone, or for the impact on frontier policies more generally. In particular, it integrates a complicated web of environmental, social economic, and political data in a manner which utilizes traditional geographic methodology but adds and incorporates a deliberate political and policy dimension.

A major finding is that the problems of the frontier zone are indeed an aggravated microcosm of the general issues dominating relations between the two States. Second, that the policies for meeting those problems have not been designed with the interests of frontier dwellers in the forefront and there have been adverse and inadvertent impacts in the frontier zone on both sides as a result. In this sense, no matter what the policies of Mexico and the USA may be, the peoples of the Rio Grande see abundant merit in co-operating more closely in a remote and harsh geographical habitat. Informal arrangements have been developed for them to do so, a clear recognition of the existence and significance of the trans-frontier region as an entity for international planning. In Europe such trans-frontier regions have already developed many differing kinds of co-operative institutions at local level (House 1980, 470–2). In the socialist world such a concept does not seem to exist, nor are there comparable transnational institutions. Wherever there is a marked asymmetry of relationships across an international boundary—and in this sense the US–Mexican case is a dramatic instance of developed–developing world interaction—there is difficulty in developing trans-frontier regions. Fears of dependency, domination, exploitation, and neocolonialism abound, but it is precisely across such boundaries that the first fruits of a commitment by the affluent North to the impoverished South could be most directly and profitably transmitted.

Anyone using the model developed for this study should be aware of certain difficulties encountered. It was at times problematic to identify and differentiate transactions, perceptions, or the contribution by many actors at the regional (intermediate) and national (core) levels, though those performed at the local (frontier, periphery) level were usually clear. The distance–decay effects of particular transactions from the frontier zone into the regional and national interiors were traced and measured with difficulty. Ironically, some of the illegal transactions, highlighted by the criminal justice system, were often better documented. A problem common to all transnational studies, and not surprisingly, was the lack of a comparable data base for the two countries. This was not only a matter of the range and volume of data, but also the kind of spatial units and the time-intervals for which data was available. The harmonization of statistical sources between adjacent countries would have practical pay-offs, and not solely for scholars.

Much of the social and economic data which can be assembled will not bear the kind of sophisticated multivariate analysis which studies of the city or of social justice now commonly require. Inevitably, judgements are more qualitative and value-assessments filter in. Any investigator will incorporate his own bias and, in an ideal world the model used here should be calibrated independently by Americans, Mexicans, and *chicanos*, to detect different mental maps or cultural frameworks. Furthermore, since the two frontier-nations contain a wide diversity of internal perceptions/attitudes, and actors on the stage domestic (or internal) differences of view may also need to be accommodated.

One of the most problematic segments of the model is that concerned with perceptions and attitudes. Behavioural methodology has scarcely entered political geography, other than in electoral studies. Psychological testing, based on interviewing and sampling, usually addresses itself to specific variables and produces results scarcely capable of being generalized at regional or national levels. Interpersonal and group interactions between Mexicans, Americans, and *chicanos* are highly cosmopolitan, within and across social classes, age cohorts and between the sexes, in social as well as in economic and political associations. Diffusion from one culture into another, involves both acculturation and culture shock, feeding back into tension management. An alternative, little explored research avenue lies in the exploration of the mental maps, symbols, and images of decision-takers, the actors on the political stage, scanning their operational environment (Henrickson 1980).

Lacking at present a full behavioural understanding for the transfrontier model gaming simulation of events or the application of game theory (Harsanyi 1969; Rapoport 1974) may have a part to play in an analysis of a particular problem or policy. Simulations may be mathematical (not presently possible for the frontier model) or expressed in scenario-writing and empirical step-by-step modification. The ground rules would then become more qualitative, as in war-gaming.

The policy and plans segment of the model is more clear-cut, with more data and documentation available. Policy objectives, however, are mixed and not always readily identified, categorized, or traced. Moreover, policy may be poorly reflected in plans, these may miscarry, have unintended effects, or be ineffective. The final phase of the model, the field of tension management, is doubly important because it is the meeting place with political science researchers and students of international relations, and also because it is the test of the operational validity of the model. Tension management analysis tests for the conflict–co-operation balance at the three different scale levels within and between each country. The outcome influences attitudes to events, the general characteristics of policy, and the equilibrium between closure and openness intentions in planning for the frontier. The spatial origins, nature, and impacts of the tensions (positive and negative) are the major novel contributions the political geographer brings to this end stage, in a field already well tenanted by political scientists.

Behavioural response feeds back into the model at almost all its stages, but it must constantly be borne in mind that the policy process of Fig. 1a is rarely so coherent, sequential, or clear-cut. Disjointed incrementalism or graduated response are more characteristic, to say nothing of the irrational impulse of the politicians under severe emotional pressures from their constituents. Nevertheless, in spite of the practical limitations the model points a way forward and it is a track whose imprint is clear and convergent with the mainstream preoccupations of other social scientists.

THEORIES

It is premature to outline a general, comprehensive theory for frontier studies. At present such theory must continue to be sought by a 'building-blocks approach' from segments of relevant theory formulated for other purposes. Conflict theory (Boulding 1962) offers the dynamism, while the cybernetic theory of social communications (Deutsch 1978) is a creative and constructive means of testing tensions and proposing their management. In the composition and working of the model both structuralist and dialectical theories (Agnew 1981) are used. Pluralist decision-maker theory is the framework for the 'actors/institutions' and the 'policies/plans' segments of the model, with the theory of public choice an underlying paradigm for the analysis of objectives and trade-offs in the management of conflict or co-operation. Among theories of economic development that of cumulative causation (Myrdal 1957) is perhaps the most relevant to markedly asymmetrical cross-frontier relationships, though some would prefer the explanatory power of theories of imperialism or dependency (Fernández and Ocampo 1977). Within overtly spatial theories those of centre–periphery relationships (Gottmann 1980) and gravity-model distance decay or diffusion seem to be the most germane, though of limited intellectual coverage in the frontier model.

If the links between theories and empirical realities are to be bridged then both deductive analysis from above and inductive analysis from below will be needed. The operational model outlined essentially offers an inductive contribution. Empirical realities are apt to constrain the elegance of model or theory, just as prior adoption of ideological premises or postures limits the effectiveness of theories in their application to a real world which is to be examined, or even better, improved.

RIVERLINE BOUNDARIES

The Rio Grande is a test-bed not only for the principles and precepts of international law, both public and private, but also for the varied domestic systems for dealing with the environment, people, resources, and their transactions. It has been said that that legal system is best which most closely accords with the facts of environment and that is most closely in accord with the needs, customs, and wishes of the dominant strata of society. Most legal systems dealing with water resources originated in specific geographical environments where water was either a scarce or an abundant resource. Once adopted, laws on water rights tend to be transplanted along with migrant streams of people, into geographical environments within which they may be entirely inappropriate, even ruinous. The history of the water management of the Rio Grande basin amply chronicles the disasters or costly shortcomings of inappropriate water laws (as well as the chauvinism of law-makers), just as it highlights the problems when the issues become international and contending parties argue from entirely valid premisses of conflicting principles. There is a major field for political geographers to extend their fruitful dialogue with international lawyers beyond a preoccupation with the Law of the Sea. Not only does case law need to be modified by the realities of changing events and geographical circumstance, there are problems for which international law has yet to be codified, as in the exploitation of international aquifers, or the issue of water quality. Law must be appropriate, flexible, and comprehensive to be just but, even so, there are countless fields in which international litigation is always latent along the Rio Grande. For this reason, closer co-operation between Americans, Mexicans, and *chicanos* along the frontier needs to be constantly stimulated by policies and plans, appropriately underwritten by a harmonization of legal principle and precept, particularly relating to vital common, shared resources. Failing this, the next most desirable safeguard is to protect the interests of foreign nationals under domestic law, not only the 'human rights' of workers and deportees but the right to equity, freedom, and equality of opportunity in the Borderlands on either side of the Rio Grande. A fundamental building-block in closer harmony between two such asymmetrical international partners, and as such a pointer to that realistic, ethical, and politically desirable rapprochement between North and South on the global stage.

REFERENCES

AGNEW, J. A. (1981) "Structural and dialectical theories of political regionalism', ch. 3 in A. O. Burnett & P. J. Taylor (eds.) *Political Studies from Spatial Perspectives* (Chichester: Wiley), 275–90.

BOULDING, K. E. (1962) *Conflict and Defense: a General Theory* (New York: Harper and Row.)

CLEMENT, N. (1979) 'Institutional response to recent Border problems: survey and analysis', ch. 28 in B. W. Poulson & T. N. Osborn (eds.) *US-Mexico economic relations* (Boulder, Colorado: Westview Spec. Stud.)

DEUTSCH, K. (1968) *The Analysis of International Relations*, 2nd ed. (Prentice Hall: Englewood Cliffs, NJ).

FAGEN, R. F. (1977) 'The realities of US-Mexican relations', *Foreign Affairs*, **55,** 685–700.

FERNÁNDEZ, R. and OCAMPO, J. F. (1974) 'The Latin American Revolution: a theory of imperialism, not dependency', *Latin Am. Perspect.* **1,** 1, 30–61.

GOTTMANN, J. G. (ed.) (1980) *Centre and Periphery* (Beverly Hills: Sage Publications).

GRAYSON, G. W. (1980) 'Oil and US' Mexican relations', *J. Int.-Am. Stud. Wld. Affairs*, **21,** 4, 427–56.

HARSANYI, J. C. (1969) 'Game theory and the analysis of international relations' in J. N. Rosenau (ed.) *International Politics and Foreign Policy* (New York: Free Press), 370–9.

HENRICKSON, A. K. (1980) 'The geographical mental maps of American foreign policy-makers', *Int. pol. Sci. Rev.*, **1,** 4, 495–530.

HOUSE, J. W. (1980)|'The frontier zone: a conceptual|problem for|policy-makers'. *Int. Pol. Sci. Rev.*, **1,** 4, 456–77.

LÓPEZ-PORTILLO, PRES. (1980) *State of the Nation Address*, 1, Sept. 1980.

MANCKE, R. B. (1980) *Mexican oil and natural gas* (New York: Praeger Special Stud.).

MUMME, S. P. (1978) 'Mexican politics and the prospects for emigration policy: a policy perspective', *Int.-Am. econ. Affairs*, **32,** 1, 67–94.

MYRDAL, G. (1957) *Economic theory and under-developed regions* (London: Duckworth).

RAPOPORT, A. (ed.) (1974) *Game theory as a theory of conflict resolution* (Dordrecht: D. Reidel).

RONFELDT, D. F. (1980) *Mexico's petroleum and US policy: implications for the 1980s* (Santa Monica, Cal.: Rand Corpn.), R-2510-DOE.

TRUETT, D. B. and TRUETT, L. F. (1980) 'Mexico and the General System of Preferences', *Int.-Am. econ. Affairs*, **34,** 2, 67–85.

US CONGRESS (1977) Jt. Econ. Committee, Hearings before the Subcommittee of Inter-Am. Econ. Relns., *Recent developments in Mexico and their implications for the United States*, 95th Congr., 1st Sess., Washington DC, USGPO.

Input–output elements of the frontier transactional model (linkages)

SPATIAL

	LOCAL (PERIPHERY)		REGIONAL (INTERMEDIATE)		NATIONAL (CORE)	
	MEXICO Az	USA Bz	MEXICO Ai	USA Bi	MEXICO A	USA B
STRUCTURAL						
PERCEPTIONS/ ATTITUDES						
Ideology:						
Sense of history	Mission, *presidio*, turbulence, oppression, dependency	Expanding frontier domination, turbulence, vice	Northern reform and revolutionary tradition	Texan 'imperial' past, heritage	Unequal treaties, oppression and dependency	'Manifest continental destiny': Good Neighbour
Mythology	*Aztlán*	Texas Rangers, frontiersman	Heroic revolutionary 'ideals and heroes'	Texan 'national' identity, *macho* image	Heroes, icons and symbols of the past	Rugged frontier ethic, individualism, pioneer
Stereotypes	(of US) *gringo, gabacho,* licentious, neurotic, cold, self-assertive arrogant	(of Mex.) 'greaser', 'wetback', slow lazy, irresponsible, peasant	less extreme views away from Border	little difference from Bz	More liberal in large cities and capital. Public mistrust and scorn of USA	More liberal in NE, chauvinist in S, SW, and Chicago

Values	Border culture, strong impact US life-styles, espec. among young	Border culture, strong *chicano* elements	*Norteño* sub-culture	Convergence on US life-styles, in cities and suburbs	*Mexicanidad*; catholic faith; heroes, Spanish-Indian culture; family-based; conservative; passive	Differentiated metropolitan, urban and rural values. Individualism, work ethic, puritan ethic, democracy, freedom, market forces, minimum government

TIME DIMENSION

Shifts in attitudes, opinions, perceptions recalibrated by changing events, by manipulation through propaganda, the media or advertising. Surprising continuity of cultural traits, but diffusion of US material values south and Mexican cultural values north of the Rio Grande.

TRANSACTIONS

Labour:						
daily, weekly	out-commuters, shoppers	small-scale selective commuting	—	—	—	—
seasonal	harvest labour out to US irrigated areas	none	harvest labour diffused through Texas	none	harvest labour on contract to NW, Midwest	none
long-term (legal)	permit-holders formerly *bracero*	very few	permit-holders formerly *bracero*	very few	limited entry by quota or contract	selective professional executive, commercial
socio-economic	labourers, manual and service workers, male and female	managers, key personnel, entrepreneurs	as Az	as Bz	Az, but with more professional and technical	Bz, but selective espec. multi-national business men and managers
illegal	out-commuters for all purposes, safety valve maximum movement in this zone	no southward flow. Conflict with *chicano* residents	searchers for work in Texas	no southward flow. Conflict with *chicanos* and blacks	diffused through US, mainly to cities	Conflicts with other Hispanics and blacks

Capital exports	tourist goods, 'in-bond' manufs., farm and mine products	capital and consumer goods retail/wholesale items	oil, farm and ranch products, iron and steel goods	capital and consumer goods	oil, farm and ranch products, 'in-bond' manufactures, machinery and transport equipment	manfuactures: capital and consumer goods. Higher-value products
investment (factory)	'in-bond' plants from US	'home-based' branch 'in-bond' plant	'in-bond' plants away from Border. Controls on US ownership	Parent firms of 'in-bond' plants (Fig. 27)	US investments in Mexican firms, multinational structures	Parent firms of 'in-bond' plants (Fig. 27)
other investment	US investments in urban utilities, shops, offices, transport, tourist facilities (hotels etc.)	Net inflow of savings to US	US investments in land, mines, banking, city-based activities (especially in (Monterrey))	Limited Mexican private investment in banks, commerce etc.	Selective investment of savings	Source of multinational capital for production, trade, services
retail/ wholesale	Food drink, furniture, prescriptions, tourist goods, entertainment (low retention of tourist dollar)	Food, spirits, cigarettes, clothing, cars, consumer durables, electrical goods	Shopping hinterland up to 100–150 miles south	Distance decay of hinterland to north of Rio Grande	Exchange through regional metropoli	As A
tourism/ recreation	exploit culture, cheapness, scenery	high-quality items	Little US tourist penetration N provinces	Limited Mexican tourist penetration in Texas	Major tourist flows Mexico City, Acapulco, Tijuana	Diffusion Mexican tourism (high class)
illegal	Border smuggling, drugs out; crime; vice, including prostitution etc.	Smuggling arms, electronics, consumer durables	Concentration from region to Border crossings	Smuggling through-routes	Nation-wide networks	Nation-wide networks, espec. in New York and Midwest

Land						
Natural resources: farm and ranch / irrigated tracts Urban/indus./comm. Second homes	US investments in land purchases in Border (to 100 km) limited by law	Little reciprocal land purchase	Extensive US purchases since 19th century	Little reciprocal land purchase	Landed investment, companies, banks etc.	Selective investments in US land

TIME DIMENSION

Shifts in volume, direction, distance of flows, and intensity of interaction, e.g. peso devaluations in 1976 and 1982. Illegal transactions governed by laws and effective enforcement, but also by economic and social change in labour markets.

POLICIES/PLANS						
Scale Level:	town to town variously active across Rio Grande	as A, with greater reluctance	limited by centralization of power in Mexico City	limited by US Constitution. No treaties at State level	national, *not* Border issues paramount. Water resource management	as A
Objectives:	Development Social justice Environment Health Welfare	Development Protection of minorities Safety/public order Health	as Az Central planning	as Bz Market forces	Development, then growth; Benefits from oil; Welfare; Environment lesser priority	Economic growth Protection against inflation unemployment Social welfare Quality-of-life 1969–79 Environment
Structure: Urban	Municipal sector planning Twin-city co-operation	Land-use zoning Twin-city co-operation	*Provincia* controls *Municipio* plans; 1977–9 Decentralizn. for planning, to *Provincia*	State zoning laws fragmentary	Management of *barrios*, urban revitalization incl. industry, housing	Anti-poverty; Environmental programmes; Mass transit; Housing policy; Direct Federal intervention

	Demographic pressure	Rural depopulation	Provincial development plans	Regional Council plans (in assocn. with Federal agencies) EDDs	Sector programmes (incl. *ejido*)	Federal agencies
Rural	—	—	—			
Regional				Texas Good Neighbour Commission	Border Programme (PRONAF), 1961 Border Industrlzn. (BIP), 1965	SW Border Commission (1977)
Frontier	openness, but selective protection	co-operation, protection; exploitation of Az. Organization US Border cities	No special policies for co-operation	Protection US Border municipalities; Trend to closure by some agencies, to openness by others	*Paraestatales*, Water Resources Sec.; External Affairs Min., Co-ordinat. Commn. (1977) Nat. Reg. Devel. Commission International Boundary Waters Commission 1976 Consultative Commission	INS, US Customs, Dept. Agric.; Drugs Enforcement Admin. Dept. State; FAA; Dept. Justice

TIME DIMENSION

Policy shifts in focus, objectives, priorities, efficiency–equity ratio. Border policies subsidiary to national policy priorities and trade-offs, which may have adverse effects on the peoples of the Rio Grande.

POLITICAL SYSTEM						
Political culture (male dominated)	Local bosses, dominated by PRI and bureaucrats	City caucuses and élite groups; Citizen power.	Political bosses (*caudillos*)	One-party—Conservative. Tied to social structure	authoritarian, *machismo*, over-centralized	democratic pluralism bureaucratic

Governments	Municipio dominated by Provincia	County, city. Variably strong or weak. SMSAS	Provincia	Texas State	Federal—strong	Federal—partnership with State
Bureaucrats	Strong	Weak	Ministry representatives Paraestatales	State Development Commn. Bureaucracy weak in face of politicians	Hierarchical down to municipio. Responsive to PRI	Strong in Federal agencies. Responsive to Congress committees and caucuses
Political parties	PRI weaker in Border cities, but controls	Democratic Pty. monopoly. Machine politics. Raza Unida waxed and waned	PRI strong	Democratic Congress, Republican Governor	PRI dominant President at apex of pyramid. Patronage in 6 yr term of office	Republican President, Republican House majority, Broad 'political' church'
Élite groups	PRI politicians and bureaucrats	Businessmen—politicians in coalitions	Business leaders in Monterrey	Oil, ranching entrepreneurs	Ministers, business leaders, professions	Business leaders; Congress Committee Chairman; Trade Unions
Interest groups	Border traders peasants, workers, middle classes	Border traders, Environmentalists, chicanos	as A	oil, farm, ranch interests, Environmentalists, chicanos	peasants, workers, professions, industrialists	Unions, farmers, miners, multinationals, environmentalists, human rights activists, feminists.
Welfare	higher disease and infant mortality; less medical provision; fewer educational facilities; less welfare	above US average poor health and medical care; minority education problems; limited welfare	less favourable health or medical care than Border towns	better health and medical care; welfare still limited; minorities better integrated	polarized society; social justice; strong urban/rural contrasts in provision	Medicaid and Medicare; full range education; minority rights; human rights

Shifts in quantum and balance of functions and powers. Rigidities in Mexican structure, flexibility in Federal, State, and local relations in US.

Public opinion	little influence; traditional; conservative; manipulated	strong media and advertising; prejudiced on Az; citizen power	expressed through PRI structures	pressure on State legislature	at national level very weak	pressure on Congressmen strong
TENSION MANAGEMENT						
Conflict	crime; vice; dependency; exploitation; deprivation; curbs on out-migration; human rights of migrants in USA; unfavourable Border balance of payments	illegal aliens; effects on *chicanos* labour unions; drugs traffic	dependency; exploitation; deprivation; oil and gas as bargaining counter	illegal aliens; drugs traffic	Access to water resources; national balance of payments; access of workers to USA; control smuggling; US fishing rights; combat US arrogance	'undocumented workers'; drugs traffic; safeguarding US interests in Mexico
Co-operation	town to town: élite networks; minimize adherence to rules; maximize informal contacts; public safety (police): health services; anti-pollution measures New life-styles from US; / Tourism links; Fire protection for Mexican towns. Little co-operation in city planning	bilateral but limited negotiation, *if* agreed at federal level (health, veterinary): Border policing, little co-operation; exchange of prisoners; cultural visits		Presidential meetings (frequent) Border Commission (inoperative) IBWC; 1976 Consultative Commission	

Behavioural Response

adaptive (entropic, system-merging)	By MEXICO:	Control/suppression illegal drugs traffic, 'undocumented' migrants; freer access to Mexican market for US goods; fuller allegiance by Mexico to Pan-Americanism; abandonment of non-alignment; accommodation on oil and gas exports to the USA
	By USA:	increased quota for legal migrants; 'human rights' charter for illegal migrants, or amnesty; more open access for Mexican goods in US market; economic aid from US without political strings
	Within Mexico and USA:	More stable equilibrium between decentralization of powers and functions (to State and local levels) and more effective funding, aid, and planning from Federal centres
maladaptive (negentropic, system-sustaining) [i.e. divisive]	By MEXICO:	Refusal to meet US energy needs for gas and oil; restriction on US access to Mexican markets; more active policy links with Cuba/COMECON
	By USA:	Continuing restrictions on Mexican exports; no action on 'human rights' or quotas for immigrant Mexican workers; continuance of neocolonialist exploitation tactics; penetration by multinationals
	Internally:	Neglect of frontier-zone problems of underdevelopment and social pathology; withdrawal of functions and powers from local and regional levels; policies of economic autarchy, damaging frontier-zone trade.

INDEX